Study Guide

Chapters 1-15

College Accounting

Twenty-second Edition

James A. Heintz, DBA, CPA
Professor of Accounting
School of Business
University of Kansas

Robert W. Parry, Jr., Ph.D.
Professor of Accounting
Kelley School of Business
Indiana University

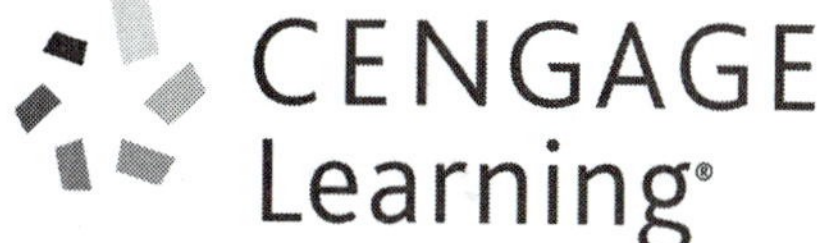

Australia • Brazil • Mexico • Singapore • United Kingdom • United States

For product information and technology assistance, contact us at **Cengage Learning Academic Resource Center, 1-800-423-0563**.

For permission to use material from this text or product, submit all requests online at **www.cengage.com/permissions**. Further permissions questions can be emailed to **permissionrequest@cengage.com**.

ISBN: 978-1-305-66766-2

Cengage Learning
20 Channel Center Street
Boston, MA 02210
USA

Cengage Learning is a leading provider of customized learning solutions with employees residing in nearly 40 different countries and sales in more than 125 countries around the world. Find your local representative at **www.cengage.com**.

Cengage Learning products are represented in Canada by Nelson Education, Ltd.

To learn more about Cengage Learning Solutions, visit **www.cengage.com**.

Purchase any of our products at your local college store or at our preferred online store **www.cengagebrain.com**.

Printed in the United States of America
Print Number: 01 Print Year: 2015

Table of Contents

CHAPTER 1
INTRODUCTION TO ACCOUNTING

LEARNING OBJECTIVES

Chapter 1 is designed to introduce you to accounting—its purpose, process, and career opportunities. Businesses that keep good accounting records benefit in many ways. Users of accounting information are able to make sound decisions, which will affect the business's future. Accounting offers many career opportunities, some of which are entry level and task oriented and others that involve decision making and planning.

Objective 1. Describe the purpose of accounting.

Accounting is the process by which businesses keep track of daily transactions and determine how the business is doing. Accounting provides needed information for its many users, from owners to government agencies and others.

Objective 2. Describe the accounting process.

The accounting process contains six major steps.

Step 1 Analyzing: Looking at information available and figuring out what to do with it. This first step in the accounting process usually occurs when the business receives some type of information, such as a bill, that needs to be properly entered into the business's records. This first step also involves deciding if the piece of information should result in an accounting entry or not.

Step 2 Recording: Entering the information, manually or via a computer, into the accounting system.

Step 3 Classifying: Grouping like items together.

Step 4 Summarizing: Aggregating many similar events to provide information that is easy to understand.

Step 5 Reporting: Communicating the results, such as profit or loss, commonly using tables of numbers to tell the financial status of the business.

Step 6 Interpreting: Examining the financial statements to evaluate the financial health of the business.

Objective 3. Define GAAP and describe the process used by FASB to develop these principles.

Generally accepted accounting principles (GAAP) are the rules that businesses must follow when preparing financial statements. The Securities and Exchange Commission (SEC) has the legal power to make these rules for firms listed on one of the U.S. stock exchanges. However, the SEC has delegated this responsibility to the Financial Accounting Standards Board (FASB).

FASB takes the following steps to develop an accounting standard:

1. The issue is placed on FASB's agenda.
2. After researching an issue, FASB issues a Preliminary Views document to offer the pros and cons of the accounting alternatives and to invite others to comment.
3. To gather additional views on the issue, the Board often holds public hearings around the country.
4. Following these hearings, the Board issues an exposure draft. This document explains the rules that FASB believes firms should follow in accounting for this event.
5. After considering feedback on the exposure draft, the Board issues an Accounting Standards Update which amends the FASB Accounting Standards Codification.

Objective 4. Define three types of business ownership structures.

Businesses can be classified according to who owns them and the specific way they are organized. A sole proprietorship is owned by one person who assumes all risks for the business and makes all business decisions. A partnership is owned by two or more persons who share the risks and decision making. Corporations have many owners (shareholders) whose risk is limited to their investment and who have little influence in business decisions.

Objective 5. Classify different types of businesses by activities.

Businesses also can be classified by the type of service or product they provide. A service business provides a service, a merchandising business purchases a product from another business to sell, and a manufacturing business makes a product to sell.

Objective 6. Identify career opportunities in accounting.

Accounting has varied and diverse opportunities, depending on the education and experience of the worker, the type of business, and the accounting processes used within the business.

Accounting clerks record, sort, and file accounting information. Bookkeepers supervise clerks, help with daily accounting work, and summarize information. Para-accountants provide many accounting, auditing, or tax services under the direct supervision of an accountant.

Public accountants offer services such as auditing, tax advice, management advisory services, and forensic accounting services. Under the Sarbanes-Oxley Act, however, they may not provide audit and management advisory services to the same company. Further, audit and tax services may be provided to the same company only if preapproved by the audit committee of the company.

Managerial accountants offer services to private businesses, such as designing accounting information systems, general accounting, cost accounting, budgeting, tax accounting, and internal auditing. Government and not-for-profit organizations also employ accountants.

Accounting is a professional field, which includes organizations and certifications for those who pass examinations and have relevant work experience.

REVIEW QUESTIONS

Instructions: Analyze each of the following items carefully before writing your answer in the column at the right.

	Question	Answer
LO 1	**1.** The purpose of accounting is to provide current information to users. For each user below, briefly describe what type of information is needed. a. Owners (present and future) b. Managers who make decisions for the business c. Creditors (present and future) d. Government agencies (state, local, and national)	
LO 5	**2.** A travel agency is an example of this type of business.	______________
LO 4	**3.** The ownership structure where owners share risks and decision making is called a(n) ________.	______________
LO 5	**4.** A(n) ________ business makes a product to sell.	______________
LO 5	**5.** A business that purchases a product from another business to sell to customers is called a(n) ________ business.	______________
LO 4	**6.** Under the ________ ownership structure, the owner's personal assets can be taken to pay creditors.	______________
LO 3	**7.** The Financial Accounting Standards Board develops procedures and guidelines called ________ to be followed in the accounting process.	______________

LO 3 **8.** The following actions are taken by FASB when developing an accounting standard. Indicate the proper sequence of events by placing a 1 through 5 in the space provided.

Step

_______ The Accounting Standards Update is issued which amends the FASB Accounting Standards Codification.

_______ Public hearings are held.

_______ An exposure draft is issued.

_______ The issue is placed on FASB's agenda.

_______ A Preliminary Views document is issued.

LO 4 **9.** The owners' risk is usually limited to their initial investment in this type of ownership structure. .... ____________________

LO 6 **10.** Is a public accounting firm permitted to provide audit and tax services to a publicly held company?.. ____________________

LO 6 **11.** By meeting education and experience requirements and passing an examination, a public accountant can achieve recognition as a(n) _____. ____________________

LO 6 **12.** The segment of accounting practice that includes fraud detection, fraud prevention, litigation support, business valuation, expert witness services, and other investigative activities is known as ________. .... ____________________

LO 2 **13.** The six major steps of the accounting process are listed in the box at the right. In front of each term, write the letter that identifies the correct description provided in the column on the left.

a. The process of entering financial information about events affecting the business

b. Aggregating similar events to provide information that is easy to understand

c. The process of sorting or grouping like things together, rather than merely keeping a simple, diary-like narrative record of numerous and varied transactions

d. The process of determining the effect of various events on the business

e. The process of deciding the importance of the information in various reports

f. The process of communicating the results of operation

_______ Analyzing

_______ Recording

_______ Classifying

_______ Summarizing

_______ Reporting

_______ Interpreting

CHAPTER 2
ANALYZING TRANSACTIONS: THE ACCOUNTING EQUATION

LEARNING OBJECTIVES

Chapter 2 continues the introductory discussion of accounting—its elements, equation, and transactions. The accounting equation provides a structure for analyzing transactions. After all transactions have been analyzed, the financial statements—income statement, statement of owner's equity, and balance sheet—are prepared. Let's look at each of these learning objectives in detail.

Objective 1. Define the accounting elements.

Accounting elements are the parts that make up the accounting equation: assets, liabilities, and owner's equity. **Assets** are items *owned* by the business that will provide future benefits. **Liabilities** are debts *owed* by the business and will require a future outflow of assets. **Owner's equity** (also called net worth or capital) is the difference between assets and liabilities. **Revenues** represent the amount a business charges customers for products sold or services provided. Revenues create an inflow of assets. **Expenses** represent an outflow of assets (or increase in liabilities) as a result of the efforts made to generate revenues.

Objective 2. Construct the accounting equation.

The accounting equation shows the relationship among assets, liabilities, and owner's equity (the accounting elements).

Assets = Liabilities + Owner's Equity

When given two of the numbers for the equation above, you can calculate the missing number by adding or subtracting.

The accounting equation may be expanded to include revenues, expenses, and drawing. Although drawing is not considered a major element in the accounting equation, it is a very special type of owner's equity account. It represents the withdrawals of assets from the business by the owner.

ASSETS (Items Owned)			=	LIABILITIES (Amts. Owed)	+	OWNER'S EQUITY (Owner's Investment)				(Earnings)		
Cash	+	Delivery Equipment	=	Accounts Payable	+	Rohan Macsen, Capital	−	Rohan Macsen, Drawing	+	Revenues	−	Expenses

Objective 3. Analyze business transactions.

Analyzing is the first step in the accounting process. Three questions must be answered: (1) What happened? (2) Which accounts are affected, and what kind of accounts are they (asset, liability, owner's equity)? (3) How is the accounting equation affected? (Accounts will increase or decrease, but the equation always remains in balance.)

Objective 4. Show the effects of business transactions on the accounting equation.

Each transaction will affect asset, liability, owner's equity, revenue, or expense accounts. For example, when an owner invests cash in the business, the asset account called *Cash* increases, and the owner's equity account *Capital* also increases.

For each transaction, you must decide what accounts are affected and whether the accounts increase or decrease. After each transaction, the equation must still be in balance.

Objective 5. Prepare and describe the purposes of a simple income statement, statement of owner's equity, and balance sheet.

After the transactions are completed, the financial statements are prepared to show the results of those transactions. As shown on page 7, all financial statements have a heading that indicates the name of the firm, title of the statement, and time period or date covered by the statement. The income statement reports revenues, expenses, and the net income for the period. The statement of owner's equity shows the beginning balance of the owner's capital account, plus investments and net income, less withdrawals to compute the ending capital balance. The balance sheet reports all assets, liabilities, and the owner's capital on a certain date and confirms that the accounting equation has remained in balance.

Note that net income computed on the income statement is transferred to the statement of owner's equity to compute Patty V's capital at the end of the month. Patty V's capital on December 31, 20--, is then transferred to the balance sheet to compute total liabilities and owner's equity.

Objective 6. Define the three basic phases of the accounting process.

The three basic phases of the accounting process are input, processing, and output. The inputs to the accounting process are the business transactions. These transactions are processed to recognize their effects on the assets, liabilities, owner's equity, revenues, and expenses of the business. The results of these events are then reported as outputs of the accounting process in the financial statements.

Patty V's Consulting Income Statement For Month Ended December 31, 20--		
Revenues		
Consulting fees		$10,000
Expenses		
Wages expense	$5,000	
Rent expense	1,500	
Phone expense	500	
Total expenses		7,000
Net income		$ 3,000

Patty V's Consulting Statement of Owner's Equity For Month Ended December 31, 20--		
Patty V, capital, December 1, 20--		$ —
Investment in December		20,000
Total investment		$20,000
Net income for December	$3,000	
Less withdrawals for December	1,000	
Increase in capital		2,000
Patty V, capital, December 31, 20--		$22,000

Patty V's Consulting Balance Sheet December 31, 20--			
Assets		Liabilities	
Cash	$ 500	Accounts payable	$ 6,500
Accounts receivable	8,000		
Computer equipment	20,000	Owner's Equity	
		Patty V, capital	22,000
		Total liabilities and	
Total assets	$28,500	owner's equity	$28,500

REVIEW QUESTIONS

Instructions: Analyze each of the following items carefully before writing your answer in the column at the right.

	Question	Answer
LO 2	1. The entire accounting process is based on one simple equation called the ________.	________
LO 1	2. An individual, association, or organization that engages in business activities is called a(n) ________.	________
LO 1	3. An item owned by a business that will provide future benefits is a(n) ________.	________
LO 1	4. Something owed to another business entity is a(n) ________.	________
LO 1	5. A(n) ________ is an unwritten promise to pay a supplier for assets purchased or a service rendered.	________
LO 2	6. The amount by which assets exceed the liabilities of a business is called ________.	________
LO 1	7. According to the ________ concept, nonbusiness assets and liabilities are not included in the business entity's records.	________
LO 2	8. Assets – Liabilities = ________.	________
LO 2	9. Assets – Owner's Equity = ________.	________
LO 2	10. Assets = Liabilities + ________.	________
LO 4	11. The outflow of assets (or increase in liabilities) as the result of efforts to produce revenue is called a(n) ________.	________
LO 4	12. When total revenues exceed total expenses, the difference is called ________.	________
LO 4	13. When expenses are greater than revenues, the difference is called ________.	________
LO 4	14. Any accounting period of 12 months' duration is called a(n) ________.	________
LO 4	15. Withdrawals, or ______, represent a reduction in owner's equity because the owner takes cash or other assets for personal use.	________
LO 5	16. The financial statement that reports the profitability of the business for a period of time is the ________.	________
LO 5	17. The financial statement that shows investments and withdrawals by the owner, as well as profit or loss generated by the business, is the ________.	________
LO 5	18. The financial statement that reports the assets, liabilities, and owner's equity on a specific date is the ________.	________

LO 5 19. On the balance sheet, assets are listed in order of ________, or the ease with which they can be converted to cash. .... ____________

EXERCISES

Exercise 1 (LO 2) THE ACCOUNTING EQUATION

Using the accounting equation provided below, compute the missing amounts.

	ASSETS	=	LIABILITIES	+	OWNER'S EQUITY
(a)	________	=	$4,000	+	$20,000
(b)	$25,000	=	$8,000	+	________
(c)	$50,000	=	________	+	$10,000

Exercise 2 (LO 2/4) THE EXPANDED ACCOUNTING EQUATION

Using the accounting equation provided below, compute the missing amounts.

	ASSETS (Items Owned)	=	LIABILITIES + (Amts. Owed)	+	OWNER'S EQUITY (Owner's Investment)				(Earnings)		
	Cash		Accounts Payable		Capital	–	Drawing	+	Revenues	–	Expenses
(a)	______	=	$60,000	+	$20,000	–	$10,000	+	$80,000	–	$60,000
(b)	$80,000	=	______	+	$35,000	–	$ 5,000	+	$70,000	–	$55,000
(c)	$90,000	=	$25,000	+	______	–	$ 2,000	+	$57,000	–	$50,000
(d)	$60,000	=	$20,000	+	$30,000	–	$ 5,000	+	______	–	$40,000
(e)	$40,000	=	$25,000	+	$40,000	–	$ 5,000	+	$30,000	–	______
(f)	$75,000	=	$20,000	+	$50,000	–	______	+	$40,000	–	$25,000

Exercise 3 (LO 5) STATEMENT OF OWNER'S EQUITY

If owner's equity was $38,000 at the beginning of the period and $45,000 at the end of the period, compute the net income or loss for the period. (There were no investments or withdrawals during the period.)

Exercise 4 (LO 2) ACCOUNTING EQUATION

If Irma Elkton, a dentist, owns office equipment amounting to $3,500, laboratory equipment amounting to $10,000, and other property that is used in the business amounting to $4,620, and owes business suppliers a total of $5,000, what is the owner's equity in the business?

Exercise 5 (LO 2) ACCOUNTING EQUATION

This is an extension of Exercise 4. One year later, the amount of Dr. Elkton's business assets has increased to a total of $22,000, and the amount of business liabilities has increased to a total of $6,000. Assuming that Dr. Elkton has not made any additional investments or withdrawals, compute the following:

(a) Owner's equity at year-end $ ____________

(b) Net income or loss for the year $ ____________

Exercise 6 (LO 3/4) EFFECTS OF TRANSACTIONS (BALANCE SHEET ACCOUNTS)

Rich Brite has started his own business. During the first month, the following transactions occurred:

(a) Invested $15,000 cash in the business, which was used to open a bank account.
(b) Purchased office equipment for cash, $4,000.
(c) Purchased a computer on account for $9,000.
(d) Paid $2,000 on account for the computer.

Using the lines provided below, show the effect of each transaction on the basic elements of the accounting equation: assets, liabilities, and owner's equity. Compute the new amounts for each element after each transaction to satisfy yourself that the accounting equation has remained in balance.

	ASSETS	=	LIABILITIES	+	OWNER'S EQUITY
(a)	______		______		______
Bal.	______		______		______
(b)	______		______		______
	______		______		______
Bal.	______		______		______
(c)	______		______		______
Bal.	______		______		______
(d)	______		______		______
Bal.	______		______		______

Exercise 7 (LO 3/4) EFFECTS OF TRANSACTIONS (REVENUE, EXPENSE, WITHDRAWALS)

In late May, Glen Ross opened a business by investing $20,000 cash and purchasing office equipment on account for $8,000. These events were properly entered in the accounting records. In June, the following transactions took place:

(a) Received $4,000 from a client for professional services rendered.
(b) Paid $1,200 office rent for the month.
(c) Paid $200 to the power company for the month's utility bill.
(d) Withdrew $600 cash for personal use.

On the first Balance (Bal.) line provided on the following page, record the amount of assets, liabilities, and owner's equity as the result of Ross's investment and purchase of office equipment in May. Then, record the effect of transactions (a) to (d) on the expanded accounting equation: Assets = Liabilities + Owner's Equity (Capital – Drawing + Revenues – Expenses). Following transaction (d), compute the new balances for each category to satisfy yourself that the accounting equation has remained in balance.

Exercise 7 (Concluded)

	ASSETS (Items Owned)	= LIABILITIES + (Amts. Owed)	OWNER'S EQUITY (Owner's Investment)		(Earnings)		
	Cash	Accounts Payable	Glen Ross, Capital	– Glen Ross, Drawing	+ Revenues	– Expenses	Description
Bal.							
(a)							
(b)							
(c)							
(d)							
Bal.							

Exercise 8 (LO 3/4) EFFECTS OF TRANSACTIONS (ALL ACCOUNTS)

Judith Moore started her own business. During the month of July, the following transactions occurred:

(a) Invested $10,000 cash in the business.
(b) Purchased office equipment for $5,500 on account.
(c) Received $900 cash from a client for services rendered.
(d) Purchased computer equipment for cash, $6,000.
(e) Received $1,500 cash from a client for services rendered.
(f) Paid $800 office rent for the month.
(g) Paid the phone bill for the month, $75.
(h) Paid $100 on account, for office equipment previously purchased.
(i) Withdrew $500 for personal use.

Required:

1. Record the effect of each of the transactions listed above on the accounting equation provided in the chart on the following page. Following transaction (i), compute the new balances for the accounts to satisfy yourself that the equation has remained in balance.

Exercise 8 (Concluded)

	ASSETS (Items Owned)		= LIABILITIES + (Amts. Owed)	OWNER'S EQUITY (Owner's Investment)		(Earnings)		
	Cash	+ Office Equipment	= Accounts Payable	+ J. Moore, Capital	– J. Moore, Drawing	+ Revenues	– Expenses	Description
(a)								
(b)								
(c)								
(d)								
(e)								
(f)								
(g)								
(h)								
(i)								
Bal.								

2. After recording the transactions in part (1), compute the following:

Total assets	$
Total liabilities	$
Owner's equity	$
Owner's equity in excess of original investment	$
Total revenues	$
Total expenses	$
Net income	$

Exercise 9 (LO 5) PREPARATION OF AN INCOME STATEMENT

Based on the transactions reported in Exercise 8, prepare an income statement for Judith Moore Enterprises for the month ended July 31, 20--, in the space provided below.

Exercise 10 (LO 5) PREPARATION OF THE STATEMENT OF OWNER'S EQUITY

Based on the transactions reported in Exercise 8, prepare a statement of owner's equity for Judith Moore Enterprises for the month ended July 31, 20--, in the space provided below.

Exercise 11 (LO 5) PREPARATION OF A BALANCE SHEET

Based on the transactions reported in Exercise 8, prepare a balance sheet as of July 31, 20--, in the space provided below.

PROBLEMS

Problem 12 (LO 2) THE ACCOUNTING EQUATION

Dr. Abe Miller is a general practitioner. As of December 31, Miller owned the following assets related to the professional practice:

Cash	$3,300	X-ray equipment	$7,000
Office equipment	4,500	Laboratory equipment	4,000

As of that date, Miller owed business suppliers as follows:

General Office Equipment Inc.	$2,000
Young Medical Supply Company	1,500
Buck Gas Company	1,200

Required:

1. Compute the amount of assets, liabilities, and owner's equity as of December 31.

   ASSETS = LIABILITIES + OWNER'S EQUITY

   ______________ ______________ ______________

2. Assuming that during January there is an increase of $4,600 in Dr. Miller's business assets and an increase of $2,500 in business liabilities, compute the resulting accounting equation as of January 31.

   ASSETS = LIABILITIES + OWNER'S EQUITY

   ______________ ______________ ______________

3. Assuming that during February there is a decrease of $1,500 in assets and a decrease of $1,200 in liabilities, compute the resulting accounting equation as of February 28.

   ASSETS = LIABILITIES + OWNER'S EQUITY

   ______________ ______________ ______________

4. Assuming that Dr. Miller made no additional investments or withdrawals, compute the net income or loss for each month.

Problem 13 (LO 3/4) EFFECT OF TRANSACTIONS ON ACCOUNTING EQUATION

Susan Cole started her own consulting business in October 20--. During the first month, the following transactions occurred:

(a) Invested $12,000 cash in the business.
(b) Purchased office equipment for $7,500 on account.
(c) Purchased computer equipment for cash, $800.
(d) Received $700 cash from a client for services rendered.
(e) Paid $600 office rent for the month.
(f) Paid student assistant wages for the month, $150.
(g) Paid one-year insurance premium, $200.
(h) Paid $3,000 on account for the office equipment purchased in transaction (b).
(i) Withdrew cash for personal use, $100.

Problem 13 (Concluded)

Required:

1. Record the effect of each of the transactions from the previous page on the accounting equation chart provided below. Following transaction (i), compute the new amounts in the accounts.

	ASSETS			= LIABILITIES +	OWNER'S EQUITY				
	(Items Owned)			(Amts. Owed)	(Owner's Investment)		(Earnings)		
	Cash	+ Office Equip.	+ Prepaid Insur.	= Accounts Payable	+ S. Cole, Capital	– S. Cole, Drawing	+ Revenues	– Expenses	Description
(a)									
(b)									
(c)									
(d)									
(e)									
(f)									
(g)									
(h)									
(i)									
Bal.									

2. After recording the transactions, compute the following:

Total assets .... $ ______

Total liabilities .... $ ______

Owner's equity .... $ ______

Change in owner's equity from original investment .... $ ______

Total revenues .... $ ______

Total expenses .... $ ______

Net income (loss) .... $ ______

Name ______________________________

Problem 14 (LO 5) INCOME STATEMENT

Based on the transactions in Problem 13, prepare an income statement for Susan Cole Consulting Services for the month ended October 31, 20--, in the space provided below.

Problem 15 (LO 5) STATEMENT OF OWNER'S EQUITY

Based on the transactions in Problem 13, prepare a statement of owner's equity for Susan Cole Consulting Services for the month ended October 31, 20--, in the space provided below.

Problem 16 (LO 5) BALANCE SHEET

Based on the transactions in Problem 13, prepare a balance sheet as of October 31, 20--, in the space provided below.

Problem 17 (LO 3/4/5) ANALYZE THE EFFECTS OF BUSINESS TRANSACTIONS ON THE ACCOUNTING EQUATION AND PREPARE FINANCIAL STATEMENTS

Stuart Cassady is opening a typing service. During the first month (April 20--), the following transactions occurred:

(a) Invested $10,000 in the business.
(b) Purchased office supplies for $200 cash.
(c) Purchased office supplies for $800, $400 on account and $400 in cash.
(d) Received typing fees of $300 cash.
(e) Paid the rent, $600.
(f) Withdrew $100 for personal use.
(g) Earned typing fees of $600, $200 in cash and $400 on account.
(h) Made partial payment for office supplies in transaction (c) of $200.
(i) Received $200 cash for typing fees earned on account in transaction (g).

Required:

1. Record the effect of each transaction on the accounting equation below. Following transaction (i), compute new amounts for each account.

	ASSETS			= LIABILITIES +	OWNER'S EQUITY				
	(Items Owned)			(Amts. Owed)	(Owner's Investment)		(Earnings)		
	Cash	+ Accounts Receivable.	+ Office Supplies	= Accounts Payable	+ S. Cassady, Capital	– S. Cassady, Drawing	+ Revenues	– Expenses	Description
(a)									
(b)									
(c)									
(d)									
(e)									
(f)									
(g)									
(h)									
(i)									
Bal.									

Problem 17 (Concluded)

2. Based on the transactions in part (1) of Problem 17, prepare an income statement, statement of owner's equity, and balance sheet for Stuart Cassady Typing Service.

Income Statement

Statement of Owner's Equity

Balance Sheet

CHAPTER 3
THE DOUBLE-ENTRY FRAMEWORK

LEARNING OBJECTIVES

Objective 1. Define the parts of a T account.

The **T account** gets its name from the fact that it resembles the letter *T*. There are three major parts of an account. The title of the account is on top. The left side of the T account is the debit side, and the right side is the credit side.

Objective 2. Foot and balance a T account.

To determine the balance of a T account, simply total the dollar amounts of the debit and credit sides. These totals are known as **footings.** The difference between the footings is called the *balance* of the account. The balance is written on the side with the larger footing.

Objective 3. Describe the effects of debits and credits on specific types of accounts.

Assets are on the left side of the accounting equation. Thus, increases are entered on the left, or debit, side; and decreases are entered on the right, or credit, side. The normal balance of an asset account is a debit.

Liabilities and owner's equity are on the right side of the equation. Thus, increases are entered on the right, or credit, side; and decreases are entered on the left, or debit, side. The normal balance of a liability and owner's capital account is a credit.

Revenues increase owner's equity. Thus, increases in revenue are recorded as credits. The normal balance of a revenue account is a credit.

Expenses decrease owner's equity. Thus, increases in expenses are recorded as debits. The normal balance of an expense account is a debit.

Withdrawals of cash and other assets by the owner for personal reasons decrease owner's equity. Thus, an increase in drawing is recorded as a debit. The normal balance of a drawing account is a debit.

The following figure should be helpful in developing your understanding of debits and credits and the accounting equation:

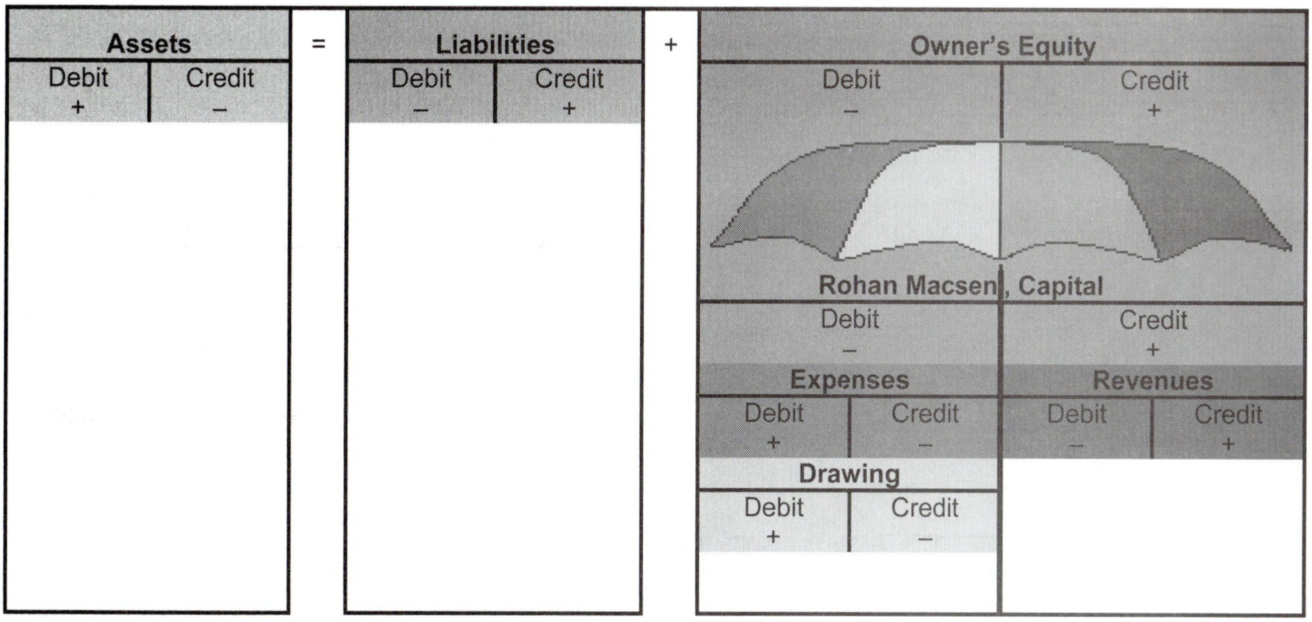

Assets		=	Liabilities		+	Owner's Equity	
Debit +	Credit −		Debit −	Credit +		Debit −	Credit +

Rohan Macsen, Capital

Debit −	Credit +

Expenses		Revenues	
Debit +	Credit −	Debit −	Credit +

Drawing	
Debit +	Credit −

Objective 4. Use T accounts to analyze transactions.

There are three basic questions that must be answered when analyzing a transaction: (1) What happened? (2) Which accounts are affected? and (3) How is the accounting equation affected? After analyzing the transaction, in every instance, debits will equal credits.

Objective 5. Prepare a trial balance and explain its purposes and linkages with the financial statements.

There are two very important rules in double-entry accounting: (1) The sum of the debits must equal the sum of the credits. This means that at least two accounts are affected by each transaction. (2) The accounting equation must remain in balance.

A **trial balance** is a list of all accounts showing the title and balance of each account. The total debits and credits must be equal. A trial balance is not a formal statement or report. It can be used as an aid in preparing the financial statements.

REVIEW QUESTIONS

Instructions: Analyze each of the following items carefully before writing your answer in the column at the right.

	Question	Answer
LO 1	**1.** A form or record used to keep track of the increases and decreases in each type of asset, liability, owner's equity, revenue, and expense is known as a(n) ________.	________
LO 1	**2.** The left side of a T account is called the ________ side.	________
LO 1	**3.** The right side of a T account is called the ________ side.	________
LO 2	**4.** The process of entering totals in the debit and credit sides of a T account is referred to as ________.	________
LO 2	**5.** The amount of the difference between the debits and credits recorded in a T account is called the ________.	________
LO 3	**6.** An increase in the asset Cash is recorded by a(n) ________.	________
LO 3	**7.** An increase in the liability Accounts Payable is recorded by a(n) ________.	________
LO 3	**8.** The normal balance of a revenue account is on the ________ side.	________
LO 3	**9.** A decrease in the liability Accounts Payable is recorded by a(n) ________.	________
LO 3	**10.** The normal balance of a liability account is on the ________ side.	________
LO 4	**11.** The fact that each transaction has a dual effect on the accounting elements provides the basis for what is called ________.	________
LO 5	**12.** A list of all of the accounts showing the title and balance of each account is called the ________.	________

EXERCISES

Exercise 1 (LO 1) DEFINING PARTS OF THE T ACCOUNT

Provided below are T accounts for the six types of accounts discussed to this point. Identify the debit and credit side of each type of account by writing debit on the debit side and credit on the credit side.

Assets | Liabilities | Owner's Capital | Owner's Drawing | Expenses | Revenues

Exercise 2 (LO 3) EFFECTS OF DEBITS AND CREDITS

Indicate whether each of the following types of accounts would normally have a debit or credit balance by circling either debit or credit in the column at the right:

Type of Account	Normal Balance (Circle one)	
(a) Assets	Debit	Credit
(b) Liabilities	Debit	Credit
(c) Owner's capital	Debit	Credit
(d) Revenues	Debit	Credit
(e) Expenses	Debit	Credit
(f) Drawing	Debit	Credit

Exercise 3 (LO 3) INCREASING AND DECREASING ACCOUNTS WITH DEBITS AND CREDITS

Provided below are T accounts representing the six types of accounts discussed. Indicate how each account would be increased and decreased by placing a (+) or (–) on the debit and credit side of each account.

Assets | Liabilities | Owner's Capital | Owner's Drawing | Expenses | Revenues

Exercise 4 (LO 4) USING T ACCOUNTS TO ANALYZE TRANSACTIONS

The following transactions were completed by Jacque Hamon, an educational consultant. Analyze each transaction and enter the amounts in the proper debit and credit positions in the T accounts at the right.

(a) Invested $3,000 cash in the business. — Cash | Jacque Hamon, Capital

(b) Received $1,000 in cash for consulting services rendered. — Cash | Professional Fees

(c) Bought office equipment from Gusse Supply Co. on account, $500. — Office Equipment | Accounts Payable

(d) Paid electric bill, $75. — Cash | Utilities Expense

Exercise 4 (Concluded)

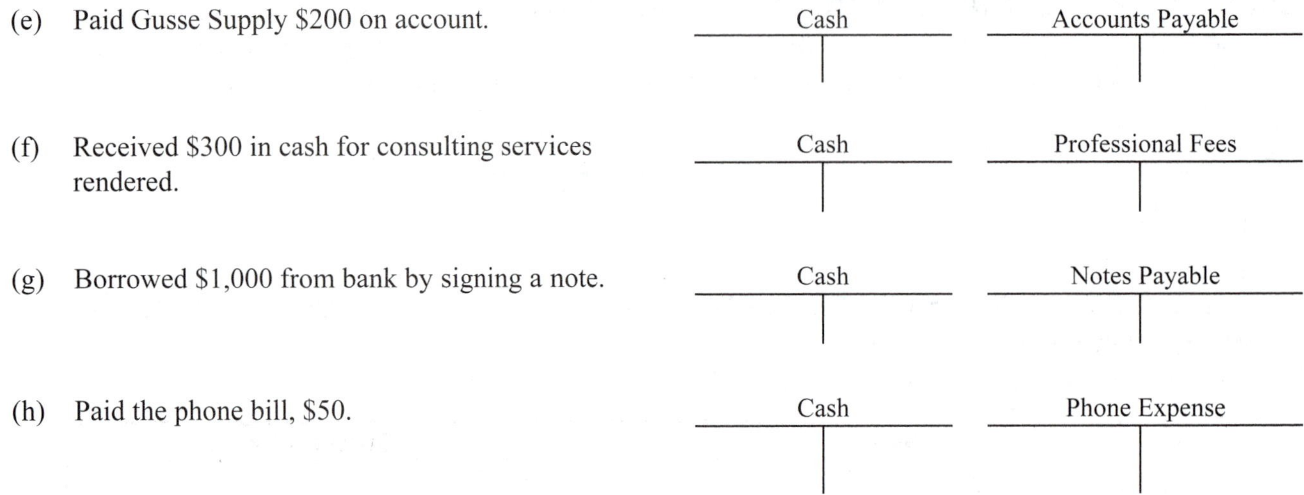

Exercise 5 (LO 4) USING T ACCOUNTS TO ANALYZE TRANSACTIONS (BALANCE SHEET ACCOUNTS)

Connie Sung has started her own typing business. During the first month, the following transactions occurred:

(a) Invested $12,000 cash in the business, and the money was deposited in a bank account.
(b) Purchased a new computer and printer on account from Stahl Electronics for $8,000.
(c) Paid the premium on a one-year insurance policy on computer equipment, $75 cash.
(d) Secured a bank loan by signing a note for $5,000.
(e) Made payment of $3,000 to Stahl Electronics on account.

Required:

Record the above transactions in the T accounts provided below.

Assets		=	Liabilities		+	Owner's Equity	
Debit +	Credit –		Debit –	Credit +		Debit –	Credit +

Assets	Liabilities	Owner's Equity
Cash	Accounts Payable	C. Sung, Capital
Office Equipment	Notes Payable	
Prepaid Insurance		

Exercise 6 (LO 4) USING T ACCOUNTS TO ANALYZE TRANSACTIONS (ALL ACCOUNTS)

In late April, Frazier Baar opened a psychiatry practice by investing $9,000 cash and purchasing a couch, chair, and leather-covered note pad on account for $2,500. These events were properly entered in the accounting records. In May, Dr. Baar began seeing patients and entered into the following transactions:

(a) Received $500 for counseling services rendered.
(b) Paid $100 for *Psychology Today* and other magazines for patients to read in the waiting room.
(c) Paid $1,200 office rent for the month.

Required:

1. Enter the balances as of May 1 in the following accounts: Cash, Office Furnishings, Accounts Payable, and F. Baar, Capital.

2. Record the May transactions in the accounts listed below.

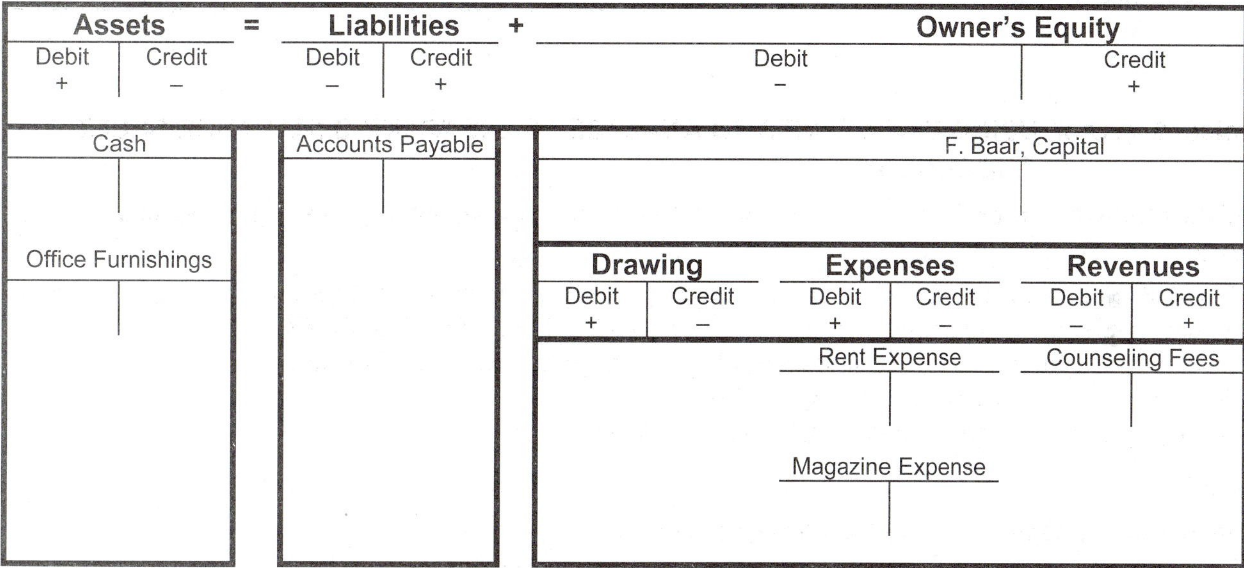

Exercise 7 (LO 2/4) USING T ACCOUNTS TO ANALYZE TRANSACTIONS, FOOTING AND BALANCING T ACCOUNTS

In January 20--, Blanca Estavez, CPA, started her own accounting practice. The following is a l[illegible] transactions for the first month:

(a) Invested $20,000 cash in the business.
(b) Purchased office supplies, $500 cash.
(c) Purchased office furniture, $6,000 cash.
(d) Purchased a computer and printer for $9,000: $5,000 cash and $4,000 on account.
(e) Paid $800 for accounting software programs.
(f) Performed accounting services and earned fees totaling $1,800: $1,200 in cash and $600 on account.
(g) Paid $700 rent for the month.
(h) Withdrew $200 for personal use.
(i) Paid $2,000 on account for the computer.

Exercise 7 (Concluded)

Required:

1. Record the transactions in the T accounts that follow.
2. After all transactions have been entered, foot and balance the T accounts.

Assets		=	Liabilities		+	Owner's Equity	
Debit +	Credit –		Debit –	Credit +		Debit –	Credit +

Assets: Cash; Accounts Receivable; Office Supplies; Office Furniture; Computer Equipment; Computer Software

Liabilities: Accounts Payable

Owner's Equity: B. Estavez, Capital

Drawing		Expenses		Revenues	
Debit +	Credit –	Debit +	Credit –	Debit –	Credit +
B. Estavez, Drawing		Rent Expense		Accounting Fees	

Exercise 8 (LO 5) PREPARE A TRIAL BALANCE

Based on the transactions recorded in Exercise 7, prepare a trial balance at the end of the first month of operations using the form provided below.

ACCOUNT	DEBIT BALANCE	CREDIT BALANCE

PROBLEMS

Problem 9 (LO 2/4/5) ANALYZING TRANSACTIONS WITH T ACCOUNTS, FOOTING AND BALANCING ACCOUNTS, AND PREPARING A TRIAL BALANCE

Jali Abdul has decided to offer his services as a promoter for local rock-n-roll bands. Following is a narrative of selected transactions completed during January, the first month of J. A. Productions' operations:

(a) Invested $10,000 in the business and opened a checking account.
(b) Purchased office furniture on account at a cost of $5,000.
(c) Purchased computer equipment for $4,500. Abdul paid $1,500 cash and promised to pay the balance over the next three months.
(d) Purchased office supplies for cash, $350.
(e) Sent letters to numerous performing groups throughout the region explaining the services available through J. A. Productions. Postage of $200 was paid in cash.
(f) Began arranging performances throughout the region after securing contracts with several groups. The phone bill came to $300 and was paid in cash.
(g) Earned promotion revenue of $2,500: $2,000 in cash and $500 on account.
(h) Paid part-time receptionist $600.
(i) Withdrew $1,000 for personal use.
(j) Paid $2,500 on account for the office furniture purchased in part (b).
(k) Collected $250 for promotional fees earned on account.

Problem 9 (Continued)

Required:

1. Record the transactions in the T accounts provided.
2. Foot and balance the accounts.
3. Prepare a trial balance of the accounts as of January 31, 20--, using the form provided.

1. and 2.

Assets		=	Liabilities		+	Owner's Equity	
Debit +	Credit −		Debit −	Credit +		Debit −	Credit +

Cash

Accounts Receivable

Office Supplies

Office Furniture

Computer Equipment

Accounts Payable

J. Abdul, Capital

Drawing		Expenses		Revenues	
Debit +	Credit −	Debit +	Credit −	Debit −	Credit +

J. Abdul, Drawing

Wages Expense

Phone Expense

Postage Expense

Promotion Fees

Problem 9 (Concluded)

3.

ACCOUNT	DEBIT BALANCE	CREDIT BALANCE

Problem 10 (LO 5) REVIEW: ACCOUNTING EQUATION AND FINANCIAL STATEMENTS

Based on the transactions recorded in Problem 9, select the information needed to fill in the blank space in the following statements:

(a) Total revenue for the month __________

(b) Total expenses for the month __________

(c) Net income for the month __________

(d) Abdul's original investment in the business __________

+ Net income for the month __________

– Owner's drawing __________

Increase in capital __________

= Owner's equity at the end of the month __________

(e) End-of-month accounting equation:

Assets	=	Liabilities	+	Owner's Equity

Problem 11 (LO 5) REVIEW: PREPARATION OF FINANCIAL STATEMENTS

Refer to the trial balance in Problem 9 and to the analysis of the change in owner's equity in Problem 10.

(a) Prepare an income statement for J. A. Productions for the month ended January 31, 20--.

(b) Prepare a statement of owner's equity for J. A. Productions for the month ended January 31, 20--.

(c) Prepare a balance sheet for J. A. Productions as of January 31, 20--.

(a)

Problem 11 (Concluded)

(b)

(c)

CHAPTER 4
JOURNALIZING AND POSTING TRANSACTIONS

LEARNING OBJECTIVES

Chapter 3 introduced the double-entry framework and illustrated the impact of debits and credits on the accounting equation and T accounts. In Chapter 4, business transactions are entered into the general journal and posted to general ledger accounts.

Objective 1. Describe the flow of data from source documents to the trial balance.

The flow of financial data from the source documents through the accounting information systems follows the steps listed below.

1. Analyze what happened by using information from source documents and the firm's chart of accounts.
2. Enter business transactions in the general journal.
3. Post entries to accounts in the general ledger.
4. Prepare a trial balance.

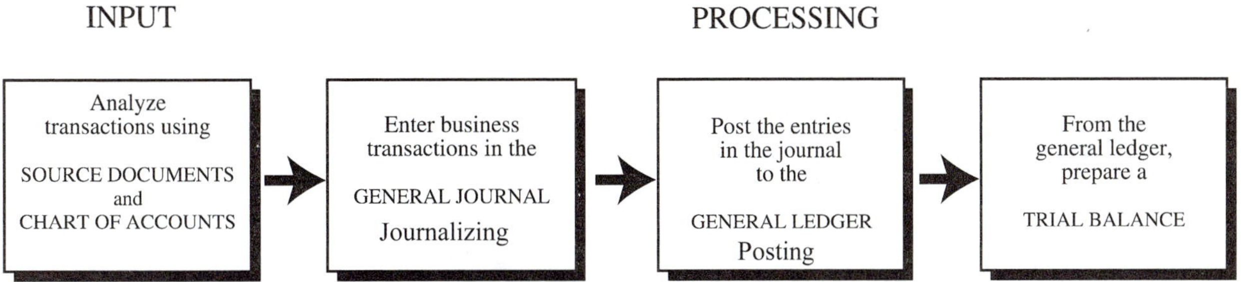

Objective 2. Describe and explain the purpose of source documents.

A **source document** provides objective information needed to record a transaction. Examples include check stubs, receipts, cash register tapes, sales invoices, and memos. Source documents are analyzed to determine which accounts should be increased or decreased.

Objective 3. Describe the chart of accounts as a means of classifying financial information.

The **chart of accounts** lists in numerical order all of the accounts being used by a business. Assets are listed first (begin with "1"); liabilities are second (begin with "2"); owner's equity accounts are third (begin with "3"); revenues are fourth (begin with "4"); and expenses are last (begin with "5"). In a three-digit account numbering system, for example, Cash may be account number 101 and Accounts Receivable may be account number 122. Spacing numbers this way permits easy addition of new accounts as the business grows.

Objective 4. Journalize transactions.

Journalizing is the process of entering information into the journal, or book of original entry. This simply means the journal is the first place a transaction is recorded. The general journal has space to enter the date of the transaction, the name of the accounts being debited and credited, the account numbers, and the amounts of the debits and credits. A brief description follows each journal entry stating the reason for the entry.

Objective 5. Post to the general ledger and prepare a trial balance.

Once the transactions are entered into the general journal, they must be **posted** to (copied to) the individual accounts, which are located in the general ledger. The accounts are in the general ledger in the chart of accounts order. That is, the assets are first, followed by liabilities, owner's equity, revenue, and expense accounts.

In this chapter, the general ledger accounts are in the form of four-column accounts. This is better than the T account because a running balance is maintained.

The **trial balance** is a listing of account balances at the end of the month—after all the transactions have been posted from the general journal to the general ledger accounts. The total of the debit balances must equal the total of the credit balances.

Objective 6. Explain how to find and correct errors.

Finding errors can be a long and frustrating process. But there are some methods to reduce the time and effort needed. The first thing to do is double check your calculations and the accuracy of the posting activities. Common errors include sliding ($230 could become $23 or $2,300) and transposing numbers ($326 could become $236). Taking the difference between the debits and credits and dividing by 9 or by 2 may help locate the error.

There are two methods of correcting errors. The **ruling method** may be used before the transaction has been posted. Under this method, you draw a line through the incorrect title or amount and write in the correct information above the ruling. The **correcting entry method** is used after an entry has been posted to the general ledger. The correcting entry increases and decreases accounts in a manner that corrects the errors made in previous transactions.

REVIEW QUESTIONS

Instructions: Analyze each of the following items carefully before writing your answer in the column at the right.

		Question	Answer
LO 1/2	**1.**	A document that provides information about a business transaction is called a(n) ________.	________
LO 3	**2.**	A list of all the accounts used by a business enterprise is called a(n) ________.	________
LO 3	**3.**	Accounts that begin with the number "3" are ________.	________
LO 3	**4.**	Expenses are accounts that begin with which number?	________
LO 4	**5.**	A document that provides a day-by-day listing of transactions of a business is called a(n) ________.	________
LO 4	**6.**	A journal is commonly referred to as a(n) ________ because it is here that the first formal accounting record is made.	________
LO 4	**7.**	Transactions affecting more than two accounts are called ________.	________
LO 4	**8.**	The act of entering transactions into a journal is called ________.	________
LO 4	**9.**	In a journal, debits are entered first; then credits are entered and indented ________ (how much space).	________
LO 5	**10.**	A complete set of all accounts used by a business is known as the ________.	________

LO 5 11. A(n) ________ account allows the accountant to keep a running balance. .... ____________________

LO 5 12. The process of copying debits and credits from the journal to the ledger accounts is called ________. .... ____________________

LO 5 13. Posting from the journal to the ledger is done ________ or at frequent intervals. .... ____________________

LO 5 14. The information in the Posting Reference columns of the journal and the ledger accounts provides a link known as a(n) ________. .... ____________________

LO 5 15. A(n) ________ is taken after transactions are posted to the general ledger accounts to be sure that debit and credit balances in the ledger are equal. .... ____________________

LO 6 16. A(n) ________ error occurs when you move a number a decimal place to the right or left. .... ____________________

LO 6 17. A(n) ________ error occurs when you use the right numbers but in the wrong order. .... ____________________

LO 6 18. Drawing a line through the incorrect amount or account title and writing correct information above it is an example of the ________ method. .... ____________________

LO 6 19. When an incorrect entry has been journalized and posted, a(n) _______ entry is required. .... ____________________

EXERCISES

Exercise 1 (LO 4) REVIEW: TRANSACTION ANALYSIS

Before a transaction is recorded in the journal, it should be analyzed to determine the following:

(a) What accounts are affected by the transaction.
(b) Whether each affected account is to be increased or decreased.
(c) Whether the increase or decrease is to be accomplished by a debit or credit.

In the following list of transactions for Abbott Service Co., indicate the names of the accounts to be debited and credited. Place a check mark in either the plus (+) or minus (–) column to indicate whether the account has been increased or decreased. The first transaction is entered as an illustration.

Transaction		Account	(+)	(–)
1. J. A. Abbott invested cash in a business enterprise.	Debit:	Cash	✓	
	Credit:	J. A. Abbott, Capital	✓	
2. Received cash for services provided.	Debit:			
	Credit:			

Transaction		Account	(+)	(–)
3. Paid cash for rent on the office.	Debit:	______	____	____
	Credit:	______	____	____
4. Purchased office equipment on account.	Debit:	______	____	____
	Credit	______	____	____
5. Paid cash to a creditor for a debt previously owed.	Debit:	______	____	____
	Credit:	______	____	____
6. Paid the phone bill for the month.	Debit:	______	____	____
	Credit:	______	____	____
7. Paid supplier for office equipment purchased in transaction (4) above.	Debit:	______	____	____
	Credit:	______	____	____
8. Paid cash for a car for the owner's personal use.	Debit:	______	____	____
	Credit:	______	____	____
9. Paid temporary secretary's wages.	Debit:	______	____	____
	Credit:	______	____	____
10. Performed services that will be paid for later.	Debit:	______	____	____
	Credit:	______	____	____

Exercise 2 (LO 4) JOURNALIZING TRANSACTIONS

Susan Poe started a business, Poe's Connections. She provides resource referral services whereby she helps businesses locate vendors of specialty products and vice versa. She charges a referral fee to her clients who may be businesses or vendors. She has a part-time clerk who enters information into a database to match requests with potential users or suppliers. Her chart of accounts is as follows:

Assets
- 101 Cash
- 122 Accounts Receivable
- 182 Office Furniture

Liabilities
- 202 Accounts Payable

Owner's Equity
- 311 Susan Poe, Capital
- 312 Susan Poe, Drawing

Revenues
- 401 Referral Fees

Expenses
- 511 Wages Expense
- 521 Rent Expense

Exercise 2 (Continued)

Required:

Enter the following transactions in the two-column journal provided on the next page.

20--		
May	1	Susan invested $5,000 cash to start the business.
	5	Purchased office furniture on account, $3,000.
	9	Paid office rent for the month, $450.
	10	Received fees for referral services, $500.
	15	Made payment on account (for office furniture), $100.
	20	Earned referral fees: $125 cash and $175 on account.
	25	Paid wages to clerk for part-time work, $400.
	28	Withdrew cash for personal use, $100.
	29	Received cash for referral services previously rendered, $150.

Exercise 2 (Concluded)

GENERAL JOURNAL

PAGE 1

DATE		DESCRIPTION	POST. REF.	DEBIT	CREDIT

Exercise 3 (LO 5) POST TO THE GENERAL LEDGER

Post the transactions from Exercise 2 to the general ledger accounts provided as follows. Be sure to enter the appropriate cross-reference information in the Posting Reference columns of the general ledger accounts and the general journal.

GENERAL LEDGER

ACCOUNT: Cash ACCOUNT NO. 101

DATE	ITEM	POST. REF.	DEBIT	CREDIT	BALANCE DEBIT	BALANCE CREDIT

ACCOUNT: Accounts Receivable ACCOUNT NO. 122

DATE	ITEM	POST. REF.	DEBIT	CREDIT	BALANCE DEBIT	BALANCE CREDIT

ACCOUNT: Office Furniture ACCOUNT NO. 182

DATE	ITEM	POST. REF.	DEBIT	CREDIT	BALANCE DEBIT	BALANCE CREDIT

ACCOUNT: Accounts Payable ACCOUNT NO. 202

DATE	ITEM	POST. REF.	DEBIT	CREDIT	BALANCE DEBIT	BALANCE CREDIT

Exercise 3 (Concluded)

GENERAL LEDGER

ACCOUNT: Susan Poe, Capital — ACCOUNT NO. 311

DATE		ITEM	POST. REF.	DEBIT	CREDIT	BALANCE	
						DEBIT	CREDIT

ACCOUNT: Susan Poe, Drawing — ACCOUNT NO. 312

DATE		ITEM	POST. REF.	DEBIT	CREDIT	BALANCE	
						DEBIT	CREDIT

ACCOUNT: Referral Fees — ACCOUNT NO. 401

DATE		ITEM	POST. REF.	DEBIT	CREDIT	BALANCE	
						DEBIT	CREDIT

ACCOUNT: Wages Expense — ACCOUNT NO. 511

DATE		ITEM	POST. REF.	DEBIT	CREDIT	BALANCE	
						DEBIT	CREDIT

ACCOUNT: Rent Expense — ACCOUNT NO. 521

DATE		ITEM	POST. REF.	DEBIT	CREDIT	BALANCE	
						DEBIT	CREDIT

Exercise 4 (LO 5) REVIEW: PREPARE A TRIAL BALANCE

After the transactions are posted in Exercise 3, prepare the trial balance.

____

____

____

ACCOUNT TITLE	ACCT. NO.	DEBIT BALANCE	CREDIT BALANCE

PROBLEMS

Problem 5 (LO 4/5) JOURNALIZING AND POSTING TRANSACTIONS FOLLOWED BY PREPARATION OF A TRIAL BALANCE

Della Jordan started her own business, D. J. Parties. For about $50 per hour, Della and a group of part-time associates serve as disc jockeys for parties held at the client's home. As part of the service, Della provides a lighting system, stereo equipment, CDs, and two disc jockeys working as a team for each party. A wide range of music is offered, and the client may provide additional CDs to be played. A chart of accounts is provided below.

D. J. Parties
Chart of Accounts

Assets		Owner's Equity	
101	Cash	311	Della Jordan, Capital
122	Accounts Receivable	312	Della Jordan, Drawing
181	Stereo Equipment		
182	Office Furniture	Revenue	
183	CDs	401	Disc Jockey Fees
184	Lighting Equipment		
185	Van	Expenses	
		511	Wages Expense
Liabilities		521	Rent Expense
202	Accounts Payable	525	Phone Expense
		538	Gas Expense

Problem 5 (Continued)

The following transactions occurred during May, the first month of operation:

20--		
May	1	Jordan invested $30,000 cash in the business. The funds were deposited in a business checking account.
	3	Purchased stereo equipment and speaker systems from Big Al's Discount Stereo for $7,000: $3,000 cash and $4,000 on account.
	4	Purchased compact discs and tapes for $2,500.
	4	Purchased lighting equipment for $2,000.
	5	Purchased office furniture on account, $500.
	7	Purchased a van to be used to haul the equipment to the clients' homes, $9,500.
	18	Earned fees for services rendered, $3,800: $800 cash and $3,000 on account.
	20	Paid part-time associates for work performed, $600.
	21	Made payment on account for stereo equipment bought on May 3, $1,500.
	25	Paid for gas for the van, $40.
	27	Paid phone bill, $80.
	28	Received cash for services previously rendered, $1,500.
	29	Paid part-time associates, $1,100.
	30	Paid rent, $500.
	30	Made payment on account for stereo equipment bought on May 3, $1,200.
	30	Jordan made withdrawal for personal use, $1,000.

Required:

1. Enter the transactions in the two-column journal provided on pages 45–46. Use journal page 1 for transactions through May 20. Enter the remainder on page 2.
2. Post the transactions from the journal to the general ledger accounts on pages 47–50.
3. Prepare a trial balance.

Name ______________________________

Problem 5 (Continued)

1. *[Instructor: Account numbers in Post. Ref. column are entered when completing requirement 2.]*

GENERAL JOURNAL

PAGE 1

DATE		DESCRIPTION	POST. REF.	DEBIT	CREDIT

Problem 5 (Continued)

GENERAL JOURNAL

PAGE 2

	DATE	DESCRIPTION	POST. REF.	DEBIT	CREDIT	
1						1
2						2
3						3
4						4
5						5
6						6
7						7
8						8
9						9
10						10
11						11
12						12
13						13
14						14
15						15
16						16
17						17
18						18
19						19
20						20
21						21
22						22
23						23
24						24
25						25
26						26
27						27
28						28
29						29
30						30
31						31
32						32
33						33

Name ______________________________

Problem 5 (Continued)

2.

GENERAL LEDGER

ACCOUNT: Cash ACCOUNT NO. 101

DATE	ITEM	POST. REF.	DEBIT	CREDIT	BALANCE DEBIT	BALANCE CREDIT

ACCOUNT: Accounts Receivable ACCOUNT NO. 122

DATE	ITEM	POST. REF.	DEBIT	CREDIT	BALANCE DEBIT	BALANCE CREDIT

ACCOUNT: Stereo Equipment ACCOUNT NO. 181

DATE	ITEM	POST. REF.	DEBIT	CREDIT	BALANCE DEBIT	BALANCE CREDIT

Problem 5 (Continued)

ACCOUNT: Office Furniture ACCOUNT NO. 182

DATE	ITEM	POST. REF.	DEBIT	CREDIT	BALANCE	
					DEBIT	CREDIT

ACCOUNT: CDs ACCOUNT NO. 183

DATE	ITEM	POST. REF.	DEBIT	CREDIT	BALANCE	
					DEBIT	CREDIT

ACCOUNT: Lighting Equipment ACCOUNT NO. 184

DATE	ITEM	POST. REF.	DEBIT	CREDIT	BALANCE	
					DEBIT	CREDIT

ACCOUNT: Van ACCOUNT NO. 185

DATE	ITEM	POST. REF.	DEBIT	CREDIT	BALANCE	
					DEBIT	CREDIT

ACCOUNT: Accounts Payable ACCOUNT NO. 202

DATE	ITEM	POST. REF.	DEBIT	CREDIT	BALANCE	
					DEBIT	CREDIT

Problem 5 (Continued)

ACCOUNT: Della Jordan, Capital ACCOUNT NO. 311

DATE	ITEM	POST. REF.	DEBIT	CREDIT	BALANCE DEBIT	BALANCE CREDIT

ACCOUNT: Della Jordan, Drawing ACCOUNT NO. 312

DATE	ITEM	POST. REF.	DEBIT	CREDIT	BALANCE DEBIT	BALANCE CREDIT

ACCOUNT: Disc Jockey Fees ACCOUNT NO. 401

DATE	ITEM	POST. REF.	DEBIT	CREDIT	BALANCE DEBIT	BALANCE CREDIT

ACCOUNT: Wages Expense ACCOUNT NO. 511

DATE	ITEM	POST. REF.	DEBIT	CREDIT	BALANCE DEBIT	BALANCE CREDIT

ACCOUNT: Rent Expense ACCOUNT NO. 521

DATE	ITEM	POST. REF.	DEBIT	CREDIT	BALANCE DEBIT	BALANCE CREDIT

Problem 5 (Concluded)

ACCOUNT: Phone Expense ACCOUNT NO. 525

DATE		ITEM	POST. REF.	DEBIT	CREDIT	BALANCE	
						DEBIT	CREDIT

ACCOUNT: Gas Expense ACCOUNT NO. 538

DATE		ITEM	POST. REF.	DEBIT	CREDIT	BALANCE	
						DEBIT	CREDIT

3.

ACCOUNT TITLE	ACCT. NO.	DEBIT BALANCE	CREDIT BALANCE

Name ____________________

Problem 6 (LO 5) REVIEW: PREPARATION OF FINANCIAL STATEMENTS

From the information in Problem 5, prepare an income statement, a statement of owner's equity, and a balance sheet.

Problem 6 (Concluded)

Problem 7

1. (LO 6) CORRECTION OF ERRORS: The Ruling Method

The following journal entries were made but not posted. On January 1, $500 cash was withdrawn by the owner for personal use (R. J. Hammond) but was charged to Wages Expense. On January 2, $230 was paid on account. Make corrections using the ruling method.

GENERAL JOURNAL PAGE

	DATE		DESCRIPTION	POST. REF.	DEBIT	CREDIT	
1	20-- Jan.	1	Wages Expense		500 00		1
2			Cash			500 00	2
3			Paid R. J. Hammond				3
4							4
5		2	Accounts Payable		320 00		5
6			Cash			320 00	6
7			Payment on account				7
8							8

Problem 7 (Concluded)

2. (LO 6) CORRECTION OF ERRORS: The Correcting Entry Method

On January 10, Office Equipment was debited for $800 when the debit should have been to Office Supplies. Since the entry has been posted, show the appropriate correcting entry made in the general journal on January 15.

GENERAL JOURNAL PAGE

	DATE		DESCRIPTION	POST. REF.	DEBIT	CREDIT	
1							1
2							2
3							3
4							4
5							5
6							6
7							7
8							8

CHAPTER 5
ADJUSTING ENTRIES AND THE WORK SHEET

LEARNING OBJECTIVES

We are coming to the end of the accounting cycle, and certain things must be done at the end of the period that are not done during the regular accounting period. In Chapter 5, adjusting entries and the work sheet are presented.

Objective 1. Prepare end-of-period adjustments.

In Chapters 2 through 4, we learned how to account for business transactions—events based primarily on arm's length exchanges with other parties. During the accounting period, however, other changes occur which affect the financial condition of the business. For example, supplies are being used, equipment is wearing out, insurance is expiring, and employees may have earned wages that have not yet been paid. It is important for information reported on the financial statements to accurately reflect the results of business transactions with outside parties and other activities taking place inside the business. Therefore, adjustments must be made at the end of the accounting period to properly report assets and liabilities on the balance sheet and to comply with the revenue recognition and matching principles. The **revenue recognition principle** states that revenues should be recognized when earned, regardless of when cash is received from the customer. Revenues are considered earned when a service is provided or a product sold. Similarly, the **expense recognition principle** states that expenses should be recognized when incurred, regardless of when cash is paid. Expenses are generally considered incurred when services are received or assets are consumed. The proper matching of revenues earned during an accounting period with the expenses incurred to produce the revenues is often referred to as the **matching principle**. This approach offers the best measure of net income.

Objective 2. Post adjusting entries to the general ledger.

After the adjusting entries are journalized, the next step is to post them to the general ledger. The word "Adjusting" is written in the Item column in the general ledger, and each adjustment is posted to the proper general ledger account.

Objective 3. Prepare a work sheet.

The work sheet is a tool used by accountants to help organize work done at the end of the accounting period. This document is not a formal part of the accounting system. Therefore, information recorded here has no effect on the accounts or financial statements. The main purposes of the work sheet are to prepare the adjusting entries and accumulate information that will be used in the preparation of the financial statements. Five steps are taken to prepare a work sheet.

Step 1 Prepare a trial balance to ensure that the general ledger is in balance before adjusting the accounts.

Step 2 Analyze and enter the adjusting entries in the Adjustments columns of the work sheet. Every adjustment must have an equal debit and credit; and upon completion, the total debits and credits must be equal in the Adjustments columns.

Step 3 Prepare the adjusted trial balance. Every account appearing in the Trial Balance columns will be extended to the Adjusted Trial Balance columns and include any changes due to the adjusting entries. Upon completion, the total of the debits and credits in the Adjusted Trial Balance columns must be equal.

Step 4 Extend the balances in the adjusted trial balance to either the Income Statement or Balance Sheet columns. All revenue and expenses are extended to the Income Statement columns. All other accounts (assets, liabilities, owner's capital, owner's drawing) are extended to the Balance Sheet columns.

Step 5 Complete the work sheet. Initially, the totals of the Income Statement columns will not be equal. Similarly, the totals of the Balance Sheet columns will not be equal. If the Income Statement Credit column exceeds the Income Statement Debit column, the difference represents net income. If the Income Statement Debit column exceeds the Income Statement Credit column, the difference represents net loss. The difference in the Balance Sheet columns will be exactly the same as the difference in the Income Statement columns. The amount of net income should be added to the Income Statement Debit column and the Balance Sheet Credit column for total debits to equal total credits for all four columns. If there is a net loss, this amount should be added to the Income Statement Credit column and the Balance Sheet Debit column.

Partial Work Sheet

	For Net Income					**For Net Loss**			
	Income Statement		**Balance Sheet**			**Income Statement**		**Balance Sheet**	
	Debit	**Credit**	**Debit**	**Credit**		**Debit**	**Credit**	**Debit**	**Credit**
	2,500	3,200	6,200	5,500		3,000	2,500	7,000	7,500
Net Income	**700**			**700**	**Net Loss**		**500**	**500**	
	3,200	3,200	6,200	6,200		3,000	3,000	7,500	7,500
	Apart						Together		

Objective 4. Describe methods for finding errors on the work sheet.

The following tips may help in finding errors on the work sheet:

1. Check the addition of all columns.
2. Check the addition and subtraction required when extending to the Adjusted Trial Balance columns.
3. Make sure the adjusted account balances have been extended to the appropriate columns.
4. Make sure that the net income or net loss has been added to the appropriate columns.

Objective 5. Journalize adjusting entries from the work sheet.

Once the adjustments have been "penciled in" on the work sheet, the next step is to journalize the adjusting entries. "Adjusting Entries" is written in the Description column in the general journal, and the adjusting entries are copied from the work sheet into the general journal.

Objective 6. Explain the cash, modified cash, and accrual bases of accounting.

The *accrual basis* of accounting recognizes revenues when earned, regardless of when cash is received from the customer. Likewise, expenses are recognized when incurred, regardless of when they are actually paid. The *cash basis* is used by some small businesses and by individuals for income tax purposes. With the cash basis, no revenue or expenses are recognized until cash is actually received or paid.

The *modified cash basis* is a combination of the accrual and cash methods. Revenues and most expenses are recorded only when cash is received or paid (like the cash basis). However, when cash is paid for assets with useful lives greater than one accounting period, exceptions are made. Cash payments like these are recorded as assets, and adjustments are made each period as under the accrual basis. Figure 5-25 in the text compares these methods in different types of transactions.

REVIEW QUESTIONS

Instructions: Analyze each of the following items carefully before writing your answer in the column at the right.

	Question	Answer
LO 1	**1.** The revenue recognition principle requires revenues to be recognized when ________.	________
LO 1	**2.** The **expense recognition principle** states that expenses should be recognized when	________
LO 1	**3.** The matching principle in accounting requires the matching of ________ and ________.	________
LO 1	**4.** The asset account Supplies is adjusted to the income statement account entitled ________.	________
LO 1	**5.** The asset account Prepaid Insurance is adjusted to the income statement account entitled ________.	________
LO 1	**6.** The adjustment to Wages Expense will also affect a liability account called ________.	________
LO 1	**7.** The period of time a plant asset is expected to help produce revenues is called its ________.	________
LO 1	**8.** The purpose of ________ is to spread the cost of a plant asset over its useful life.	________
LO 1	**9.** A plant asset's original cost less salvage value is called ________.	________
LO 1	**10.** A ________ has a credit balance and is deducted from the related asset account on the balance sheet.	________
LO 1	**11.** The depreciation adjusting entry consists of a debit to Depreciation Expense and a credit to ________.	________
LO 1	**12.** The difference between the original cost of a plant asset and its accumulated depreciation is called ________.	________
LO 3	**13.** A ________ is helpful in preparing end-of-period adjustments and financial statements.	________
LO 3	**14.** The first two monetary columns of a work sheet are called the ________ columns.	________
LO 3	**15.** To which columns of the work sheet are asset and liability accounts extended?	________
LO 3	**16.** To which columns of the work sheet are revenue and expense accounts extended?	________
LO 3	**17.** To which columns of the work sheet are the capital and drawing accounts extended?	________

LO 3 18. If the total of the Income Statement Credit column exceeds the total of the Debit column, the business has earned ________. .... ______________________

LO 6 19. In the ________ basis of accounting, revenues are recorded when earned and expenses are recorded when incurred, regardless of when cash is received or paid. .... ______________________

LO 6 20. In the ________ basis of accounting, revenues are recorded only when cash is received and expenses are recorded only when cash is paid. .... ______________________

LO 6 21. The ________ basis of accounting uses the cash basis for revenues and most expenses. .... ______________________

LO 6 22. Many small professional ________ businesses use the modified cash basis of accounting. .... ______________________

EXERCISES

Exercise 1 (LO 1) PREPARING END-OF-PERIOD ADJUSTMENTS: SUPPLIES

The beginning balance of the supplies account was $300. During the year, additional supplies costing $600 were purchased and entered as debits to the supplies account. An end-of-period inventory determined that $200 worth of supplies are still on hand.

Required:

1. Determine the balance of the supplies account just prior to making any end-of-period adjustments. ______________________
2. When preparing the balance sheet, what should be reported for Supplies at the end of the year? ______________________
3. Determine the balance of the supplies expense account just prior to making any end-of-period adjustments. ______________________
4. When preparing the income statement, what should be reported for Supplies Expense? (What was the cost of the supplies used?) ______________________
5. What adjustment must be made to the supplies and supplies expense accounts? ______________________

Exercise 2 (LO 1) PREPARING END-OF-PERIOD ADJUSTMENTS: DEPRECIATION

Office equipment with an expected life of 10 years and no salvage value was purchased on January 1 for $5,000. Assume the business has no other office equipment and straight-line depreciation is used.

Required:

1. What is the balance of the office equipment account at the end of the year? ______________________
2. What expense amount should be reported on the income statement for the use of the office equipment? ______________________
3. What book value should be reported on the balance sheet for the office equipment at the end of the first year? ______________________
4. What adjustment must be made at the end of the year to report information about the office equipment on the income statement and balance sheet? ______________________

Exercise 3 (LO 1/2) PREPARING, JOURNALIZING, AND POSTING ADJUSTING ENTRIES: SUPPLIES

The Maddie Hays modeling agency began the current period with office supplies that cost $1,225. During the period, additional supplies costing $4,545 were purchased. At the end of the accounting period, December 31, 20--, only $800 in supplies remain.

Required:

1. Enter the appropriate adjusting entry in a two-column journal.
2. Post this entry to the ledger accounts provided on the next page.

Exercise 3 (Concluded)

1.

GENERAL JOURNAL

PAGE 5

	DATE		DESCRIPTION	POST. REF.	DEBIT	CREDIT	
1							1
2							2
3							3
4							4
5							5

2.

GENERAL LEDGER

ACCOUNT: Supplies ACCOUNT NO. 141

DATE		ITEM	POST. REF.	DEBIT	CREDIT	BALANCE DEBIT	BALANCE CREDIT
20-- Jan.	1	Balance	✓			1,225.00	
Feb.	12		J2	4,545.00		5,770.00	

ACCOUNT: Supplies Expense ACCOUNT NO. 524

DATE		ITEM	POST. REF.	DEBIT	CREDIT	BALANCE DEBIT	BALANCE CREDIT

Exercise 4 (LO 1/2) PREPARING, JOURNALIZING, AND POSTING ADJUSTING ENTRIES: DEPRECIATION

The Billy Willis Detective Agency began the accounting period by purchasing three cars that cost a total of $75,000. The estimated useful life of these cars is only two years with no salvage value.

Required:

1. Enter the appropriate adjusting entry at the end of the first year in a two-column journal. Willis uses straight-line depreciation.
2. Post this entry to the ledger accounts provided on the next page.

Exercise 4 (Concluded)

1. GENERAL JOURNAL PAGE 5

	DATE		DESCRIPTION	POST. REF.	DEBIT	CREDIT	
1							1
2							2
3							3
4							4

2. GENERAL LEDGER

ACCOUNT: Automobiles ACCOUNT NO. 185

DATE		ITEM	POST. REF.	DEBIT	CREDIT	BALANCE DEBIT	BALANCE CREDIT
20-- Jan.	2		J1	75 0 0 0 00		75 0 0 0 00	

ACCOUNT: Accumulated Depreciation—Automobiles ACCOUNT NO. 185.1

DATE		ITEM	POST. REF.	DEBIT	CREDIT	BALANCE DEBIT	BALANCE CREDIT

ACCOUNT: Depreciation Expense—Automobiles ACCOUNT NO. 541

DATE		ITEM	POST. REF.	DEBIT	CREDIT	BALANCE DEBIT	BALANCE CREDIT

Exercise 5 (LO 1/2) PREPARING, JOURNALIZING, AND POSTING ADJUSTING ENTRIES: PREPAID INSURANCE AND WAGES PAYABLE

On June 1, the Straw Basket Herb Farm purchased a one-year liability insurance policy for $600.

As of June 30, an additional $120 was earned by the employees but not yet paid.

Required:

1. Enter the appropriate adjusting entries at the end of June in the following general journal.
2. Post the entries to the ledger accounts provided.

1.

GENERAL JOURNAL

PAGE 6

	DATE		DESCRIPTION	POST. REF.	DEBIT	CREDIT	
1							1
2							2
3							3
4							4
5							5
6							6
7							7

2.

GENERAL LEDGER

ACCOUNT: Prepaid Insurance ACCOUNT NO. 145

DATE		ITEM	POST. REF.	DEBIT	CREDIT	BALANCE	
						DEBIT	CREDIT
20-- June	1		J2	600 00		600 00	

ACCOUNT: Wages Payable ACCOUNT NO. 219

DATE		ITEM	POST. REF.	DEBIT	CREDIT	BALANCE	
						DEBIT	CREDIT

Exercise 5 (Concluded)

ACCOUNT: Wages Expense ACCOUNT NO. 511

DATE		ITEM	POST. REF.	DEBIT	CREDIT	BALANCE DEBIT	BALANCE CREDIT
20--							
June	14		J5	500 00		500 00	
	28		J5	500 00		1000 00	

ACCOUNT: Insurance Expense ACCOUNT NO. 535

DATE		ITEM	POST. REF.	DEBIT	CREDIT	BALANCE DEBIT	BALANCE CREDIT

Exercise 6 (LO 6) CASH BASIS OF ACCOUNTING

In the space provided, indicate which account is debited and which account is credited, using the **cash basis** of accounting. If no entry is made, write "NO ENTRY."

1. Paid rent, $500.

____

____

2. Purchased typewriter (office equipment) for $300.

____

____

3. Revenue for week: $300 cash, $200 on account.

____

____

4. Purchased fax machine (office equipment) for $400, on account.

____

____

5. Made payment on fax machine, $100.

____

____

Exercise 7 (LO 6) MODIFIED CASH BASIS OF ACCOUNTING

In the space provided, indicate which account is debited and which account is credited, using the **modified cash basis** of accounting. If no entry is made, write "NO ENTRY."

1. Paid electricity bill, $50.

2. Purchased office equipment for $500, on account.

3. Revenue for week: $500 cash, $200 on account.

4. Wages earned but not paid, $500.

5. Made payment on office equipment previously purchased, $25.

Exercise 8 (LO 6) ACCRUAL BASIS OF ACCOUNTING

In the space provided, indicate which account is debited and which account is credited, using the **accrual basis** of accounting. If no entry is made, write "NO ENTRY."

1. Purchased supplies (prepaid asset), $500, on account.

2. Revenue for week: $400 cash, $250 on account.

3. Wages earned but not paid, $250.

Exercise 8 (Concluded)

4. Made payment on account, $50, for supplies previously purchased.

5. Depreciation on long-term assets, $300.

PROBLEMS

Problem 9 (LO1/3) PREPARING ADJUSTMENTS AND THE WORK SHEET

Kim Ho offers employment counseling to middle managers unemployed due to corporate downsizing. On January 1 of the current year, Ho purchased office equipment with an expected life of 12 years and no salvage value. Computer equipment with an expected life of four years and no salvage value was purchased on July 1 of the current year. Ho uses straight-line depreciation. Office supplies on hand at year-end amounted to $150. Employees earned $300 in wages that have not yet been paid. Provided are the general ledger accounts as of December 31, prior to adjustment.

Required:

1. Using the ledger accounts, complete the Trial Balance columns of the year-end work sheet provided.
2. Prepare the necessary year-end adjustments.
3. Complete the work sheet.

GENERAL LEDGER

ACCOUNT: Cash ACCOUNT NO. 101

DATE		ITEM	POST. REF.	DEBIT	CREDIT	BALANCE DEBIT	BALANCE CREDIT
20--							
Dec.	1	Balance	✔			2,400.00	
	21		J20	10,800.00		13,200.00	
	27		J20		4,200.00	9,000.00	

ACCOUNT: Office Supplies ACCOUNT NO. 142

DATE		ITEM	POST. REF.	DEBIT	CREDIT	BALANCE DEBIT	BALANCE CREDIT
20--							
Dec.	1	Balance	✔			200.00	
	6		J20	300.00		500.00	

Problem 9 (Continued)

ACCOUNT: Office Equipment — ACCOUNT NO. 181

DATE		ITEM	POST. REF.	DEBIT	CREDIT	BALANCE DEBIT	BALANCE CREDIT
20-- Dec.	1	Balance	✔			6,000.00	

ACCOUNT: Accumulated Depreciation—Office Equipment — ACCOUNT NO. 181.1

DATE		ITEM	POST. REF.	DEBIT	CREDIT	BALANCE DEBIT	BALANCE CREDIT

ACCOUNT: Computer Equipment — ACCOUNT NO. 187

DATE		ITEM	POST. REF.	DEBIT	CREDIT	BALANCE DEBIT	BALANCE CREDIT
20-- Dec.	1	Balance	✔			8,000.00	

ACCOUNT: Accumulated Depreciation—Computer Equipment — ACCOUNT NO. 187.1

DATE		ITEM	POST. REF.	DEBIT	CREDIT	BALANCE DEBIT	BALANCE CREDIT

ACCOUNT: Accounts Payable — ACCOUNT NO. 202

DATE		ITEM	POST. REF.	DEBIT	CREDIT	BALANCE DEBIT	BALANCE CREDIT
20-- Dec.	1	Balance	✔				300.00
	6		J20		200.00		500.00
	27		J20	100.00			400.00

Problem 9 (Continued)

ACCOUNT: Wages Payable ACCOUNT NO. 219

DATE		ITEM	POST. REF.	DEBIT	CREDIT	BALANCE DEBIT	BALANCE CREDIT

ACCOUNT: Kim Ho, Capital ACCOUNT NO. 311

DATE		ITEM	POST. REF.	DEBIT	CREDIT	BALANCE DEBIT	BALANCE CREDIT
20-- Dec.	1	Balance	✔				10 2 0 0 00

ACCOUNT: Kim Ho, Drawing ACCOUNT NO. 312

DATE		ITEM	POST. REF.	DEBIT	CREDIT	BALANCE DEBIT	BALANCE CREDIT
20-- Dec.	1	Balance	✔			1 5 0 0 00	
	30		J20	1 0 0 0 00		2 5 0 0 00	

ACCOUNT: Counseling Fees ACCOUNT NO. 401

DATE		ITEM	POST. REF.	DEBIT	CREDIT	BALANCE DEBIT	BALANCE CREDIT
20-- Dec.	1	Balance	✔				22 0 0 0 00
	31		J20		10 1 7 0 00		32 1 7 0 00

Problem 9 (Continued)

ACCOUNT: Wages Expense ACCOUNT NO. 511

DATE		ITEM	POST. REF.	DEBIT	CREDIT	BALANCE DEBIT	BALANCE CREDIT
20-- Dec.	1	Balance	✓			7,000.00	
	31		J20	1,500.00		8,500.00	

ACCOUNT: Rent Expense ACCOUNT NO. 521

DATE		ITEM	POST. REF.	DEBIT	CREDIT	BALANCE DEBIT	BALANCE CREDIT
20-- Dec.	1	Balance	✓			4,400.00	
	4		J20	1,200.00		5,600.00	

ACCOUNT: Supplies Expense ACCOUNT NO. 524

DATE		ITEM	POST. REF.	DEBIT	CREDIT	BALANCE DEBIT	BALANCE CREDIT

ACCOUNT: Utilities Expense ACCOUNT NO. 533

DATE		ITEM	POST. REF.	DEBIT	CREDIT	BALANCE DEBIT	BALANCE CREDIT
20-- Dec.	1	Balance	✓			1,300.00	
	31		J20	570.00		1,870.00	

Name ______________________

Problem 9 (Continued)

ACCOUNT: Depreciation Expense—Office Equipment ACCOUNT NO. 541

DATE		ITEM	POST. REF.	DEBIT	CREDIT	BALANCE DEBIT	BALANCE CREDIT

ACCOUNT: Depreciation Expense—Computer Equipment ACCOUNT NO. 542

DATE		ITEM	POST. REF.	DEBIT	CREDIT	BALANCE DEBIT	BALANCE CREDIT

ACCOUNT: Miscellaneous Expense ACCOUNT NO. 549

DATE		ITEM	POST. REF.	DEBIT	CREDIT	BALANCE DEBIT	BALANCE CREDIT
20— Dec.	1	Balance	✔			600.00	
	22		J20	200.00		800.00	

Problem 9 (Continued)

1., 2., and 3.

KIM HO EMPLOYMENT

WORK

FOR YEAR ENDED

	ACCOUNT TITLE	TRIAL BALANCE		ADJUSTMENTS	
		DEBIT	CREDIT	DEBIT	CREDIT
1					
2					
3					
4					
5					
6					
7					
8					
9					
10					
11					
12					
13					
14					
15					
16					
17					
18					
19					
20					
21					
22					
23					
24					
25					
26					
27					
28					
29					
30					
31					

Name ____________________

Problem 9 (Concluded)

COUNSELING SERVICES

SHEET

DECEMBER 31, 20--

ADJUSTED TRIAL BALANCE		INCOME STATEMENT		BALANCE SHEET		
DEBIT	CREDIT	DEBIT	CREDIT	DEBIT	CREDIT	
						1
						2
						3
						4
						5
						6
						7
						8
						9
						10
						11
						12
						13
						14
						15
						16
						17
						18
						19
						20
						21
						22
						23
						24
						25
						26
						27
						28
						29
						30
						31

Problem 10 (LO 1/3) PREPARING ADJUSTMENTS AND THE WORK SHEET

The trial balance for Juan's Speedy Delivery Service as of September 30, 20--, is shown on the work sheet that follows.

Data to complete the adjustments are as follows:

(a) Supplies inventory as of September 30, $450.
(b) Insurance expired, $200.
(c) Depreciation on delivery equipment, $350.
(d) Wages earned by employees but not paid as of September 30, $215.

Required:

1. Enter the adjustments in the Adjustments columns on the work sheet.
2. Complete the work sheet.

1. and 2.

JUAN'S SPEEDY

WORK

FOR MONTH ENDED

	ACCOUNT TITLE	TRIAL BALANCE DEBIT	TRIAL BALANCE CREDIT	ADJUSTMENTS DEBIT	ADJUSTMENTS CREDIT
1	Cash	1,545.00			
2	Accounts Receivable	850.00			
3	Supplies	725.00			
4	Prepaid Insurance	1,500.00			
5	Delivery Equipment	6,300.00			
6	Accum. Depr.—Delivery Equip.				
7	Accounts Payable		980.00		
8	Wages Payable				
9	Juan Garcia, Capital		9,000.00		
10	Juan Garcia, Drawing	1,200.00			
11	Delivery Fees		5,240.00		
12	Wages Expense	1,475.00			
13	Advertising Expense	420.00			
14	Rent Expense	750.00			
15	Supplies Expense				
16	Phone Expense	180.00			
17	Insurance Expense				
18	Repair Expense	190.00			
19	Oil and Gas Expense	85.00			
20	Depreciation Expense—Del. Equip.				
21		15,220.00	15,220.00		
22					
23					

Problem 10 (Concluded)

DELIVERY SERVICE

SHEET

SEPTEMBER 30, 20--

ADJUSTED TRIAL BALANCE		INCOME STATEMENT		BALANCE SHEET		
DEBIT	CREDIT	DEBIT	CREDIT	DEBIT	CREDIT	
						1
						2
						3
						4
						5
						6
						7
						8
						9
						10
						11
						12
						13
						14
						15
						16
						17
						18
						19
						20
						21
						22
						23

Problem 11 (LO 4) FINDING AND CORRECTING ERRORS ON A WORK SHEET

A work sheet for George Green's Landscaping Service follows. It should include these adjustments.

(a) Ending inventory of supplies as of July 31, $350.
(b) Insurance expired as of July 31, $225.
(c) Depreciation on tractor, $460.
(d) Wages earned but not paid as of July 31, $320.

Required:

Errors have been intentionally placed in this work sheet. Review the work sheet for addition mistakes, transpositions, and other errors and make all necessary corrections.

(*Note:* Errors are intentional.)

GREEN'S LANDSCAPING

WORK

FOR MONTH ENDED

	ACCOUNT TITLE	TRIAL BALANCE DEBIT	TRIAL BALANCE CREDIT	ADJUSTMENTS DEBIT	ADJUSTMENTS CREDIT
1	Cash	1,825.00			
2	Accounts Receivable	720.00			
3	Supplies	600.00			(a) 350.00
4	Prepaid Insurance	850.00			(b) 225.00
5	Tractor	6,550.00			(c) 460.00
6	Accum. Depr.—Tractor				
7	Accounts Payable		520.00		
8	Wages Payable				(d) 320.00
9	George Green, Capital		8,250.00		
10	George Green, Drawing	1,200.00			
11	Landscaping Fees		6,100.00		
12	Wages Expense	1,540.00		(d) 320.00	
13	Advertising Expense	250.00			
14	Rent Expense	775.00			
15	Supplies Expense			(a) 350.00	
16	Phone Expense	140.00			
17	Utilities Expense	220.00			
18	Insurance Expense			(b) 225.00	
19	Depr. Expense—Tractor			(c) 460.00	
20	Miscellaneous Expense	200.00			
21		14,870.00	14,870.00	1,355.00	1,355.00
22	Net Income				
23					

Name ______________________________

Problem 11 (Concluded)

SERVICE

SHEET

JULY 31, 20--

ADJUSTED TRIAL BALANCE		INCOME STATEMENT		BALANCE SHEET		
DEBIT	CREDIT	DEBIT	CREDIT	DEBIT	CREDIT	
1825 00				1825 00		1
720 00				720 00		2
250 00				250 00		3
650 00				650 00		4
6090 00				6090 00		5
						6
	520 00				520 00	7
	320 00		320 00			8
	8250 00				8250 00	9
1200 00		1200 00				10
	6100 00		6100 00			11
1540 00		1540 00			1840 00	12
250 00		250 00				13
775 00		775 00				14
350 00		350 00				15
140 00		140 00				16
220 00		220 00				17
225 00		225 00				18
460 00		460 00				19
200 00		200 00				20
13355 00	15190 00	2417 00	6420 00	8347 00	8770 00	21
		1720 00			1720 00	22
		4137 00	6420 00	8347 00	10490 00	23

Problem 12 (LO 6) CASH, MODIFIED CASH, AND ACCRUAL BASES

Mark Mosley has his own consulting business. Listed below are selected transactions from the month of April.

Apr.	1	Paid office rent, $500.
	2	Purchased office supplies, $250.
	3	Purchased office equipment on account, $1,000.
	4	Earned consulting fees: $400 cash, $150 on account.
	5	Paid phone bill, $48.
	6	Purchased one-year insurance policy, $200.
	7	Paid $100 on account (for office equipment previously purchased).
	8	Received $150 on account from a customer (previously owed).
	9	Recorded depreciation on office equipment for month, $50.

Required:

Record the transactions in the space provided, using the following bases:

1. The cash basis.
2. The modified cash basis.
3. The accrual basis.

Name ______________________

Problem 12 (Continued)

1. Cash Basis

GENERAL JOURNAL PAGE

DATE	DESCRIPTION	POST. REF.	DEBIT	CREDIT

Problem 12 (Continued)

2. Modified Cash Basis

GENERAL JOURNAL PAGE

	DATE		DESCRIPTION	POST. REF.	DEBIT	CREDIT	
1							1
2							2
3							3
4							4
5							5
6							6
7							7
8							8
9							9
10							10
11							11
12							12
13							13
14							14
15							15
16							16
17							17
18							18
19							19
20							20
21							21
22							22
23							23
24							24
25							25
26							26
27							27
28							28
29							29
30							30

Name ____________________

Problem 12 (Concluded)

3. Accrual Basis

GENERAL JOURNAL PAGE

DATE		DESCRIPTION	POST. REF.	DEBIT	CREDIT

CHAPTER 5 APPENDIX DEPRECIATION METHODS

APPENDIX LEARNING OBJECTIVES

In Chapter 5, the straight-line method of depreciation was illustrated. In the appendix to Chapter 5, three additional methods are explained. These methods are used when a different schedule of expenses provides a more appropriate matching with the revenues generated.

Objective 1. **Prepare a depreciation schedule using the straight-line method.**
Objective 2. **Prepare a depreciation schedule using the sum-of-the-years'-digits method.**
Objective 3. **Prepare a depreciation schedule using the double-declining-balance method.**
Objective 4. **Prepare a depreciation schedule for tax purposes using the Modified Accelerated Cost Recovery System.**

Apx. Exercise 1 (LO 1) STRAIGHT-LINE DEPRECIATION

Office equipment was purchased on January 1 at a cost of $48,000. It has an estimated useful life of four years and a salvage value of $6,000. Prepare a depreciation schedule showing the depreciation expense, accumulated depreciation, and book value for each year under the straight-line method.

STRAIGHT-LINE DEPRECIATION

Apx. Exercise 2 (LO 2) SUM-OF-THE-YEARS'-DIGITS DEPRECIATION

Using the information given in Exercise 1, prepare a depreciation schedule showing the depreciation expense, accumulated depreciation, and book value for each year under the sum-of-the-years'-digits method.

SUM-OF-THE-YEARS'-DIGITS DEPRECIATION

Apx. Exercise 3 (LO 3) DOUBLE-DECLINING-BALANCE DEPRECIATION

Using the information given in Exercise 1, prepare a depreciation schedule showing the depreciation expense, accumulated depreciation, and book value for each year under the double-declining-balance method.

DOUBLE-DECLINING-BALANCE DEPRECIATION

Apx. Exercise 4 (LO 4) DEPRECIATION UNDER THE MODIFIED ACCELERATED COST RECOVERY SYSTEM

Using the information given in Exercise 1 and the rates shown in Figure 5A-4 of the text, prepare a depreciation schedule showing the depreciation expense, accumulated depreciation, and book value for each year under the Modified Accelerated Cost Recovery System. For tax purposes, assume that the office equipment has a useful life of five years. (The IRS schedule will spread depreciation over six years.) Round to the nearest dollar.

MODIFIED ACCELERATED COST RECOVERY SYSTEM

CHAPTER 6
FINANCIAL STATEMENTS AND THE CLOSING PROCESS

LEARNING OBJECTIVES

Chapter 5 introduced the work sheet and demonstrated how it is used to prepare year-end adjustments. Chapter 6 completes the discussion of the work sheet by illustrating its role in the preparation of financial statements and closing entries. The purpose of the post-closing trial balance is also explained. It is prepared after closing entries have been posted to the general ledger accounts.

Objective 1. Prepare financial statements with the aid of a work sheet.

The work sheet contains almost all the information needed to prepare the income statement, the statement of owner's equity, and the balance sheet. Numbers can be taken directly from the Income Statement columns for the income statement. The owner's capital account must be reviewed before completing the statement of owner's equity. If additional investments were made, they must be added to the beginning capital balance to compute the total investment. The net income (or net loss) is added to the total investment, and withdrawals (drawing) are subtracted, giving the ending owner's equity. The balance sheet is prepared using the ending owner's equity balance reported on the statement of owner's equity and the permanent accounts listed in the Balance Sheet columns of the work sheet.

Objective 2. Journalize and post closing entries.

After the work sheet is completed, the financial statements are prepared. Then the adjusting and closing entries are journalized and posted. All temporary accounts need zero balances to begin the new accounting period. The closing process has four journal entries:

1. to close revenue account(s) to Income Summary,
2. to close expense accounts to Income Summary,
3. to close Income Summary to the owner's capital account, and
4. to close Drawing to the owner's capital account.

Objective 3. Prepare a post-closing trial balance.

The **post-closing trial balance** lists all the permanent accounts that have balances to begin the new accounting period. It is prepared to prove the equality of the debit and credit balances in the general ledger accounts following the closing process. Since temporary accounts (drawing, revenues, and expenses) are closed at the end of the period, they do not appear on the post-closing trial balance.

Objective 4. List and describe the steps in the accounting cycle.

This chapter concludes the accounting cycle that began in Chapter 1. The 10 steps are as follows:

During the Accounting Period

1. Analyze source documents.
2. Journalize the transactions.
3. Post to the general ledger accounts.

End of Accounting Period

4. Prepare a trial balance.
5. Determine and prepare the needed adjustments on the work sheet.

6. Complete an end-of-period work sheet.
7. Journalize and post the adjusting entries.
8. Prepare an income statement, a statement of owner's equity, and a balance sheet.
9. Journalize and post the closing entries.
10. Prepare a post-closing trial balance.

REVIEW QUESTIONS

Instructions: Analyze each of the following items carefully before writing your answer in the column at the right.

		Question	Answer
LO 1	**1.**	The work sheet provides most of the needed information to prepare which three financial statements?	________________
LO 1	**2.**	The income statement contains which two major types of accounts?	________________
LO 1	**3.**	The statement of owner's equity adds ________ to the owner's investment and subtracts ________.	________________ ________________
LO 1	**4.**	Amounts owed that will be paid within a year are called ________.	________________
LO 1	**5.**	Expenses are listed on the income statement in the order they appear on the chart of accounts or in descending order by _______ amount.	________________
LO 1	**6.**	To find if the owner made any additional investments during the period, we must review the _______ account in the general ledger.	________________
LO 1	**7.**	When net income and additional investments are greater than withdrawals, the difference is called a(n) ________ in capital for the month.	________________
LO 1	**8.**	When the balance sheet is shown in ________ form, liabilities and owner's equity sections are placed below the assets section.	________________
LO 1	**9.**	When the balance sheet is shown in ________ form, assets are on the left and liabilities and owner's equity are on the right.	________________
LO 1	**10.**	A(n) ________ balance sheet groups similar items together such as current assets and current liabilities.	________________
LO 1	**11.**	Cash and assets that will be converted to cash or consumed within a year or the normal operating cycle are called ________ assets. ...	________________
LO 1	**12.**	The ________ is the period of time required to purchase supplies and services and convert them back into cash.	________________
LO 1	**13.**	Accounts Payable and Wages Payable are classified as ________ liabilities.	________________
LO 2	**14.**	Assets, liabilities, and the owner's capital account accumulate information across accounting periods; they are called ________ accounts.	________________

LO 2 15. Revenue, expense, and drawing accounts accumulate information for the specific period only, then they go back to ________ balances. ____________

LO 2 16. Because revenue, expense, and drawing accounts are closed each accounting period, they are called ________ accounts. .... ____________

LO 2 17. The ________ account is used to summarize the effects of revenue and expense accounts; it is then closed to the capital account. .... ____________

LO 2 18. When closing entries are posted to the general ledger, the word ________ is written in the Item column of each general ledger account affected. .... ____________

LO 3 19. The ________ trial balance only lists permanent accounts. .... ____________

LO 4 20. The ________ begins with analyzing source documents and ends with the post-closing trial balance. .... ____________

EXERCISES

Exercise 1 (LO 1) REVIEW: COMPUTE NET INCOME

From the information given below, compute net income. ____________

Revenue:	Delivery Fees	$4,826
Expenses:	Wages Expense	2,700
	Rent Expense	350
	Supplies Expense	55
	Insurance Expense	33
	Depreciation Expense	100

Exercise 2 (LO 1) REVIEW: COMPUTE OWNER'S EQUITY

Using the net income from Exercise 1 and the following information, compute the (a) increase to owner's equity and (b) ending owner's equity balance. Assume no additional investments were made by the owner.

(a) ____________

(b) ____________

Beginning owner's equity:	$5,680
Withdrawals by owner:	1,000

Exercise 3 (LO 2) THE CLOSING PROCESS

Based upon Exercises 1 and 2 above, list the accounts that must be closed at the end of the accounting cycle (in addition to the income summary account).

____

____

____

____

____

____

____

PROBLEMS

Problems 4–9

To complete Problems 4 through 9, use the completed work sheet for Collins Cycle Service as of April 30, 20--, below and the general ledger on pages 88-92.

COLLINS CYCLE

WORK

FOR MONTH ENDED

	ACCOUNT TITLE	TRIAL BALANCE DEBIT	TRIAL BALANCE CREDIT	ADJUSTMENTS DEBIT	ADJUSTMENTS CREDIT
1	Cash	4800 00			
2	Supplies	826 00			(a) 326 00
3	Prepaid Insurance	1300 00			(b) 200 00
4	Repair Equipment	2600 00			
5	Accum. Depr.—Repair Equip.		400 00		(c) 400 00
6	Accounts Payable		1300 00		
7	Wages Payable				(d) 100 00
8	Jean Collins, Capital		6000 00		
9	Jean Collins, Drawing	300 00			
10	Repair Fees		2839 00		
11	Wages Expense	275 00		(d) 100 00	
12	Rent Expense	400 00			
13	Supplies Expense			(a) 326 00	
14	Phone Expense	38 00			
15	Insurance Expense			(b) 200 00	
16	Depreciation Exp.—Repair Equip.			(c) 400 00	
17		10539 00	10539 00	1026 00	1026 00
18					
19					

Problems 4–9 (Concluded)

SERVICE

SHEET

APRIL 30, 20--

ADJUSTED TRIAL BALANCE		INCOME STATEMENT		BALANCE SHEET		
DEBIT	CREDIT	DEBIT	CREDIT	DEBIT	CREDIT	
4800 00				4800 00		1
500 00				500 00		2
1100 00				1100 00		3
2600 00				2600 00		4
	800 00				800 00	5
	1300 00				1300 00	6
	100 00				100 00	7
	6000 00				6000 00	8
300 00				300 00		9
	2839 00		2839 00			10
375 00		375 00				11
400 00		400 00				12
326 00		326 00				13
38 00		38 00				14
200 00		200 00				15
400 00		400 00				16
11039 00	11039 00	1739 00	2839 00	9300 00	8200 00	17
		1100 00			1100 00	18
		2839 00	2839 00	9300 00	9300 00	19

Problem 4 REVIEW: PREPARE ADJUSTING ENTRIES

Journalize the adjusting entries and post them to the general ledger accounts. The balances shown in the general ledger accounts are *trial balance* amounts—that is, before adjusting and closing entries are entered.

GENERAL JOURNAL

PAGE 2

	DATE		DESCRIPTION	POST. REF.	DEBIT	CREDIT	
1							1
2							2
3							3
4							4
5							5
6							6
7							7
8							8
9							9
10							10
11							11
12							12
13							13

Use these ledger accounts for Problems 4 and 8.

GENERAL LEDGER

ACCOUNT Cash ACCOUNT NO. 101

DATE		ITEM	POST. REF.	DEBIT	CREDIT	BALANCE	
						DEBIT	CREDIT
20-- Apr.	30	Balance	✓			4 8 0 0 00	

ACCOUNT Supplies ACCOUNT NO. 141

DATE		ITEM	POST. REF.	DEBIT	CREDIT	BALANCE	
						DEBIT	CREDIT
20-- Apr.	30	Balance	✓			8 2 6 00	

Problems 4 and 8 (Continued)

ACCOUNT Prepaid Insurance ACCOUNT NO. 145

DATE		ITEM	POST. REF.	DEBIT	CREDIT	BALANCE DEBIT	BALANCE CREDIT
20-- Apr.	30	Balance	✓			1,300 00	

ACCOUNT Repair Equipment ACCOUNT NO. 188

DATE		ITEM	POST. REF.	DEBIT	CREDIT	BALANCE DEBIT	BALANCE CREDIT
20-- Apr.	30	Balance	✓			2,600 00	

ACCOUNT Accumulated Depreciation—Repair Equipment ACCOUNT NO. 188.1

DATE		ITEM	POST. REF.	DEBIT	CREDIT	BALANCE DEBIT	BALANCE CREDIT
20-- Apr.	1	Balance	✓				400 00

ACCOUNT Accounts Payable ACCOUNT NO. 202

DATE		ITEM	POST. REF.	DEBIT	CREDIT	BALANCE DEBIT	BALANCE CREDIT
20-- Apr.	30	Balance	✓				1,300 00

Problems 4 and 8 (Continued)

ACCOUNT Wages Payable ACCOUNT NO. 219

DATE		ITEM	POST. REF.	DEBIT	CREDIT	BALANCE DEBIT	BALANCE CREDIT

ACCOUNT Jean Collins, Capital ACCOUNT NO. 311

DATE		ITEM	POST. REF.	DEBIT	CREDIT	BALANCE DEBIT	BALANCE CREDIT
20-- Apr.	1	Balance	✓				5 0 0 0 00
	15		J1		1 0 0 0 00		6 0 0 0 00

ACCOUNT Jean Collins, Drawing ACCOUNT NO. 312

DATE		ITEM	POST. REF.	DEBIT	CREDIT	BALANCE DEBIT	BALANCE CREDIT
20-- Apr.	30	Balance	✓			3 0 0 00	

ACCOUNT Income Summary ACCOUNT NO. 313

DATE		ITEM	POST. REF.	DEBIT	CREDIT	BALANCE DEBIT	BALANCE CREDIT

Problems 4 and 8 (Continued)

ACCOUNT Repair Fees ACCOUNT NO. 401

DATE		ITEM	POST. REF.	DEBIT	CREDIT	BALANCE DEBIT	BALANCE CREDIT
20-- Apr.	30	Balance	✓				2,839.00

ACCOUNT Wages Expense ACCOUNT NO. 511

DATE		ITEM	POST. REF.	DEBIT	CREDIT	BALANCE DEBIT	BALANCE CREDIT
20-- Apr.	30	Balance	✓			275.00	

ACCOUNT Rent Expense ACCOUNT NO. 521

DATE		ITEM	POST. REF.	DEBIT	CREDIT	BALANCE DEBIT	BALANCE CREDIT
20-- Apr.	30	Balance	✓			400.00	

ACCOUNT Supplies Expense ACCOUNT NO. 524

DATE		ITEM	POST. REF.	DEBIT	CREDIT	BALANCE DEBIT	BALANCE CREDIT

Problems 4 and 8 (Continued)

ACCOUNT Phone Expense ACCOUNT NO. 525

DATE		ITEM	POST. REF.	DEBIT	CREDIT	BALANCE DEBIT	BALANCE CREDIT
20--							
Apr.	30	Balance	✓			38 00	

ACCOUNT Insurance Expense ACCOUNT NO. 535

DATE		ITEM	POST. REF.	DEBIT	CREDIT	BALANCE DEBIT	BALANCE CREDIT

ACCOUNT Depreciation Expense—Repair Equipment ACCOUNT NO. 542

DATE		ITEM	POST. REF.	DEBIT	CREDIT	BALANCE DEBIT	BALANCE CREDIT

Problem 5 (LO 1) PREPARE AN INCOME STATEMENT

Prepare the income statement.

Problem 6 (LO 2) PREPARE A STATEMENT OF OWNER'S EQUITY

Prepare the statement of owner's equity. Be sure to check the capital account in the general ledger.

Problem 7 (LO 1) PREPARE A BALANCE SHEET

Prepare the balance sheet in report form.

Problem 8 (LO 2) JOURNALIZING AND POSTING CLOSING ENTRIES

Journalize the closing entries and post them to the general ledger accounts. (The general ledger accounts can be found on pages 88-92.)

GENERAL JOURNAL

PAGE 2

DATE		DESCRIPTION	POST. REF.	DEBIT	CREDIT

Problem 9 (LO 3) PREPARE A POST-CLOSING TRIAL BALANCE

Prepare the post-closing trial balance.

ACCOUNT TITLE	ACCT. NO.	DEBIT BALANCE	CREDIT BALANCE

CHAPTER 6 APPENDIX
STATEMENT OF CASH FLOWS

APPENDIX LEARNING OBJECTIVES

In Chapter 6, we reviewed in greater detail the preparation of three financial statements: the income statement, statement of owner's equity, and balance sheet. A fourth important financial statement is the statement of cash flows. The main purpose of this statement is to report the sources and uses of cash. These sources and uses are categorized into three types of business activities: operating, investing, and financing.

Objective 1. Classify business transactions as operating, investing, or financing.

Operating activities include those cash flows that are related to the revenues and expenses reported on the income statement. Examples include cash received for services performed and the payment of cash for expenses.

Investing activities are those transactions associated with buying and selling long-term assets, lending money, and collecting the principal on the related loans.

Financing activities are those cash transactions with owners and creditors. Examples include cash received from the owner to finance the operations and cash paid to the owner as withdrawals. Financing activities also include the receipt of cash from loans and the repayment of the loans.

Objective 2. Prepare a statement of cash flows by analyzing and categorizing a series of business transactions.

The main body of the statement of cash flows consists of three sections: operating, investing, and financing activities.

Name of Business		
Statement of Cash Flows		
For Period Ended Date		
Cash flows from operating activities:		
Cash received from customers		$ x,xxx.xx
List cash paid for various expenses	$ (xxx.xx)	
Total cash paid for operations		(x,xxx.xx)
Net cash provided by (used for) operating activities		$ xxx.xx
Cash flows from investing activities:		
List cash received from the sale of long-term assets and other investing activities	$ x,xxx.xx	
List cash paid for the purchase of long-term assets and other investing activities	(x,xxx.xx)	
Net cash provided by (used for) investing activities		x,xxx.xx
Cash flows from financing activities:		
List cash received from owners and creditors	$ x,xxx.xx	
List cash paid to owners and creditors	(xxx.xx)	
Net cash provided by (used for) financing activities		x,xxx.xx
Net increase (decrease) in cash		$ xxx.xx

Apx. Exercise 1 REVIEW: ENTERING TRANSACTIONS IN T ACCOUNTS

Sung Joon Lee opened an overseas mailing business, "Lee's Quick Sail." The following transactions occurred during August of the current year. Enter the transactions in the cash T account provided on the next page, identifying each with its corresponding letter.

(a) Lee invested $5,000 in the business.
(b) Paid office rent, $500.
(c) Bought supplies for the month, $200.
(d) Lee made an additional investment in the business, $1,000.
(e) Bought a new scale for $1,200: $700 cash and $500 on account.
(f) Received $600 for mailing services.
(g) Paid $200 on loan [see transaction (e)].
(h) Paid electricity bill, $64.
(i) Paid gas bill, $70.
(j) Received $900 for mailing services.
(k) Paid part-time employee, $90.
(l) Lee withdrew cash for personal use, $400.

Apx. Exercise 1 (Concluded)

CASH	

Apx. Exercise 2 REVIEW: FOOTING AND BALANCING A T ACCOUNT

Foot and balance the T account in Exercise 1. The cash balance at the end of August is _______ .

Apx. Problem 3 (LO 1) CLASSIFYING BUSINESS TRANSACTIONS AS OPERATING, INVESTING, OR FINANCING

Label each transaction in the cash T account of Exercise 1 as an operating (O), an investing (I), or a financing (F) activity.

Apx. Problem 4 (LO 2) PREPARING A STATEMENT OF CASH FLOWS BY ANALYZING BUSINESS TRANSACTIONS

Prepare a statement of cash flows based on the transactions and cash T account in Exercises 1 and 2, and Problem 3.

CHAPTER 7
ACCOUNTING FOR CASH

LEARNING OBJECTIVES

Managing cash is an essential part of every business's operations. In Chapter 7, we explore the cash account—setting up a bank account, writing checks and making deposits, preparing a bank reconciliation and the journal entries needed, operating a petty cash fund, establishing a change fund and using a cash short and over account.

Objective 1. Describe how to open and use a checking account.

Most banks have standard procedures for opening and using a **checking account.** They begin with a signature card, whereby the depositor's Social Security number or EIN number and signature are provided. Preparing deposit tickets, endorsing properly, and writing checks are parts of using a checking account wisely.

Objective 2. Prepare a bank reconciliation and related journal entries.

On a monthly basis, banks send **bank statements** to their checking account customers. The bank statement must be reconciled—compared to the checkbook. Adjustments are made to the ending bank balance and the checkbook balance until they are equal. Once the bank reconciliation is prepared, any changes to the book (checkbook) balance will require journal entries.

Objective 3. Establish and use a petty cash fund.

A **petty cash fund** is both convenient and cost effective. Rather than writing checks for small amounts, costing time and money, a sum of money is set aside for petty (small) cash payments during the month. Vouchers are issued for all money paid out; the petty cash fund is replenished at the end of the month (brought back up to its original amount). A journal entry is made to record all of the expenses shown in the petty cash record.

Objective 4. Establish a change fund and use the cash short and over account.

Businesses that receive cash from customers generally need to establish a change fund of currency and coins to use in handling cash sales. When many cash transactions occur, there often will be a difference between what the cash register tape says and the amount of cash actually found in the drawer. An account called Cash Short and Over is used to account for these differences. At the end of the month, if there is more cash short than over, it is an expense to the business. If there is more cash over than short, it is a revenue to the business.

REVIEW QUESTIONS

Instructions: Analyze each of the following items carefully before writing your answer in the column at the right.

		Question	Answer
LO 1	**1.**	To open a checking account, each person authorized to sign checks must fill out a(n) ________.	________
LO 1	**2.**	A(n) ________ lists items being deposited to a checking account.	________
LO 1	**3.**	Each check deposited is identified by its ________.	________
LO 1	**4.**	A(n) ________ consists of stamping or writing the depositor's name and other information on the back of a check.	________
LO 1	**5.**	A(n) ________ endorsement consists of a signature on the back of a check.	________
LO 1	**6.**	A(n) ________ endorsement consists of a signature together with words such as "For Deposit."	________
LO 1	**7.**	Depositors using ATMs must first key in their _______.	________
LO 1	**8.**	A(n) ________ is a document ordering a bank to pay cash from the depositor's account.	________
LO 1	**9.**	The ________ is the bank on which a check is drawn.	________
LO 1	**10.**	The ________ is the person being paid the cash.	________
LO 1	**11.**	The ________ is the depositor who orders the bank to pay the cash.	________
LO 1	**12.**	Space is contained to record all relevant information about a check on its ________.	________
LO 1	**13.**	A statement issued to the depositor once a month is called a ________.	________
LO 1	**14.**	Checks paid by the bank and returned to the depositor are called ________.	________
LO 2	**15.**	The process of bringing the bank and book balances into agreement is called preparing a(n) ________.	________
LO 2	**16.**	Checks issued during the period but not yet processed by the bank are called ________.	________
LO 2	**17.**	Deposits made but not yet recorded by the bank are called _______.	________
LO 2	**18.**	Bank charges for services are called ________.	________
LO 2	**19.**	Checks deposited but not paid because the drawer did not have enough money in the account are called ________ checks.	________
LO 2	**20.**	Transactions can be completed by ________ rather than by the manual process of writing checks or using cash.	________
LO 3	**21.**	A fund called the ________ is established to pay for small items with cash.	________

LO 3 **22.** A receipt called a(n) ________ is prepared for every payment from the petty cash fund. .... ______________________

LO 3 **23.** The ________ is a special multi-column record where petty cash payments are recorded. .... ______________________

LO 3 **24.** At the end of the month, the petty cash fund is ________, or brought up to its original amount. .... ______________________

LO 4 **25.** The cash short and over account is used when actual cash on hand is different from what is on the ________ tape plus the change fund. ______________________

LO 4 **26.** When actual cash on hand exceeds what is on the register tape plus the change fund, this difference is a(n) ________. .... ______________________

LO 4 **27.** When actual cash on hand is less than what is on the register tape plus the change fund, this difference is a(n) ________. .... ______________________

EXERCISES

Exercise 1 (LO1) PREPARE DEPOSIT TICKET

Using the deposit ticket shown below, enter the following information:

Date:	March 28, 20--	Checks:	33-11	$202
Currency:	$318		123-666	48
Coin:	33		2-9	211

PEOPLE'S BANK
Wilkes-Barre, PA 18704-1456

Date____________________ 20_____

CHECKS AND OTHER ITEMS ARE RECEIVED FOR DEPOSIT SUBJECT TO THE TERMS AND CONDITIONS OF THIS FINANCIAL INSTITUTION'S ACCOUNT AGREEMENT.

____
SIGN HERE ONLY IF CASH RECEIVED FROM DEPOSIT

⑆0631 12094⑆ 0001632475⑈

DEPOSIT TICKET

CURRENCY		
COIN		
CHECKS		
TOTAL FROM OTHER SIDE		
SUBTOTAL		
LESS CASH RECEIVED		
NET DEPOSIT		

Exercise 2 (LO1) PREPARE CHECK AND STUB

During the month of October, you made the following payments by check. Fill in the stubs and write the checks. Use the blank checks provided on page 104. Enter $825.50 as the balance brought forward on Check No. 138, and add a deposit for $85 on October 10.

Oct.	3	Issued Check No. 138 to Emerald Lawn Care, Inc., for work done on the shrubbery around the office building, $125. (Miscellaneous Expense)
	8	Issued Check No. 139 to Maxwell Office Supply for stationery, $85.90. (Office Supplies)
	10	Issued Check No. 140 to Wesley's Towing for cost of towing company car to repair shop, $50. (Automobile Expense)

Exercise 2 (Concluded)

No. 138

DATE ______ 20____
TO ______
FOR ______

ACCT. ______

	DOLLARS	CENTS
BAL BRO'T FOR'D		
AMT. DEPOSITED		
TOTAL		
AMT. THIS CHECK		
BAL CAR'D FOR'D		

No. 138 60-55/313

______ 20____

PAY TO THE ORDER OF ______ $ ______

______ Dollars

FOR CLASSROOM USE ONLY

PEOPLE'S BANK
Wilkes-Barre, PA 18704-1456

MEMO ______ BY ______

⑆1300555 16 3247 5⑈

No. 139

DATE ______ 20____
TO ______
FOR ______

ACCT. ______

	DOLLARS	CENTS
BAL BRO'T FOR'D		
AMT. DEPOSITED		
TOTAL		
AMT. THIS CHECK		
BAL CAR'D FOR'D		

No. 139 60-55/313

______ 20____

PAY TO THE ORDER OF ______ $ ______

______ Dollars

FOR CLASSROOM USE ONLY

PEOPLE'S BANK
Wilkes-Barre, PA 18704-1456

MEMO ______ BY ______

⑆1300555 16 3247 5⑈

No. 140

DATE ______ 20____
TO ______
FOR ______

ACCT. ______

	DOLLARS	CENTS
BAL BRO'T FOR'D		
AMT. DEPOSITED		
TOTAL		
AMT. THIS CHECK		
BAL CAR'D FOR'D		

No. 140 60-55/313

______ 20____

PAY TO THE ORDER OF ______ $ ______

______ Dollars

FOR CLASSROOM USE ONLY

PEOPLE'S BANK
Wilkes-Barre, PA 18704-1456

MEMO ______ BY ______

⑆1300555 16 3247 5⑈

Exercise 3 (LO2) BANK RECONCILIATION PROCEDURES

The bank reconciliation is a process of matching the checkbook balance with the bank statement balance—adding and subtracting items until the two are equal. In the exercise below, indicate which action is taken.

a. Add to checkbook balance.

b. Subtract from checkbook balance.

c. Add to bank statement balance.

d. Subtract from bank statement balance.

________ 1. Deposits in transit

________ 2. Error in checkbook whereby a check for $128 was entered into the checkbook as $182

________ 3. NSF check

________ 4. Checks outstanding (not yet processed by the bank)

________ 5. Bank service fees

________ 6. Credit memo, telling depositor that a note was collected

________ 7. Error in checkbook whereby a check for $181 was entered into the checkbook as $118

Exercise 4 (LO 2) PREPARE JOURNAL ENTRIES FOR BANK RECONCILIATION

Based on the following bank reconciliation, prepare the necessary journal entries as of January 28, 20--:

Bank statement balance, January 28		$1,896.00
Add: Deposits in transit:		
1/26	$118.00	
1/28	92.00	210.00
		$2,106.00
Deduct: Outstanding checks:		
No. 683	$ 23.00	
No. 685	6.50	
No. 687	102.50	
No. 688	13.00	
No. 689	208.00	353.00
Adjusted bank balance		$1,753.00
Book balance, January 28		$1,994.00
Add: Error on check*	$ 28.00	
Note collected**	142.00	170.00
		$2,164.00
Deduct: Unrecorded ATM withdrawal***	$ 30.00	
Service charge	11.00	
NSF check	370.00	411.00
Adjusted book balance		$1,753.00

*Accounts Payable was debited.
**Credit Notes Receivable.
***Debit Gail Bennett, Drawing.

Exercise 4 (Concluded)

GENERAL JOURNAL PAGE

DATE		DESCRIPTION	POST. REF.	DEBIT	CREDIT

Exercise 5 (LO3) PETTY CASH JOURNAL ENTRIES

Based on the following petty cash information, prepare journal entries to establish the petty cash fund and to replenish the fund at the end of the month.

1. On March 1, a check is written for $100 to establish a petty cash fund.
2. During the month, the following petty cash payments are made:

Phone Expense	$ 3.50
Automobile Expense	11.00
Postage Expense	4.50
B. Crenshaw, Drawing	35.00
Charitable Contributions Expense	25.00
Miscellaneous Expense	3.00

Exercise 5 (Concluded)

GENERAL JOURNAL PAGE 1

	DATE		DESCRIPTION	POST. REF.	DEBIT	CREDIT	
1							1
2							2
3							3
4							4
5							5
6							6
7							7
8							8
9							9
10							10
11							11
12							12

Exercise 6 (LO4) CASH SHORT AND OVER JOURNAL ENTRIES

Based on the following information, prepare weekly entries for cash receipts from service fees and cash short and over. A change fund of $100 is maintained.

Aug.	5	Cash in drawer:	$318.00	Cash register amount:	$218.00
	12		402.00		300.00
	19		388.00		292.00
	26		411.50		309.50

Exercise 6 (Concluded)

GENERAL JOURNAL

PAGE 1

	DATE		DESCRIPTION	POST. REF.	DEBIT	CREDIT	
1							1
2							2
3							3
4							4
5							5
6							6
7							7
8							8
9							9
10							10
11							11
12							12
13							13
14							14
15							15
16							16
17							17
18							18
19							19

PROBLEMS

Problem 7 (LO2) BANK RECONCILIATION AND RELATED JOURNAL ENTRIES

The following information relates to the bank account of the Mini Donut House:

Balance, March 31, per check stub		$2,923
Balance, March 31, per bank statement		3,199
March deposits not shown on bank statement	$ 302	
	206	508
Bank service charge shown on bank statement		14
Unrecorded ATM withdrawal*		60
NSF check shown on bank statement		153

Error on Check No. 144, where stub shows $132, but the check was made in the amount of $123. Accounts Payable was originally debited.

Checks outstanding, March 31, are as follows:

No. 148	$201.00
No. 151	300.00
No. 155	501.00

*Funds were withdrawn by the owner, Paolo Goes, for personal use.

Required:

1. Prepare the bank reconciliation.
2. Prepare the required journal entries.

Problem 7 (Continued)

1.

Problem 7 (Concluded)

2.

GENERAL JOURNAL

PAGE 1

	DATE	DESCRIPTION	POST. REF.	DEBIT	CREDIT	
1						1
2						2
3						3
4						4
5						5
6						6
7						7
8						8
9						9
10						10
11						11
12						12
13						13
14						14
15						15
16						16
17						17
18						18
19						19
20						20
21						21
22						22
23						23
24						24
25						25
26						26
27						27
28						28
29						29

Problem 8 (LO3) PETTY CASH PAYMENTS RECORD AND JOURNAL ENTRIES

On April 1, the Fitzgibbons Furniture Repair Shop established a petty cash fund of $200. The following cash payments were made from the petty cash fund during the first two weeks of April. The fund was replenished to the $200 level on April 16.

Apr.	1	Paid $5.28 for postage due on a package received. Petty Cash Voucher No. 10.
	5	Made a $25 contribution to the Washington Township Baseball League. Petty Cash Voucher No. 11.
	6	Reimbursed $6.25 to an employee for phone calls made from a pay phone. Petty Cash Voucher No. 12.
	8	Paid $22 for office supplies. Petty Cash Voucher No. 13.
	10	Paid $32 for a newspaper advertisement. Petty Cash Voucher No. 14.
	12	Paid $33 for an oil change for the company truck. Petty Cash Voucher No. 15.
	14	Paid $20 for postage stamps. Petty Cash Voucher No. 16.
	15	Made a $25 contribution to the Girl Scouts. Petty Cash Voucher No. 17.

Required:

1. Prepare the journal entry to establish the petty cash fund.
2. Enter the above payments in the petty cash payments record provided on page 113.
3. Prove the petty cash payments record.
4. Prepare the journal entry to replenish the fund on April 16.

Problem 8 (Continued)
2. and 3.

PETTY CASH PAYMENTS FOR MONTH OF 20-- PAGE 1

					DISTRIBUTION OF PAYMENTS								
	DAY	DESCRIPTION	VOU. NO.	TOTAL AMOUNT	TRUCK EXPENSE	POSTAGE EXPENSE	CHARIT. CONTRIB. EXPENSE	PHONE EXPENSE	OFFICE SUPPLIES	ADVERT. EXPENSE	ACCOUNT	AMOUNT	
1													1
2													2
3													3
4													4
5													5
6													6
7													7
8													8
9													9
10													10
11													11
12													12
13													13
14													14
15													15
16													16
17													17
18													18
19													19
20													20
21													21
22													22

Problem 8 (Concluded)
1. and 4.

GENERAL JOURNAL PAGE 1

	DATE		DESCRIPTION	POST. REF.	DEBIT	CREDIT	
1							1
2							2
3							3
4							4
5							5
6							6
7							7
8							8
9							9
10							10
11							11
12							12

Problem 9 (LO4) CASH SHORT AND OVER JOURNAL ENTRIES

Mackie's Salon deposits cash weekly. A record of cash register receipts for the month of April is shown below. A change fund of $100 is maintained.

Apr.	2	Cash in drawer:	$298.00	Cash register amount:	$196.50
	9		286.50		192.00
	16		293.50		193.50
	23		306.00		204.50
	30		301.50		203.00

Required:

Prepare weekly journal entries for cash receipts from service fees, showing cash short and over when needed.

Problem 9 (Concluded)

GENERAL JOURNAL

PAGE 1

	DATE		DESCRIPTION	POST. REF.	DEBIT	CREDIT	
1							1
2							2
3							3
4							4
5							5
6							6
7							7
8							8
9							9
10							10
11							11
12							12
13							13
14							14
15							15
16							16
17							17
18							18
19							19
20							20
21							21
22							22
23							23
24							24
25							25
26							26
27							27
28							28
29							29
30							30
31							31
32							32

CHAPTER 8
PAYROLL ACCOUNTING: EMPLOYEE EARNINGS AND DEDUCTIONS

LEARNING OBJECTIVES

Payroll accounting is an important part of any business, partly because it is such a significant expense and partly because so many laws govern its record keeping. In Chapter 8, we examine the payroll records that employers are required to keep and also those records that help run the business efficiently.

Objective 1. Distinguish between employees and independent contractors.

An **employee** is one who works under the control and direction of an employer. The employer controls how and when the job is to be done, determines working hours, and in general is responsible for all aspects of the employee's work. An **independent contractor**, on the other hand, performs a service for a fee and does not work under the control and direction of the company paying for his or her service. This is an important distinction because employers are required to maintain payroll records and file many reports for their employees but must file only one form for independent contractors.

Objective 2. Calculate employee earnings and deductions.

Three steps are required to determine how much to pay an employee for a pay period. (1) Calculate the employee's total earnings for the pay period. (2) Determine the amounts of deductions for the same pay period. (3) Subtract deductions from total earnings. The deductions may be required by law—for example, Social Security and Medicare taxes and federal and state income taxes—or by agreement with the employer—for example, insurance deductions and savings bond deductions.

Objective 3. Describe and prepare payroll records.

Three types of payroll records are used to accumulate required information for federal and state tax purposes: the payroll register, the payroll check (or record of direct deposit) with earnings statement attached, and the employee earnings record.

The **payroll register** is a multi-column form that accumulates the necessary data to prepare the journal entry. Detailed information on earnings, taxable earnings, deductions, and net pay is provided for each employee and for the employees in total.

The **payroll check** (or record of direct deposit) is prepared from information in the payroll register. The detachable earnings statement attached to the employee's check shows the gross earnings, total deductions, and net pay.

A separate record of each employee's earnings is called an **employee earnings record.** This information is also obtained from the payroll register. The earnings record is designed so that quarterly and annual totals can be accumulated in order for the employer to prepare several reports.

Objective 4. Account for employee earnings and deductions.

The payroll register provides all the information needed to prepare the journal entry for any pay period. The total gross earnings is debited to a wages and salaries expense account, and each deduction is credited to a current liability account. The difference between gross earnings and total deductions is called **net pay** and is credited to Cash.

Objective 5. Describe various payroll record-keeping methods.

In addition to a manual system of preparing all the necessary payroll records, payroll processing centers and electronic systems can be used to prepare the same records.

A **payroll processing center** is a business that sells payroll record-keeping services. An **electronic system** is a computer system based on a software package that performs all payroll record keeping and prepares payroll checks or EFTs.

REVIEW QUESTIONS

Instructions: Analyze each of the following items carefully before writing your answer in the column at the right.

	Question	Answer
LO 1	**1.** A(n) ________ is one who works under the control and direction of an employer.	____________
LO 1	**2.** A(n) ________ performs a service for a fee and does not work under the control and direction of the company paying for the service.	____________
LO 2	**3.** What three steps are required to determine how much to pay an employee for a pay period?	____________ ____________ ____________
LO 2	**4.** Compensation for managerial or administrative services, normally expressed in biweekly, monthly, or annual terms, is called ________.	____________
LO 2	**5.** Compensation for skilled or unskilled labor, normally expressed in terms of hours, weeks, or units produced, is called ________.	____________
LO 2	**6.** When compensation is based on time, ________ are helpful for keeping a record of the time worked by each employee.	____________
LO 2	**7.** An employee's total earnings is also called ________.	____________
LO 2	**8.** An employee's total earnings less all the deductions is called ______.	____________
LO 2	**9.** What are the three major categories of deductions from an employee's paycheck?	____________ ____________ ____________
LO 2	**10.** David Astin is married with two children, holds only one job, and has a spouse who is not employed. What number of withholding allowances is Astin entitled to claim, assuming that he does not anticipate large itemized deductions?	____________

LO 2 11. Upon employment, each employee is required to furnish the employer a Form ________ that details, among other things, the number of withholding allowances and marital status. .... ____________

LO 2 12. Name the four factors that determine the amount to be withheld from an employee's gross pay each pay period. .... ____________

____

____

____

LO 3 13. A form used to assemble the data required at the end of each payroll period is called a(n) ________. .... ____________

LO 3 14. A method of payment in which the employee's net pay is placed directly in the employee's bank account is called a(n) ________. ..... ____________

LO 3 15. A separate, detailed record of each employee's earnings is called a(n) ________ . ... ____________

LO 5 16. Name two approaches in addition to a manual system used to accumulate and record payroll information. .... ____________

____

EXERCISES

Exercise 1 (LO 2) COMPUTING OVERTIME PAY RATE

Lu-yin Cheng receives a regular salary of $2,500 a month and is entitled to overtime pay at the rate of 1½ times the regular hourly rate for any time worked in excess of 40 hours per week. Compute Cheng's overtime hourly rate.

Exercise 2 (LO 2) COMPUTING GROSS PAY

Roger Watkins earns a regular hourly rate of $12.50 and receives time and a half for any time worked over 8 hours per weekday. Roger earns double time for hours worked on Saturday or Sunday. During the past week, Roger worked 8 hours each day Monday through Wednesday, 5 hours on Thursday, 12 hours on Friday, and 6 hours on Saturday. Compute Watkins's gross pay.

Exercise 3 (LO 2) COMPUTING NET PAY

Bill Burry is married, has three children, and claims five withholding allowances for federal income tax purposes. Burry's gross pay for the week was $683. Using the federal income tax withholding tables provided in Figure 8-4 of the text and the information provided below, compute Burry's net pay for the week.

(a) Social Security tax rate is 6.2% (Burry's prior earnings equaled $23,455).
(b) Medicare tax rate is 1.45%.
(c) State income tax is 2% of gross earnings.
(d) City income tax is 1% of gross earnings.
(e) Contribution to pension plan is $25.
(f) Health insurance deduction is $8.50.

Exercise 4 (LO 4) JOURNALIZING PAYROLL TRANSACTIONS

Using the information provided in Exercise 3, enter the payment of Bill Burry's wages in a general journal. Assume a pay period ending on July 31, 20--.

GENERAL JOURNAL PAGE 1

	DATE	DESCRIPTION	POST. REF.	DEBIT	CREDIT	
1						1
2						2
3						3
4						4
5						5
6						6
7						7
8						8
9						9
10						10

Exercise 5 (LO 3, 4) PAYROLL JOURNAL ENTRIES

The following data were taken from the payroll register of United Processors as of May 14, 20--.

Regular earnings	$6,516.00
Overtime earnings	710.00
Total earnings	______
Deductions:	
Federal income tax	______
Social Security tax	448.01
Medicare tax	104.78
Pension plan	134.00
Health insurance	260.00
United Way	190.00
Net pay	$5,394.21

Required:

1. Determine the missing amounts.
2. Prepare the journal entry for the payroll, crediting Cash for the net pay.

1.

Exercise 5 (Concluded)

2.

GENERAL JOURNAL

PAGE

	DATE		DESCRIPTION	POST. REF.	DEBIT	CREDIT	
1							1
2							2
3							3
4							4
5							5
6							6
7							7
8							8
9							9
10							10
11							11
12							12

PROBLEMS

Problem 6 (LO 2, 3, 4) PAYROLL REGISTER AND PAYROLL JOURNAL ENTRIES

Earl Wilson operates a business known as Wilson Enterprises. Listed below are the name, number of allowances claimed, marital status, total hours worked, and hourly rate of each employee. All hours worked in excess of 40 a week are paid for at the rate of time and a half.

The employer uses a weekly federal income tax withholding table. A portion of this weekly table is provided in Chapter 8 of your textbook. Social Security tax is withheld at the rate of 6.2%, Medicare tax is withheld at the rate of 1.45%, state income tax is withheld at the rate of 3.5%, and city earnings tax is withheld at the rate of 1%. Kagan, Kennedy, Scalia, and Sotomayor each have $15 withheld this payday for group life insurance. Each employee, except Ginsberg, has $5 withheld for health insurance. All of the employees use payroll deduction to the credit union for varying amounts as listed below. Alito, Kennedy, and Thomas each have $18.25 withheld this payday under a savings bond purchase plan.

Wilson Enterprises follows the practice of drawing a single check for the net amount of the payroll and depositing the check in a special payroll account at the bank. Individual paychecks are then drawn for the amount due each employee. The checks issued this payday were numbered consecutively beginning with Check No. 531.

Wilson Enterprises
Payroll Information for the Week Ended January 15, 20--

Name	Allow-ances	Marital Status	Total Hours Worked	Regular Hourly Rate	Credit Union Deposit	Cumul. Earnings thru 1/8
Alito, Samuel	3	M	45	$12.00	$114.00	$525.00
Breyer, Susan	2	M	50	10.00	110.00	680.00
Ginsberg, Ruth	3	M	43	11.00	97.90	500.00
Kagan, Ellen	2	S	48	11.00	114.40	625.00
Kennedy, Tony	3	M	43	13.00	115.70	730.00
Roberts, John	5	M	40	17.00	136.00	850.00
Scalia, Anton	2	S	38	9.00	68.40	425.00
Sotomayor, Sonja	4	M	47	11.00	111.10	[illegible]
Thomas, Clarence	1	S	60	10.00	140.00	615.00

Required:

1. Prepare a payroll register for Wilson Enterprises for the pay period ended January 15, 20--. Use the form provided on pages 124–125. (In the Taxable Earnings/Unemployment Compensation column, enter the same amounts as in the Social Security column.)
2. Assuming that the wages for the week ended January 15 were paid on January 17, enter the payment in the general journal provided on page 125.

Problem 6 (Continued)

1.

PAYROLL REGISTER

					EARNINGS				TAXABLE EARNINGS	
	NAME	EMP. NO.	NO. ALLOW.	MARIT. STATUS	REGULAR	OVERTIME	TOTAL	CUMULATIVE TOTAL	UNEMPLOY. COMP.	SOCIAL SECURITY
1										
2										
3										
4										
5										
6										
7										
8										
9										
10										
11										
12										
13										
14										

Problem 6 (Concluded)

FOR PERIOD ENDED 20--

DEDUCTIONS												
FEDERAL INC. TAX	SOC. SEC. TAX	MEDICARE TAX	STATE INC. TAX	CITY EARN. TAX	LIFE INS.	HEALTH INS.	CREDIT UNION	OTHER	TOTAL	NET PAY	CK. NO.	
												1
												2
												3
												4
												5
												6
												7
												8
												9
												10
												11
												12
												13
												14

2.

GENERAL JOURNAL

PAGE 1

	DATE	DESCRIPTION	POST. REF.	DEBIT	CREDIT	
1						1
2						2
3						3
4						4
5						5
6						6
7						7
8						8
9						9
10						10
11						11
12						12
13						13

Problem 7 (LO 3) EMPLOYEE EARNINGS RECORD

The current employee earnings record for Susan Breyer is provided below and on page 127. Using the information provided in Problem 6, update Breyer's earnings record to reflect the January 15 payroll. Although this information should have been entered earlier, complete the required information at the bottom of the earnings record. The necessary information is provided below.

Name:	Susan Breyer
Address:	422 Long Plain Rd.
	Leverett, MA 01054
Employee No.:	2
Gender:	Female
Department:	Sanitation
Occupation:	Janitor
S.S. No.:	336-56-7534
Marital Status:	Married
Allowances:	4
Pay Rate:	$10 per hour
Birth Date:	7/6/69
Date Employed:	6/22/--

EMPLOYEE EARNINGS RECORD

20 -- PERIOD ENDED	EARNINGS REGULAR	EARNINGS OVERTIME	EARNINGS TOTAL	EARNINGS CUMULATIVE TOTAL	TAXABLE EARNINGS UNEMPLOY. COMP.	TAXABLE EARNINGS SOCIAL SECURITY	DEDUCTIONS FEDERAL INCOME TAX	DEDUCTIONS SOCIAL SECURITY TAX
Jan. 1	300 00		300 00	300 00	300 00	300 00	0 00	18 60
8	380 00		380 00	680 00	380 00	380 00	7 00	23 56

GENDER		DEPARTMENT	OCCUPATION	SOCIAL SECURITY NO.	MARITAL STATUS	ALLOW-ANCES
M	F					

Problem 7 (Concluded)

FOR PERIOD ENDED 20--

DEDUCTIONS																				
MEDICARE TAX		STATE INCOME TAX		CITY EARNINGS TAX		LIFE INSUR.		HEALTH INSUR.		CREDIT UNION		OTHER			TOTAL		NET PAY		CK. NO.
4	35	10	50	3	00			5	00	40	00				81	45	218	55	321
5	51	13	30	3	80			5	00	56	00				114	17	265	83	422

PAY RATE	DATE OF BIRTH	DATE HIRED	NAME/ADDRESS	EMP. NO.

CHAPTER 9
PAYROLL ACCOUNTING: EMPLOYER TAXES AND REPORTS

LEARNING OBJECTIVES

Chapter 8 discussed taxes levied on the employee and withheld by the employer. None of these taxes was an expense of the employer. In Chapter 9, we examine several taxes that represent an additional payroll expense imposed directly on the employer.

Objective 1. Describe and calculate employer payroll taxes.

Most employers are subject to a matching portion of the Social Security and Medicare taxes and to federal and state unemployment taxes. The employer's **Social Security and Medicare taxes** are levied on employers at the same rates and on the same bases as the employee Social Security and Medicare taxes. The **FUTA** tax is levied only on employers. The purpose of this tax is to raise funds to administer the federal/state unemployment compensation program. The **SUTA** tax is also levied only on employers. The purpose of this tax is to raise funds to pay unemployment benefits.

The Social Security, FUTA, and SUTA taxes are calculated from the accumulated amounts found in the Taxable Earnings columns in the payroll register. The Medicare tax is calculated from the Earnings—Total column.

Objective 2. Account for employer payroll taxes expense.

To journalize employer payroll taxes, debit the total of the employer Social Security, Medicare, FUTA, and SUTA taxes to a single account entitled Payroll Taxes Expense. The liabilities for the Social Security, Medicare, FUTA, and SUTA taxes payable normally are credited to separate accounts. The general format of this entry appears below.

Account	Debit	Credit
Payroll Taxes Expense	xx	
Social Security Tax Payable		xx
Medicare Tax Payable		xx
FUTA Tax Payable		xx
SUTA Tax Payable		xx

Objective 3. Describe employer reporting and payment responsibilities.

Employer payroll reporting and payment responsibilities fall in six areas.

1. Federal income tax withholding and Social Security and Medicare taxes
2. FUTA taxes
3. SUTA taxes
4. Employee Wage and Tax Statement (Form W-2)
5. Summary of employee wages and taxes (Form W-3)
6. Employment eligibility notification (Form I-9)

The due date for federal income tax withholding and Social Security and Medicare taxes varies, depending on the amount of these taxes. Deposits are made using EFTPS. In addition, a Form 941 must be completed each quarter and filed with the IRS.

The federal unemployment taxes must be computed on a quarterly basis. In addition, Form 940 must be filed with the IRS by the beginning of the second week of February.

Deposit rules and forms for state unemployment taxes vary among the states. Deposits usually are required on a quarterly basis.

Employers must furnish each employee with a Wage and Tax Statement (Form W-2) by January 31 of each year. Information needed to complete this form is contained in the employee earnings records. The employer also must file Form W-3 with the Social Security Administration by the last day of February. This form summarizes the employee earnings and tax information from Forms W-2.

The purpose of Form I-9 is to document that each employee is authorized to work in the United States. It must be completed by the employee and employer and retained by the employer.

Objective 4. Describe and account for workers' compensation insurance.

Workers' compensation insurance provides insurance for employees who suffer a work-related illness or injury. The cost of the insurance depends on the number of employees, the riskiness of the job, and the company's accident history. The employer usually pays the premium at the beginning of the year, based on the estimated annual payroll, and makes an adjustment at the end of the year when the actual annual payroll is known.

REVIEW QUESTIONS

Instructions: Analyze each of the following items carefully before writing your answer in the column at the right.

		Question	Answer
LO 1	**1.**	Name the four payroll taxes paid by the employer.	______________ ______________ ______________ ______________
LO 1	**2.**	The textbook uses a Social Security tax rate of 6.2% applied to maximum employee earnings of ________.	______________
LO 1	**3.**	The ________ is a key source of information for computing employer payroll taxes.	______________
LO 1	**4.**	Individuals who own and run their own business are considered ____.	______________
LO 1	**5.**	The law requires persons earning net self-employment income of $400 or more to pay a(n) ________.	______________
LO 1	**6.**	The textbook uses a FUTA tax rate of 0.6% applied to maximum employee earnings of ________.	______________
LO 2	**7.**	When journalizing the employer's payroll taxes, debit the total of the employer Social Security, Medicare, FUTA, and SUTA taxes to a single account entitled ________.	______________
LO 3	**8.**	Name the three taxes that are associated with Form 941.	______________ ______________ ______________
LO 3	**9.**	In addition to making quarterly deposits, employers are required to file an annual report of federal unemployment tax on Form ________.	______________

LO 3 10. By January 31 of each year, employers must furnish each employee with a(n) ________. .... ____________________

LO 3 11. ________ documents that an employee is authorized to work in the United States. .... ____________________

LO 4 12. ________ provides insurance for employees who suffer a work-related illness or injury. .... ____________________

EXERCISES

Exercise 1 (LO 1) CALCULATION OF EMPLOYER PAYROLL TAXES

Sylvania Bookstore pays a SUTA tax of 5.4% and a FUTA tax of 0.6%. The total taxable wages for unemployment compensation on a certain payday amount to $16,800. Compute the unemployment taxes payable to the state and federal government.

Exercise 2 (LO 2) CALCULATION OF PAYROLL TAXES AND PREPARATION OF JOURNAL ENTRIES

The Totals line from Wong Drug Store's payroll register for the week ended December 31, 20--, is shown on pages 132 and 133.

Payroll taxes are imposed as follows:

Social Security tax	6.2%
Medicare tax	1.45%
FUTA tax	0.6%
SUTA tax	5.4%

Required:

1. Prepare the journal entry for payment of this payroll on December 31, 20--.
2. Prepare the journal entry for the employer's payroll taxes for the period ended December 31, 20--.

Exercise 2 (Continued)

PAYROLL REGISTER

	NAME	EMPL. NO.	NO. ALLOW.	MARIT. STATUS	EARNINGS				TAXABLE EARNINGS	
					REGULAR	OVERTIME	TOTAL	CUMULATIVE TOTAL	UNEMPLOY. COMP.	SOCIAL SECURITY
1	Totals				4,200 00	500 00	4,700 00	203,700 00	300 00	3,600 00
2										
3										
4										
5										
6										
7										
8										
9										
10										

1. and 2.

GENERAL JOURNAL

PAGE 1

	DATE		DESCRIPTION	POST. REF.	DEBIT	CREDIT	
1							1
2							2
3							3
4							4
5							5
6							6
7							7
8							8
9							9
10							10
11							11
12							12
13							13
14							14
15							15
16							16

Exercise 2 (Concluded)

FOR PERIOD ENDED December 31, 20--

DEDUCTIONS									
FEDERAL INC. TAX	SOC. SEC. TAX	MEDICARE TAX	HEALTH INS.	CREDIT UNION	OTHER	TOTAL	NET PAY	CK. NO.	
420 00	223 20	68 15	80 00	200 00		991 35	3,708 65		1
									2
									3
									4
									5
									6
									7
									8
									9
									10

Exercise 3 (LO1/2) TOTAL COST OF AN EMPLOYEE

Compute the total annual cost to an employer of employing a person whose gross salary is $45,000. (Assume a 5.4% state unemployment tax rate and a FUTA tax rate of 0.6%, both on the first $7,000 of earnings, an employer's Social Security tax rate of 6.2% on the first $118,500 of earnings and a Medicare tax rate of 1.45% on gross earnings.)

Exercise 4 (LO 3) JOURNAL ENTRIES FOR PAYMENT OF PAYROLL TAXES

The general ledger of GNU Co. includes the following accounts and balances related to payroll as of October 15 of the current year:

Social Security Tax Payable	$12,400
Medicare Tax Payable	2,900
FUTA Tax Payable	540
SUTA Tax Payable	4,320
Employee Federal Income Tax Payable	7,780

Required:

Journalize the payment of the employee federal income taxes and Social Security and Medicare taxes on October 15, 20--, and the deposit of the FUTA and SUTA taxes on October 31, 20--.

GENERAL JOURNAL

PAGE

	DATE	DESCRIPTION	POST. REF.	DEBIT	CREDIT	
1						1
2						2
3						3
4						4
5						5
6						6
7						7
8						8
9						9
10						10
11						11
12						12
13						13
14						14

Exercise 5 (LO 4) WORKERS' COMPENSATION INSURANCE AND ADJUSTMENT

Curtis Company paid a premium of $360 for workers' compensation insurance based on the estimated payroll as of the beginning of the year. Based on actual payroll as of the end of the year, the actual premium is $397. Prepare the adjusting entry to reflect the underpayment of the insurance premium.

GENERAL JOURNAL PAGE 1

	DATE		DESCRIPTION	POST. REF.	DEBIT	CREDIT	
1							1
2							2
3							3
4							4
5							5

PROBLEMS

Problem 6 (LO 1/2) CALCULATING PAYROLL TAXES EXPENSE AND PREPARING JOURNAL ENTRY

A partial payroll register for the pay period ended August 31, 20--, is provided on the following page for the Astroscope Company.

Required:

1. Compute the total earnings subject to federal and state unemployment taxes and the Social Security tax by completing the Taxable Earnings columns of the payroll register.
2. Assume the company is in a state with an unemployment tax rate of 5.4% and a FUTA tax rate of 0.6%, both on the first $7,000 of earnings. The Social Security tax rate is 6.2% on the first $118,500 of earnings, and the Medicare tax rate is 1.45% on gross earnings. Compute the state and federal unemployment taxes and the Social Security and Medicare taxes on the lines provided on page 136.
3. Prepare the entry for the employer's payroll taxes in the general journal provided on page 137.

Problem 6 (Continued)

1.

PAYROLL REGISTER

	NAME	NO. ALLOW.	MARIT. STATUS	EARNINGS: REGULAR	EARNINGS: OVERTIME	EARNINGS: TOTAL	EARNINGS: CUMULATIVE TOTAL	TAXABLE EARNINGS: UNEMPLOY. COMP.	TAXABLE EARNINGS: SOCIAL SECURITY
1	Coolie, Betty					350 00	7,150 00		
2	Covar, Mike					200 00	6,800 00		
3	Hagen, Frank					375 00	6,200 00		
4	Gutierrez, Bob					1,540 00	47,300 00		
5	Moten, Alice					1,500 00	50,500 00		
6	Rice, Darlene					3,300 00	121,400 00		
7									

2.

Problem 6 (Concluded)

3.

GENERAL JOURNAL

PAGE 1

	DATE		DESCRIPTION	POST. REF.	DEBIT	CREDIT	
1							1
2							2
3							3
4							4
5							5
6							6
7							7
8							8
9							9

Problem 7 (LO 2/3) JOURNALIZING AND POSTING PAYROLL ENTRIES

Rock Creek Company has five employees. All are paid on a monthly basis. The fiscal year of the business is March 1 to February 28. Payroll taxes are imposed as follows:

Social Security tax to be withheld from employees' wages and imposed on the employer, 6.2% each on the first $118,500 of earnings.

Medicare tax to be withheld from employees' wages and imposed on the employer, 1.45% each on gross earnings.

SUTA tax imposed on the employer, 5.4% on the first $7,000 of earnings.

FUTA tax imposed on the employer, 0.6% on the first $7,000 of earnings.

The accounts kept by Rock Creek Company include the following:

Account Number	Title	Balance on March 1
101	Cash	$62,500.00
211	Employee Federal Income Tax Payable	3,375.00
212	Social Security Tax Payable	4,740.00
213	Medicare Tax Payable	1,110.00
218	Savings Bond Deductions Payable	1,200.00
221	FUTA Tax Payable	320.00
222	SUTA Tax Payable	2,670.00
511	Wages and Salaries Expense	0.00
530	Payroll Taxes Expense	0.00

Problem 7 (Continued)

Following is a narrative of selected transactions relating to payrolls and payroll taxes that occurred during the months of March and April:

Mar.	15	Paid $9,225.00 covering the following February taxes:		
		Employee federal income tax withheld		$3,375.00
		Social Security tax		4,740.00
		Medicare tax		1,110.00
		Total		$9,225.00
	31	March payroll:		
		Total wages and salaries expense		$39,000.00
		Less amounts withheld:		
		Employee federal income tax	$3,690.00	
		Social Security tax	2,418.00	
		Medicare tax	565.50	
		Savings bond deductions payable	1,200.00	7,873.50
		Net amount paid		$31,126.50
	31	Purchased savings bonds for employees, $2,400.00		
	31	Data for completing employer's payroll taxes expense for March:		
		Social Security taxable wages		$39,000.00
		Unemployment taxable wages		12,000.00
Apr.	15	Paid $9,657.00 covering the following March taxes:		
		Employee federal income tax payable		$ 3,690.00
		Social Security tax		4,836.00
		Medicare tax		1,131.00
	30	Paid SUTA tax for the quarter, $3,318.00		
	30	Paid FUTA tax, $392.00		

Required:

1. Using a general journal, journalize the preceding transactions.
2. Open T accounts for the payroll expense and liabilities. Enter the beginning balances and post the transactions recorded in the journal.

Problem 7 (Continued)

1.

GENERAL JOURNAL

PAGE

	DATE		DESCRIPTION	POST. REF.	DEBIT	CREDIT	
1							1
2							2
3							3
4							4
5							5
6							6
7							7
8							8
9							9
10							10
11							11
12							12
13							13
14							14
15							15
16							16
17							17
18							18
19							19
20							20
21							21
22							22
23							23
24							24
25							25
26							26
27							27
28							28
29							29
30							30

Problem 7 (Continued)

GENERAL JOURNAL

PAGE

	DATE		DESCRIPTION	POST. REF.	DEBIT	CREDIT	
1							1
2							2
3							3
4							4
5							5
6							6
7							7
8							8
9							9
10							10
11							11
12							12
13							13
14							14

2.

Cash 101

Employee Federal Income Tax Payable 211

Social Security Tax Payable 212

Medicare Tax Payable 213

Problem 7 (Concluded)

Savings Bond Deductions Payable 218	

FUTA Tax Payable 221	

SUTA Tax Payable 222	

Wages and Salaries Expense 511	

Payroll Taxes Expense 530	

Problem 8 (LO 4) WORKERS' COMPENSATION INSURANCE AND ADJUSTMENT

Jackson Manufacturing estimated its total payroll for the coming year to be $630,000. The workers' compensation insurance premium rate is 0.35%.

Required:

1. Calculate the estimated workers' compensation insurance premium and prepare the journal entry for the payment as of January 2, 20--.
2. Assume Jackson Manufacturing's actual payroll for the year is $658,000. Calculate the total insurance premium owed. Prepare a journal entry as of December 31, 20--, to record the adjustment for the underpayment. The actual payment of the additional insurance premium will take place in January of the next year.
3. Assume, instead, that Jackson Manufacturing's actual payroll for the year is $607,000. Prepare a journal entry as of December 31, 20--, for the total amount that should be refunded. The refund will not be received until the next year.

1., 2., and 3.

GENERAL JOURNAL PAGE 1

	DATE		DESCRIPTION	POST. REF.	DEBIT	CREDIT	
1							1
2							2
3							3
4							4
5							5
6							6
7							7
8							8
9							9
10							10
11							11
12							12
13							13
14							14

CHAPTER 10
ACCOUNTING FOR SALES AND CASH RECEIPTS

LEARNING OBJECTIVES

Chapter 10 introduces the merchandising business: sales transactions and the related new accounts, a new ledger, and a new schedule. Merchandise sales transactions are shown in general journal format.

Objective 1. Describe merchandise sales transactions.

Retail businesses make sales on account, as well as cash sales and credit card sales. Sales tickets and cash register receipts are produced for customers and for accounting purposes.

Wholesale businesses also make sales on account, but the process is more complicated and includes purchase orders and sales invoices. Credit approval is required for sales on account.

Both types of businesses have sales returns (merchandise returned for a refund) and allowances (reductions in price because of defects, damage, or other problems with the merchandise).

Objective 2. Describe and use merchandise sales accounts.

Accounting for sales transactions requires four general ledger accounts: Sales, Sales Tax Payable, Sales Returns and Allowances, and Sales Discounts. Sales is a revenue account; Sales Tax Payable is a liability account; and Sales Returns and Allowances and Sales Discounts are contra-revenue accounts.

When a sale is made and sales tax is added to the sale, the liability account (Sales Tax Payable) is credited for the amount of tax that will be remitted to the government. Therefore, when merchandise is returned for a credit (Sales Returns and Allowances), the customer is also refunded the amount of the sales tax (Sales Tax Payable is debited).

Cash discounts are given to business customers who pay within a discount period such as 10 days. This encourages prompt payment of bills. When a discount is taken, the sales discounts account is debited for the amount of the discount.

Net sales is determined by deducting the contra-revenue accounts (Sales Returns and Allowances and Sales Discounts) from gross sales.

Objective 3. Describe and use the accounts receivable ledger.

The accounts receivable account in the general ledger provides a record of the total amount owed to a business by its customers. To help run the business, a record also is needed of the amount owed by individual customers. The accounts receivable subsidiary ledger provides this information.

When an accounts receivable subsidiary ledger is used, the accounts receivable account in the general ledger is a "controlling account." The accounts receivable ledger is "subsidiary" to this account. Transactions are posted daily from the general journal to both the general ledger and the accounts receivable ledger.

Objective 4. Prepare a schedule of accounts receivable.

Once all daily postings are completed to individual accounts, the balance in the accounts receivable general ledger account must agree with the sum of the customer balances in the accounts receivable ledger. The schedule of accounts receivable is prepared at the end of the month to verify that the total of customer balances equals the balance in the controlling account, Accounts Receivable.

REVIEW QUESTIONS

Instructions: Analyze each of the following items carefully before writing your answer in the column at the right.

		Question	Answer
LO 1	**1.**	A(n) ________ business purchases merchandise such as clothing, furniture, or computers to sell to its customers.	____________
LO 1	**2.**	A(n) ________ is a transfer of merchandise from one individual or business to another in exchange for cash or a promise to pay cash.	____________
LO 1	**3.**	A(n) ________ is a document created as evidence of a sale for a retail business.	____________
LO 1	**4.**	A written order to buy merchandise, called a(n) ________, is received from a customer.	____________
LO 1	**5.**	A(n) ________ is prepared when merchandise ordered is shipped to a customer.	____________
LO 1	**6.**	Merchandise returned by a customer for a refund is called a(n) ________.	____________
LO 1	**7.**	Reductions in price of merchandise granted because of defect or damage are called ________.	____________
LO 1	**8.**	When credit is given for merchandise returned or for an allowance, a(n) ________ is issued.	____________
LO 2	**9.**	The sales account is a ________ account.	____________
LO 2	**10.**	When a sale on account is made, ________ is debited.	____________
LO 2	**11.**	When a sale is made with sales tax, a liability account, called ________, is credited for the amount of the sales tax.	____________
LO 2	**12.**	Sales Returns and Allowances is a contra- ________ account.	____________
LO 2	**13.**	A(n) ________ is granted for prompt payment by customers who buy merchandise on account.	____________
LO 2	**14.**	Sales Discounts is a contra- ________ account.	____________
LO 3	**15.**	A record of each customer's account balance is contained in the ________ ledger.	____________
LO 3	**16.**	To indicate that the accounts receivable ledger has been posted, a slash and a ________ are entered in the Posting Reference column of the general journal.	____________
LO 3	**17.**	Sales returns and allowances are posted to both the general ledger and the ________ ledger.	____________
LO 3	**18.**	When a collection is received on account, ________ is credited.	____________
LO 4	**19.**	The ________ is a listing of the balances of all customers who owe money at the end of the month.	____________
LO 4	**20.**	The schedule of accounts receivable is used to verify that the sum of the accounts receivable ledger balances equals the ________ balance.	____________

EXERCISES

Exercise 1 (LO 1) SALES DOCUMENTS

The following is a copy of a purchase order received from Custom Builders, Inc., by Rogers Building Supplies, Inc. Assuming you are employed by Rogers Building Supplies, Inc., prepare a sales invoice (No. 491) dated July 18 billing Custom Builders, Inc., for the items specified in their Order No. A208. The unit prices are as follows: #6 insulated steel doors, $290.00 each and #28 pine, six-panel doors, $125 each. Indicate terms of 30 days.

Purchase Order *Order No.* **A208**

Date July 15, 20--

Terms 30 days

CUSTOM BUILDERS, INC.
2001 HILLSIDE DR.
BLOOMINGTON, IN 47401-2287

To
Rogers Building Supplies, Inc.
So. Adams
Bloomington, IN 47401-3663

Quantity	Description	Price
10	#6 Insulated steel doors	290.00
15	#28 Pine, six-panel doors	125.00

Deliver no goods without a written order on this form. *By* E. Taylor

Exercise 1 (Concluded)

Invoice Invoice No. Date Your Order No. Terms	ROGERS BUILDING SUPPLIES, INC. So. Adams, Bloomington, IN 47401-3663 Sold to		
Quantity	Description	Unit Price	Amount

Exercise 2 (LO 1) SALES DOCUMENTS

On July 28, Custom Builders, Inc., returned one #6 insulated steel door to Rogers Building Supplies, Inc., for credit. Using the blank form on page 147, prepare a credit memorandum (No. 17) covering the cost of the door sold on July 18.

Exercise 2 (Concluded)

Credit Memorandum	ROGERS BUILDING SUPPLIES, INC.
No.	So. Adams, Bloomington, IN 47401-3663
Date	To
We credit your account as follows:	

Quantity	Description	Unit Price	Amount

Exercise 3 (LO 2/3) SALES AND SALES RETURNS AND ALLOWANCES TRANSACTIONS

Record the following transactions in a general journal, assuming a 5% sales tax.

(a) Sold $230 of merchandise, plus sales tax, on account. R. B. Jones, Sale No. 28.
(b) R. B. Jones returned $30 worth of merchandise for a credit.
(c) R. B. Jones paid the balance of the account in cash.
(d) Sold $300 of merchandise, plus sales tax, for cash.
(e) Merchandise returned for cash refund, $15.

Exercise 3 (Concluded)

GENERAL JOURNAL PAGE

	DATE	DESCRIPTION	POST. REF.	DEBIT	CREDIT	
1						1
2						2
3						3
4						4
5						5
6						6
7						7
8						8
9						9
10						10
11						11
12						12
13						13
14						14
15						15
16						16
17						17
18						18
19						19
20						20
21						21
22						22
23						23
24						24

Exercise 4 (LO2) COMPUTING NET SALES

Based on the following information, compute net sales.

Gross sales	$5,010
Sales returns and allowances	565
Sales discounts	97

Exercise 5 (LO3) SALES TRANSACTIONS

Diana Brewer operates the Floor and Window Treatment Center and completed the following transactions related to sales of merchandise on account during the month of February. Sales tax of 5% was included in the amount of each sale.

Feb. 2 Sold wallpaper supplies to Dresson Homes, $98.95; terms, n/30. Sale No. 255.
12 Sold paint to Ray Acuff, $105; terms, n/30. Sale No. 256.
23 Sold miniblinds to Clydette Rupert, $114.83; terms, n/30. Sale No. 257.
24 Sold decorator items to Marty Staple, $35.55; terms, n/30. Sale No. 258.
25 Sold paint to Angel Burtin, $25.57; terms, n/30. Sale No. 259.

Required:

Enter the above transactions in a general journal.

GENERAL JOURNAL

PAGE

	DATE	DESCRIPTION	POST. REF.	DEBIT	CREDIT	
1						1
2						2
3						3
4						4
5						5
6						6
7						7
8						8
9						9
10						10
11						11
12						12
13						13
14						14
15						15
16						16
17						17
18						18
19						19
20						20
21						21
22						22
23						23
24						24
25						25

Exercise 6 (LO 3) CASH RECEIPTS TRANSACTIONS

Diana Brewer of the Floor and Window Treatment Center received cash during the month of March as described below.

Mar. 2 Received cash from Dresson Homes on account, $98.95.
12 Received cash from Ray Acuff on account, $105.
15 Made cash sale to Jean Granite, $404.76, plus 5% sales tax.
18 Made cash sale to Bill Green, $2,380.95, plus 5% sales tax.
23 Received cash from Clydette Rupert on account, $114.83.
24 Received cash from Marty Staple on account, $35.55.
25 Received cash from Angel Burtin on account, $25.57.
31 Cash sales for the month were $22,000, including 5% sales tax (from cash register tape).
31 Credit card sales for the month were $28,000, including 5% sales tax. Bank credit card expense is $560.

Required:

Enter the above transactions in the general journal below and on the next page.

GENERAL JOURNAL

PAGE

	DATE		DESCRIPTION	POST. REF.	DEBIT	CREDIT	
1							1
2							2
3							3
4							4
5							5
6							6
7							7
8							8
9							9
10							10
11							11
12							12
13							13
14							14
15							15
16							16
17							17
18							18
19							19
20							20

Exercise 6 (Concluded)

GENERAL JOURNAL

PAGE

	DATE		DESCRIPTION	POST. REF.	DEBIT	CREDIT	
1							1
2							2
3							3
4							4
5							5
6							6
7							7
8							8
9							9
10							10
11							11
12							12
13							13
14							14
15							15
16							16
17							17
18							18
19							19
20							20
21							21
22							22
23							23
24							24
25							25
26							26
27							27
28							28
29							29
30							30
31							31
32							32
33							33
34							34

PROBLEMS

Problem 7 (LO 2/3) SALES, SALES RETURNS AND ALLOWANCES, AND CASH RECEIPTS TRANSACTIONS

The following information represents transactions for Kwan Chu's Fish Market for the month of July 20--. Sales tax is 6%.

July	1	Sold merchandise on account to B. A. Smith, $137.50, plus sales tax. Sale No. 33.
	3	B. A. Smith returned merchandise worth $15, plus sales tax, for a credit. Credit Memo No.11.
	5	Sold merchandise on account to L. L. Unis, $218, plus sales tax. Sale No. 34.
	7	Cash sales for the week were $325.44, plus sales tax.
	10	Sold merchandise on account to W. P. Clark, $208, plus sales tax. Sale No. 35.
	11	Received $129.85 from B. A. Smith, on account.
	13	W. P. Clark returned merchandise worth $22, plus sales tax, for a credit. Credit Memo No. 12.
	14	Cash sales for the week were $411.20, plus sales tax.
	16	Sold merchandise on account to B. A. Smith, $282.50, plus sales tax. Sale No. 36.
	17	Received $231.08 from L. L. Unis, on account.
	21	Cash sales for the week were $292.50, plus sales tax.
	24	Sold merchandise on account to L. L. Unis, $224.50, plus sales tax. Sale No. 37.
	28	Cash sales for the week were $300.50, plus sales tax.
	31	Received $197.16 from W. P. Clark, on account.

Required:

Using the information provided, record the transactions in the general journal below and on pages 153–154.

GENERAL JOURNAL PAGE

	DATE		DESCRIPTION	POST. REF.	DEBIT	CREDIT	
1							1
2							2
3							3
4							4
5							5
6							6
7							7
8							8
9							9
10							10
11							11
12							12
13							13
14							14
15							15

Problem 7 (Continued)

GENERAL JOURNAL

PAGE

	DATE		DESCRIPTION	POST. REF.	DEBIT	CREDIT	
1							1
2							2
3							
4							
5							5
6							6
7							7
8							8
9							9
10							10
11							11
12							12
13							13
14							14
15							15
16							16
17							17
18							18
19							19
20							20
21							21
22							22
23							23
24							24
25							25
26							26
27							27
28							28
29							29
30							30

Problem 7 (Concluded)

GENERAL JOURNAL

PAGE

DATE		DESCRIPTION	POST. REF.	DEBIT	CREDIT

Problem 8 (LO 3/4) SALES, LEDGERS, AND SCHEDULE OF ACCOUNTS RECEIVABLE

H. K. Smythe operates Leather All, a leather shop that sells luggage, handbags, business cases, and other leather goods. During the month of May, the following sales on account were made:

May	3	Sold merchandise on account to T. A. Pigdon, $247.50, plus sales tax of $14.85. Sale No. 51.
	4	Sold merchandise on account to J. R. Feyton, $55, plus sales tax of $3.30. Sale No. 52.
	6	Sold merchandise on account to P. C. McMurdy, $99, plus sales tax of $5.94. Sale No. 53.
	10	Sold merchandise on account to J. T. Messer, $175, plus sales tax of $10.50. Sale No. 54.
	12	Sold merchandise on account to A. F. Schlitz, $355, plus sales tax of $21.30. Sale No. 55.
	13	Sold merchandise on account to J. R. Feyton, $215, plus sales tax of $12.90. Sale No. 56.
	20	Sold merchandise on account to P. C. McMurdy, $400, plus sales tax of $24.00. Sale No. 57.
	28	Sold merchandise on account to J. T. Messer, $255, plus sales tax of $15.30. Sale No. 58.

Required:

1. Enter the above transactions in the general journal provided below and on page 156 (start with page 7).
2. Post the entries to the general ledger and accounts receivable ledger on pages 156–158.
3. Prepare a schedule of accounts receivable as of May 31.

1. **GENERAL JOURNAL** PAGE

	DATE		DESCRIPTION	POST. REF.	DEBIT	CREDIT	
1							1
2							2
3							3
4							4
5							5
6							6
7							7
8							8
9							9
10							10
11							11
12							12
13							13
14							14
15							15
16							16
17							17
18							18
19							19
20							20

Problem 8 (Continued)

GENERAL JOURNAL

PAGE

	DATE		DESCRIPTION	POST. REF.	DEBIT	CREDIT	
1							1
2							2
3							3
4							4
5							5
6							6
7							7
8							8
9							9
10							10
11							11
12							12
13							13
14							14
15							15
16							16
17							17
18							18
19							19

2.

GENERAL LEDGER

ACCOUNT Accounts Receivable ACCOUNT NO. 122

DATE		ITEM	POST. REF.	DEBIT	CREDIT	BALANCE DEBIT	BALANCE CREDIT
20-- May	1	Balance	✓			8 3 4 00	

Problem 8 (Continued)

ACCOUNT Sales Tax Payable ACCOUNT NO. 231

DATE	ITEM	POST. REF.	DEBIT	CREDIT	BALANCE	
					DEBIT	CREDIT

ACCOUNT Sales ACCOUNT NO. 401

DATE	ITEM	POST. REF.	DEBIT	CREDIT	BALANCE	
					DEBIT	CREDIT

ACCOUNTS RECEIVABLE LEDGER

NAME J. R. Feyton

ADDRESS 6022 Columbia, St. Louis, MO 63139-1906

DATE	ITEM	POST. REF.	DEBIT	CREDIT	BALANCE

Problem 8 (Continued)

NAME P. C. McMurdy

ADDRESS 1214 N. 2nd St., E. St. Louis, IL 62201-2679

DATE		ITEM	POST. REF.	DEBIT	CREDIT	BALANCE
20-- May	1	Balance	✓			125 00

NAME J. T. Messer

ADDRESS P.O. Box 249, Chesterfield, MO 63017-3901

DATE		ITEM	POST. REF.	DEBIT	CREDIT	BALANCE
20-- May	1	Balance	✓			177 00

NAME T. A. Pigdon

ADDRESS 1070 Purcell, University City, MO 63130-1546

DATE		ITEM	POST. REF.	DEBIT	CREDIT	BALANCE
20-- May	1	Balance	✓			280 00

NAME A. F. Schlitz

ADDRESS 800 Lindbergh Blvd., St. Louis, MO 63166-1546

DATE		ITEM	POST. REF.	DEBIT	CREDIT	BALANCE
20-- May	1	Balance	✓			252 00

Problem 8 (Concluded)

3.

Problem 9 (LO 2/3) SALES, SALES RETURNS AND ALLOWANCES, CASH RECEIPTS, AND LEDGERS

Paula Angelillis operates the Hard-to-Find Auto Parts Store. Much of her business is by mail. The following transactions related to sales and cash receipts occurred during June:

June 1 Received $300 from A. K. Wells, including $14.29 of sales tax, for field cash sale. (Field cash sales are not included in cash register tapes.)
5 Received $125.60 from L. Strous on account.
10 Received $263.25 from D. Manning on account.
12 Q. Striker returned merchandise for credit. The sales price was $215, plus sales tax of $10.75.
18 Received $58.25 from D. Warding on account.
20 Received $1,000 from B. L. Stryker, including $47.62 tax (field cash sale).
21 Received $29.99 from L. Clese on account.
24 R. Popielarz returned merchandise for credit. Sales price was $116.25, plus sales tax of $5.81.
27 Received $426 from L. LeCount on account.
30 Cash and bank credit card sales for the month were $8,200, plus sales tax of $410. Bank credit card expense is $80.

Required:

1. Enter each transaction in the general journal provided on pages 160–161 (start with page 8).
2. Post the entries to the general and accounts receivable ledgers (pages 161–164).

Problem 9 (Continued)

1. **GENERAL JOURNAL** PAGE

DATE		DESCRIPTION	POST. REF.	DEBIT	CREDIT

Problem 9 (Continued)

GENERAL JOURNAL

PAGE

	DATE		DESCRIPTION	POST. REF.	DEBIT	CREDIT	
1							1
2							2
3							3
4							4
5							5
6							6
7							7
8							8
9							9
10							10
11							11
12							12
13							13
14							14
15							15
16							16
17							17

2.

GENERAL LEDGER

ACCOUNT Cash ACCOUNT NO. 101

DATE		ITEM	POST. REF.	DEBIT	CREDIT	BALANCE	
						DEBIT	CREDIT
20-- June	1	Balance	✓			13,200.25	

Problem 9 (Continued)

ACCOUNT Accounts Receivable ACCOUNT NO. 122

DATE		ITEM	POST. REF.	DEBIT	CREDIT	BALANCE DEBIT	BALANCE CREDIT
20-- June	1	Balance	✓			1,250 90	

ACCOUNT Sales Tax Payable ACCOUNT NO. 231

DATE		ITEM	POST. REF.	DEBIT	CREDIT	BALANCE DEBIT	BALANCE CREDIT
20-- June	1	Balance	✓				125 00

ACCOUNT Sales ACCOUNT NO. 401

DATE		ITEM	POST. REF.	DEBIT	CREDIT	BALANCE DEBIT	BALANCE CREDIT

ACCOUNT Sales Returns and Allowances ACCOUNT NO. 401.1

DATE		ITEM	POST. REF.	DEBIT	CREDIT	BALANCE DEBIT	BALANCE CREDIT

Problem 9 (Continued)

ACCOUNT Bank Credit Card Expense ACCOUNT NO. 513

DATE		ITEM	POST. REF.	DEBIT	CREDIT	BALANCE	
						DEBIT	CREDIT

ACCOUNTS RECEIVABLE LEDGER

NAME L. Clese

ADDRESS 875 Glenway Drive, Glendale, MO 63122-4112

DATE		ITEM	POST. REF.	DEBIT	CREDIT	BALANCE
20-- June	1	Balance	✓			29 99

NAME L. LeCount

ADDRESS 1439 East Broad Street, Columbus, OH 43205-9892

DATE		ITEM	POST. REF.	DEBIT	CREDIT	BALANCE
20-- June	1	Balance	✓			426 00

NAME D. Manning

ADDRESS 2101 Cumberland Road, Noblesville, IN 47870-2435

DATE		ITEM	POST. REF.	DEBIT	CREDIT	BALANCE
20-- June	1	Balance	✓			263 25

Problem 9 (Concluded)

NAME R. Popielarz

ADDRESS 3001 Hillcrest Drive, Dallas, PA 18612-6854

DATE		ITEM	POST. REF.	DEBIT	CREDIT	BALANCE
20-- June	1	Balance	✓			122 06

NAME Q. Striker

ADDRESS 4113 Main Street, Beech Grove, IN 46107-9643

DATE		ITEM	POST. REF.	DEBIT	CREDIT	BALANCE
20-- June	1	Balance	✓			225 75

NAME L. Strous

ADDRESS 2215 N. State Road 135, Greenwood, IN 46142-6432

DATE		ITEM	POST. REF.	DEBIT	CREDIT	BALANCE
20-- June	1	Balance	✓			125 60

NAME D. Warding

ADDRESS 1100 W. Main Street, Carmel, IN 46032-2364

DATE		ITEM	POST. REF.	DEBIT	CREDIT	BALANCE
20-- June	1	Balance	✓			58 25

CHAPTER 11
ACCOUNTING FOR PURCHASES AND CASH PAYMENTS

LEARNING OBJECTIVES

Chapter 11 continues the study of merchandise transactions. In this chapter, purchases and cash payments are emphasized, and another new ledger and new schedule are introduced. As was done in Chapter 10, merchandise purchases transactions are shown in general journal format.

Objective 1. Describe merchandise purchases transactions.

For a merchandising business, **purchases** refers to merchandise acquired for resale. Several important documents are used in the purchasing process of a merchandising business. A **purchase requisition** is a form used to request the purchasing department to purchase merchandise or other property. A **purchase order** is a written order to buy goods from a specific vendor (supplier). A **receiving report** is prepared upon receipt of merchandise and indicates what merchandise has been received. An **invoice** is a document prepared by the seller as a bill for the merchandise shipped. To the seller, this is a sales invoice. To the buyer, it is called a **purchase invoice.**

The accounting department compares the purchase invoice with the purchase requisition, purchase order, and receiving report. If the invoice is for the goods ordered at the correct price, the invoice is paid by the due date.

When credit terms such as 2/10, n/30 are offered by the seller, a **cash discount** is available to the buyer if the bill is paid within the discount period. Another type of discount, called a **trade discount,** is often offered by manufacturers and wholesalers. This discount is a reduction from the list or catalog price. By simply adjusting the trade discount percentages, companies can avoid the cost of reprinting catalogs every time there is a change in price.

Objective 2. Describe and use merchandise purchases accounts and compute gross profit.

To account for merchandise purchases transactions, four new accounts are used. These are **Purchases, Purchases Returns and Allowances, Purchases Discounts,** and **Freight-In.**

Purchases is an account to which the cost of merchandise (i.e., inventory acquired for resale) is debited.

Purchases Returns and Allowances is a contra-purchases account to which returns of merchandise and price reductions are credited. This account is subtracted from Purchases on the income statement.

Purchases Discounts is a contra-purchases account to which any cash discounts allowed on purchases are credited. This account is subtracted from Purchases on the income statement.

Freight-In is an adjunct-purchases account to which transportation charges on merchandise purchases are debited. This account is added to Purchases on the income statement.

FOB shipping point means that transportation charges are paid by the buyer. **FOB destination** means that transportation charges are paid by the seller.

Gross profit is computed using the following format:

Sales			$xxxx	
Less: Sales returns and allowances		$xxxx		
Sales discounts		xxxx	xxxx	
Net sales				$xxxx
Cost of goods sold:				
Merchandise inventory, beginning of period			$xxxx	
Purchases		$xxxx		
Less: Purchases returns and allowances	$xxxx			
Purchases discounts	xxxx	xxxx		
Net purchases		$xxxx		
Add freight-in		xxxx		
Cost of goods purchased			xxxx	
Goods available for sale			$xxxx	
Less merchandise inventory, end of period			xxxx	
Cost of goods sold				xxxx
Gross profit				$xxxx

Objective 3. Describe and use the accounts payable ledger.

The accounts payable account in the general ledger provides a record of the total amount owed by a business to its suppliers. To help run the business, a record also is needed of the amount owed to each supplier. The accounts payable subsidiary ledger provides this information.

When an accounts payable subsidiary ledger is used, the accounts payable account in the general ledger is a "controlling account." The accounts payable ledger is "subsidiary" to this account. Transactions are posted daily from the general journal to both the general ledger and the accounts payable ledger.

Objective 4. Prepare a schedule of accounts payable.

The Accounts Payable balance in the general ledger should equal the sum of the supplier balances in the accounts payable ledger. A listing of supplier accounts and balances is called a **schedule of accounts payable.** This schedule is usually prepared at the end of the month to verify that the sum of the accounts payable ledger balances equals the Accounts Payable balance.

REVIEW QUESTIONS

Instructions: Analyze each of the following items carefully before writing your answer in the column at the right.

	Question	Answer
LO 1	**1.** For a merchandising business, ________ refers to merchandise acquired for resale.	________________
LO 1	**2.** A(n) ________ is a form used to request the purchasing department to purchase merchandise or other property.	________________
LO 1	**3.** A(n) ________ is a written order to buy goods from a specific vendor (supplier).	________________

LO 1	**4.**	When the merchandise is received, a(n) ________ indicating what has been received is prepared.	____________________
LO 1	**5.**	To the buyer, a document prepared by the seller as a bill for the merchandise shipped is called a(n) ________.	____________________
LO 1	**6.**	In the credit terms 2/10, n/30, the 2 represents a(n) ________.	____________________
LO 1	**7.**	A(n) ________ is a type of discount offered by manufacturers and wholesalers as a reduction from the list or catalog price offered to different classes of customers.	____________________
LO 2	**8.**	List the four accounts used with merchandise purchases transactions.	____________________
			____________________
			____________________
			____________________
LO 2	**9.**	FOB shipping point means that transportation charges are paid by the ________.	____________________
LO 2	**10.**	FOB destination means that transportation charges are paid by the ________.	____________________
LO 2	**11.**	Cost of merchandise available for sale less the end-of-period merchandise inventory is called ________.	____________________
LO 2	**12.**	Net sales minus cost of merchandise sold is called ________.	____________________
LO 3	**13.**	A separate ledger containing an individual account payable for each supplier is called a(n) ________.	____________________
LO 3	**14.**	To indicate that the accounts payable ledger has been posted, a slash and a _______ are entered in the Posting Reference column of the general journal.	____________________
LO 3	**15.**	If a buyer returns merchandise or is given an allowance for damaged merchandise, the account ________ is credited for the dollar amount..	____________________
LO 3	**16.**	Purchases returns and allowances are posted to both the general ledger and the _______ ledger.	____________________
LO 3	**17.**	When a payment is made on account, _______ is debited.	____________________
LO 4	**18.**	To verify that the sum of the accounts payable ledger balances equals the Accounts Payable balance, a(n) ________ is prepared.	____________________

EXERCISES

Exercise 1 (LO 1) PURCHASE REQUISITION

You are employed by Eberle Hardware, a retail hardware business, as manager of the lawn and garden department. On October 1, 20--, after completing an inventory, you decide that the following merchandise should be ordered:

15	All steel rubber-tire wheelbarrows	24	Spade shovels
25	Garden hose, 1/2", 50 ft.	6	Long-handle spade shovels
3	Power mower, 21" cut	12	Spade forks
5	Heavy duty rototillers		

You would like delivery within 10 days and should be notified upon receipt of the merchandise. Using the form provided below, prepare the purchase requisition.

Eberle Hardware

110 E. Kirkwood Ave.
Indianapolis, IN 46011-3274

Purchase Requisition

Requisition No. 502

Required for Department ______________________ Date Issued ______________

Advise ______________________ On Delivery Date Required ______________

Quantity	Description

Approved By ______________________ Requisition Placed By ______________________

DEPARTMENT MANAGER'S MEMORANDUM

Issued To ______________________

Purchase Order No. ______________________

Date ______________________

NOTE: The department manager's memorandum at the bottom of the form should not be completed until after the purchase order is placed in Exercise 2.

Exercise 2 (LO 1) PURCHASE ORDER

Assume you are acting as purchasing agent for Eberle Hardware. On October 2, 20--, order the merchandise specified on Requisition No. 502 in Exercise 1 from Wesner's Supply, 1476 S. Spurr Drive, Miami, FL 33161-1516. Use the purchase order form provided below specifying shipment by AAA freight FOB destination; unit prices as follows:

All steel rubber-tire wheelbarrows	$ 20.35
Garden hose, 1/2", 50 ft.	4.65
Power mower, 21" cut	180.75
Heavy duty rototillers	291.50
Spade shovels	7.45
Long-handle spade shovels	9.30
Spade forks	7.70

After preparing the purchase order, fill in the department manager's memorandum at the bottom of Purchase Requisition No. 502 prepared in Exercise 1. Assume the requisition was approved by Scott Roturt.

Eberle Hardware

110 E. Kirkwood Ave.
Indianapolis, IN 46011-3274

Purchase Order

Order No. 361

Date ______________

To ______________ Deliver By ______________

______________ Ship via ______________

______________ FOB ______________

Quantity	Description	Unit Price	Total

By ______________

Exercise 3 (LO 1) PURCHASE INVOICES

The purchase invoice below received from Wesner's Supply has been referred to you for verification. Compare it with Purchase Order No. 361 in Exercise 2 and verify (a) the quantities ordered, (b) the quantities shipped, (c) the unit prices, (d) the extensions, and (e) the total amount of the invoice. For each item that has been verified, report any discrepancies detected.

INVOICE NO	SOLD TO	SHIP TO
	Eberle Hardware 110 E. Kirkwood Ave. Indianapolis, IN 46011-3274	same

WS Wesner's Supply
1476 So. Spurr Drive, Miami, FL 33161-1516

INVOICE DATE	YOUR ORDER NO & DATE	DATE SHIPPED
Oct. 7, 20--	361 Oct. 2, 20--	Oct. 7, 20--

REQUISITION NO	OUR ORDER NO

TERMS	FOB	CAR INITIALS & NO	HOW SHIPPED & ROUTE	SHIPPED FROM
2/10, n/30	Destination		Freight AAA	Miami

QUANTITY SHIPPED	DESCRIPTION	UNIT PRICE	EXTENSION
15	All steel rubber-tire wheelbarrows	$ 20.35	$ 305.25
25	Garden hose, 1/2", 50 ft.	4.65	116.25
4	Power mower, 21" cut	291.50	1,166.00
5	Heavy duty rototillers	180.75	903.75
24	Spade shovels	7.95	178.80
6	Long-handle spade shovels	9.30	57.00
12	Spade forks	7.70	92.40
			$2,819.45

Exercise 4 (LO 1) TRADE DISCOUNT

Skirvin Enterprises purchased merchandise with a list price of $800, less a trade discount of 10%. Compute the amount to be paid.

Exercise 5 (LO 1) CASH DISCOUNT

Geisel's Boating Supplies purchased life preservers and other boating equipment for resale costing $1,200, terms 3/10, n/60.

1. If Geisel makes payment within the discount period, how much will be paid?

2. If the invoice terms were 2/10, n/30, compute the cash discount available to Geisel's if payment is made within the discount period.

Exercise 6 (LO 2) GROSS PROFIT

The following information was taken from the records of Hi-Fi Specialists for the month of August 20--:

Sales	$257,800
Sales returns and allowances	1,900
Sales discounts	400
Merchandise inventory, August 1	38,000
Merchandise inventory, August 31	32,000
Purchases	200,000
Purchases returns and allowances	10,200
Purchases discounts	4,000
Freight-In	2,000

Required:

Using the form on page 172, show the computation of gross profit on the income statement for the month of August.

Exercise 6 (Concluded)

Exercise 7 (LO 3) JOURNALIZING PURCHASES AND CASH PAYMENTS

The following transactions occurred during the month of November at O'Henesy Office Equipment and Supply:

Nov. 5 Purchased the following merchandise on account; unit prices are given:

20	Mini-shredders	$ 63.95
10	Hi-speed printer-scanners	900.00
5	Laptop computers	1,995.00

The purchase has a trade discount of 15% and credit terms of 2/10, n/30.

15 Issued a check for the amount due on the November 5 purchase.

Required:

1. Journalize the above transactions in the general journal below.
2. Give the appropriate general journal entry if the payment is not made until December 5.

1. and 2.

GENERAL JOURNAL PAGE

	DATE		DESCRIPTION	POST. REF.	DEBIT	CREDIT	
1							1
2							2
3							3
4							4
5							5
6							6
7							7
8							8
9							9
10							10
11							11

Supporting calculations:

PROBLEMS

Problem 8 (LO2/3) JOURNALIZING AND POSTING PURCHASES TRANSACTIONS

J. R. Lang, owner of Lang's Galleria, made the following purchases of merchandise on account during the month of November 20--:

Nov.	2	Purchase Invoice No. 611, $4,145, from Ford Distributors.
	5	Purchase Invoice No. 216, $2,165, from Mueller Wholesaler.
	15	Purchase Invoice No. 399, $2,895, from Grant White & Co.
	19	Purchase Invoice No. 106, $1,845, from Bailey & Hinds, Inc.
	22	Purchase Invoice No. 914, $3,225, from Ford Distributors.
	28	Purchase Invoice No. 661, $2,175, from Jackson Company.
	30	Purchase Invoice No. 716, $3,500, from Mueller Wholesaler.

Required:

1. Record the transactions in the general journal (page 9) on page 175.
2. Post from the journal to the general ledger accounts and the accounts payable ledger accounts (pages 176–177).

Name ______________________________

Problem 8 (Continued)

1.

GENERAL JOURNAL

PAGE

	DATE	DESCRIPTION	POST. REF.	DEBIT	CREDIT	
1						1
2						2
3						3
4						4
5						5
6						6
7						7
8						8
9						9
10						10
11						11
12						12
13						13
14						14
15						15
16						16
17						17
18						18
19						19
20						20
21						21
22						22
23						23
24						24
25						25
26						26
27						27
28						28
29						29
30						30

Problem 8 (Continued)

2.

GENERAL LEDGER

ACCOUNT Accounts Payable ACCOUNT NO. 202

DATE		ITEM	POST. REF.	DEBIT	CREDIT	BALANCE DEBIT	BALANCE CREDIT

ACCOUNT Purchases ACCOUNT NO. 501

DATE		ITEM	POST. REF.	DEBIT	CREDIT	BALANCE DEBIT	BALANCE CREDIT

ACCOUNTS PAYABLE LEDGER

NAME Bailey & Hinds, Inc.

ADDRESS

DATE		ITEM	POST. REF.	DEBIT	CREDIT	BALANCE

Problem 8 (Concluded)

NAME Ford Distributors

ADDRESS

DATE		ITEM	POST. REF.	DEBIT	CREDIT	BALANCE

NAME Grant White & Co.

ADDRESS

DATE		ITEM	POST. REF.	DEBIT	CREDIT	BALANCE

NAME Jackson Company

ADDRESS

DATE		ITEM	POST. REF.	DEBIT	CREDIT	BALANCE

NAME Mueller Wholesaler

ADDRESS

DATE		ITEM	POST. REF.	DEBIT	CREDIT	BALANCE

Problem 9 (LO 2/3/4) PURCHASES TRANSACTIONS AND SCHEDULE OF ACCOUNTS PAYABLE

Tom Bowers operates a business under the name of Tom's Sporting Goods. The books include a general journal and an accounts payable ledger. The following transactions are related to purchases for the month of February:

Feb.	3	Purchased merchandise from Ringer's on account, $498.64. Invoice No. 611; terms 2/10, n/30.
	4	Purchased merchandise on account from Klein Brothers, $780.11. Invoice No. 112; terms 30 days.
	11	Purchased merchandise from Corleon's on account, $2,300.00. Invoice No. 432; terms 30 days.
	15	Received a credit memorandum from Ringer's for $30.00 for merchandise returned that had been purchased on account.

Required:

1. Enter the above transactions in the general journal provided below (page 5).
2. Post from the journal to the general ledger and accounts payable ledger on pages 179–180.
3. Prepare a schedule of accounts payable as of February 28.

1.

GENERAL JOURNAL

PAGE

	DATE		DESCRIPTION	POST. REF.	DEBIT	CREDIT	
1							1
2							2
3							3
4							4
5							5
6							6
7							7
8							8
9							9
10							10
11							11
12							12
13							13
14							14
15							15

Problem 9 (Continued)
2.

GENERAL LEDGER

ACCOUNT Accounts Payable ACCOUNT NO. 202

DATE		ITEM	POST. REF.	DEBIT	CREDIT	BALANCE DEBIT	BALANCE CREDIT
20-- Feb.	1	Balance	✓				3,125.50

ACCOUNT Purchases ACCOUNT NO. 501

DATE		ITEM	POST. REF.	DEBIT	CREDIT	BALANCE DEBIT	BALANCE CREDIT
20-- Feb.	1	Balance	✓			2,500.00	

ACCOUNT Purchases Returns and Allowances ACCOUNT NO. 501.1

DATE		ITEM	POST. REF.	DEBIT	CREDIT	BALANCE DEBIT	BALANCE CREDIT
20-- Feb.	1	Balance	✓				200.00

Problem 9 (Concluded)

ACCOUNTS PAYABLE LEDGER

NAME Corleon's

ADDRESS 1894 Winthrop Ave., White Plains, NY 10606-6915

DATE		ITEM	POST. REF.	DEBIT	CREDIT	BALANCE
20-- Feb.	1	Balance	✓			1 6 2 5 50

NAME Klein Brothers

ADDRESS 1728 Camino Real, San Antonio, TX 78238-4420

DATE		ITEM	POST. REF.	DEBIT	CREDIT	BALANCE
20-- Feb.	1	Balance	✓			6 2 5 00

NAME Ringer's

ADDRESS 1500 North Street, Bakersfield, CA 93301-4747

DATE		ITEM	POST. REF.	DEBIT	CREDIT	BALANCE
20-- Feb.	1	Balance	✓			8 7 5 00

3.

Problem 10 (LO 3/4) CASH PAYMENTS TRANSACTIONS AND SCHEDULE OF ACCOUNTS PAYABLE

Chris Bultman operates a retail shoe store called Bultman Shoes. The books include a general journal and an accounts payable ledger. The following transactions are related to cash payments for the month of August:

Aug.	1	Issued Check No. 47 for $900.00 in payment of rent (Rent Expense) for August.
	3	Issued Check No. 48 to Blue Suede Shoes Company in payment on account, $640.00, less 2% discount.
	9	Issued Check No. 49 to Style-Rite in payment on account, $800.00, less 3% discount.
	14	Issued Check No. 50 for $125.28 in payment of utility bill (Utilities Expense).
	20	Issued Check No. 51 to Baldo Company in payment for cash purchase, $525.00.
	22	Issued Check No. 52 to West Coast Shoes in payment on account, $625.00. A discount of 2% was lost because Bultman neglected to pay the invoice within the discount period.
	27	Issued Check No. 53 for $2,000.00 to Bultman for a cash withdrawal for personal use.

Required:

1. Enter the above transactions in the general journal (page 4) on page 182.
2. Post from the journal to the general ledger and accounts payable ledger accounts provided on pages 183–185.
3. Prepare a schedule of accounts payable for Bultman Shoes on August 31, 20--, using the form on page 185.

Problem 10 (Continued)

1.

GENERAL JOURNAL

PAGE

DATE		DESCRIPTION	POST. REF.	DEBIT	CREDIT

Problem 10 (Continued)
2.

GENERAL LEDGER

ACCOUNT Cash ACCOUNT NO. 101

DATE		ITEM	POST. REF.	DEBIT	CREDIT	BALANCE DEBIT	BALANCE CREDIT
20-- Aug.	1	Balance	✓			25,000 00	

ACCOUNT Accounts Payable ACCOUNT NO. 202

DATE		ITEM	POST. REF.	DEBIT	CREDIT	BALANCE DEBIT	BALANCE CREDIT
20-- Aug.	1	Balance	✓				3,366 00

ACCOUNT C. Bultman, Drawing ACCOUNT NO. 312

DATE		ITEM	POST. REF.	DEBIT	CREDIT	BALANCE DEBIT	BALANCE CREDIT
20-- Aug.	1	Balance	✓			14,000 00	

ACCOUNT Purchases ACCOUNT NO. 501

DATE		ITEM	POST. REF.	DEBIT	CREDIT	BALANCE DEBIT	BALANCE CREDIT
20-- Aug.	1	Balance	✓			54,265 43	

Problem 10 (Continued)

ACCOUNT Purchases Discounts ACCOUNT NO. 501.2

DATE		ITEM	POST. REF.	DEBIT	CREDIT	BALANCE DEBIT	BALANCE CREDIT
20-- Aug.	1	Balance	✓				325 20

ACCOUNT Rent Expense ACCOUNT NO. 521

DATE		ITEM	POST. REF.	DEBIT	CREDIT	BALANCE DEBIT	BALANCE CREDIT
20-- Aug.	1	Balance	✓			7200 00	

ACCOUNT Utilities Expense ACCOUNT NO. 533

DATE		ITEM	POST. REF.	DEBIT	CREDIT	BALANCE DEBIT	BALANCE CREDIT
20-- Aug.	1	Balance	✓			822 87	

ACCOUNTS PAYABLE LEDGER

NAME Blue Suede Shoes Company

ADDRESS 2805 South Meridian, Indianapolis, IN 46225-3460

DATE		ITEM	POST. REF.	DEBIT	CREDIT	BALANCE
20-- Aug.	1	Balance	✓			640 00

Problem 10 (Concluded)

NAME Style-Rite

ADDRESS 6500 9th Street, New Orleans, LA 70115-1122

DATE		ITEM	POST. REF.	DEBIT	CREDIT	BALANCE
20-- Aug.	1	Balance	✓			1 2 0 0 00

NAME West Coast Shoes

ADDRESS 705 Rialto Avenue, Fresno, CA 93705-7845

DATE		ITEM	POST. REF.	DEBIT	CREDIT	BALANCE
20-- Aug.	1	Balance	✓			1 5 2 6 00

3.

Problem 11 (LO 3) CASH PAYMENTS TRANSACTIONS

The following cash payments were made by Demis Music Company during the month of July:

July 5 Paid $600 for rent. Issued Check No. 222.

12 Purchased $3,250 in merchandise from Hamilton Music Company. Issued Check No. 223.

18 Made a payment on account to Martinez Guitar Company for $4,500, less a 2% discount for paying within the discount period. Issued Check No. 224.

25 Paid $2,000 to First National Bank to pay off a note. Issued Check No. 225.

31 Anna Demis withdrew $5,500 from the business for personal use. Issued Check No. 226.

Required:

Enter the above transactions in a general journal.

GENERAL JOURNAL

PAGE

	DATE	DESCRIPTION	POST. REF.	DEBIT	CREDIT	
1						1
2						2
3						3
4						4
5						5
6						6
7						7
8						8
9						9
10						10
11						11
12						12
13						13
14						14
15						15
16						16
17						17
18						18
19						19
20						20

CHAPTER 11 APPENDIX
THE NET-PRICE METHOD OF RECORDING PURCHASES

LEARNING OBJECTIVES

Objective 1. Describe the net-price method of recording purchases.

Under the net-price method, purchases are recorded at the net amount, assuming that all cash discounts will be taken.

Objective 2. Record purchases and cash payments using the net-price method.

At the time of purchase, Purchases is debited and Accounts Payable is credited for the gross price less the cash discount. If payment is made within the discount period, Accounts Payable is debited and Cash is credited for the net price. If payment is not made until after the discount period, Accounts Payable is debited for the net price, Purchases Discounts Lost is debited for the discount lost, and Cash is credited for the gross price.

Apx. Exercise (LO 1/2) PURCHASES AND CASH PAYMENTS TRANSACTIONS

Jiang's Accessory Shop had the following transactions during April:

Apr. 2 Purchased merchandise on account from Sag's Apparel for $2,000, terms 2/10, n/30.
5 Purchased merchandise on account from Lee's Wholesale for $1,800, terms 1/10, n/30.
11 Paid the amount due to Sag's Apparel for the purchase on April 2.
25 Paid the amount due to Lee's Wholesale for the purchase on April 5.

Required:

1. Prepare general journal entries for these transactions using the gross-price method.
2. Prepare general journal entries for these transactions using the net-price method.

1.

GENERAL JOURNAL

PAGE

	DATE	DESCRIPTION	POST. REF.	DEBIT	CREDIT	
1						1
2						2
3						3
4						4
5						5
6						6
7						7
8						8
9						9
10						10
11						11
12						12
13						13

Apx. Exercise (Concluded)

2.

GENERAL JOURNAL

PAGE

DATE	DESCRIPTION	POST. REF.	DEBIT	CREDIT

CHAPTER 12
SPECIAL JOURNALS

LEARNING OBJECTIVES

Chapter 12 continues the study of sales, cash receipts, purchases, and cash payments transactions in a merchandising business. The focus is on how to account for these transactions more efficiently. Four special journals that speed up and simplify the recording process are introduced.

Objective 1. Describe, explain the purpose of, and identify transactions recorded in special journals.

A **special journal** is a journal designed for recording only certain kinds of transactions. The types of special journals used by a business should depend on the types of transactions that occur frequently for the business. Four special journals commonly used by businesses are the sales journal, cash receipts journal, purchases journal, and cash payments journal.

Objective 2. Describe and use the sales journal.

The **sales journal** saves time and energy by simplifying the recording and posting of transactions. It is a "special journal" used to record only credit sales of merchandise.

Credit sales affect Accounts Receivable (debit), Sales (credit), and, if there is a sales tax, Sales Tax Payable (credit). The sales journal provides separate columns for Accounts Receivable Debit, Sales Credit, and Sales Tax Payable Credit. The column totals are posted monthly to the general ledger accounts. Individual customer accounts in the accounts receivable ledger are posted daily.

Objective 3. Describe and use the cash receipts journal.

Like the sales journal, a **cash receipts journal** saves time and energy in recording and posting transactions. Any time cash is received, the cash receipts journal is the book of original entry, and Cash is always debited. Column headings are established for Cash and other accounts that are frequently used, such as Sales (credit), Accounts Receivable (credit), Bank Credit Card Expense (debit), and Sales Tax Payable (credit). There usually also is a General Credit column for accounts that do not have a special column.

As with other special journals, column totals are posted at the end of the month. Daily postings are made for items in the General Credit column, as well as to the accounts receivable ledger.

Objective 4. Describe and use the purchases journal.

A **purchases journal** is a special journal used to record only purchases of merchandise on account. This journal may have only a single column for Purchases Debit/Accounts Payable Credit Alternatively, there may be three columns for Purchases Debit, Freight-In Debit, and Accounts Payable Credit.

Each general ledger account used in the purchases journal requires only one posting each period. Individual supplier accounts in the accounts payable ledger are posted daily.

Objective 5. Describe and use the cash payments journal.

A **cash payments journal** is a special journal used to record only cash payments transactions. The column headings of the cash payments journal will be those accounts that are most frequently affected by the company's cash payments transactions. Column totals are posted to the general ledger accounts at the end of the month. Items in the General Debit column are posted daily. Individual supplier accounts in the accounts payable ledger also are posted daily.

REVIEW QUESTIONS

Instructions: Analyze each of the following items carefully before writing your answer in the column at the right.

		Question	Answer
LO 1	1.	A journal designed for recording only certain kinds of transactions is called a ________.	________
LO 1	2.	Transactions that occur infrequently, and adjusting and closing entries usually are recorded in the ________.	________
LO 2	3.	A sale is recorded in a sales journal by entering what four pieces of information?	________ ________ ________ ________
LO 2	4.	A(n) ________ journal is a special journal used to record only sales of merchandise on account.	________
LO 2	5.	Sales returns and allowances are generally recorded in the ________ journal.	________
LO 2	6.	Each sales journal entry is posted to the accounts receivable ledger ____________.	________
LO 3	7.	Any time the cash receipts journal is used, a debit is made to ____________.	________
LO 3	8.	The cash receipts journal is a special journal used to record only ___________ transactions.	________
LO 3	9.	Each amount in the General Credit column of the cash receipts journal is posted ________.	________
LO 4	10.	A(n) ________ is a special journal used to record only purchases of merchandise on account.	________
LO 4	11.	Purchases returns and allowances are recorded in the ________.	________
LO 4	12.	The purchases journal for a company like Northern Micro, whose suppliers generally pay the freight charges, would have only a single column labeled Purchases Debit/ ________.	________
LO 4	13.	A separate ledger containing an individual account payable for each supplier is called a(n) ________.	________
LO 4	14.	Each purchases journal entry is posted to the accounts payable ledger ___________.	________
LO 5	15.	A(n) ________ is a special journal used to record only cash payments transactions.	________

LO 5 **16.** Any time the cash payments journal is used, a credit is made to the account called ________. .... ______________________

LO 5 **17.** A cash payment is recorded in the cash payments journal by entering what four pieces of information? .... ______________________

____

____

____

LO 5 **18.** Each amount in the General Debit column of the cash payments journal is posted ________. .... ______________________

EXERCISES

Exercise 1 (LO 1) RECORDING TRANSACTIONS IN THE PROPER JOURNAL

Indicate the proper journal in which to record each transaction below by placing an "X" in the appropriate box.

	Journal				
Transaction	**Sales**	**Cash Receipts**	**Purchases**	**Cash Payments**	**General**
a. Made payment to supplier on account.					
b. Sold old delivery equipment for cash.					
c. Sold merchandise on account.					
d. Purchased merchandise for cash.					
e. Returned merchandise to supplier for credit.					
f. Invested additional funds in the business.					
g. Purchased merchandise on account.					

Exercise 2 (LO 2) SALES JOURNAL

Diana Brewer operates the Floor and Window Treatment Center and completed the following transactions related to sales of merchandise on account during the month of February. Sales tax of 5% was included in the amount of each sale.

Feb. 2 Sold wallpaper supplies to Dresson Homes, $98.95, terms n/30. Sale No. 255.
12 Sold paint to Ray Acuff, $105, terms n/30. Sale No. 256.
23 Sold miniblinds to Clydette Rupert, $114.83, terms n/30. Sale No. 257.
24 Sold decorator items to Marty Staple, $35.55, terms n/30. Sale No. 258.
25 Sold paint to Angel Burtin, $25.57, terms n/30. Sale No. 259.

Exercise 2 (Concluded)

Required:

1. Enter the transactions from the previous page in the sales journal.
2. Total and rule the journal.

1. and 2.

SALES JOURNAL PAGE

	DATE		SALE NO.	TO WHOM SOLD	POST. REF.	ACCOUNTS RECEIVABLE DEBIT	SALES CREDIT	SALES TAX PAYABLE CREDIT	
1									1
2									2
3									3
4									4
5									5
6									6
7									7

Exercise 3 (LO 3) CASH RECEIPTS JOURNAL

Diana Brewer of the Floor and Window Treatment Center received cash during the month of March as described below.

Mar. 2 Received cash from Dresson Homes on account, $98.95.
12 Received cash from Ray Acuff on account, $105.
15 Made cash sale to Jean Granite, $404.76, plus 5% sales tax.
18 Made cash sale to Bill Green, $2,380.95, plus 5% sales tax.
23 Received cash from Clydette Rupert on account, $114.83.
24 Received cash from Marty Staple on account, $35.55.
25 Received cash from Angel Burtin on account, $25.57.
31 Made cash sales for the month of $22,000, including 5% sales tax (from cash register tape).
31 Made credit card sales for the month of $28,000, including 5% sales tax.

Required:

1. Enter the above transactions in the cash receipts journal on page 193.
2. Total and rule the journal.

Exercise 3 (Concluded)

1. and 2.

CASH RECEIPTS JOURNAL

PAGE

	DATE		ACCOUNT CREDITED	POST. REF.	GENERAL CREDIT	ACCOUNTS RECEIVABLE CREDIT	SALES CREDIT	SALES TAX PAYABLE CREDIT	CASH DEBIT	
1										1
2										2
3										3
4										4
5										5
6										6
7										7
8										8
9										9
10										10
11										11

Exercise 4 (LO 4) PURCHASES JOURNAL

Tom Bowers operates a business under the name of Tom's Sporting Goods. The books of original entry include a purchases journal and a general journal, in which entries such as Purchase Returns and Allowances are recorded. An accounts payable ledger is used to maintain a record of the amount owed to suppliers. The following transactions are related to purchases for the month of February:

Feb. 3 Purchased merchandise from Ringer's on account, $498.64, Invoice No. 611, terms 2/10, n/30.

4 Purchased merchandise on account from Klein Brothers, $780.11, Invoice No. 112, terms 30 days.

11 Purchased merchandise from Corleon's on account, $2,300, Invoice No. 432, terms 30 days.

15 Received a credit memo from Ringer's for $30 for merchandise returned that had been purchased on account.

Required:

Enter the above transactions in the following purchases journal and general journal:

PURCHASES JOURNAL

PAGE

	DATE		INVOICE NO.	FROM WHOM PURCHASED	POST. REF.	PURCHASES DEBIT ACCTS. PAY. CREDIT	
1							1
2							2
3							3
4							4
5							5

Exercise 4 (Concluded)

GENERAL JOURNAL PAGE

	DATE		DESCRIPTION	POST. REF.	DEBIT	CREDIT	
1							1
2							2
3							3

Exercise 5 (LO 5) CASH PAYMENTS JOURNAL

The following cash payments were made by Demis Music Company during the month of July:

July 5 Paid $600 for rent. Issued Check No. 222.
12 Purchased $3,250 in merchandise from Hamilton Music Company. Issued Check No. 223.
18 Made a payment on account to Martinez Guitar Company for $4,500, less a 2% discount for paying within the discount period. Issued Check No. 224.
25 Paid $2,000 to First National Bank to pay off a note. Issued Check No. 225.
31 Anna Demis withdrew $5,500 from the business for personal use. Issued Check No. 226.

Required:

1. Enter the above transactions in the cash payments journal.
2. Total, rule, and prove the journal.

1. and 2.

CASH PAYMENTS JOURNAL PAGE

	DATE		CK. NO.	ACCOUNT DEBITED	POST. REF.	GENERAL DEBIT	ACCOUNTS PAYABLE DEBIT	PURCHASES DEBIT	PURCHASES DISCOUNTS CREDIT	CASH CREDIT	
1											1
2											2
3											3
4											4
5											5
6											6
7											7

PROBLEMS

Problem 6 (LO 2/3) SALES JOURNAL AND CASH RECEIPTS JOURNAL

The following information represents transactions for Kwan Chu's Fish Market for the month of July 20--. Sales tax is 6%.

July	1	Sold merchandise on account to B. A. Smith, $137.50, plus sales tax. Sale No. 33.
	3	B. A. Smith returned merchandise, $15, plus sales tax, for a credit. Credit Memo No. 11.
	5	Sold merchandise on account to L. L. Unis, $218, plus sales tax. Sale No. 34.
	7	Made cash sales for the week, $325.44, plus sales tax.
	10	Sold merchandise on account to W. P. Clark, $208, plus sales tax. Sale No. 35.
	11	Received $129.85 from B. A. Smith, on account.
	13	W. P. Clark returned merchandise, $22, plus sales tax, for a credit. Credit Memo No. 12.
	14	Made cash sales for the week, $411.20, plus sales tax.
	16	Sold merchandise on account to B. A. Smith, $282.50, plus sales tax. Sale No. 36.
	17	Received $231.08 from L. L. Unis, on account.
	21	Made cash sales for the week, $292.50, plus sales tax.
	24	Sold merchandise on account to L. L. Unis, $224.50, plus sales tax. Sale No. 37.
	28	Made cash sales for the week, $300.50, plus sales tax.
	31	Received $197.16 from W. P. Clark, on account.

Required:

1. Using the information provided, record the transactions in the sales journal, cash receipts journal, or general journal as required.
2. Total and rule the column totals.

1. and 2.

GENERAL JOURNAL PAGE

	DATE		DESCRIPTION	POST. REF.	DEBIT	CREDIT	
1							1
2							2
3							3
4							4
5							5
6							6
7							7
8							8
9							9
10							10

Problem 6 (Concluded)

SALES JOURNAL

PAGE

	DATE	SALE NO.	TO WHOM SOLD	POST. REF.	ACCOUNTS RECEIVABLE DEBIT	SALES CREDIT	SALES TAX PAYABLE CREDIT	
1								1
2								2
3								3
4								4
5								5
6								6
7								7
8								8

CASH RECEIPTS JOURNAL

PAGE

	DATE	ACCOUNT CREDITED	POST. REF.	GENERAL CREDIT	ACCOUNTS RECEIVABLE CREDIT	SALES CREDIT	SALES TAX PAYABLE CREDIT	CASH DEBIT	
1									1
2									2
3									3
4									4
5									5
6									6
7									7
8									8
9									9
10									10

Problem 7 (LO 2) SALES JOURNAL, GENERAL LEDGER, AND ACCOUNTS RECEIVABLE LEDGER

H. K. Smythe operates Leather All, a leather shop that sells luggage, handbags, business cases, and other leather goods. During the month of May, the following sales on account were made:

May	3	Sold merchandise on account to T. A. Pigdon, $247.50, plus sales tax of $14.85. Sale No. 51.
	4	Sold merchandise on account to J. R. Feyton, $55, plus sales tax of $3.30. Sale No. 52.
	6	Sold merchandise on account to P. C. McMurdy, $99, plus sales tax of $5.94. Sale No. 53.
	10	Sold merchandise on account to J. T. Messer, $175, plus sales tax of $10.50. Sale No. 54.
	12	Sold merchandise on account to A. F. Schlitz, $355, plus sales tax of $21.30. Sale No. 55.
	13	Sold merchandise on account to J. R. Feyton, $215, plus sales tax of $12.90. Sale No. 56.
	20	Sold merchandise on account to P. C. McMurdy, $400, plus sales tax of $24. Sale No. 57.
	28	Sold merchandise on account to J. T. Messer, $255, plus sales tax of $15.30. Sale No. 58.

Required:

1. Enter the above transactions in the sales journal (page 1) provided below.
2. Post the entries in the sales journal to the accounts receivable ledger on pages 198–199.
3. Total and verify the column totals and rule the sales journal. Complete the summary postings to the general ledger on page 198.

1. and 3.

SALES JOURNAL PAGE 1

	DATE	SALE NO.	TO WHOM SOLD	POST. REF.	ACCOUNTS RECEIVABLE DEBIT	SALES CREDIT	SALES TAX PAYABLE CREDIT	
1								1
2								2
3								3
4								4
5								5
6								6
7								7
8								8
9								9
10								10

Problem 7 (Continued)

3.

GENERAL LEDGER

ACCOUNT Accounts Receivable ACCOUNT NO. 122

DATE		ITEM	POST. REF.	DEBIT	CREDIT	BALANCE DEBIT	BALANCE CREDIT
20-- May	1	Balance	✓			834 00	

ACCOUNT Sales Tax Payable ACCOUNT NO. 231

DATE		ITEM	POST. REF.	DEBIT	CREDIT	BALANCE DEBIT	BALANCE CREDIT

ACCOUNT Sales ACCOUNT NO. 401

DATE		ITEM	POST. REF.	DEBIT	CREDIT	BALANCE DEBIT	BALANCE CREDIT

2.

ACCOUNTS RECEIVABLE LEDGER

NAME J. R. Feyton

ADDRESS 6022 Columbia, St. Louis, MO 63139-1906

DATE		ITEM	POST. REF.	DEBIT	CREDIT	BALANCE

Problem 7 (Concluded)

NAME P. C. McMurdy

ADDRESS 1214 N. 2nd St., E. St. Louis, IL 62201-2679

DATE		ITEM	POST. REF.	DEBIT	CREDIT	BALANCE
20-- May	1	Balance	✓			125 00

NAME J. T. Messer

ADDRESS P.O. Box 249, Chesterfield, MO 63017-3901

DATE		ITEM	POST. REF.	DEBIT	CREDIT	BALANCE
20-- May	1	Balance	✓			177 00

NAME T. A. Pigdon

ADDRESS 1070 Purcell, University City, MO 63130-1546

DATE		ITEM	POST. REF.	DEBIT	CREDIT	BALANCE
20-- May	1	Balance	✓			280 00

NAME A. F. Schlitz

ADDRESS 800 Lindbergh Blvd., St. Louis, MO 63166-1546

DATE		ITEM	POST. REF.	DEBIT	CREDIT	BALANCE
20-- May	1	Balance	✓			252 00

Problem 8 (LO 3) CASH RECEIPTS JOURNAL, GENERAL JOURNAL, GENERAL LEDGER, AND ACCOUNTS RECEIVABLE LEDGER

Paula Angelillis operates Hard-to-Find Auto Parts Store. Much of her business is by mail. The books of original entry include a cash receipts journal and a general journal. The following transactions related to sales and cash receipts occurred during June:

June	1	Received $300 from A. K. Wells, including $14.29 of sales tax, for field cash sale. (Field cash sales are not included in cash register tapes.)
	5	Received $125.60 from L. Strous on account.
	10	Received $263.25 from D. Manning on account.
	12	Q. Striker returned merchandise for credit. The sales price was $215, plus sales tax of $10.75.
	18	Received $58.25 from D. Warding on account.
	20	Received $1,000 from B. L. Stryker, including $47.62 tax (field cash sale).
	21	Received $29.99 from L. Clese on account.
	24	R. Popielarz returned merchandise for credit. The sales price was $116.25, plus sales tax of $5.81.
	27	Received $426 from L. LeCount on account.
	30	Made cash and bank credit card sales for the month of $8,200, plus sales tax of $410. Bank credit card expense is $80.

Required:

1. Enter each transaction in either the cash receipts journal (page 18) or the general journal (page 5) provided. Total, verify the totals, and rule the cash receipts journal.
2. Make the individual postings required from the cash receipts journal and the general journal to the general and accounts receivable ledgers.
3. Make the summary postings from the cash receipts journal to the general ledger.

1.

GENERAL JOURNAL

PAGE 5

	DATE		DESCRIPTION	POST. REF.	DEBIT	CREDIT	
1							1
2							2
3							3
4							4
5							5
6							6
7							7
8							8
9							9
10							10

Problem 8 (Continued)

CASH RECEIPTS JOURNAL

PAGE 18

	DATE	ACCOUNT CREDITED	POST. REF.	GENERAL CREDIT	ACCOUNTS REC. CREDIT	SALES CREDIT	SALES TAX PAYABLE CREDIT	BANK CR. CARD EXP. DEBIT	CASH DEBIT	
1										1
2										2
3										3
4										4
5										5
6										6
7										7
8										8
9										9
10										10
11										11
12										12

2. and 3.

GENERAL LEDGER

ACCOUNT Cash ACCOUNT NO. 101

DATE		ITEM	POST. REF.	DEBIT	CREDIT	BALANCE	
						DEBIT	CREDIT
20-- June	1	Balance	✓			13,200.25	

ACCOUNT Accounts Receivable ACCOUNT NO. 122

DATE		ITEM	POST. REF.	DEBIT	CREDIT	BALANCE	
						DEBIT	CREDIT
20-- June	1	Balance	✓			1,250.90	

Problem 8 (Continued)

ACCOUNT Sales Tax Payable ACCOUNT NO. 231

DATE		ITEM	POST. REF.	DEBIT	CREDIT	BALANCE DEBIT	BALANCE CREDIT
20-- June	1	Balance	✓				125 00

ACCOUNT Sales ACCOUNT NO. 401

DATE		ITEM	POST. REF.	DEBIT	CREDIT	BALANCE DEBIT	BALANCE CREDIT

ACCOUNT Sales Returns and Allowances ACCOUNT NO. 401.1

DATE		ITEM	POST. REF.	DEBIT	CREDIT	BALANCE DEBIT	BALANCE CREDIT

ACCOUNT Bank Credit Card Expense ACCOUNT NO. 513

DATE		ITEM	POST. REF.	DEBIT	CREDIT	BALANCE DEBIT	BALANCE CREDIT

Name ______________________________

Problem 8 (Continued)

ACCOUNTS RECEIVABLE LEDGER

NAME L. Clese

ADDRESS 875 Glenway Drive, Glendale, MO 63122-4112

DATE		ITEM	POST. REF.	DEBIT	CREDIT	BALANCE
20-- June	1	Balance	✓			29.99

NAME L. LeCount

ADDRESS 1439 East Broad Street, Columbus, OH 43205-9892

DATE		ITEM	POST. REF.	DEBIT	CREDIT	BALANCE
20-- June	1	Balance	✓			426.00

NAME D. Manning

ADDRESS 2101 Cumberland Road, Noblesville, IN 47870-2435

DATE		ITEM	POST. REF.	DEBIT	CREDIT	BALANCE
20-- June	1	Balance	✓			263.25

Problem 8 (Concluded)

NAME R. Popielarz

ADDRESS 3001 Hillcrest Drive, Dallas, PA 18612-6854

DATE		ITEM	POST. REF.	DEBIT	CREDIT	BALANCE
20-- June	1	Balance	✓			1,222.06

NAME Q. Striker

ADDRESS 4113 Main Street, Beech Grove, IN 46107-9643

DATE		ITEM	POST. REF.	DEBIT	CREDIT	BALANCE
20-- June	1	Balance	✓			2,255.75

NAME L. Strous

ADDRESS 2215 N. State Road 135, Greenwood, IN 46142-6432

DATE		ITEM	POST. REF.	DEBIT	CREDIT	BALANCE
20-- June	1	Balance	✓			1,256.60

NAME D. Warding

ADDRESS 1100 W. Main Street, Carmel, IN 46032-2364

DATE		ITEM	POST. REF.	DEBIT	CREDIT	BALANCE
20-- June	1	Balance	✓			58.25

Problem 9 (LO 4) PURCHASES JOURNAL, GENERAL LEDGER, AND ACCOUNTS PAYABLE LEDGER

J. R. Lang, owner of Lang's Galleria, made the following purchases of merchandise on account during the month of November 20--.

Nov.	2	Purchase Invoice No. 611, $4,145, from Ford Distributors.
	5	Purchase Invoice No. 216, $2,165, from Mueller Wholesaler.
	15	Purchase Invoice No. 399, $2,895, from Grant White & Co.
	19	Purchase Invoice No. 106, $1,845, from Bailey & Hinds, Inc.
	22	Purchase Invoice No. 914, $3,225, from Ford Distributors.
	28	Purchase Invoice No. 661, $2,175, from Jackson Company.
	30	Purchase Invoice No. 716, $3,500, from Mueller Wholesaler.

Required:

1. Record the transactions in the purchases journal (page 9). Total and rule the journal.
2. Post from the purchases journal to the general ledger accounts and to the accounts payable ledger accounts.

1.

PURCHASES JOURNAL

PAGE 9

	DATE	INVOICE NO.	FROM WHOM PURCHASED	POST. REF.	PURCHASES DEBIT ACCTS. PAY. CREDIT	
1						1
2						2
3						3
4						4
5						5
6						6
7						7
8						8
9						9
10						10

2.

GENERAL LEDGER

ACCOUNT Accounts Payable ACCOUNT NO. 202

DATE	ITEM	POST. REF.	DEBIT	CREDIT	BALANCE DEBIT	BALANCE CREDIT

Problem 9 (Continued)

ACCOUNT Purchases ACCOUNT NO. 501

DATE		ITEM	POST. REF.	DEBIT	CREDIT	BALANCE DEBIT	BALANCE CREDIT

ACCOUNTS PAYABLE LEDGER

NAME Bailey & Hinds, Inc.

ADDRESS

DATE		ITEM	POST. REF.	DEBIT	CREDIT	BALANCE

NAME Ford Distributors

ADDRESS

DATE		ITEM	POST. REF.	DEBIT	CREDIT	BALANCE

NAME Grant White & Co.

ADDRESS

DATE		ITEM	POST. REF.	DEBIT	CREDIT	BALANCE

Problem 9 (Concluded)

NAME Jackson Company

ADDRESS

DATE		ITEM	POST. REF.	DEBIT	CREDIT	BALANCE

NAME Mueller Wholesaler

ADDRESS

DATE		ITEM	POST. REF.	DEBIT	CREDIT	BALANCE

Problem 10 (LO 5) CASH PAYMENTS JOURNAL, GENERAL LEDGER, AND ACCOUNTS PAYABLE LEDGER

Chris Bultman operates a retail shoe store. The following transactions are related to cash payments for the month of August:

Aug.	1	Issued Check No. 47 for $900 in payment of rent (Rent Expense) for August.
	3	Issued Check No. 48 to Blue Suede Shoes Company in payment on account, $640, less 2% discount.
	9	Issued Check No. 49 to Style-Rite in payment on account, $800, less 3% discount.
	14	Issued Check No. 50 for $125.28 in payment of utility bill (Utilities Expense).
	20	Issued Check No. 51 to Baldo Company in payment for cash purchase, $525.
	22	Issued Check No. 52 to West Coast Shoes in payment on account, $625. A discount of 2% was lost because Bultman neglected to pay the invoice within the discount period.
	27	Issued Check No. 53 for $2,000 to Bultman for a cash withdrawal for personal use.

Required:

1. Enter the above transactions in the cash payments journal (page 9).
2. Enter the totals, rule, and prove the journal.
3. Complete individual postings to the general ledger and accounts payable ledger and summary postings to the general ledger. The relevant accounts are provided on pages 208–210.

Problem 10 (Continued)

1. and 2.

CASH PAYMENTS JOURNAL

PAGE 9

	DATE		CK. NO.	ACCOUNT DEBITED	POST. REF.	GENERAL DEBIT	ACCOUNTS PAYABLE DEBIT	PURCHASES DEBIT	PURCHASES DISCOUNTS CREDIT	CASH CREDIT	
1											1
2											2
3											3
4											4
5											5
6											6
7											7
8											8
9											9
10											10

3.

GENERAL LEDGER

ACCOUNT Cash ACCOUNT NO. 101

DATE		ITEM	POST. REF.	DEBIT	CREDIT	BALANCE DEBIT	BALANCE CREDIT
20-- Aug.	1	Balance	✓			25 0 0 0 00	

ACCOUNT Accounts Payable ACCOUNT NO. 202

DATE		ITEM	POST. REF.	DEBIT	CREDIT	BALANCE DEBIT	BALANCE CREDIT
20-- Aug.	1	Balance	✓				3 3 6 6 00

Problem 10 (Continued)

ACCOUNT C. Bultman, Drawing ACCOUNT NO. 312

DATE		ITEM	POST. REF.	DEBIT	CREDIT	BALANCE DEBIT	BALANCE CREDIT
20-- Aug.	1	Balance	✓			14,000.00	

ACCOUNT Purchases ACCOUNT NO. 501

DATE		ITEM	POST. REF.	DEBIT	CREDIT	BALANCE DEBIT	BALANCE CREDIT
20-- Aug.	1	Balance	✓			54,265.43	

ACCOUNT Purchases Discounts ACCOUNT NO. 501.2

DATE		ITEM	POST. REF.	DEBIT	CREDIT	BALANCE DEBIT	BALANCE CREDIT
20-- Aug.	1	Balance	✓				325.20

ACCOUNT Rent Expense ACCOUNT NO. 521

DATE		ITEM	POST. REF.	DEBIT	CREDIT	BALANCE DEBIT	BALANCE CREDIT
20-- Aug.	1	Balance	✓			7,200.00	

ACCOUNT Utilities Expense ACCOUNT NO. 533

DATE		ITEM	POST. REF.	DEBIT	CREDIT	BALANCE DEBIT	BALANCE CREDIT
20-- Aug.	1	Balance	✓			822.87	

Problem 10 (Concluded)

ACCOUNTS PAYABLE LEDGER

NAME Blue Suede Shoes Company

ADDRESS

DATE		ITEM	POST. REF.	DEBIT	CREDIT	BALANCE
20-- Aug.	1	Balance	✓			640 00

NAME Style-Rite

ADDRESS

DATE		ITEM	POST. REF.	DEBIT	CREDIT	BALANCE
20-- Aug.	1	Balance	✓			1200 00

NAME West Coast Shoes

ADDRESS

DATE		ITEM	POST. REF.	DEBIT	CREDIT	BALANCE
20-- Aug.	1	Balance	✓			1526 00

CHAPTER 13
ACCOUNTING FOR MERCHANDISE INVENTORY

LEARNING OBJECTIVES

Merchandise inventory plays an important role in determining the amount of net income on the income statement. For a merchandising business, the cost of goods sold is the largest individual expense on the income statement. In this chapter, you will learn how to determine the dollar amounts assigned to the cost of goods sold and ending merchandise inventory.

Objective 1. Explain the impact of merchandise inventory on the financial statements.

It is important to report accurately the dollar amount of merchandise inventory on the income statement. An error in counting the physical ending merchandise inventory will not only affect the current year's net income but will also affect the following year's net income. This is because the ending merchandise inventory for the current year becomes the beginning merchandise inventory for the following year. In the year that the error in counting the merchandise inventory is made, the statement of owner's equity and balance sheet will also be in error. However, at the end of the second year, the income statement will be in error, but the statement of owner's equity and balance sheet will be correctly stated. This is because an ending inventory error in the first year "washes out" over the two-year period.

Objective 2. Describe the two principal systems of accounting for merchandise inventory—the periodic system and the perpetual system.

There are two principal systems of accounting for inventory: (1) the periodic system and (2) the perpetual system.

Under the **periodic system**, the current merchandise inventory and the cost of goods sold are not determined until the end of the accounting period when a **physical inventory** is taken. The purchases account is debited for the cost of all goods purchased. The balance in the merchandise inventory account is merely a record of the most recent physical inventory.

Under the **perpetual system**, the merchandise inventory account is debited for the cost of all goods bought, including freight charges, and credited for the cost of all goods sold. In addition, this account is debited when customers return merchandise and credited when returns, allowances, and discounts are granted by suppliers. The balance of the merchandise inventory account represents the cost of goods on hand at all times.

Objective 3. Compute the costs allocated to the ending inventory and cost of goods sold using different inventory methods.

A **physical inventory** is a count of all the goods that have not been sold. This is normally done when the inventory is at its lowest level, which corresponds with the end of the company's **natural business year**. Only goods that are the property of the firm should be included in a physical inventory. Goods held on **consignment** and goods shipped **FOB shipping point** as of the balance sheet date should be excluded. Goods shipped **FOB destination** and in transit as of the balance sheet date should be included in the inventory count. Because prices are constantly changing, there are four acceptable methods to assigning costs to the ending inventory.

When each unit of inventory can be specifically identified, the **specific identification method** can be used. To use this method, inventory items must be physically different from each other or must have serial numbers.

The **first-in, first-out (FIFO)** method assumes that the first goods bought are the first goods sold. Therefore, the latest goods bought remain in inventory.

Another method of allocating merchandise cost is called the **weighted-average method, or average cost method**. This costing method is based on the average cost of identical units. The weighted average is calculated by dividing the total cost of merchandise available for sale by the total number of units available for sale. To compute the cost of goods sold, simply multiply the number of units sold by the weighted-average cost per unit.

A fourth method of allocating merchandise cost is called the **last-in, first-out (LIFO) method**. It assumes that the sales in the period were made from the most recently purchased goods. Therefore, the earliest goods bought remain in inventory. It is important to emphasize that this method is used to allocate costs to inventory. In most cases, it does not correspond to the physical flow of merchandise. When prices are rising, net income calculated by using the LIFO method will be less than net income calculated by using either the FIFO or the weighted-average method.

When a firm uses a **perpetual inventory system**, a continuous record is maintained for the quantities and costs of goods on hand at all times. Perpetual inventories do not eliminate the need for taking periodic physical inventories. If a difference is found between the physical count and the amount in the perpetual inventory records, the adjustment to merchandise inventory is required. This adjustment is illustrated in Chapter 14.

The **lower-of-cost-or-market method** is used whenever the replacement cost of the ending inventory is less than its actual cost. When this happens, the following entry is made:

Loss on Write-Down of Inventory	xxx	
Merchandise Inventory		xxx

This practice is consistent with the practice of conservatism.

Objective 4. Estimate the ending inventory and cost of goods sold by using the gross profit and retail inventory methods.

Businesses using the periodic inventory method must estimate their ending inventory and cost of goods sold in order to provide interim financial statements. Two generally accepted methods are the gross profit method and the retail inventory method.

Under the **gross profit method**, the firm's normal gross profit percentage [(net sales – cost of goods sold)/net sales] can be used to estimate the cost of goods sold and ending inventory. Cost of goods sold can be estimated by multiplying the gross profit percentage by the net sales and subtracting this amount from net sales.

The **retail inventory method** requires keeping records of both the cost and selling (retail) prices of all goods purchased. The percentage of total goods available for sale at cost divided by the total goods available for sale at retail is used to estimate cost of goods sold and ending inventory.

REVIEW QUESTIONS

Instructions: Analyze each of the following items carefully before writing your answer in the column at the right.

	Question	Answer
LO 1	1. Understating the ending inventory for the year 20-1 will cause net income for the year 20-1 to be ________.	____________________
LO 1	2. Overstating the ending inventory for the year 20-1 will cause net income for the year 20-2 to be ________.	____________________
LO 2	3. The two principal systems of accounting for inventory are the ________ and ________.	____________________ ____________________

LO 2 **4.** Under the ________ system, the merchandise inventory account is debited for the cost of all goods purchased. .... ____________________

LO 3 **5.** The process of counting all the goods on hand at the end of the period is called taking a(n) ________. .... ____________________

LO 3 **6.** A fiscal year that starts and ends at the time the stock of goods is normally at its lowest level is known as a(n) ________. .... ____________________

LO 3 **7.** A special form used to record information when taking a physical inventory is called a(n) ________. .... ____________________

LO 3 **8.** In the term "FOB shipping point," FOB stands for ________. .... ____________________

LO 3 **9.** If goods are shipped "FOB ________," the seller pays for shipping and the goods are the property of the selling company until received by the buying company. .... ____________________

LO 3 **10.** Name the four methods of assigning cost to the ending inventory and cost of goods sold. . ... ____________________

____

____

____

LO 3 **11.** A costing method that assumes the first goods bought were the first goods sold and, therefore, the latest goods bought remain in inventory is called ________. .... ____________________

LO 3 **12.** A costing method that assumes the sales in the period were made from the most recently purchased goods and, therefore, the earliest goods bought remain in inventory is called ______. .... ____________________

LO 3 **13.** When prices are rising, the cost method that will result in the highest net income is ________. .... ____________________

LO 3 **14.** When prices are rising, the cost method that will result in the lowest ending inventory is ________. .... ____________________

LO 3 **15.** In the application of "lower-of-cost-or-market," the term "market" refers to ________. .... ____________________

LO 3 **16.** The practice of conservatism states we should never anticipate ________ but always anticipate ________. .... ____________________

____

LO 3 **17.** The difference between the cost and market value is considered a loss due to holding ________. .... ____________________

LO 3 **18.** The dollar amount of the loss due to holding inventory is normally charged to an account entitled ________. .... ____________________

LO 4 **19.** Under the ________ method, the firm's normal gross profit can be used to estimate the cost of goods sold and ending inventory. .... ____________________

LO 4 **20.** The ________ method of estimating inventory requires keeping records of both the cost and selling (retail) prices of all goods purchased. ..... ____________________

EXERCISES

Exercise 1 (LO 2) JOURNAL ENTRIES FOR PERIODIC AND PERPETUAL INVENTORY METHODS

The following inventory transactions occurred for Riegler Company during the month of April:

Apr.	2	Purchased merchandise on account, \$2,500.
	5	Purchased merchandise for cash, \$3,000.
	10	Sold merchandise on account for \$500. The cost of the merchandise sold was \$300.
	15	Sold merchandise that cost \$250 for \$400 cash.

Required:

1. Prepare general journal entries for the above transactions. Assume the periodic inventory system is used.
2. Prepare general journal entries for the above transactions. Assume the perpetual inventory system is used.

Name ____________________

Exercise 1 (Continued)
1. Periodic Inventory System

GENERAL JOURNAL

PAGE

	DATE		DESCRIPTION	POST. REF.	DEBIT	CREDIT	
1							1
2							2
3							3
4							4
5							5
6							6
7							7
8							8
9							9
10							10
11							11
12							12
13							13
14							14
15							15
16							16
17							17
18							18
19							19
20							20
21							21
22							22
23							23
24							24
25							25
26							26
27							27
28							28
29							29
30							30
31							31
32							32
33							33

Exercise 1 (Concluded)
2. Perpetual Inventory System

GENERAL JOURNAL

PAGE

	DATE		DESCRIPTION	POST. REF.	DEBIT	CREDIT	
1							1
2							2
3							3
4							4
5							5
6							6
7							7
8							8
9							9
10							10
11							11
12							12
13							13
14							14
15							15
16							16
17							17
18							18
19							19
20							20
21							21
22							22
23							23
24							24
25							25
26							26
27							27
28							28
29							29
30							30
31							31
32							32
33							33

Exercise 2 (LO 3) COMPUTING COST OF GOODS SOLD, ENDING INVENTORY, AND GROSS PROFIT

Sally Holvey operates Sally's Used Cars. Sally uses the specific identification costing method for determining ending inventory and cost of goods sold. Provided below is a list of the cars that were available for sale during the past month with the cost and selling price if sold. Based on this information, compute the cost of goods sold, cost of the ending inventory, and gross profit.

Year	Model	Cost	Selling Price
2011	Mercury Grand Marquis	$12,000	$13,450
2011	Ford Explorer	21,500	
2011	Ford Focus	12,400	13,992
2009	Ford Mustang	13,200	14,450
2008	Honda Accord	10,200	12,900
2008	Jeep Wrangler	11,400	
2008	Porsche 911	42,500	49,900
2010	Porsche Boxster	32,500	34,200
2007	Honda CR-V	10,500	
2009	BMW M5	39,500	
1993	BMW 325i	4,200	

Exercise 3 (LO 3) LOWER-OF-COST-OR-MARKET

Keast Enterprises has four items of inventory with costs and market values at year-end as follows:

Item	Cost	Market Value
1	$20,000	$18,000
2	45,000	48,000
3	18,000	16,000
4	88,000	90,000

Compute the amount of Keast's inventory at year-end using the lower-of-cost-or-market method applied to:

a. The total inventory.
b. Each item in the inventory.

Exercise 4 (LO 4) RETAIL INVENTORY METHOD

Tyrone Sales Company started in the retail business on July 1. Net purchases to December 31 amounted to \$140,000, and the goods were marked to sell at retail for \$200,000. Net sales amounted to \$160,000. Using the retail method, compute the approximate cost of the inventory on December 31.

PROBLEMS

Problem 5 (LO 3) FIFO, LIFO, AND WEIGHTED-AVERAGE

Hickman Equipment Co. sells stereo equipment and is interested in the effect that the inventory method has on the information provided in the financial statements. You have been asked to demonstrate the impact of various inventory methods for one item of merchandise handled by Hickman. Use the information provided below for your analysis.

	Units	Unit Price	Total Cost
Beginning inventory	50	$120	$ 6,000
Purchases during period:			
1st purchase	80	130	10,400
2nd purchase	100	150	15,000
3rd purchase	70	160	11,200
Total	300		$42,600

Number of units sold: 280
Net sales revenue for the period: $54,000

Required:
Compute cost of goods sold, ending inventory, and gross profit using the FIFO, LIFO, and weighted-average cost methods.

FIFO Inventory Method

Date 20-1/ 20-2		Cost of Goods Sold			Cost of Ending Inventory		
		Units	Unit Price	Total	Units	Unit Price	Total

Problem 5 (Concluded)

LIFO Inventory Method

Date 20-1/ 20-2		Cost of Goods Sold Units	Unit Price	Total	Cost of Ending Inventory Units	Unit Price	Total

Weighted-Average Method

Problem 6 (LO 4) GROSS PROFIT METHOD OF ESTIMATING INVENTORY

The normal gross profit of Zello Company is 30%. The store was destroyed by fire the night of May 27, but the records were saved. The accounts show that the inventory at the start of the year cost $120,000, net purchases to May 27 were $140,000, and net sales to date were $230,000.

Required:

Calculate the estimated cost of the goods destroyed by the fire.

Problem 7 (LO 4) RETAIL INVENTORY METHOD

Assume the following information for Vargo Company:

	Cost	Retail
Inventory, June 1	$200,000	$300,000
Net purchases for June	400,000	700,000
Net sales for June		780,000

Required:

Estimate the June 30 inventory using the retail inventory method.

CHAPTER 13 APPENDIX PERPETUAL INVENTORY METHOD: LIFO AND MOVING-AVERAGE METHODS

APPENDIX LEARNING OBJECTIVES

In Chapter 13, you learned how to apply the LIFO and weighted-average inventory methods under the **periodic inventory system**. In the appendix to Chapter 13, the **perpetual inventory system** is illustrated. Recall that all calculations under the periodic system are done at the end of the accounting period. Under the perpetual system, costs are computed every time merchandise is purchased and sold. These costs are used to maintain a running record of the cost of goods sold to date and the balance of inventory on hand.

Objective 1. Compute the costs allocated to the ending inventory and cost of goods sold using the perpetual LIFO inventory method.

LIFO has layers. Under perpetual LIFO, each time inventory is purchased, a new layer of inventory is formed. Each time inventory is sold, it is assumed that the units came from the most recently purchased layer, followed by the next most recently purchased layer.

Objective 2. Compute the costs allocated to the ending inventory and cost of goods sold using the perpetual moving-average inventory method.

When using the perpetual moving-average inventory method, each time inventory is purchased, a new average cost per unit is calculated. When inventory is sold, the most recent average cost is used to measure cost of goods sold and the remaining inventory on hand.

APPENDIX EXERCISES

Apx. Exercise 1 (LO 1) PERPETUAL LIFO INVENTORY METHOD

The beginning inventory, purchases, and sales for Smaltz Sailing Company for the month of September are provided below.

Date	Beginning Inventory and Purchases		Sales
	Units	Cost/Unit	Units
Sept. 1 (BI)	100	$6.00	
	100	6.20	
	200	6.30	
Sept. 10			250
Sept. 15	600	6.50	
Sept. 30			300
BI: Beginning Inventory			

Required:

Calculate the total amount assigned to cost of goods sold during September and the ending inventory on September 30 using the perpetual LIFO inventory method.

Apx. Exercise 1 (Concluded)

Date	Purchases			Cost of Goods Sold				Inventory on Hand				
	Units	Cost/ Unit	Total	Units	Cost/ Unit	CGS	Cum. CGS	Layer	Units	Cost/ Unit	Layer Cost	Total
9/1 (BI)												
9/10												
9/15												
9/30												
Cost of Goods Sold during September												

BI: Beginning Inventory

Apx. Exercise 2 (LO 2) PERPETUAL MOVING-AVERAGE INVENTORY METHOD

Required:

Using the inventory data provided in Apx. Exercise 1, calculate the total amount assigned to cost of goods sold during September and the ending inventory on September 30 using the perpetual moving-average inventory method.

	Purchases			Cost of Goods Sold				Inventory on Hand and Average Cost per Unit			
Date	Units	Cost/ Unit	Total	Units	Cost/ Unit	CGS	Cum. CGS	Cost of Purchase or (Sale)	Cost of Inventory on Hand	Units on Hand	Average Cost/ Unit
9/1 (BI)											
9/10											
9/15											
9/30											
Cost of Goods Sold during September											

BI: Beginning Inventory

Apx. Exercise 3 (LO 1) PERPETUAL LIFO INVENTORY METHOD

The beginning inventory, purchases, and sales for McGuire Flag Company for the month of October are provided below.

Date	Beginning Inventory and Purchases		Sales
	Units	Cost/Unit	Units
Oct. 1 (BI)	100 150 250	$3.00 3.20 3.50	
Oct. 8			450
Oct. 20	300	3.80	
Oct. 31			200
BI: Beginning Inventory			

Required:

Calculate the total amount to be assigned to cost of goods sold during October and the ending inventory on October 31 using the perpetual LIFO inventory method.

Apx. Exercise 3 (Concluded)

Date	Purchases			Cost of Goods Sold				Inventory on Hand				
	Units	Cost/ Unit	Total	Units	Cost/ Unit	CGS	Cum. CGS	Layer	Units	Cost/ Unit	Layer Cost	Total
10/1 (BI)												
10/8												
10/20												
10/31												
Cost of Goods Sold during October												

BI: Beginning Inventory

Apx. Exercise 4 (LO 2) PERPETUAL MOVING-AVERAGE INVENTORY METHOD

Required:

Using the inventory data provided in Apx. Exercise 3, calculate the total amount assigned to cost of goods sold during October and the ending inventory on October 31 using the perpetual moving-average inventory method.

	Purchases			Cost of Goods Sold				Inventory on Hand and Average Cost per Unit			
Date	Units	Cost/ Unit	Total	Units	Cost/ Unit	CGS	Cum. CGS	Cost of Purchase or (Sale)	Cost of Inventory on Hand	Units on Hand	Average Cost/ Unit
10/1 (BI)											
10/8											
10/20											
10/31											
Cost of Goods Sold during October											

BI: Beginning Inventory

APPENDIX PROBLEMS

Apx. Problem 5 (LO 1) PERPETUAL LIFO INVENTORY METHOD

The beginning inventory, purchases, and sales for Snyder Ball Company for the month of February are provided below.

Date	Beginning Inventory and Purchases		Sales
	Units	Cost/ Unit	Units
Feb. 1 (BI)	30 70	$6.70 6.90	
Feb. 3	400	7.10	
Feb. 5			250
Feb. 11	700	7.20	
Feb. 13			500
Feb. 16	300	7.50	
Feb. 18	500	7.70	
Feb. 24			600
Feb. 25			50
Feb. 28	300	8.00	
BI: Beginning Inventory			

Required:

Calculate the total amount to be assigned to cost of goods sold during February and the ending inventory on February 28 using the perpetual LIFO inventory method.

Apx. Problem 5 (Continued)

Date	Purchases			Cost of Goods Sold				Inventory on Hand				
	Units	Cost/ Unit	Total	Units	Cost/ Unit	CGS	Cum. CGS	Layer	Units	Cost/ Unit	Layer Cost	Total
2/1 (BI)												
2/3												
2/5												
2/11												
2/13												
2/16												

Apx. Problem 5 (Concluded)

Date	Purchases			Cost of Goods Sold				Inventory on Hand				
	Units	Cost/ Unit	Total	Units	Cost/ Unit	CGS	Cum. CGS	Layer	Units	Cost/ Unit	Layer Cost	Total
2/18												
2/24												
2/25												
2/28												
Cost of Goods Sold during February												

BI: Beginning Inventory

Apx. Problem 6 (LO 2) PERPETUAL MOVING-AVERAGE INVENTORY METHOD

Required:

Using the inventory data provided in Apx. Problem 5, calculate the total amount assigned to cost of goods sold during February and the ending inventory on February 28 using the perpetual moving-average inventory method.

Date	Purchases			Cost of Goods Sold				Inventory on Hand and Average Cost per Unit			
	Units	Cost/ Unit	Total	Units	Cost/ Unit	CGS	Cum. CGS	Cost of Purchase or (Sale)	Cost of Inventory on Hand	Units on Hand	Average Cost/ Unit
2/1 (BI)											
2/3											
2/5											
2/11											
2/13											
2/16											
2/18											
2/24											
2/25											
2/28											
Cost of Goods Sold during February											

BI: Beginning Inventory

Apx. Problem 7 (LO 1) PERPETUAL LIFO INVENTORY METHOD

The beginning inventory, purchases, and sales for Rafalko Candy Company for the month of July are provided below.

Date	Beginning Inventory and Purchases		Sales
	Units	Cost/ Unit	Units
July 1	50	$5.90	
(BI)	50	6.10	
July 5	400	6.20	
July 7			300
July 12	300	6.40	
July 15			200
July 18	100	6.50	
July 20	600	6.80	
July 24			800
July 27			100
July 31	100	6.90	
BI: Beginning Inventory			

Required:

Calculate the total amount to be assigned to cost of goods sold during July and the ending inventory on July 31 using the perpetual LIFO inventory method.

Apx. Problem 7 (Continued)

Date	Purchases Units	Purchases Cost/ Unit	Purchases Total	Cost of Goods Sold Units	Cost of Goods Sold Cost/ Unit	Cost of Goods Sold CGS	Cost of Goods Sold Cum. CGS	Inventory on Hand Layer	Inventory on Hand Units	Inventory on Hand Cost/ Unit	Inventory on Hand Layer Cost	Inventory on Hand Total
7/1 (BI)												
7/5												
7/7												
7/12												
7/15												
7/18												

Apx. Problem 7 (Concluded)

Date	Purchases			Cost of Goods Sold				Inventory on Hand				
	Units	Cost/ Unit	Total	Units	Cost/ Unit	CGS	Cum. CGS	Layer	Units	Cost/ Unit	Layer Cost	Total
7/20												
7/24												
7/27												
7/31												
Cost of Goods Sold during July												

BI: Beginning Inventory

Apx. Problem 8 (LO 2) PERPETUAL MOVING-AVERAGE INVENTORY METHOD

Required:

Using the inventory data provided in Apx. Problem 7, calculate the total amount assigned to cost of goods sold during July and the ending inventory on July 31 using the perpetual moving-average inventory method.

	Purchases			Cost of Goods Sold				Inventory on Hand and Average Cost per Unit			
Date	Units	Cost/ Unit	Total	Units	Cost/ Unit	CGS	Cum. CGS	Cost of Purchase or (Sale)	Cost of Inventory on Hand	Units on Hand	Average Cost/ Unit
7/1 (BI)											
7/5											
7/7											
7/12											
7/15											
7/18											
7/20											
7/24											
7/27											
7/31											
Cost of Goods Sold during July											

BI: Beginning Inventory

CHAPTER 14 ADJUSTMENTS AND THE WORK SHEET FOR A MERCHANDISING BUSINESS

LEARNING OBJECTIVES

Chapter 14 covers the end-of-period adjustments and the preparation of a work sheet for a merchandising business. Adjustments for merchandise inventory and unearned revenue are emphasized.

Objective 1. Prepare an adjustment for merchandise inventory using the periodic inventory system.

During the year, the purchase and sale of merchandise is not entered in the merchandise inventory account. Thus, at the end of the year, it is necessary to adjust the merchandise inventory account to properly reflect the amount of inventory on hand. This is accomplished by removing the beginning inventory from the books (the current balance), and entering the ending inventory, based on a physical count. This adjustment is made on the work sheet in a two-step process as shown below. This technique is used so that all of the information required to compute cost of goods sold is available in the Income Statement columns of the work sheet.

Account Title	Trial Balance		Adjustments		Adjusted Trial Balance		Income Statement		Balance Sheet	
	Debit	Credit	Debit	Credit	Debit	Credit	Debit	Credit	Debit	Credit
Merchandise Inventory	20		**(Step 2) 30**	*20 (Step 1)*	30		*BI*	**EI**	30	
Income Summary			*(Step 1) 20*	**30 (Step 2)**	*20*	**30**	*20*	**30**		
Purchases	80						80	Purchases		

Step 1: Remove beginning inventory	*Income Summary*	*20*	
	Merchandise Inventory		*20*
Step 2: Insert ending inventory	**Merchandise Inventory**	**30**	
	Income Summary		**30**

BI: Beginning Inventory ($20); EI: Ending Inventory ($30)

Cost of goods sold:	
Merchandise inventory, January 1	*$ 20*
Purchases	80
Goods available for sale	$100
Less merchandise inventory, December 31	**30**
Cost of goods sold	$ 70

Objective 2. Prepare an adjustment for unearned revenue.

A liability account is created when cash is received before the product or service is provided. This liability is called **unearned revenue**. If all, or part, of the revenue has been earned by the end of the period, an adjustment is made in order to reduce the liability, Unearned Revenue, and increase the related revenue account.

The entry to record receipt of cash for revenue to be earned later is as follows:

Cash	XXX	
Unearned Revenue		XXX

The entry when all, or part, of revenue has been earned is as follows:

Unearned Revenue	xxx	
Sales		xxx

Objective 3. Prepare a work sheet for a merchandising business.

At the end of the accounting period, a work sheet is prepared to make the remaining steps of the accounting cycle easier. The work sheet is similar to the one you learned about in Chapter 5 for a service business, except for the new accounts introduced for a merchandising business and the unearned revenue account that was introduced in this chapter.

Adjusting entries are entered on the work sheet, including adjustments for supplies used, insurance expired, depreciation, and wages earned but not paid. From the Adjusted Trial Balance columns, all amounts are extended to either the Income Statement columns or the Balance Sheet columns of the work sheet.

Of particular importance is the method of extending the amounts for Merchandise Inventory and Income Summary on the work sheet. Merchandise Inventory is extended in the usual manner. The adjusted balance is extended to the Adjusted Trial Balance columns and then to the Balance Sheet columns. However, both the debit *and* credit adjustments to Income Summary are extended to the Adjusted Trial Balance columns and then to the Income Statement columns (see table below). The debit to Income Summary represents the beginning balance of Merchandise Inventory. The credit to Income Summary represents the ending balance of Merchandise Inventory. Both amounts are used on the income statement. Thus, both amounts are extended to the Income Statement columns.

The other accounts identified with merchandise accounting will be extended into the Income Statement columns of the work sheet. Also, any unearned revenue that has been earned as of the balance sheet date will be adjusted into revenue (see table below).

WORK SHEET

	Trial Balance		Adjustments		Adj. Trial Balance		Income Statement		Balance Sheet	
	Dr.	Cr.	Dr.	Cr.	Dr.	Cr.	Dr.	Cr.	Dr.	Cr.
Merchandise Inv.	BI		EI	BI	EI				EI	
Unearned Rev.		xx	xx			xx				xx
Income Summary			BI	EI	BI	EI	BI	EI		
Revenue		xx		xx		xx		xx		
Sales		xx				xx		xx		
Sales Ret. & Allow.	xx				xx		xx			
Sales Discounts	xx				xx		xx			
Purchases	xx				xx		xx			
Purch. Ret. & Allow.		xx				xx		xx		
Purch. Discounts		xx				xx		xx		
Freight-In	xx				xx		xx			

All of the accounts needed to arrive at net income for a merchandising business are in the Income Statement columns of the work sheet. The difference between the debits and credits in the Income Statement columns and between the debits and credits in the Balance Sheet columns will equal either net income or net loss.

Objective 4. Journalize adjusting entries for a merchandising business.

Just because adjusting entries were analyzed and placed on the work sheet does not mean that they have been entered into the accounts in the general ledger. Adjusting entries need to be entered in the general journal and posted to the general ledger. This information can be taken from the Adjustments columns of the work sheet.

Objective 5. Prepare adjusting journal entries under the perpetual inventory system.

Under the perpetual inventory system, the merchandise inventory and cost of goods sold accounts are continually updated throughout the year to reflect purchases and sales of inventory. Comparative entries under the periodic and perpetual inventory systems are shown below.

Transaction	Periodic System			Perpetual System		
1. Purchased merchandise on account, $100.	Purchases Accounts Payable	100	 100	Merchandise Inventory Accounts Payable	100	 100
2. Sold merchandise on account, $60. The cost of the merchandise sold was $50.	Accounts Receivable Sales	60	 60	Accounts Receivable Sales Cost of Goods Sold Merchandise Inventory	60 50	 60 50
3. Periodic system: Beginning inventory, $40. Ending inventory, $90.	Income Summary Merchandise Inventory Merchandise Inventory Income Summary	40 90	 40 90			
4. Perpetual system: Ending balance of merchandise inventory, $100. Ending inventory based on physical count, $90.				Inventory Short and Over Merchandise Inventory	10	 10

REVIEW QUESTIONS

Instructions: Analyze each of the following items carefully before writing your answer in the column at the right.

	Question	Answer
LO 1	**1.** At the end of an accounting period, a(n) ________ is used to analyze and prepare adjustments and to determine the amount of net income or net loss for the time period.	____________________
LO 1	**2.** The amount of inventory on hand at the end of the accounting period is determined by taking a(n) ________ of the goods on hand.	____________________
LO 1	**3.** Under the periodic system of adjusting for the ending inventory, the beginning inventory is removed from the merchandise inventory account with a(n) ________ , and a debit is entered into the ________ account.	____________________ ____________________
LO 1	**4.** Under the periodic system of accounting for the ending inventory, the ending inventory is entered by debiting Merchandise Inventory and crediting the ________ account.	____________________

LO 1 **5.** Purchases less purchases returns and allowances and purchases discounts equals ________. .... ____________________

LO 1 **6.** Beginning inventory plus net purchases and freight-in equals ________. .... ____________________

LO 1 **7.** Merchandise available for sale less ending inventory is equal to ________. .... ____________________

LO 1 **8.** On the work sheet, both the debit and credit amounts of the income summary account are extended to the ________ and the ________ columns of the work sheet. .... ____________________ ____________________

LO 1 **9.** Purchases Returns and Allowances and Purchases Discounts are deducted from the ________ account on the income statement. ...... ____________________

LO 2 **10.** The cash received in advance of delivering a product or performing a service is called ________. .... ____________________

LO 2 **11.** Unearned revenue is reported as a(n) ________ on the balance sheet. ____________________

LO 2 **12.** At the end of an accounting period, unearned revenue is adjusted into a(n) ________ account for the amount of revenue that has been earned. .... ____________________

LO 2 **13.** Purchases Returns and Allowances and Purchases Discounts are classified as ________ accounts. .... ____________________

LO 3 **14.** The first step in preparing a work sheet is to prepare the ________. ____________________

LO 3 **15.** On the work sheet, amounts are extended from the Adjusted Trial Balance columns to the ________ and ________ columns. .... ____________________ ____________________

LO 3 **16.** If credits exceed debits on the Income Statement columns of the work sheet, this represents a net ________. .... ____________________

LO 3 **17.** The most helpful aid in entering adjustments into the general journal is the ________. .... ____________________

LO 5 **18.** Under the perpetual inventory system, ________ is debited when inventory is purchased. .... ____________________

LO 5 **19.** Under the perpetual inventory system, ________ is (are) debited when inventory is sold. .... ____________________

EXERCISES

Exercise 1 (LO 1) ADJUSTING ENTRIES FOR MERCHANDISE INVENTORY

Kendall's TV and Appliances had merchandise inventory of $60,300 at the beginning of the year and $54,800 at the end of the year. Prepare the necessary adjusting entries in a general journal.

GENERAL JOURNAL PAGE

	DATE		DESCRIPTION	POST. REF.	DEBIT	CREDIT	
1							1
2							2
3							3
4							4
5							5
6							6
7							7

Exercise 2 (LO 1) CALCULATION OF COST OF GOODS SOLD

The following amounts are known for Casey's Card and Gift Shop:

Beginning merchandise inventory	$33,000
Ending merchandise inventory	41,000
Purchases	86,000
Purchases returns and allowances	4,500
Purchases discounts	2,500
Freight-in	1,000

Prepare the cost of goods sold section of the income statement for Casey's Card and Gift Shop.

Exercise 3 (LO 2) ADJUSTMENT FOR UNEARNED REVENUE

The following transactions took place for Hamilton Theaters. Journalize these transactions in a general journal.

Feb. 22 Sold 2,000 season tickets at $25 each, receiving cash of $50,000. Received cash before the services were provided.

Dec. 31 An end-of-period adjustment is needed to recognize that $45,000 in ticket revenue has been earned.

GENERAL JOURNAL PAGE

	DATE		DESCRIPTION	POST. REF.	DEBIT	CREDIT	
1							1
2							2
3							3
4							4
5							5
6							6
7							7

Exercise 4 (LO 4) JOURNALIZING ADJUSTING ENTRIES

The partial work sheet below is taken from the books of Long Auto Repair for the year ended December 31, 20--.

Long Auto Repair
Work Sheet (Partial)
For Year Ended December 31, 20--

	ACCOUNT TITLE	TRIAL BALANCE DEBIT	TRIAL BALANCE CREDIT	ADJUSTMENTS DEBIT	ADJUSTMENTS CREDIT	
1	Merchandise Inventory	60,000.00		(b) 57,000.00	(a) 60,000.00	1
2	Supplies	6,000.00			(d) 3,200.00	2
3	Building	150,000.00				3
4	Accum. Depr.—Building		45,000.00		(e) 8,000.00	4
5	Wages Payable				(f) 2,400.00	5
6	Unearned Repair Revenue		6,000.00	(c) 5,000.00		6
7	Income Summary			(a) 60,000.00	(b) 57,000.00	7
8	Repair Revenue		30,000.00		(c) 5,000.00	8
9	Wages Expense	39,000.00		(f) 2,400.00		9
10	Supplies Expense			(d) 3,200.00		10
11	Depr. Exp.—Building			(e) 8,000.00		11
12						12
13						13
14						14
15						15

Journalize the above adjustments in a general journal.

Exercise 4 (Concluded)

GENERAL JOURNAL

PAGE

	DATE		DESCRIPTION	POST. REF.	DEBIT	CREDIT	
1							1
2							2
3							3
4							4
5							5
6							6
7							7
8							8
9							9
10							10
11							11
12							12
13							13
14							14
15							15
16							16
17							17
18							18
19							19
20							20

Exercise 5 (LO 5) JOURNAL ENTRIES UNDER THE PERPETUAL INVENTORY SYSTEM

Bahita Business Supplies entered into the following transactions. Prepare journal entries under the perpetual inventory system.

Aug. 1 Purchased merchandise on account from Gul Paper, $10,000.
5 Purchased merchandise for cash, $5,000.
10 Sold merchandise on account to Padam Medical Services for $2,000. The merchandise cost $1,500.

GENERAL JOURNAL

PAGE

DATE	DESCRIPTION	POST. REF.	DEBIT	CREDIT

Exercise 6 (LO 5) PREPARE ADJUSTING ENTRY FOR A MERCHANDISING BUSINESS: PERPETUAL INVENTORY SYSTEM

On December 31, Ranjit Enterprises completed a physical count of its inventory. Although the merchandise inventory account shows a balance of $8,000, the physical count comes to $7,800. Prepare the appropriate adjusting entry under the perpetual inventory system.

GENERAL JOURNAL PAGE

	DATE		DESCRIPTION	POST. REF.	DEBIT	CREDIT	
1							1
2							2
3							3
4							4
5							5
6							6
7							7
8							8

PROBLEMS

Problem 7 (LO 1/2/3) PREPARE A WORK SHEET

The work sheet provided on pages 248–249 is taken from the books of Ocean Beach Sail Shop, a business owned by Nicole Smith. Adjustment information is provided below. Smith uses the periodic inventory system.

(a and b) Based on a physical count, merchandise inventory on hand as of December 31, 20--, $36,000.
(c) Supplies remaining at end of the year, $2,350.
(d) Unexpired insurance on December 31, $1,875.
(e) Depreciation expense on the building for 20--, $7,000.
(f) Depreciation expense on the store equipment for 20--, $2,800.
(g) Unearned tour revenue as of December 31, $2,700.
(h) Wages earned but not paid as of December 31, $1,100.

Required:

1. Complete the Adjustments columns. Identify each adjustment with its corresponding letter.
2. Complete the work sheet.

Problem 7 (Continued)
1. and 2.

Ocean Beach

Work

For Year Ended

	ACCOUNT TITLE	TRIAL BALANCE DEBIT	TRIAL BALANCE CREDIT	ADJUSTMENTS DEBIT	ADJUSTMENTS CREDIT
1	Cash	27,000.00			
2	Accounts Receivable	9,000.00			
3	Merchandise Inventory	31,000.00			
4	Supplies	7,500.00			
5	Prepaid Insurance	4,900.00			
6	Land	40,000.00			
7	Building	60,000.00			
8	Accum. Depr.—Building		25,000.00		
9	Store Equipment	29,000.00			
10	Accum. Depr.—Store Equipment		9,000.00		
11	Accounts Payable		7,600.00		
12	Wages Payable				
13	Sales Tax Payable		6,100.00		
14	Unearned Tour Revenue		6,800.00		
15	Mortgage Payable		43,000.00		
16	N. Smith, Capital		124,590.00		
17	N. Smith, Drawing	33,000.00			
18	Income Summary				
19	Sales		122,000.00		
20	Sales Returns and Allowances	4,200.00			
21	Tour Revenue				
22	Purchases	38,000.00			
23	Purchases Returns and Allowances		2,600.00		
24	Purchases Discounts		1,400.00		
25	Freight-In	2,500.00			
26	Wages Expense	47,000.00			
27	Advertising Expense	4,800.00			
28	Supplies Expense				
29	Phone Expense	1,800.00			
30	Utilities Expense	7,600.00			
31	Insurance Expense				
32	Depr. Expense—Building				
33	Depr. Expense—Store Equipment				
34	Miscellaneous Expense	790.00			
35		348,090.00	348,090.00		
36					
37					
38					

Problem 7 (Concluded)

Sail Shop

Sheet

December 31, 20--

ADJUSTED TRIAL BALANCE		INCOME STATEMENT		BALANCE SHEET	
DEBIT	CREDIT	DEBIT	CREDIT	DEBIT	CREDIT

Problem 8 (LO 4) JOURNALIZING ADJUSTING ENTRIES

From the work sheet prepared for Ocean Beach Sail Shop (Problem 7), record the adjusting entries in a general journal.

GENERAL JOURNAL

PAGE

	DATE	DESCRIPTION	POST. REF.	DEBIT	CREDIT	
1						1
2						2
3						3
4						4
5						5
6						6
7						7
8						8
9						9
10						10
11						11
12						12
13						13
14						14
15						15
16						16
17						17
18						18
19						19
20						20
21						21
22						22
23						23
24						24
25						25
26						26
27						27
28						28
29						29
30						30

CHAPTER 14 APPENDIX
EXPENSE METHOD OF ACCOUNTING FOR PREPAID EXPENSES

LEARNING OBJECTIVES

The appendix to Chapter 14 covers the expense method of accounting for prepaid expenses.

Objective 1. Use the expense method of accounting for prepaid expenses.

Under the **expense method** of accounting for prepaid expenses, supplies and other prepaid items are entered as **expenses** when purchased. Under this method, we must adjust the accounts at the end of each accounting period to record the **unused** portions as assets.

Objective 2. Make the appropriate adjusting entries when the expense method is used for prepaid expenses.

To illustrate the appropriate entries, let's assume that the following entry was made on November 1, 20--, when six months' office rent was paid in advance:

20--			
Nov. 1	Office Rent Expense	6,000	
	Cash		6,000
	Paid six months' office rent in advance		

At the end of December, adjusting entries must be made to prepare year-end financial statements. The office has been used for two months. Thus, the office expense for the year should be $2,000 ($1,000 per month × 2). This leaves $4,000 that should be recorded as an asset, Prepaid Office Rent. The following adjusting entry is made for office rent:

20--	Adjusting Entry		
Dec. 31	Prepaid Office Rent	4,000	
	Office Rent Expense		4,000

As shown in the T accounts below, after this entry is posted, the office rent expense account has a debit balance of $2,000 ($6,000 – $4,000). This amount is reported on the income statement as an operating expense. The prepaid office rent account has a debit balance of $4,000. It is reported on the balance sheet as a current asset.

Prepaid Office Rent

Debit		Credit	
Adj. Dec. 31	4,000		

Office Rent Expense

Debit		Credit	
Nov. 1	6,000		
		Adj. Dec. 31	4,000
Bal. Dec. 31	2,000		

Apx. Exercise 1 (LO 2) EXPENSE METHOD OF ACCOUNTING FOR PREPAID EXPENSES

Dalton's Fishery paid $2,400 for a one-year insurance premium on its delivery van on October 1. The following entry was made:

20--			
Oct. 1	Insurance Expense	2,400	
	Cash		2,400
	Paid insurance premium		

Insurance coverage started on October 1. Prepare the adjusting entry on December 31.

GENERAL JOURNAL PAGE

	DATE		DESCRIPTION	POST. REF.	DEBIT	CREDIT	
1							1
2							2
3							3
4							4
5							5

Apx. Exercise 2 (LO 1/2) EXPENSE METHOD OF ACCOUNTING FOR PREPAID EXPENSES

On August 21, Georgio's Dry Goods purchased supplies costing $6,000 for cash. This amount was debited to the supplies expense account. At the end of the year, an inventory shows that supplies costing $1,000 still remain. Prepare the entries for the purchase and year-end adjustment.

GENERAL JOURNAL PAGE

	DATE		DESCRIPTION	POST. REF.	DEBIT	CREDIT	
1							1
2							2
3							3
4							4
5							5
6							6
7							7
8							8
9							9
10							10

CHAPTER 15
FINANCIAL STATEMENTS AND YEAR-END ACCOUNTING FOR A MERCHANDISING BUSINESS

LEARNING OBJECTIVES

Chapter 15 covers the year-end accounting process as it applies to a merchandising business—the work sheet, closing and reversing entries, and the financial statements. In addition, financial ratios are introduced for the merchandising business.

Objective 1. Prepare a single-step and multiple-step income statement for a merchandising business.

The **single-step** form of income statement lists all revenue items and their total first, followed by all expense items and their total. The difference, which is either net income or net loss, is then calculated.

The **multiple-step income statement** contains the computation of net sales and cost of goods sold. It also reports gross profit, income from operations, and net income. The multiple-step income statement begins with gross sales less deductions to arrive at *net sales*. Then, cost of goods sold is calculated—beginning inventory plus net purchases and freight-in, less ending inventory. Net sales minus cost of goods sold results in *gross profit*. Then, operating expenses are subtracted, resulting in income from operations. Finally, other revenue and expenses not from operations (such as interest) are included to compute *net income*.

Objective 2. Prepare a statement of owner's equity.

The statement of owner's equity summarizes all changes in the owner's equity, including net income or loss and any additional investments or withdrawals by the owner.

Objective 3. Prepare a classified balance sheet.

The **classified balance sheet** distinguishes between *current* and long-term assets and liabilities. Current assets include cash and assets that will be converted to cash or consumed within the year or operating cycle (whichever is longer). Property, plant, and equipment are assets with long useful lives and much less liquidity. Current liabilities are generally due within a year and require the use of current assets. Long-term liabilities extend longer than one year.

Objective 4. Compute standard financial ratios.

Financial ratios help evaluate the current financial condition and profitability of a company. **Working capital** is current assets minus current liabilities; it tells whether a business has enough current assets to meet current operating debts.

The **current** and **quick ratios** measure a firm's ability to pay its current liabilities. The current ratio is calculated by dividing current assets by current liabilities. The desirable ratio is 2:1 ($2 of current assets for every $1 of current liabilities). **Quick assets** include cash and other very liquid assets—such as accounts receivable. The quick ratio is calculated by dividing quick assets by current liabilities. The desirable ratio is 1:1.

Return on owner's equity is calculated by dividing net income by average owner's equity (beginning equity plus ending equity, divided by 2). This rate of return can be compared with other years' rates and with other businesses' rates.

The **accounts receivable turnover** is determined by dividing net credit sales by average accounts receivable. This number is then divided into 365 days to determine the average number of days credit customers are taking to pay for their purchases.

Inventory turnover reveals how many times merchandise inventory "turned over" or was sold during the period. It is calculated by dividing cost of goods sold by the average inventory (beginning inventory plus ending inventory, divided by 2). This number is then divided into 365 days to determine the average number of days merchandise is held before it is sold.

Objective 5. Prepare closing entries for a merchandising business.

As with a service business, closing entries for a merchandising business are facilitated by the work sheet. All temporary accounts are closed—sales, contra-sales accounts, purchases, contra-purchases accounts, and expenses. The income summary account already contains two entries for merchandise inventory adjustments (debited to remove the old balance; credited to enter the new balance). First, all income statement accounts with credit balances are debited, crediting the income summary account. Then, all income statement accounts with debit balances are credited, debiting the income summary account. The balance in the income summary account is then transferred to the owner's equity account; a credit balance (indicating net income) is debited to close the income summary account. Finally, the drawing account is closed to the owner's capital account.

After the closing entries are posted, the post-closing trial balance is prepared. It reflects balances after the adjusting and closing entries are posted; only permanent accounts still have balances.

Objective 6. Prepare reversing entries.

Year-end adjusting entries may be reversed in the next accounting period if it helps to simplify entries to be made in the new year. Except for the first year of operation, **reversing entries** are helpful whenever an adjusting entry has increased an asset or liability account from a zero balance. The reversing entries are made on the first day of the new accounting period.

REVIEW QUESTIONS

Instructions: Analyze each of the following items carefully before writing your answer in the column at the right.

		Question	Answer
LO 1	1.	The primary purpose of the ________ is to serve as an aid in preparing the financial statements.	____________
LO 1	2.	The ________ form of income statement lists all revenue items first, followed by all expense items and their totals.	____________
LO 1	3.	Gross sales less sales returns and allowances is called ________.	____________
LO 1	4.	________ is the result of net sales less cost of goods sold.	____________
LO 1	5.	When operating expenses are subtracted from gross profit, the result is called ________.	____________
LO 1	6.	After other revenues are added and other expenses are subtracted, the final result is called ________.	____________

LO 2	7. The statement of owner's equity shows the net _______ or _______ in owner's equity for the period.	____________ ____________
LO 3	8. The report form of a(n) ________ balance sheet distinguishes between current and long-term assets and between current and long-term liabilities.	____________
LO 3	9. The speed with which assets can be converted to cash is called ________.	____________
LO 3	10. The difference between the cost of a long-term asset and the amount of accumulated depreciation is called ________ or book value.	____________
LO 3	11. ________ are obligations that are due within one year or during the normal operating cycle of the business, whichever is longer.	____________
LO 3	12. A(n) ________ is an example of a long-term liability based on a written agreement evidencing a debt secured by property.	____________
LO 4	13. The difference between current assets and current liabilities is called ________.	____________
LO 4	14. The ________ ratio is current assets divided by current liabilities.	____________
LO 4	15. ________ assets include cash and all other current assets that can be quickly converted to cash.	____________
LO 4	16. The ________ ratio is calculated by dividing net income by average owner's equity.	____________
LO 4	17. The ________ measures the number of times the accounts receivable were collected during the accounting period.	____________
LO 4	18. The ________ measures the number of times merchandise is sold during the accounting period.	____________
LO 5	19. All ________ owner's equity accounts are closed at the end of the accounting period.	____________
LO 5	20. The purpose of the ________ is to prove that the general ledger is in balance at the beginning of the new accounting period and that all temporary accounts have zero balances.	____________
LO 6	21. A reversing entry is the opposite of a(n) ________ entry.	____________
LO 6	22. Adjusting entries that increase an asset or liability account from a(n) ________ balance may be reversed.	____________

EXERCISES

Exercise 1 (LO 1) MULTIPLE-STEP INCOME STATEMENT

From the information below, prepare a multiple-step income statement for Morse Motor Company for the year ended December 31, 20-1.

Merchandise Inventory, January 1, 20-1	$ 28,900
Merchandise Inventory, December 31, 20-1	29,600
Sales	118,300
Sales Returns and Allowances	1,000
Sales Discounts	280
Interest Revenue	1,900
Purchases	68,000
Purchases Returns and Allowances	2,140
Purchases Discounts	1,360
Freight-In	540
Wages Expense	23,200
Rent Expense	8,000
Supplies Expense	900
Phone Expense	2,600
Utilities Expense	3,800
Insurance Expense	1,000
Depreciation Expense—Equipment	2,000
Miscellaneous Expense	300
Interest Expense	700

Name ______________________________

Exercise 1 (Concluded)

Exercise 2 (LO 2/3) PREPARE A STATEMENT OF OWNER'S EQUITY AND CLASSIFIED BALANCE SHEET

From the information below and the income statement prepared for Exercise 1, prepare a statement of owner's equity and a report form of a classified balance sheet for Morse Motor Company as of December 31, 20-1.

Cash	$19,200
Accounts Receivable	28,500
Merchandise Inventory	29,600
Supplies	1,800
Prepaid Insurance	1,100
Equipment	32,000
Accumulated Depreciation—Equipment	4,000
Accounts Payable	18,620
Wages Payable	280
Sales Tax Payable	480
Mortgage Payable—current portion	1,200
Mortgage Payable	8,000
K. T. Morse, Capital, January 1, 20-1	66,740
K. T. Morse, Drawing (during year)	8,000
Additional investment by K. T. Morse, May 1, 20-1	10,000

Exercise 2 (Concluded)

Exercise 3 (LO 4) FINANCIAL RATIOS

From the Morse Motor Company financial statements prepared in Exercises 1 and 2, compute the following ratios: (Net credit sales for the year were $88,000; accounts receivable on January 1 was $24,200.)

1. Working capital

2. Current ratio

3. Quick ratio

4. Return on owner's equity

5. Accounts receivable turnover

6. Inventory turnover

Exercise 4 (LO 5/6) CLOSING AND REVERSING ENTRIES

Based on the foregoing information provided for Morse Motor Company in Exercises 1-3, prepare closing and reversing entries in the general journal on page 262. Adjusting entries are shown below.

Account	Debit	Credit
Income Summary	28,900	
Merchandise Inventory		28,900
Merchandise Inventory	29,600	
Income Summary		29,600
Insurance Expense	1,000	
Prepaid Insurance		1,000
Depreciation Expense	2,000	
Accumulated Depreciation—Equipment		2,000
Supplies Expense	900	
Supplies		900
Wages Expense	280	
Wages Payable		280

Exercise 4 (Concluded)

GENERAL JOURNAL

PAGE

DATE		DESCRIPTION	POST. REF.	DEBIT	CREDIT

PROBLEMS

Problem 5 (REVIEW) COMPLETE A WORK SHEET

Complete the work sheet for Clark's Clothing Store on pages 264–265 by using the adjustment information provided below.

(a and b) Merchandise Inventory, December 31, 20-1, $12,400.

(c) Unused supplies on December 31, 20-1, $2,100.

(d) Expired insurance on December 31, 20-1, $500.

(e) Depreciation expense on building for the year, $10,000.

(f) Depreciation expense on fixtures for the year, $2,000.

(g) Wages accrued (earned but not yet paid), $380.

(h) Unearned revenues on December 31, 20-1, $3,000.

Problem 5 (Continued)

Clark's Clothing

Work

For Year Ended

	ACCOUNT TITLE	TRIAL BALANCE		ADJUSTMENTS	
		DEBIT	CREDIT	DEBIT	CREDIT
1	Cash	16,400.00			
2	Accounts Receivable	7,100.00			
3	Merchandise Inventory	28,000.00			
4	Supplies	3,000.00			
5	Prepaid Insurance	2,000.00			
6	Land	10,000.00			
7	Building	100,000.00			
8	Accum. Depr.—Building		10,000.00		
9	Fixtures	33,000.00			
10	Accum. Depr.—Fixtures		6,000.00		
11	Accounts Payable		9,000.00		
12	Wages Payable				
13	Sales Tax Payable		1,200.00		
14	Unearned Revenue		10,000.00		
15	Mortgage Payable		58,000.00		
16	Alex Clark, Capital		73,300.00		
17	Alex Clark, Drawing	12,500.00			
18	Income Summary				
19	Sales		225,500.00		
20	Sales Returns and Allowances	2,000.00			
21	Sales Discounts	500.00			
22	Purchases	68,500.00			
23	Purchases Returns and Allowances		1,200.00		
24	Purchases Discounts		1,300.00		
25	Freight-In	440.00			
26	Wages Expense	19,800.00			
27	Advertising Expense	700.00			
28	Rent Expense	82,660.00			
29	Supplies Expense				
30	Phone Expense	2,100.00			
31	Utilities Expense	1,800.00			
32	Insurance Expense				
33	Depr. Expense—Building				
34	Depr. Expense—Fixtures				
35	Miscellaneous Expense	600.00			
36	Interest Expense	4,400.00			
37		395,500.00	395,500.00		
38	Net Income				
39					

Problem 5 (Concluded)

Store

Sheet

December 31, 20-1

ADJUSTED TRIAL BALANCE		INCOME STATEMENT		BALANCE SHEET	
DEBIT	CREDIT	DEBIT	CREDIT	DEBIT	CREDIT

Problem 6 (LO 1/2/3) PREPARATION OF AN INCOME STATEMENT, STATEMENT OF OWNER'S EQUITY, AND BALANCE SHEET

Based on the work sheet for Clark's Clothing Store, prepare the following financial statements:

1. Multiple-step income statement.
2. Statement of owner's equity. (Alex made no additional investments during the year.)
3. Classified balance sheet. (Mortgage Payable—current portion is $1,000.)

1. (See page 267)

2.

Problem 6 (Continued)

1.

Problem 6 (Concluded)

3.

Problem 7 (LO 4) FINANCIAL RATIOS

For Clark's Clothing Store, calculate the following financial statement ratios. (*Note*: Net credit sales for the year were $115,000, and accounts receivable on January 1 was $8,400.)

1. Working capital

2. Current ratio

3. Quick ratio

4. Return on owner's equity

5. Accounts receivable turnover

6. Inventory turnover

Problem 8 (LO 5/6) ADJUSTING, CLOSING, AND REVERSING ENTRIES

From the work sheet prepared for Clark's Clothing Store (Problem 5), record the adjusting, closing, and reversing entries on the general journal page below and on the next page.

GENERAL JOURNAL

PAGE

DATE		DESCRIPTION	POST. REF.	DEBIT	CREDIT

Problem 8 (Concluded)

GENERAL JOURNAL

PAGE

DATE		DESCRIPTION	POST. REF.	DEBIT	CREDIT

NOTES

NOTES

NOTES

NOTES

NOTES

NOTES

NOTES

NOTES

NOTES

NOTES

NOTES

END PAGE OF

STUDY GUIDE

Working Papers

Chapters 1-15

College Accounting

Twenty-second Edition

James A. Heintz, DBA, CPA
Professor of Accounting
School of Business
University of Kansas

Robert W. Parry, Jr., Ph.D.
Professor of Accounting
Kelley School of Business
Indiana University

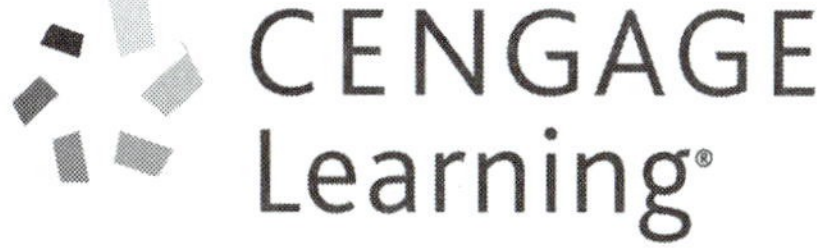

Australia • Brazil • Mexico • Singapore • United Kingdom • United States

ISBN: 978-1-305-66766-2

Cengage Learning
20 Channel Center Street
Boston, MA 02210
USA

Cengage Learning is a leading provider of customized learning solutions with employees residing in nearly 40 different countries and sales in more than 125 countries around the world. Find your local representative at **www.cengage.com**.

Cengage Learning products are represented in Canada by Nelson Education, Ltd.

To learn more about Cengage Learning Solutions, visit **www.cengage.com**.

Purchase any of our products at your local college store or at our preferred online store **www.cengagebrain.com**.

Printed in the United States of America
Print Number: 01 Print Year: 2015

Table of Contents

Name Jonathan Lond ACCT 1110-03

Exercise 1-1A

1.	D.	Owners	a. Whether the firm can pay its bills on time
2.	B.	Managers	b. Detailed, up-to-date information to measure business performance (and plan for future operations)
3.	A.	Creditors	c. To determine taxes to be paid and whether other regulations are met
4.	C.	Government agencies	d. The firm's current financial condition

Exercise 1-2A

Order	Accounting Process	Definition
2.	Recording	Entering financial info about events in the accounting system.
4.	Summarizing	Taking the financial data from the report and putting it all in an easy to get format.
5.	Reporting	Showing the results using tables of numbers.
1.	Analyzing	Looking at financial events and thinking about their affects on the business.
6.	Interpreting	Deciding the meaning and purpose of the financial information.
3.	Classifying	The sorting and grouping of similar items.

Exercise 1-1B

Users	Information
Owners (present and future):	________________
	________________
	________________
Managers:	________________
	________________
	________________
Creditors (present and future):	________________
	________________
	________________
Government agencies:	________________
	________________
	________________

Exercise 1-2B

Letter	Accounting Process
________	Analyzing
________	Recording
________	Classifying
________	Summarizing
________	Reporting
________	Interpreting

Definition

a. Telling the results
b. Looking at events that have taken place and thinking about how they affect the business
c. Deciding the importance of the various reports
d. Aggregating many similar events to provide information that is easy to understand
e. Sorting and grouping like items together
f. Entering financial information into the accounting system

Name Jonathan Land ACCT 1110-03

Exercise 2-1A

Item	Account	Classification
Money in bank	Cash	
Office supplies	Supplies	
Money owed	Accounts Payable	
Office chairs	Office Furniture	
Net worth of owner	John Smith, Capital	
Money withdrawn by owner	John Smith, Drawing	
Money owed by customers	Accounts Receivable	

Exercise 2-2A

Assets	=	Liabilities	+	Owner's Equity
$44,000	=	$27,000	+	$17,000
$32,000	=	$18,000	+	$14,000
$27,000	=	$7,000	+	$20,000

Exercise 2-3A

	Assets	=	Liabilities	+	Owner's Equity
(a)					
Bal.					
(b)					
Bal.					
(c)					
Bal.					
(d)					
Bal.					

Exercise 2-4A

	Assets	=	Liabilities	+	Owner's Equity: Capital	−	Drawing	+	Revenues	−	Expenses	Description
Bal. from E 2-3A												
(d)												
(e)												
(f)												
(g)												
(h)												
(i)												
(j)												
(k)												
Bal.												

Name ______________________________

Exercise 2-5A

Account	Classification	Financial Statement
Cash		
Rent Expense		
Accounts Payable		
Service Fees		
Supplies		
Wages Expense		
Ramon Martinez, Drawing		
Ramon Martinez, Capital		
Prepaid Insurance		
Accounts Receivable		

Exercise 2-6A

Exercise 2-7A

Problem 2-8A

	Assets	=	Liabilities	+	Owner's Equity
1.	$26,960		$7550		$19,410
2.	$35,500		$10,910		$24,590
3.	$32,040		$12,910		$19,130

Problem 2-9A: See page WP-7

Problem 2-10A

Name ______________________

Problem 2-9A

	Assets				= Liabilities +	Owner's Equity				
	(Items Owned)				(Amts. Owed)	(Owner's Investment)		(Earnings)		
	Cash	+ Accounts Receivable	+ Office Supplies	+ Prepaid Insurance	= Accounts Payable	+ J. Pembroke, Capital	– J. Pembroke, Drawing	+ Revenues	– Expenses	Description
(a)										
(b)										
(c)										
(d)										
(e)										
(f)										
(g)										
Bal.										

Problem 2-11A

Problem 2-12A

Name ______________________________

Exercise 2-1B

Account	Classification
Cash	______________
Accounts Payable	______________
Supplies	______________
Bill Jones, Drawing	______________
Prepaid Insurance	______________
Accounts Receivable	______________
Bill Jones, Capital	______________

Exercise 2-2B

Assets	=	Liabilities	+	Owner's Equity
______________	=	$20,000	+	$ 5,000
$30,000	=	$15,000	+	______________
$20,000	=	______________	+	$10,000

Exercise 2-3B

	Assets	=	Liabilities	+	Owner's Equity
(a)	______________		______________		______________
Bal.	______________		______________		______________
(b)	______________		______________		______________
Bal.	______________		______________		______________
(c)	______________		______________		______________
	______________		______________		______________
Bal.	______________		______________		______________
(d)	______________		______________		______________
Bal.	______________		______________		______________

Exercise 2-4B

	Assets	=	Liabilities	+	Owner's Equity							Description
					Capital	–	Drawing	+	Revenues	–	Expenses	
Bal. from E 2-3B												
(d)												
(e)												
(f)												
(g)												
(h)												
(i)												
(j)												
(k)												
Bal.												

Exercise 2-5B

Account	Classification	Financial Statement
Cash		
Rent Expense		
Accounts Payable		
Service Fees		
Supplies		
Wages Expense		
Amanda Wong, Drawing		
Amanda Wong, Capital		
Prepaid Insurance		
Accounts Receivable		

Exercise 2-6B

Exercise 2-7B

Problem 2-8B

	Assets	=	Liabilities	+	Owner's Equity
1.					
2.					
3.					

Problem 2-9B: See page WP-13

Problem 2-10B

Problem 2-9B

	Assets					= Liabilities	+	Owner's Equity							
	(Items Owned)					(Amts. Owed)		(Owner's Investment)				(Earnings)			
	Cash	+	Accounts Receivable	+	Office Supplies	+	Prepaid Insurance	=	Accounts Payable	+	D. Segal, Capital	–	D. Segal, Drawing	+	Revenues	–	Expenses	Description

	Cash	Accounts Receivable	Office Supplies	Prepaid Insurance	Accounts Payable	D. Segal, Capital	D. Segal, Drawing	Revenues	Expenses	Description
(a)										
(b)										
(c)										
(d)										
(e)										
(f)										
(g)										
Bal.										

Problem 2-11B

Problem 2-12B

Mastery Problem

1.

	Assets (Items Owned)						= Liabilities (Amts. Owed)	+ Owner's Equity (Owner's Investment)		(Earnings)		
	Cash	+ Accts. Rec.	+ Sup-plies	+ Prepaid Ins.	+ Tools	+ Van	= Accts. Payable	+ L. Vozniak, Capital	– L. Vozniak, Drawing	+ Rev.	– Exp.	Description
(a)												
(b)												
(c)												
(d)												
(e)												
(f)												
(g)												
(h)												
(i)												
(j)												
(k)												
(l)												
(m)												
(n)												
(o)												
(p)												
2. Bal.												

Mastery Problem (Continued)

3.

4.

Mastery Problem (Concluded)

5.

Challenge Problem

Cash from customers		
Cash paid for wages		
Cash paid for rent		
Cash paid for utilities		
Cash paid for insurance		
Cash paid for supplies		
Cash paid for phone		
Total cash paid for operating items		
Difference between cash received from customers and		
cash paid for goods and services		

Name ______________________________

Exercise 3-1A

Cash	
500	100
400	200
600	

Exercise 3-2A

a. The cash account is increased with a .... ____________

b. The owner's capital account is increased with a .... ____________

c. The delivery equipment account is increased with a .... ____________

d. The cash account is decreased with a .... ____________

e. The liability account Accounts Payable is increased with a .... ____________

f. The revenue account Delivery Fees is increased with a .... ____________

g. The asset account Accounts Receivable is increased with a .... ____________

h. The rent expense account is increased with a .... ____________

i. The owner's drawing account is increased with a .... ____________

Exercise 3-3A

1. and 2.

Cash	

Richard Gibbs, Capital	

Supplies	

Utilities Expense	

Exercise 3-4A

Account	Debit or Credit
1. Cash	__________
2. Wages Expense	__________
3. Accounts Payable	__________
4. Owner's Drawing	__________
5. Supplies	__________
6. Owner's Capital	__________
7. Equipment	__________

Exercises 3-5A and 3-6A: See page WP-21

Exercises 3-5A and 3-6A

Assets		=	Liabilities		+	Owner's Equity	
Dr. +	Cr. –		Dr. –	Cr. +		Dr. –	Cr. +

Drawing		Expenses		Revenues	
Dr. +	Cr. –	Dr. +	Cr. –	Dr. –	Cr. +

Exercise 3-7A

Assets		=	Liabilities		+	Owner's Equity	
Dr. +	Cr. –		Dr. –	Cr. +		Dr. –	Cr. +

Drawing		Expenses		Revenues	
Dr. +	Cr. –	Dr. +	Cr. –	Dr. –	Cr. +

Problem 3-15A (Concluded)

2.

3.

Exercise 3-1B

Accounts Payable	
300	450
250	350
	150

Exercise 3-2B

a. The asset account Prepaid Insurance is increased with a.................................. ______________

b. The owner's drawing account is increased with a.. ______________

c. The asset account Accounts Receivable is decreased with a .... ______________

d. The liability account Accounts Payable is decreased with a.............................. ______________

e. The owner's capital account is increased with a.. ______________

f. The revenue account Professional Fees is increased with a.............................. ______________

g. The expense account Repair Expense is increased with a .... ______________

h. The asset account Cash is decreased with a .... ______________

i. The asset account Delivery Equipment is decreased with a.............................. ______________

Exercise 3-3B

1. and 2.

Cash	

Roberto Alvarez, Capital	

Supplies	

Utilities Expense	

Name ______________________________

Exercise 3-4B

	Account	Debit or Credit
1.	Cash	____________
2.	Rent Expense	____________
3.	Notes Payable	____________
4.	Owner's Drawing	____________
5.	Accounts Receivable	____________
6.	Owner's Capital	____________
7.	Tools	____________

Exercises 3-5B and 3-6B: See page WP-32

Exercises 3-5B and 3-6B

Assets		=	Liabilities		+	Owner's Equity	
Dr. +	Cr. –		Dr. –	Cr. +		Dr. –	Cr. +

Drawing		Expenses		Revenues	
Dr. +	Cr. –	Dr. +	Cr. –	Dr. –	Cr. +

Exercise 3-7B

Assets		=	Liabilities		+	Owner's Equity	
Dr. +	Cr. –		Dr. –	Cr. +		Dr. –	Cr. +

Drawing		Expenses		Revenues	
Dr. +	Cr. –	Dr. +	Cr. –	Dr. –	Cr. +

Exercise 3-8B

ACCOUNT	DEBIT BALANCE	CREDIT BALANCE

Name ______________________________

Exercise 3-9B

ACCOUNT	DEBIT BALANCE	CREDIT BALANCE

Exercise 3-10B

Exercise 3-11B

Exercise 3-12B

Problem 3-13B

1. and 2.

Assets		=	Liabilities		+	Owner's Equity	
Dr. +	Cr. –		Dr. –	Cr. +		Dr. –	Cr. +

Drawing		Expenses		Revenues	
Dr. +	Cr. –	Dr. +	Cr. –	Dr. –	Cr. +

Problem 3-13B (Concluded)

3.

ACCOUNT	DEBIT BALANCE	CREDIT BALANCE

Problem 3-14B

1.

a. Total revenue for the month .... ______

b. Total expenses for the month .... ______

c. Net income for the month .... ______

2.

a. Sue Jantz's original investment in the business .... ______

+ Net income for the month .... ______

– Owner's drawing .... ______

Increase in capital .... ______

= Ending owner's equity .... ______

b. End-of-month accounting equation:

Assets	=	Liabilities	+	Owner's Equity
______		______		______

Problem 3-15B

1.

Problem 3-15B (Concluded)

2.

3.

Mastery Problem

1. and 2.

Assets		=	Liabilities		+	Owner's Equity	
Dr. +	Cr. −		Dr. −	Cr. +		Dr. −	Cr. +

Drawing		Expenses		Revenues	
Dr. +	Cr. −	Dr. +	Cr. −	Dr. −	Cr. +

Mastery Problem (Continued)

3.

ACCOUNT	DEBIT BALANCE	CREDIT BALANCE

4.

Mastery Problem (Concluded)

5.

6.

Challenge Problem

1.

2.

Exercise 4-1A

1.	________	Check stubs or check register	a. A good or service has been sold.
2.	________	Purchase invoice from suppliers (vendors)	b. Cash has been received by the business.
3.	________	Sales tickets or invoices to customers	c. Cash has been paid by the business.
4.	________	Receipts or cash register tapes	d. Goods or services have been purchased by the business.

Exercise 4-2A

Transaction	Debit	Credit
1. Invested cash in the business, $5,000.		
2. Paid office rent, $500.		
3. Purchased office supplies on account, $300.		
4. Received cash for services rendered (fees), $400.		
5. Paid cash on account, $50.		
6. Rendered services on account, $300.		
7. Received cash for an amount owed by a customer, $100.		

Exercise 4-3A

Exercise 4-3A (Concluded)

Total Debits: **Total Credits:**

Exercise 4-4A

GENERAL JOURNAL PAGE 1

	DATE		DESCRIPTION	POST. REF.	DEBIT	CREDIT	
1							1
2							2
3							3
4							4
5							5
6							6
7							7
8							8
9							9
10							10
11							11
12							12
13							13
14							14
15							15
16							16
17							17
18							18
19							19
20							20
21							21
22							22
23							23
24							24

Name ______________________________

Exercise 4-4A (Concluded)

GENERAL JOURNAL

PAGE 2

	DATE	DESCRIPTION	POST. REF.	DEBIT	CREDIT	
1						1
2						2
3						3
4						4
5						5
6						6
7						7
8						8
9						9
10						10
11						11
12						12
13						13
14						14
15						15
16						16
17						17
18						18
19						19
20						20
21						21
22						22
23						23
24						24
25						25
26						26
27						27
28						28
29						29
30						30
31						31
32						32
33						33
34						34
35						35
36						36

Exercise 4-5A

GENERAL LEDGER

ACCOUNT ACCOUNT NO.

DATE		ITEM	POST. REF.	DEBIT	CREDIT	BALANCE DEBIT	BALANCE CREDIT

ACCOUNT ACCOUNT NO.

DATE		ITEM	POST. REF.	DEBIT	CREDIT	BALANCE DEBIT	BALANCE CREDIT

ACCOUNT ACCOUNT NO.

DATE		ITEM	POST. REF.	DEBIT	CREDIT	BALANCE DEBIT	BALANCE CREDIT

Exercise 4-5A (Continued)

ACCOUNT ______________________________ ACCOUNT NO. ________

DATE		ITEM	POST. REF.	DEBIT	CREDIT	BALANCE DEBIT	BALANCE CREDIT

ACCOUNT ______________________________ ACCOUNT NO. ________

DATE		ITEM	POST. REF.	DEBIT	CREDIT	BALANCE DEBIT	BALANCE CREDIT

ACCOUNT ______________________________ ACCOUNT NO. ________

DATE		ITEM	POST. REF.	DEBIT	CREDIT	BALANCE DEBIT	BALANCE CREDIT

ACCOUNT ______________________________ ACCOUNT NO. ________

DATE		ITEM	POST. REF.	DEBIT	CREDIT	BALANCE DEBIT	BALANCE CREDIT

Exercise 4-5A (Continued)

ACCOUNT ACCOUNT NO.

DATE		ITEM	POST. REF.	DEBIT	CREDIT	BALANCE DEBIT	BALANCE CREDIT

ACCOUNT ACCOUNT NO.

DATE		ITEM	POST. REF.	DEBIT	CREDIT	BALANCE DEBIT	BALANCE CREDIT

ACCOUNT ACCOUNT NO.

DATE		ITEM	POST. REF.	DEBIT	CREDIT	BALANCE DEBIT	BALANCE CREDIT

ACCOUNT ACCOUNT NO.

DATE		ITEM	POST. REF.	DEBIT	CREDIT	BALANCE DEBIT	BALANCE CREDIT

ACCOUNT ACCOUNT NO.

DATE		ITEM	POST. REF.	DEBIT	CREDIT	BALANCE DEBIT	BALANCE CREDIT

Exercise 4-5A (Concluded)

ACCOUNT TITLE	ACCT. NO.	DEBIT BALANCE	CREDIT BALANCE

Exercise 4-6A

Exercise 4-6A (Concluded)

Name ______________________________

Exercise 4-7A

Exercise 4-7A (Concluded)

Exercise 4-8A

GENERAL JOURNAL

PAGE

DATE		DESCRIPTION	POST. REF.	DEBIT	CREDIT
May	17	Office Equipment		400 00	
		Cash			400 00
		Purchased copy paper			
	23	Cash	101	1000 00	
		Service Fees	401		1000 00
		Received cash for services previously earned			

Problem 4-10A

2. (For 1. and 3., see page WP-68.)

GENERAL JOURNAL

PAGE 7

DATE	DESCRIPTION	POST. REF.	DEBIT	CREDIT

Problem 4-10A (Continued)

GENERAL JOURNAL

PAGE 8

	DATE		DESCRIPTION	POST. REF.	DEBIT	CREDIT	
1							1
2							2
3							3
4							4
5							5
6							6
7							7
8							8
9							9
10							10
11							11
12							12
13							13
14							14
15							15
16							16
17							17
18							18
19							19
20							20
21							21
22							22
23							23
24							24
25							25
26							26
27							27
28							28
29							29
30							30
31							31
32							32
33							33
34							34
35							35
36							36

Problem 4-10A (Continued)

GENERAL JOURNAL

PAGE 9

DATE	DESCRIPTION	POST. REF.	DEBIT	CREDIT

Problem 4-10A (Continued)

1. and 3.

ACCOUNT Cash **GENERAL LEDGER** ACCOUNT NO. 101

DATE	ITEM	POST. REF.	DEBIT	CREDIT	BALANCE DEBIT	BALANCE CREDIT

Problem 4-10A (Continued)

ACCOUNT Accounts Receivable ACCOUNT NO. 122

DATE	ITEM	POST. REF.	DEBIT	CREDIT	BALANCE DEBIT	BALANCE CREDIT

ACCOUNT Office Supplies ACCOUNT NO. 142

DATE	ITEM	POST. REF.	DEBIT	CREDIT	BALANCE DEBIT	BALANCE CREDIT

ACCOUNT Office Equipment ACCOUNT NO. 181

DATE	ITEM	POST. REF.	DEBIT	CREDIT	BALANCE DEBIT	BALANCE CREDIT

ACCOUNT Delivery Truck ACCOUNT NO. 185

DATE	ITEM	POST. REF.	DEBIT	CREDIT	BALANCE DEBIT	BALANCE CREDIT

Problem 4-10A (Continued)

ACCOUNT Accounts Payable ACCOUNT NO. 202

DATE	ITEM	POST. REF.	DEBIT	CREDIT	BALANCE DEBIT	BALANCE CREDIT

ACCOUNT Jim Andrews, Capital ACCOUNT NO. 311

DATE	ITEM	POST. REF.	DEBIT	CREDIT	BALANCE DEBIT	BALANCE CREDIT

ACCOUNT Jim Andrews, Drawing ACCOUNT NO. 312

DATE	ITEM	POST. REF.	DEBIT	CREDIT	BALANCE DEBIT	BALANCE CREDIT

ACCOUNT Delivery Fees ACCOUNT NO. 401

DATE	ITEM	POST. REF.	DEBIT	CREDIT	BALANCE DEBIT	BALANCE CREDIT

Problem 4-10A (Continued)

ACCOUNT Wages Expense ACCOUNT NO. 511

DATE		ITEM	POST. REF.	DEBIT	CREDIT	BALANCE DEBIT	BALANCE CREDIT

ACCOUNT Advertising Expense ACCOUNT NO. 512

DATE		ITEM	POST. REF.	DEBIT	CREDIT	BALANCE DEBIT	BALANCE CREDIT

ACCOUNT Rent Expense ACCOUNT NO. 521

DATE		ITEM	POST. REF.	DEBIT	CREDIT	BALANCE DEBIT	BALANCE CREDIT

ACCOUNT Phone Expense ACCOUNT NO. 525

DATE		ITEM	POST. REF.	DEBIT	CREDIT	BALANCE DEBIT	BALANCE CREDIT

Problem 4-10A (Continued)

ACCOUNT Electricity Expense ACCOUNT NO. 533

DATE	ITEM	POST. REF.	DEBIT	CREDIT	BALANCE DEBIT	BALANCE CREDIT

ACCOUNT Charitable Contributions Expense ACCOUNT NO. 534

DATE	ITEM	POST. REF.	DEBIT	CREDIT	BALANCE DEBIT	BALANCE CREDIT

ACCOUNT Gas and Oil Expense ACCOUNT NO. 538

DATE	ITEM	POST. REF.	DEBIT	CREDIT	BALANCE DEBIT	BALANCE CREDIT

ACCOUNT Miscellaneous Expense ACCOUNT NO. 549

DATE	ITEM	POST. REF.	DEBIT	CREDIT	BALANCE DEBIT	BALANCE CREDIT

Problem 4-10A (Concluded)

4.

ACCOUNT TITLE	ACCT. NO.	DEBIT BALANCE	CREDIT BALANCE

Problem 4-11A

GENERAL JOURNAL

PAGE

	DATE		DESCRIPTION	POST. REF.	DEBIT	CREDIT	
1							1
2							2
3							3
4							4
5							5
6							6
7							7
8							8
9							9
10							10
11							11
12							12
13							13
14							14
15							15
16							16
17							17
18							18
19							19
20							20

Exercise 4-1B

1. Cash register tape
2. Sales ticket (issued to customer)
3. Purchase invoice (received from supplier or vendor)
4. Check stub

Exercise 4-2B

Transaction	Debit	Credit
1. Invested cash in the business, $1,000.	____________	____________
2. Performed services on account, $200.	____________	____________
3. Purchased office equipment on account, $500.	____________	____________
4. Received cash on account for services previously rendered, $200.	____________	____________
5. Made a payment on account, $100.	____________	____________

Exercise 4-3B

Total Debits:	Total Credits:
____________	____________
____________	____________
____________	____________
____________	____________

Exercise 4-4B

GENERAL JOURNAL

PAGE 1

	DATE	DESCRIPTION	POST. REF.	DEBIT	CREDIT	
1						1
2						2
3						3
4						4
5						5
6						6
7						7
8						8
9						9
10						10
11						11
12						12
13						13
14						14
15						15
16						16
17						17
18						18
19						19
20						20
21						21
22						22
23						23
24						24
25						25
26						26
27						27
28						28
29						29
30						30
31						31
32						32
33						33
34						34
35						35
36						36

Name ______________________________

Exercise 4-4B (Concluded)

GENERAL JOURNAL

PAGE 2

	DATE	DESCRIPTION	POST. REF.	DEBIT	CREDIT	
1						1
2						2
3						3
4						4
5						5
6						6
7						7
8						8
9						9
10						10
11						11
12						12
13						13
14						14
15						15
16						16
17						17
18						18
19						19
20						20
21						21
22						22
23						23
24						24
25						25
26						26
27						27
28						28
29						29
30						30
31						31
32						32
33						33
34						34
35						35
36						36

Exercise 4-5B

GENERAL LEDGER

ACCOUNT ACCOUNT NO.

DATE	ITEM	POST. REF.	DEBIT	CREDIT	BALANCE DEBIT	BALANCE CREDIT

ACCOUNT ACCOUNT NO.

DATE	ITEM	POST. REF.	DEBIT	CREDIT	BALANCE DEBIT	BALANCE CREDIT

ACCOUNT ACCOUNT NO.

DATE	ITEM	POST. REF.	DEBIT	CREDIT	BALANCE DEBIT	BALANCE CREDIT

Exercise 4-5B (Continued)

ACCOUNT ACCOUNT NO.

DATE		ITEM	POST. REF.	DEBIT	CREDIT	BALANCE	
						DEBIT	CREDIT

ACCOUNT ACCOUNT NO.

DATE		ITEM	POST. REF.	DEBIT	CREDIT	BALANCE	
						DEBIT	CREDIT

ACCOUNT ACCOUNT NO.

DATE		ITEM	POST. REF.	DEBIT	CREDIT	BALANCE	
						DEBIT	CREDIT

ACCOUNT ACCOUNT NO.

DATE		ITEM	POST. REF.	DEBIT	CREDIT	BALANCE	
						DEBIT	CREDIT

Exercise 4-5B (Continued)

ACCOUNT ACCOUNT NO.

DATE		ITEM	POST. REF.	DEBIT	CREDIT	BALANCE DEBIT	BALANCE CREDIT

ACCOUNT ACCOUNT NO.

DATE		ITEM	POST. REF.	DEBIT	CREDIT	BALANCE DEBIT	BALANCE CREDIT

ACCOUNT ACCOUNT NO.

DATE		ITEM	POST. REF.	DEBIT	CREDIT	BALANCE DEBIT	BALANCE CREDIT

ACCOUNT ACCOUNT NO.

DATE		ITEM	POST. REF.	DEBIT	CREDIT	BALANCE DEBIT	BALANCE CREDIT

ACCOUNT ACCOUNT NO.

DATE		ITEM	POST. REF.	DEBIT	CREDIT	BALANCE DEBIT	BALANCE CREDIT

Exercise 4-5B (Concluded)

ACCOUNT TITLE	ACCT. NO.	DEBIT BALANCE	CREDIT BALANCE

Exercise 4-6B

Exercise 4-6B (Concluded)

Problem 4-10B

2. (For 1. and 3., see page WP-98.)

GENERAL JOURNAL

PAGE 7

	DATE		DESCRIPTION	POST. REF.	DEBIT	CREDIT	
1							1
2							2
3							3
4							4
5							5
6							6
7							7
8							8
9							9
10							10
11							11
12							12
13							13
14							14
15							15
16							16
17							17
18							18
19							19
20							20
21							21
22							22
23							23
24							24
25							25
26							26
27							27
28							28
29							29
30							30
31							31
32							32
33							33
34							34

Problem 4-10B (Continued)

GENERAL JOURNAL

PAGE 8

DATE		DESCRIPTION	POST. REF.	DEBIT	CREDIT

Problem 4-10B (Continued)

GENERAL JOURNAL

PAGE 9

	DATE		DESCRIPTION	POST. REF.	DEBIT	CREDIT	
1							1
2							2
3							3
4							4
5							5
6							6
7							7
8							8
9							9
10							10
11							11
12							12
13							13
14							14
15							15
16							16
17							17
18							18
19							19
20							20
21							21
22							22
23							23
24							24
25							25
26							26
27							27
28							28
29							29
30							30
31							31
32							32
33							33
34							34
35							35
36							36

Problem 4-10B (Continued)

1. and 3.

GENERAL LEDGER

ACCOUNT Cash ACCOUNT NO. 101

DATE	ITEM	POST. REF.	DEBIT	CREDIT	BALANCE DEBIT	BALANCE CREDIT

ACCOUNT Accounts Receivable ACCOUNT NO. 122

DATE	ITEM	POST. REF.	DEBIT	CREDIT	BALANCE DEBIT	BALANCE CREDIT

Problem 4-10B (Continued)

ACCOUNT Tailoring Supplies ACCOUNT NO. 141

DATE	ITEM	POST. REF.	DEBIT	CREDIT	BALANCE	
					DEBIT	CREDIT

ACCOUNT Tailoring Equipment ACCOUNT NO. 183

DATE	ITEM	POST. REF.	DEBIT	CREDIT	BALANCE	
					DEBIT	CREDIT

ACCOUNT Accounts Payable ACCOUNT NO. 202

DATE	ITEM	POST. REF.	DEBIT	CREDIT	BALANCE	
					DEBIT	CREDIT

ACCOUNT Ann Taylor, Capital ACCOUNT NO. 311

DATE	ITEM	POST. REF.	DEBIT	CREDIT	BALANCE	
					DEBIT	CREDIT

Problem 4-10B (Continued)

ACCOUNT Ann Taylor, Drawing ACCOUNT NO. 312

DATE	ITEM	POST. REF.	DEBIT	CREDIT	BALANCE DEBIT	BALANCE CREDIT

ACCOUNT Tailoring Fees ACCOUNT NO. 401

DATE	ITEM	POST. REF.	DEBIT	CREDIT	BALANCE DEBIT	BALANCE CREDIT

ACCOUNT Wages Expense ACCOUNT NO. 511

DATE	ITEM	POST. REF.	DEBIT	CREDIT	BALANCE DEBIT	BALANCE CREDIT

ACCOUNT Advertising Expense ACCOUNT NO. 512

DATE	ITEM	POST. REF.	DEBIT	CREDIT	BALANCE DEBIT	BALANCE CREDIT

Problem 4-10B (Continued)

ACCOUNT Rent Expense ACCOUNT NO. 521

DATE	ITEM	POST. REF.	DEBIT	CREDIT	BALANCE DEBIT	BALANCE CREDIT

ACCOUNT Phone Expense ACCOUNT NO. 525

DATE	ITEM	POST. REF.	DEBIT	CREDIT	BALANCE DEBIT	BALANCE CREDIT

ACCOUNT Electricity Expense ACCOUNT NO. 533

DATE	ITEM	POST. REF.	DEBIT	CREDIT	BALANCE DEBIT	BALANCE CREDIT

ACCOUNT Miscellaneous Expense ACCOUNT NO. 549

DATE	ITEM	POST. REF.	DEBIT	CREDIT	BALANCE DEBIT	BALANCE CREDIT

Problem 4-10B (Concluded)

4.

ACCOUNT TITLE	ACCT. NO.	DEBIT BALANCE	CREDIT BALANCE

Name ______________________________

Problem 4-11B

GENERAL JOURNAL

PAGE

	DATE		DESCRIPTION	POST. REF.	DEBIT	CREDIT	
1							1
2							2
3							3
4							4
5							5
6							6
7							7
8							8
9							9
10							10
11							11
12							12
13							13
14							14
15							15
16							16
17							17
18							18
19							19
20							20
21							21
22							22
23							23

Mastery Problem

1.

GENERAL JOURNAL PAGE 1

	DATE		DESCRIPTION	POST. REF.	DEBIT	CREDIT	
1							1
2							2
3							3
4							4
5							5
6							6
7							7
8							8
9							9
10							10
11							11
12							12
13							13
14							14
15							15
16							16
17							17
18							18
19							19
20							20
21							21
22							22
23							23
24							24
25							25
26							26
27							27
28							28
29							29
30							30
31							31
32							32
33							33
34							34
35							35

Mastery Problem (Continued)

GENERAL JOURNAL

PAGE 2

	DATE		DESCRIPTION	POST. REF.	DEBIT	CREDIT	
1							1
2							2
3							3
4							4
5							5
6							6
7							7
8							8
9							9
10							10
11							11
12							12
13							13
14							14
15							15
16							16
17							17
18							18
19							19
20							20
21							21
22							22
23							23
24							24
25							25
26							26
27							27
28							28
29							29
30							30
31							31
32							32
33							33
34							34
35							35

Mastery Problem (Continued)

GENERAL JOURNAL

PAGE 3

DATE		DESCRIPTION	POST. REF.	DEBIT	CREDIT

Mastery Problem (Continued)

2.

ACCOUNT Cash **GENERAL LEDGER** ACCOUNT NO. 101

DATE		ITEM	POST. REF.	DEBIT	CREDIT	BALANCE DEBIT	BALANCE CREDIT

ACCOUNT Office Supplies ACCOUNT NO. 142

DATE		ITEM	POST. REF.	DEBIT	CREDIT	BALANCE DEBIT	BALANCE CREDIT

ACCOUNT Athletic Equipment ACCOUNT NO. 183

DATE		ITEM	POST. REF.	DEBIT	CREDIT	BALANCE DEBIT	BALANCE CREDIT

Mastery Problem (Continued)

ACCOUNT Basketball Facilities ACCOUNT NO. 184

DATE	ITEM	POST. REF.	DEBIT	CREDIT	BALANCE	
					DEBIT	CREDIT

ACCOUNT Accounts Payable ACCOUNT NO. 202

DATE	ITEM	POST. REF.	DEBIT	CREDIT	BALANCE	
					DEBIT	CREDIT

ACCOUNT Barry Bird, Capital ACCOUNT NO. 311

DATE	ITEM	POST. REF.	DEBIT	CREDIT	BALANCE	
					DEBIT	CREDIT

ACCOUNT Barry Bird, Drawing ACCOUNT NO. 312

DATE	ITEM	POST. REF.	DEBIT	CREDIT	BALANCE	
					DEBIT	CREDIT

Name ________________________________

Mastery Problem (Continued)

ACCOUNT Registration Fees ACCOUNT NO. 401

DATE		ITEM	POST. REF.	DEBIT	CREDIT	BALANCE DEBIT	BALANCE CREDIT

ACCOUNT Wages Expense ACCOUNT NO. 511

DATE		ITEM	POST. REF.	DEBIT	CREDIT	BALANCE DEBIT	BALANCE CREDIT

ACCOUNT Advertising Expense ACCOUNT NO. 512

DATE		ITEM	POST. REF.	DEBIT	CREDIT	BALANCE DEBIT	BALANCE CREDIT

Mastery Problem (Continued)

ACCOUNT Food Expense ACCOUNT NO. 524

DATE	ITEM	POST. REF.	DEBIT	CREDIT	BALANCE DEBIT	BALANCE CREDIT

ACCOUNT Phone Expense ACCOUNT NO. 525

DATE	ITEM	POST. REF.	DEBIT	CREDIT	BALANCE DEBIT	BALANCE CREDIT

ACCOUNT Utilities Expense ACCOUNT NO. 533

DATE	ITEM	POST. REF.	DEBIT	CREDIT	BALANCE DEBIT	BALANCE CREDIT

ACCOUNT Postage Expense ACCOUNT NO. 536

DATE	ITEM	POST. REF.	DEBIT	CREDIT	BALANCE DEBIT	BALANCE CREDIT

Mastery Problem (Concluded)

3.

ACCOUNT TITLE	ACCT. NO.	DEBIT BALANCE	CREDIT BALANCE

Challenge Problem

1. and 2.

3.

Fred Phaler Consulting

Trial Balance

June 30, 20--

ACCOUNT TITLE	ACCT. NO.	DEBIT BALANCE	CREDIT BALANCE
Cash	101		
Accounts Receivable	122		
Office Supplies	142		
Accounts Payable	202		
Fred Phaler, Capital	311		
Fred Phaler, Drawing	312		
Professional Fees	401		
Wages Expense	511		
Rent Expense	521		
Phone Expense	525		
Automobile Expense	526		
Utilities Expense	533		

Exercise 5-1A

(Balance Sheet) Supplies		(Income Statement) Supplies Expense	

GENERAL JOURNAL PAGE

	DATE	DESCRIPTION	POST. REF.	DEBIT	CREDIT	
1						1
2						2
3						3
4						4
5						5
6						6

Exercise 5-2A

(Balance Sheet) Prepaid Insurance		(Income Statement) Insurance Expense	

GENERAL JOURNAL PAGE

	DATE	DESCRIPTION	POST. REF.	DEBIT	CREDIT	
1						1
2						2
3						3
4						4
5						5
6						6

Exercise 5-3A

(Income Statement)
Wages Expense

(Balance Sheet)
Wages Payable

GENERAL JOURNAL PAGE

	DATE		DESCRIPTION	POST. REF.	DEBIT	CREDIT	
1							1
2							2
3							3
4							4

Exercise 5-4A

(Income Statement)
Depr. Expense—Delivery Equipment

(Balance Sheet)
Accum. Depr.—Delivery Equipment

GENERAL JOURNAL PAGE

	DATE		DESCRIPTION	POST. REF.	DEBIT	CREDIT	
1							1
2							2
3							3
4							4

Exercise 5-5A

Exercise 5-6A

1.

(Balance Sheet) Supplies		(Income Statement) Supplies Expense	
TB 580			
Bal. ______			

2.

(Balance Sheet) Supplies		(Income Statement) Supplies Expense	
TB 435			
Bal. ______			

Exercise 5-7A

1.

(Balance Sheet) Prepaid Insurance		(Income Statement) Insurance Expense	
TB 1,450			
Bal. ______			

2.

(Balance Sheet) Prepaid Insurance		(Income Statement) Insurance Expense	
TB 1,350			
Bal. ______			

Exercise 5-8A

GENERAL JOURNAL

PAGE 9

DATE		DESCRIPTION	POST. REF.	DEBIT	CREDIT
		Adjusting Entries			
20-- Dec.	31	Supplies Expense		85 00	
		Supplies			85 00
	31	Wages Expense		220 00	
		Wages Payable			220 00

Exercise 5-8A (Concluded)

GENERAL LEDGER

ACCOUNT Supplies ACCOUNT NO. 141

DATE		ITEM	POST. REF.	DEBIT	CREDIT	BALANCE DEBIT	BALANCE CREDIT
20-- Dec.	1	Balance	✓			150 00	
	15		J8	50 00		200 00	

ACCOUNT Wages Payable ACCOUNT NO. 219

DATE		ITEM	POST. REF.	DEBIT	CREDIT	BALANCE DEBIT	BALANCE CREDIT

ACCOUNT Wages Expense ACCOUNT NO. 511

DATE		ITEM	POST. REF.	DEBIT	CREDIT	BALANCE DEBIT	BALANCE CREDIT
20-- Dec.	1	Balance	✓			900 00	
	15		J8	300 00		1200 00	

ACCOUNT Supplies Expense ACCOUNT NO. 523

DATE		ITEM	POST. REF.	DEBIT	CREDIT	BALANCE DEBIT	BALANCE CREDIT

Exercise 5-9A

Jim Jacobs' Furniture Repair

Work Sheet (Partial)

For Year Ended December 31, 20--

ACCOUNT TITLE	TRIAL BALANCE		ADJUSTMENTS		ADJUSTED TRIAL BALANCE	
	DEBIT	CREDIT	DEBIT	CREDIT	DEBIT	CREDIT
Cash	100 00				100 00	
Supplies	850 00				200 00	
Prepaid Insurance	900 00				300 00	
Delivery Equipment	3600 00				3600 00	
Accum. Depr.—Delivery Equip.		600 00				800 00
Wages Payable						100 00
Jim Jacobs, Capital		4000 00				4000 00
Repair Fees		1650 00				1650 00
Wages Expense	600 00				700 00	
Advertising Expense	200 00				200 00	
Supplies Expense					650 00	
Insurance Expense					600 00	
Depr. Exp.—Delivery Equip.					200 00	
	6250 00	6250 00			6550 00	6550 00

Exercise 5-10A

GENERAL JOURNAL

PAGE

	DATE		DESCRIPTION	POST. REF.	DEBIT	CREDIT	
1							1
2							2
3							3
4							4
5							5
6							6
7							7
8							8
9							9
10							10
11							11
12							12
13							13
14							14
15							15

Exercise 5-11A

	Income Statement		Balance Sheet	
	Debit	Credit	Debit	Credit
Cash				
Accounts Receivable				
Supplies				
Prepaid Insurance				
Delivery Equipment				
Accum. Depr.—Delivery Equip.				
Accounts Payable				
Wages Payable				
Owner, Capital				
Owner, Drawing				
Delivery Fees				
Wages Expense				
Rent Expense				
Supplies Expense				
Insurance Expense				
Depr. Exp.—Delivery Equip.				

Exercise 5-12A

	Income Statement		Balance Sheet	
	Debit	Credit	Debit	Credit
Net Income				
Net Loss				

Name ______________________________

Exercise 5-13A

	Cash Basis	Modified Cash Basis	Accrual Basis
1. Purchase supplies on account.			
2. Make payment on asset previously purchased.			
3. Purchase supplies for cash.			
4. Purchase insurance for cash.			
5. Pay cash for wages.			
6. Pay cash for phone expense.			
7. Pay cash for new equipment.			
8. Wages earned but not paid.			
9. Prepaid item purchased, partly used.			
10. Depreciation on long-term assets.			

Problem 5-14A

Mason's Delivery

Work

For Month Ended

	ACCOUNT TITLE	TRIAL BALANCE DEBIT	TRIAL BALANCE CREDIT	ADJUSTMENTS DEBIT	ADJUSTMENTS CREDIT
1	Cash	1,600.00			
2	Accounts Receivable	940.00			
3	Supplies	635.00			
4	Prepaid Insurance	1,200.00			
5	Delivery Equipment	6,400.00			
6	Accum. Depr.—Delivery Equip.				
7	Accounts Payable		1,220.00		
8	Wages Payable				
9	Jill Mason, Capital		8,000.00		
10	Jill Mason, Drawing	1,400.00			
11	Delivery Fees		6,200.00		
12	Wages Expense	1,500.00			
13	Advertising Expense	460.00			
14	Rent Expense	800.00			
15	Supplies Expense				
16	Phone Expense	165.00			
17	Insurance Expense				
18	Repair Expense	230.00			
19	Oil and Gas Expense	90.00			
20	Depr. Exp.—Delivery Equip.				
21		15,420.00	15,420.00		
22					
23					
24					
25					
26					
27					
28					
29					
30					
31					
32					
33					

Name ______________________________

Problem 5-14A (Concluded)

Service

Sheet

September 30, 20--

ADJUSTED TRIAL BALANCE		INCOME STATEMENT		BALANCE SHEET		
DEBIT	CREDIT	DEBIT	CREDIT	DEBIT	CREDIT	
						1
						2
						3
						4
						5
						6
						7
						8
						9
						10
						11
						12
						13
						14
						15
						16
						17
						18
						19
						20
						21
						22
						23
						24
						25
						26
						27
						28
						29
						30
						31
						32
						33

Problem 5-15A

Campus Delivery

Work

For Month Ended

	ACCOUNT TITLE	TRIAL BALANCE DEBIT	TRIAL BALANCE CREDIT	ADJUSTMENTS DEBIT	ADJUSTMENTS CREDIT
1	Cash	980 00			
2	Accounts Receivable	590 00			
3	Supplies	575 00			
4	Prepaid Insurance	1 300 00			
5	Van	5 800 00			
6	Accumulated Depreciation—Van				
7	Accounts Payable		960 00		
8	Wages Payable				
9	Jason Armstrong, Capital		10 000 00		
10	Jason Armstrong, Drawing	600 00			
11	Delivery Fees		2 600 00		
12	Wages Expense	1 800 00			
13	Advertising Expense	380 00			
14	Rent Expense	900 00			
15	Supplies Expense				
16	Phone Expense	220 00			
17	Insurance Expense				
18	Repair Expense	315 00			
19	Oil and Gas Expense	100 00			
20	Depreciation Expense—Van				
21		13 560 00	13 560 00		
22					
23					
24					
25					
26					
27					
28					
29					
30					
31					
32					
33					

Problem 5-15A (Concluded)

Service

Sheet

November 30, 20--

ADJUSTED TRIAL BALANCE		INCOME STATEMENT		BALANCE SHEET		
DEBIT	CREDIT	DEBIT	CREDIT	DEBIT	CREDIT	
						1
						2
						3
						4
						5
						6
						7
						8
						9
						10
						11
						12
						13
						14
						15
						16
						17
						18
						19
						20
						21
						22
						23
						24
						25
						26
						27
						28
						29
						30
						31
						32
						33

Problem 5-16A

1. **GENERAL JOURNAL** PAGE 5

	DATE		DESCRIPTION	POST. REF.	DEBIT	CREDIT	
1							1
2							2
3							3
4							4
5							5
6							6
7							7
8							8
9							9
10							10
11							11
12							12
13							13
14							14
15							15
16							16
17							17
18							18
19							19
20							20
21							21
22							22
23							23
24							24
25							25
26							26
27							27
28							28
29							29
30							30
31							31
32							32
33							33
34							34
35							35
36							36

Problem 5-16A (Continued)

2. **GENERAL LEDGER**

ACCOUNT Supplies ACCOUNT NO. 141

DATE		ITEM	POST. REF.	DEBIT	CREDIT	BALANCE DEBIT	BALANCE CREDIT
20-- Nov.	1		J1	475 00		475 00	
	15		J4	100 00		575 00	

ACCOUNT Prepaid Insurance ACCOUNT NO. 145

DATE		ITEM	POST. REF.	DEBIT	CREDIT	BALANCE DEBIT	BALANCE CREDIT
20-- Nov.	1		J1	1,300 00		1,300 00	

ACCOUNT Accumulated Depreciation—Van ACCOUNT NO. 185.1

DATE		ITEM	POST. REF.	DEBIT	CREDIT	BALANCE DEBIT	BALANCE CREDIT

ACCOUNT Wages Payable ACCOUNT NO. 219

DATE		ITEM	POST. REF.	DEBIT	CREDIT	BALANCE DEBIT	BALANCE CREDIT

Problem 5-16A (Concluded)

GENERAL LEDGER

ACCOUNT Wages Expense ACCOUNT NO. 511

DATE		ITEM	POST. REF.	DEBIT	CREDIT	BALANCE DEBIT	BALANCE CREDIT
20-- Nov.	15		J3	900 00		900 00	
	26		J4	900 00		1800 00	

ACCOUNT Supplies Expense ACCOUNT NO. 523

DATE		ITEM	POST. REF.	DEBIT	CREDIT	BALANCE DEBIT	BALANCE CREDIT

ACCOUNT Insurance Expense ACCOUNT NO. 535

DATE		ITEM	POST. REF.	DEBIT	CREDIT	BALANCE DEBIT	BALANCE CREDIT

ACCOUNT Depreciation Expense—Van ACCOUNT NO. 541

DATE		ITEM	POST. REF.	DEBIT	CREDIT	BALANCE DEBIT	BALANCE CREDIT

Name ______________________________

Problem 5-17A: See pages 130 and 131

Exercise 5-1B

(Balance Sheet)
Supplies

(Income Statement)
Supplies Expense

GENERAL JOURNAL PAGE

	DATE	DESCRIPTION	POST. REF.	DEBIT	CREDIT	
1						1
2						2
3						3
4						4
5						5
6						6

Exercise 5-2B

(Balance Sheet)
Prepaid Insurance

(Income Statement)
Insurance Expense

GENERAL JOURNAL PAGE

	DATE	DESCRIPTION	POST. REF.	DEBIT	CREDIT	
1						1
2						2
3						3
4						4
5						5
6						6

Problem 5-17A

Joyce Lee's

Work

For Month Ended

	ACCOUNT TITLE	TRIAL BALANCE DEBIT	TRIAL BALANCE CREDIT	ADJUSTMENTS DEBIT	ADJUSTMENTS CREDIT
1	Cash	1 7 2 5 00			
2	Accounts Receivable	9 6 0 00			
3	Supplies	5 2 5 00			
4	Prepaid Insurance	9 3 0 00			
5	Office Equipment	5 4 5 0 00			
6	Accum. Depr.—Office Equipment				
7	Accounts Payable		4 8 0 00		
8	Wages Payable				
9	Joyce Lee, Capital		7 5 0 0 00		
10	Joyce Lee, Drawing	1 1 2 5 00			
11	Professional Fees		5 7 0 0 00		
12	Wages Expense	1 4 2 0 00			
13	Advertising Expense	3 5 0 00			
14	Rent Expense	7 0 0 00			
15	Supplies Expense				
16	Phone Expense	1 3 0 00			
17	Utilities Expense	1 9 0 00			
18	Insurance Expense				
19	Depr. Expense—Office Equipment				
20	Miscellaneous Expense	1 7 5 00			
21		13 6 8 0 00	13 6 8 0 00		
22					
23					
24					
25					
26					
27					
28					
29					
30					
31					

Name ______________________________

Problem 5-17A (Concluded)

Tax Service

Sheet

March 31, 20--

ADJUSTED TRIAL BALANCE		INCOME STATEMENT		BALANCE SHEET		
DEBIT	CREDIT	DEBIT	CREDIT	DEBIT	CREDIT	
						1
						2
						3
						4
						5
						6
						7
						8
						9
						10
						11
						12
						13
						14
						15
						16
						17
						18
						19
						20
						21
						22
						23
						24
						25
						26
						27
						28
						29
						30
						31

Exercise 5-3B

(Income Statement)
Wages Expense

(Balance Sheet)
Wages Payable

GENERAL JOURNAL PAGE

	DATE		DESCRIPTION	POST. REF.	DEBIT	CREDIT	
1							1
2							2
3							3
4							4

Exercise 5-4B

(Income Statement)
Depr. Expense—Delivery Equipment

(Balance Sheet)
Accum. Depr.—Delivery Equipment

GENERAL JOURNAL PAGE

	DATE		DESCRIPTION	POST. REF.	DEBIT	CREDIT	
1							1
2							2
3							3
4							4

Exercise 5-5B

Exercise 5-6B

1.

(Balance Sheet) Supplies		(Income Statement) Supplies Expense	
TB 540			
Bal. ______			

2.

(Balance Sheet) Supplies		(Income Statement) Supplies Expense	
TB 330			
Bal. ______			

Exercise 5-7B

1.

(Balance Sheet) Prepaid Insurance		(Income Statement) Insurance Expense	
TB 960			
Bal. ______			

2.

(Balance Sheet) Prepaid Insurance		(Income Statement) Insurance Expense	
TB 1,135			
Bal. ______			

Exercise 5-8B

GENERAL JOURNAL

PAGE 7

DATE		DESCRIPTION	POST. REF.	DEBIT	CREDIT
		Adjusting Entries			
20-- July	31	Insurance Expense		320 00	
		Prepaid Insurance			320 00
	31	Depreciation Expense—Cleaning Equipment		145 00	
		Accumulated Depreciation—Cleaning Equipment			145 00

Exercise 5-8B (Concluded)

GENERAL LEDGER

ACCOUNT Prepaid Insurance ACCOUNT NO. 145

DATE		ITEM	POST. REF.	DEBIT	CREDIT	BALANCE DEBIT	BALANCE CREDIT
20-- July	1	Balance	✓			3 2 0 00	
	15		J6	6 4 0 00		9 6 0 00	

ACCOUNT Accumulated Depreciation—Cleaning Equipment ACCOUNT NO. 183.1

DATE		ITEM	POST. REF.	DEBIT	CREDIT	BALANCE DEBIT	BALANCE CREDIT
20-- July	1	Balance	✓				8 7 0 00

ACCOUNT Insurance Expense ACCOUNT NO. 535

DATE		ITEM	POST. REF.	DEBIT	CREDIT	BALANCE DEBIT	BALANCE CREDIT

ACCOUNT Depreciation Expense—Cleaning Equipment ACCOUNT NO. 541

DATE		ITEM	POST. REF.	DEBIT	CREDIT	BALANCE DEBIT	BALANCE CREDIT

Exercise 5-9B

Jasmine Kah's Auto Detailing
Work Sheet (Partial)
For Month Ended June 30, 20--

	ACCOUNT TITLE	TRIAL BALANCE		ADJUSTMENTS		ADJUSTED TRIAL BALANCE		
		DEBIT	CREDIT	DEBIT	CREDIT	DEBIT	CREDIT	
1	Cash	150.00				150.00		1
2	Supplies	520.00				90.00		2
3	Prepaid Insurance	750.00				200.00		3
4	Cleaning Equipment	5,400.00				5,400.00		4
5	Accum. Depr.—Cleaning Equip.		850.00				1,150.00	5
6	Wages Payable						250.00	6
7	Jasmine Kah, Capital		4,600.00				4,600.00	7
8	Detailing Fees		2,220.00				2,220.00	8
9	Wages Expense	700.00				950.00		9
10	Advertising Expense	150.00				150.00		10
11	Supplies Expense					430.00		11
12	Insurance Expense					550.00		12
13	Depr. Exp.—Cleaning Equip.					300.00		13
14		7,670.00	7,670.00			8,220.00	8,220.00	14
15								15
16								16
17								17
18								18
19								19
20								20
21								21
22								22
23								23
24								24
25								25

Exercise 5-10B

GENERAL JOURNAL

PAGE

	DATE		DESCRIPTION	POST. REF.	DEBIT	CREDIT	
1							1
2							2
3							3
4							4
5							5
6							6
7							7
8							8
9							9
10							10
11							11
12							12
13							13
14							14
15							15

Exercise 5-11B

	Income Statement		Balance Sheet	
	Debit	**Credit**	**Debit**	**Credit**
Cash				
Accounts Receivable				
Supplies				
Prepaid Insurance				
Automobile				
Accum. Depr.—Automobile				
Accounts Payable				
Wages Payable				
Owner, Capital				
Owner, Drawing				
Service Fees				
Wages Expense				
Supplies Expense				
Utilities Expense				
Insurance Expense				
Depr. Exp.—Automobile				

Exercise 5-12B

	Income Statement		Balance Sheet	
	Debit	**Credit**	**Debit**	**Credit**
Net Income				
Net Loss				

Name ______________________________

Exercise 5-13B

	Cash Basis	Modified Cash Basis	Accrual Basis
1. Office Equipment Cash Purchased equipment for cash			
2. Office Equipment Accounts Payable Purchased equipment on account			
3. Cash Revenue Cash receipts for week			
4. Accounts Receivable Revenue Services performed on account			
5. Prepaid Insurance Cash Purchased prepaid asset			
6. Supplies Accounts Payable Purchased prepaid asset			
7. Phone Expense Cash Paid phone bill			
8. Wages Expense Cash Paid wages for month			
9. Accounts Payable Cash Made payment on account			
10. Supplies Expense Supplies			

Exercise 5-13B (Concluded)

	Cash Basis	Modified Cash Basis	Accrual Basis
11. Wages Expense Wages Payable			
12. Depreciation Expense—Office Equipment Accum. Depr.—Office Equipment			

This page intentionally left blank.

Problem 5-14B

Louie's Lawn

Work

For Month Ended

	ACCOUNT TITLE	TRIAL BALANCE DEBIT	TRIAL BALANCE CREDIT	ADJUSTMENTS DEBIT	ADJUSTMENTS CREDIT
1	Cash	1,375.00			
2	Accounts Receivable	880.00			
3	Supplies	490.00			
4	Prepaid Insurance	800.00			
5	Lawn Equipment	5,700.00			
6	Accum. Depr.—Lawn Equipment				
7	Accounts Payable		780.00		
8	Wages Payable				
9	Louie Long, Capital		6,500.00		
10	Louie Long, Drawing	1,250.00			
11	Lawn Service Fees		6,100.00		
12	Wages Expense	1,145.00			
13	Advertising Expense	540.00			
14	Rent Expense	725.00			
15	Supplies Expense				
16	Phone Expense	160.00			
17	Insurance Expense				
18	Repair Expense	250.00			
19	Depr. Expense—Lawn Equipment				
20	Miscellaneous Expense	65.00			
21		13,380.00	13,380.00		
22					
23					
24					
25					
26					
27					
28					
29					
30					
31					
32					
33					

Problem 5-14B (Concluded)

Service

Sheet

March 31, 20--

ADJUSTED TRIAL BALANCE		INCOME STATEMENT		BALANCE SHEET		
DEBIT	CREDIT	DEBIT	CREDIT	DEBIT	CREDIT	
						1
						2
						3
						4
						5
						6
						7
						8
						9
						10
						11
						12
						13
						14
						15
						16
						17
						18
						19
						20
						21
						22
						23
						24
						25
						26
						27
						28
						29
						30
						31
						32
						33

Problem 5-15B

Nolan's Home

Work

For Month Ended

ACCOUNT TITLE	TRIAL BALANCE		ADJUSTMENTS	
	DEBIT	CREDIT	DEBIT	CREDIT
Cash	830 00			
Accounts Receivable	760 00			
Supplies	625 00			
Prepaid Insurance	950 00			
Automobile	6500 00			
Accum. Depr.—Automobile				
Accounts Payable		1500 00		
Wages Payable				
Val Nolan, Capital		9900 00		
Val Nolan, Drawing	1100 00			
Appraisal Fees		3000 00		
Wages Expense	1560 00			
Advertising Expense	420 00			
Rent Expense	1050 00			
Supplies Expense				
Phone Expense	255 00			
Insurance Expense				
Repair Expense	270 00			
Oil and Gas Expense	80 00			
Depr. Expense—Automobile				
	14400 00	14400 00		

Problem 5-15B (Concluded)

Appraisals

Sheet

October 31, 20--

	ADJUSTED TRIAL BALANCE		INCOME STATEMENT		BALANCE SHEET		
	DEBIT	CREDIT	DEBIT	CREDIT	DEBIT	CREDIT	
							1
							2
							3
							4
							5
							6
							7
							8
							9
							10
							11
							12
							13
							14
							15
							16
							17
							18
							19
							20
							21
							22
							23
							24
							25
							26
							27
							28
							29
							30
							31
							32
							33

Problem 5-16B

1. **GENERAL JOURNAL** PAGE 3

DATE		DESCRIPTION	POST. REF.	DEBIT	CREDIT

Problem 5-16B (Continued)

2. **GENERAL LEDGER**

ACCOUNT Supplies ACCOUNT NO. 141

DATE		ITEM	POST. REF.	DEBIT	CREDIT	BALANCE DEBIT	BALANCE CREDIT
20-- Oct.	2		J1	625.00		625.00	

ACCOUNT Prepaid Insurance ACCOUNT NO. 145

DATE		ITEM	POST. REF.	DEBIT	CREDIT	BALANCE DEBIT	BALANCE CREDIT
20-- Oct.	3		J1	950.00		950.00	

ACCOUNT Accumulated Depreciation—Automobile ACCOUNT NO. 185.1

DATE		ITEM	POST. REF.	DEBIT	CREDIT	BALANCE DEBIT	BALANCE CREDIT

Problem 5-16B (Continued)

ACCOUNT Wages Payable — ACCOUNT NO. 219

DATE		ITEM	POST. REF.	DEBIT	CREDIT	BALANCE DEBIT	BALANCE CREDIT

ACCOUNT Wages Expense — ACCOUNT NO. 511

DATE		ITEM	POST. REF.	DEBIT	CREDIT	BALANCE DEBIT	BALANCE CREDIT
20-- Oct.	15		J2	700 00		700 00	
	26		J2	860 00		1560 00	

ACCOUNT Supplies Expense — ACCOUNT NO. 523

DATE		ITEM	POST. REF.	DEBIT	CREDIT	BALANCE DEBIT	BALANCE CREDIT

Problem 5-16B (Concluded)

ACCOUNT Insurance Expense ACCOUNT NO. 535

DATE	ITEM	POST. REF.	DEBIT	CREDIT	BALANCE	
					DEBIT	CREDIT

ACCOUNT Depreciation Expense—Automobile ACCOUNT NO. 541

DATE	ITEM	POST. REF.	DEBIT	CREDIT	BALANCE	
					DEBIT	CREDIT

Problem 5-17B

Dick Ady's

Work

For Month Ended

	ACCOUNT TITLE	TRIAL BALANCE DEBIT	TRIAL BALANCE CREDIT	ADJUSTMENTS DEBIT	ADJUSTMENTS CREDIT
1	Cash	1,365.00			
2	Accounts Receivable	845.00			
3	Supplies	620.00			
4	Prepaid Insurance	1,150.00			
5	Office Equipment	6,400.00			
6	Accum. Depr.—Office Equipment				
7	Accounts Payable		735.00		
8	Wages Payable				
9	Dick Ady, Capital		7,800.00		
10	Dick Ady, Drawing	1,200.00			
11	Professional Fees		6,350.00		
12	Wages Expense	1,495.00			
13	Advertising Expense	380.00			
14	Rent Expense	850.00			
15	Supplies Expense				
16	Phone Expense	205.00			
17	Utilities Expense	285.00			
18	Insurance Expense				
19	Depr. Expense—Office Equipment				
20	Miscellaneous Expense	90.00			
21		14,885.00	14,885.00		
22					
23					
24					
25					
26					
27					
28					
29					
30					
31					
32					

Name ______________________________

Problem 5-17B (Concluded)

Bookkeeping Service

Sheet

July 31, 20--

ADJUSTED TRIAL BALANCE		INCOME STATEMENT		BALANCE SHEET		
DEBIT	CREDIT	DEBIT	CREDIT	DEBIT	CREDIT	
						1
						2
						3
						4
						5
						6
						7
						8
						9
						10
						11
						12
						13
						14
						15
						16
						17
						18
						19
						20
						21
						22
						23
						24
						25
						26
						27
						28
						29
						30
						31
						32

Mastery Problem

1.

Kristi Williams Family

Work

For Year Ended

	ACCOUNT TITLE	TRIAL BALANCE DEBIT	TRIAL BALANCE CREDIT	ADJUSTMENTS DEBIT	ADJUSTMENTS CREDIT
1	Cash	8,730.00			
2	Office Supplies	700.00			
3	Prepaid Insurance	600.00			
4	Office Equipment	18,000.00			
5					
6	Computer Equipment	6,000.00			
7					
8	Notes Payable		8,000.00		
9	Accounts Payable		500.00		
10	Kristi Williams, Capital		11,400.00		
11	Kristi Williams, Drawing	3,000.00			
12	Client Fees		35,800.00		
13	Wages Expense	9,500.00			
14	Rent Expense	6,000.00			
15					
16	Utilities Expense	2,170.00			
17					
18					
19					
20	Miscellaneous Expense	1,000.00			
21		55,700.00	55,700.00		
22					
23					
24					
25					
26					
27					
28					
29					
30					
31					
32					

Name ______________________________

Mastery Problem (Continued)

Counseling Services

Sheet

December 31, 20--

ADJUSTED TRIAL BALANCE		INCOME STATEMENT		BALANCE SHEET		
DEBIT	CREDIT	DEBIT	CREDIT	DEBIT	CREDIT	
						4
						5
						6
						7
						8
						9
						10
						11
						12
						13
						14
						15
						16
						17
						18
						19
						20
						21
						22
						23
						24
						25
						26
						27
						28
						29
						30
						31
						32

Mastery Problem (Concluded)

2.

GENERAL JOURNAL

PAGE

	DATE	DESCRIPTION	POST. REF.	DEBIT	CREDIT	
1						1
2						2
3						3
4						4
5						5
6						6
7						7
8						8
9						9
10						10
11						11
12						12
13						13
14						14
15						15
16						16
17						17
18						18
19						19
20						20
21						21
22						22
23						23
24						24
25						25
26						26
27						27
28						28
29						29
30						30
31						31
32						32
33						33
34						34
35						35

Name ______________________________

Challenge Problem

See pages 156–157 for work sheet for Challenge Problem.

Challenge Problem

1.

Diane Kiefner's Wilderness

Work

For Summer

	ACCOUNT TITLE	TRIAL BALANCE DEBIT	TRIAL BALANCE CREDIT	ADJUSTMENTS DEBIT	ADJUSTMENTS CREDIT
1	Cash	11,500.00			
2					
3					
4					
5	Diane Kiefner, Capital		15,000.00		
6	Tour Revenue		10,000.00		
7	Advertising Supplies Expense	1,000.00			
8	Food Expense	2,000.00			
9	Equipment Rental Expense	3,000.00			
10	Travel Expense	4,000.00			
11	Kayak Expense	3,500.00			
12					
13		25,000.00	25,000.00		
14					
15					
16					
17					
18					
19					

Challenge Problem (Concluded)

Kayaking Tours

Sheet

Ended 20--

ADJUSTED TRIAL BALANCE		INCOME STATEMENT		BALANCE SHEET		
DEBIT	CREDIT	DEBIT	CREDIT	DEBIT	CREDIT	
						1
						2
						3
						4
						5
						6
						7
						8
						9
						10
						11
						12
						13
						14
						15
						16
						17
						18
						19

2.

APPENDIX: DEPRECIATION METHODS

Exercise 5Apx-1A

Straight-Line Depreciation

Year	Depreciable Cost	×	Rate	=	Depreciation Expense	Accumulated Depreciation End of Year	Book Value End of Year

Exercise 5Apx-2A

Sum-of-the-Years'-Digits

Year	Depreciable Cost	×	Rate	=	Depreciation Expense	Accumulated Depreciation End of Year	Book Value End of Year

Exercise 5Apx-3A

Double-Declining-Balance Method

Year	Book Value Beginning of Year	×	Rate	=	Depreciation Expense	Accumulated Depreciation End of Year	Book Value End of Year

Name ______________________________

Exercise 5Apx-4A

Modified Accelerated Cost Recovery System

Year	Cost	×	Rate	=	Depreciation Expense	Accumulated Depreciation End of Year	Book Value End of Year

Exercise 5Apx-1B

Straight-Line Depreciation

Year	Depreciable Cost	×	Rate	=	Depreciation Expense	Accumulated Depreciation End of Year	Book Value End of Year

Exercise 5Apx-2B

Sum-of-the-Years'-Digits

Year	Depreciable Cost	×	Rate	=	Depreciation Expense	Accumulated Depreciation End of Year	Book Value End of Year

Exercise 5Apx-3B

Double-Declining-Balance Method

Year	Book Value Beginning of Year	×	Rate	=	Depreciation Expense	Accumulated Depreciation End of Year	Book Value End of Year

Exercise 5Apx-4B

Modified Accelerated Cost Recovery System

Year	Cost	×	Rate	=	Depreciation Expense	Accumulated Depreciation End of Year	Book Value End of Year

Name ______________________________

Exercise 6-1A

Exercise 6-2A

Exercise 6-3A

Name ______________________________

Exercise 6-4A

GENERAL JOURNAL PAGE 1

	DATE		DESCRIPTION	POST. REF.	DEBIT	CREDIT	
1							1
2							2
3							3
4							4
5							5
6							6
7							7
8							8
9							9
10							10
11							11
12							12
13							13
14							14
15							15
16							16
17							17
18							18
19							19
20							20
21							21
22							22
23							23

Exercise 6-4A (Concluded)

Name ______________________________

Exercise 6-5A

GENERAL JOURNAL

PAGE

DATE		DESCRIPTION	POST. REF.	DEBIT	CREDIT

Exercise 6-5A (Concluded)

Cash 101

Debit		Credit	
Bal.	500		

Accounts Receivable 122

Debit		Credit	
Bal.	1,500		

Wages Payable 219

Debit		Credit	
		Bal.	400

Chris Williams, Capital 311

Debit		Credit	
		Bal.	9,000

Chris Williams, Drawing 312

Debit		Credit	
Bal.	1,000		

Income Summary 313

Debit		Credit	

Golf Instruction Fees 401

Debit		Credit	
		Bal.	4,000

Wages Expense 511

Debit		Credit	
Bal.	800		

Advertising Expense 512

Debit		Credit	
Bal.	200		

Travel Expense 515

Debit		Credit	
Bal.	600		

Supplies Expense 524

Debit		Credit	
Bal.	500		

Insurance Expense 535

Debit		Credit	
Bal.	100		

Postage Expense 536

Debit		Credit	
Bal.	50		

Gas and Oil Expense 538

Debit		Credit	
Bal.	150		

Miscellaneous Expense 549

Debit		Credit	
Bal.	80		

Name ______________________________

Exercise 6-6A

GENERAL JOURNAL

PAGE

	DATE		DESCRIPTION	POST. REF.	DEBIT	CREDIT	
1							1
2							2
3							3
4							4
5							5
6							6
7							7
8							8
9							9
10							10
11							11
12							12
13							13
14							14
15							15
16							16
17							17
18							18
19							19
20							20
21							21
22							22
23							23
24							24
25							25
26							26
27							27
28							28
29							29
30							30
31							31
32							32
33							33
34							34
35							35
36							36

Exercise 6-6A (Concluded)

Accum. Depr.—Delivery Equip. 185.1

	Bal. 100

Wages Payable 219

	Bal. 200

Saburo Goto, Capital 311

	Bal. 4,000

Saburo Goto, Drawing 312

Bal. 800	

Income Summary 313

Delivery Fees 401

	Bal. 2,200

Wages Expense 511

Bal. 1,800	

Advertising Expense 512

Bal. 80	

Rent Expense 521

Bal. 500	

Supplies Expense 523

Bal. 120	

Phone Expense 525

Bal. 58	

Electricity Expense 533

Bal. 44	

Insurance Expense 535

Bal. 30	

Gas and Oil Expense 538

Bal. 38	

Depr. Exp.—Delivery Equip. 541

Bal. 100	

Miscellaneous Expense 549

Bal. 33	

Problem 6-7A

1.

2.

Problem 6-7A (Concluded)

3.

Problem 6-8A

1.

GENERAL JOURNAL

PAGE 10

	DATE		DESCRIPTION	POST. REF.	DEBIT	CREDIT	
1							1
2							2
3							3
4							4
5							5
6							6
7							7
8							8
9							9
10							10
11							11
12							12
13							13
14							14
15							15
16							16
17							17
18							18

Problem 6-8A (Continued)

2.

GENERAL JOURNAL

PAGE 11

	DATE		DESCRIPTION	POST. REF.	DEBIT	CREDIT	
1							1
2							2
3							3
4							4
5							5
6							6
7							7
8							8
9							9
10							10
11							11
12							12
13							13
14							14
15							15
16							16
17							17
18							18
19							19
20							20
21							21
22							22
23							23

1. and 2.

GENERAL LEDGER

ACCOUNT Cash ACCOUNT NO. 101

DATE		ITEM	POST. REF.	DEBIT	CREDIT	BALANCE DEBIT	BALANCE CREDIT
20-- Jan.	31	Balance	✓			3 6 7 3 00	

Name ______________________________

Problem 6-8A (Continued)

ACCOUNT Accounts Receivable ACCOUNT NO. 122

DATE		ITEM	POST. REF.	DEBIT	CREDIT	BALANCE DEBIT	BALANCE CREDIT
20-- Jan.	31	Balance	✓			1 4 5 0 00	

ACCOUNT Supplies ACCOUNT NO. 141

DATE		ITEM	POST. REF.	DEBIT	CREDIT	BALANCE DEBIT	BALANCE CREDIT
20-- Jan.	31	Balance	✓			7 0 0 00	

ACCOUNT Prepaid Insurance ACCOUNT NO. 145

DATE		ITEM	POST. REF.	DEBIT	CREDIT	BALANCE DEBIT	BALANCE CREDIT
20-- Jan.	31	Balance	✓			9 0 0 00	

ACCOUNT Delivery Equipment ACCOUNT NO. 185

DATE		ITEM	POST. REF.	DEBIT	CREDIT	BALANCE DEBIT	BALANCE CREDIT
20-- Jan.	31	Balance	✓			3 2 0 0 00	

ACCOUNT Accumulated Depreciation—Delivery Equipment ACCOUNT NO. 185.1

DATE		ITEM	POST. REF.	DEBIT	CREDIT	BALANCE DEBIT	BALANCE CREDIT

Problem 6-8A (Continued)

ACCOUNT Accounts Payable ACCOUNT NO. 202

DATE		ITEM	POST. REF.	DEBIT	CREDIT	BALANCE DEBIT	BALANCE CREDIT
20-- Jan.	31	Balance	✓				1,200.00

ACCOUNT Wages Payable ACCOUNT NO. 219

DATE		ITEM	POST. REF.	DEBIT	CREDIT	BALANCE DEBIT	BALANCE CREDIT

ACCOUNT Don Megaffin, Capital ACCOUNT NO. 311

DATE		ITEM	POST. REF.	DEBIT	CREDIT	BALANCE DEBIT	BALANCE CREDIT
20-- Jan.	31	Balance	✓				8,000.00

ACCOUNT Don Megaffin, Drawing ACCOUNT NO. 312

DATE		ITEM	POST. REF.	DEBIT	CREDIT	BALANCE DEBIT	BALANCE CREDIT
20-- Jan.	31	Balance	✓			1,100.00	

ACCOUNT Income Summary ACCOUNT NO. 313

DATE		ITEM	POST. REF.	DEBIT	CREDIT	BALANCE DEBIT	BALANCE CREDIT

Problem 6-8A (Continued)

ACCOUNT Repair Fees ACCOUNT NO. 401

DATE		ITEM	POST. REF.	DEBIT	CREDIT	BALANCE DEBIT	BALANCE CREDIT
20-- Jan.	31	Balance	✓				4,700.00

ACCOUNT Wages Expense ACCOUNT NO. 511

DATE		ITEM	POST. REF.	DEBIT	CREDIT	BALANCE DEBIT	BALANCE CREDIT
20-- Jan.	31	Balance	✓			1,750.00	

ACCOUNT Advertising Expense ACCOUNT NO. 512

DATE		ITEM	POST. REF.	DEBIT	CREDIT	BALANCE DEBIT	BALANCE CREDIT
20-- Jan.	31	Balance	✓			200.00	

ACCOUNT Rent Expense ACCOUNT NO. 521

DATE		ITEM	POST. REF.	DEBIT	CREDIT	BALANCE DEBIT	BALANCE CREDIT
20-- Jan.	31	Balance	✓			640.00	

ACCOUNT Supplies Expense ACCOUNT NO. 523

DATE		ITEM	POST. REF.	DEBIT	CREDIT	BALANCE DEBIT	BALANCE CREDIT

Problem 6-8A (Continued)

ACCOUNT Phone Expense ACCOUNT NO. 525

DATE		ITEM	POST. REF.	DEBIT	CREDIT	BALANCE DEBIT	BALANCE CREDIT
20-- Jan.	31	Balance	✓			50 00	

ACCOUNT Insurance Expense ACCOUNT NO. 535

DATE		ITEM	POST. REF.	DEBIT	CREDIT	BALANCE DEBIT	BALANCE CREDIT

ACCOUNT Gas and Oil Expense ACCOUNT NO. 538

DATE		ITEM	POST. REF.	DEBIT	CREDIT	BALANCE DEBIT	BALANCE CREDIT
20-- Jan.	31	Balance	✓			200 00	

ACCOUNT Depreciation Expense—Delivery Equipment ACCOUNT NO. 541

DATE		ITEM	POST. REF.	DEBIT	CREDIT	BALANCE DEBIT	BALANCE CREDIT

ACCOUNT Miscellaneous Expense ACCOUNT NO. 549

DATE		ITEM	POST. REF.	DEBIT	CREDIT	BALANCE DEBIT	BALANCE CREDIT
20-- Jan.	31	Balance	✓			37 00	

Problem 6-8A (Concluded)

3.

ACCOUNT TITLE	ACCT. NO.	DEBIT BALANCE	CREDIT BALANCE

Problem 6-9A

Exercise 6-1B

Exercise 6-2B

Name ______________________________

Exercise 6-3B

Exercise 6-4B

GENERAL JOURNAL

PAGE 1

DATE	DESCRIPTION	POST. REF.	DEBIT	CREDIT

Name ______________________________

Exercise 6-4B (Concluded)

Exercise 6-5B

GENERAL JOURNAL

PAGE

DATE		DESCRIPTION	POST. REF.	DEBIT	CREDIT

Exercise 6-5B (Concluded)

Cash			101
Bal.	600		

Accounts Receivable			122
Bal.	1,800		

Wages Payable			219
		Bal.	500

Mark Thrasher, Capital			311
		Bal.	8,000

Mark Thrasher, Drawing			312
Bal.	800		

Income Summary			313

Lawn Service Fees			401
		Bal.	5,000

Wages Expense			511
Bal.	400		

Advertising Expense			512
Bal.	600		

Travel Expense			515
Bal.	100		

Supplies Expense			524
Bal.	900		

Insurance Expense			535
Bal.	300		

Postage Expense			536
Bal.	40		

Gas and Oil Expense			538
Bal.	700		

Miscellaneous Expense			549
Bal.	200		

Exercise 6-6B

GENERAL JOURNAL

PAGE

DATE		DESCRIPTION	POST. REF.	DEBIT	CREDIT

Exercise 6-6B (Concluded)

Accum. Depr.—Office Equip. 181.1

	Bal. 110

Wages Payable 219

	Bal. 260

Raquel Zapata, Capital 311

	Bal. 6,000

Raquel Zapata, Drawing 312

Bal. 2,000	

Income Summary 313

Referral Fees 401

	Bal. 2,813

Wages Expense 511

Bal. 1,080	

Advertising Expense 512

Bal. 34	

Rent Expense 521

Bal. 900	

Supplies Expense 523

Bal. 322	

Phone Expense 525

Bal. 133	

Utilities Expense 533

Bal. 102	

Insurance Expense 535

Bal. 120	

Gas and Oil Expense 538

Bal. 88	

Depr. Exp.—Office Equip. 541

Bal. 110	

Miscellaneous Expense 549

Bal. 98	

Problem 6-7B

1.

2.

Problem 6-7B (Concluded)

3.

Problem 6-8B

1.

GENERAL JOURNAL PAGE 10

DATE		DESCRIPTION	POST. REF.	DEBIT	CREDIT

Problem 6-8B (Continued)

2.

GENERAL JOURNAL

PAGE 11

	DATE		DESCRIPTION	POST. REF.	DEBIT	CREDIT	
1							1
2							2
3							3
4							4
5							5
6							6
7							7
8							8
9							9
10							10
11							11
12							12
13							13
14							14
15							15
16							16
17							17
18							18
19							19
20							20
21							21
22							22
23							23

1. and 2.

GENERAL LEDGER

ACCOUNT Cash ACCOUNT NO. 101

DATE		ITEM	POST. REF.	DEBIT	CREDIT	BALANCE DEBIT	BALANCE CREDIT
20-- June	30	Balance	✓			5,285.00	

Problem 6-8B (Continued)

ACCOUNT Accounts Receivable ACCOUNT NO. 122

DATE		ITEM	POST. REF.	DEBIT	CREDIT	BALANCE DEBIT	BALANCE CREDIT
20-- June	30	Balance	✓			1,075.00	

ACCOUNT Supplies ACCOUNT NO. 141

DATE		ITEM	POST. REF.	DEBIT	CREDIT	BALANCE DEBIT	BALANCE CREDIT
20-- June	30	Balance	✓			750.00	

ACCOUNT Prepaid Insurance ACCOUNT NO. 145

DATE		ITEM	POST. REF.	DEBIT	CREDIT	BALANCE DEBIT	BALANCE CREDIT
20-- June	30	Balance	✓			500.00	

ACCOUNT Office Equipment ACCOUNT NO. 181

DATE		ITEM	POST. REF.	DEBIT	CREDIT	BALANCE DEBIT	BALANCE CREDIT
20-- June	30	Balance	✓			2,200.00	

ACCOUNT Accumulated Depreciation—Office Equipment ACCOUNT NO. 181.1

DATE		ITEM	POST. REF.	DEBIT	CREDIT	BALANCE DEBIT	BALANCE CREDIT

Problem 6-8B (Continued)

ACCOUNT Accounts Payable ACCOUNT NO. 202

DATE		ITEM	POST. REF.	DEBIT	CREDIT	BALANCE DEBIT	BALANCE CREDIT
20-- June	30	Balance	✓				1,500 00

ACCOUNT Wages Payable ACCOUNT NO. 219

DATE		ITEM	POST. REF.	DEBIT	CREDIT	BALANCE DEBIT	BALANCE CREDIT

ACCOUNT Juanita Alvarez, Capital ACCOUNT NO. 311

DATE		ITEM	POST. REF.	DEBIT	CREDIT	BALANCE DEBIT	BALANCE CREDIT
20-- June	30	Balance	✓				7,000 00

ACCOUNT Juanita Alvarez, Drawing ACCOUNT NO. 312

DATE		ITEM	POST. REF.	DEBIT	CREDIT	BALANCE DEBIT	BALANCE CREDIT
20-- June	30	Balance	✓			800 00	

ACCOUNT Income Summary ACCOUNT NO. 313

DATE		ITEM	POST. REF.	DEBIT	CREDIT	BALANCE DEBIT	BALANCE CREDIT

Problem 6-8B (Continued)

ACCOUNT Consulting Fees ACCOUNT NO. 401

DATE		ITEM	POST. REF.	DEBIT	CREDIT	BALANCE DEBIT	BALANCE CREDIT
20-- June	30	Balance	✓				4,204.00

ACCOUNT Wages Expense ACCOUNT NO. 511

DATE		ITEM	POST. REF.	DEBIT	CREDIT	BALANCE DEBIT	BALANCE CREDIT
20-- June	30	Balance	✓			1,400.00	

ACCOUNT Advertising Expense ACCOUNT NO. 512

DATE		ITEM	POST. REF.	DEBIT	CREDIT	BALANCE DEBIT	BALANCE CREDIT
20-- June	30	Balance	✓			60.00	

ACCOUNT Rent Expense ACCOUNT NO. 521

DATE		ITEM	POST. REF.	DEBIT	CREDIT	BALANCE DEBIT	BALANCE CREDIT
20-- June	30	Balance	✓			500.00	

ACCOUNT Supplies Expense ACCOUNT NO. 523

DATE		ITEM	POST. REF.	DEBIT	CREDIT	BALANCE DEBIT	BALANCE CREDIT

Problem 6-8B (Continued)

ACCOUNT Phone Expense ACCOUNT NO. 525

DATE		ITEM	POST. REF.	DEBIT	CREDIT	BALANCE DEBIT	BALANCE CREDIT
20-- June	30	Balance	✓			46 00	

ACCOUNT Electricity Expense ACCOUNT NO. 533

DATE		ITEM	POST. REF.	DEBIT	CREDIT	BALANCE DEBIT	BALANCE CREDIT
20-- June	30	Balance	✓			39 00	

ACCOUNT Insurance Expense ACCOUNT NO. 535

DATE		ITEM	POST. REF.	DEBIT	CREDIT	BALANCE DEBIT	BALANCE CREDIT

ACCOUNT Gas and Oil Expense ACCOUNT NO. 538

DATE		ITEM	POST. REF.	DEBIT	CREDIT	BALANCE DEBIT	BALANCE CREDIT
20-- June	30	Balance	✓			28 00	

ACCOUNT Depreciation Expense—Office Equipment ACCOUNT NO. 541

DATE		ITEM	POST. REF.	DEBIT	CREDIT	BALANCE DEBIT	BALANCE CREDIT

Problem 6-8B (Concluded)

ACCOUNT Miscellaneous Expense ACCOUNT NO. 549

DATE		ITEM	POST. REF.	DEBIT	CREDIT	BALANCE DEBIT	BALANCE CREDIT
20-- June	30	Balance	✓			21 00	

3.

ACCOUNT TITLE	ACCT. NO.	DEBIT BALANCE	CREDIT BALANCE

Problem 6-9B

Mastery Problem

GENERAL JOURNAL

PAGE 4

	DATE		DESCRIPTION	POST. REF.	DEBIT	CREDIT	
1							1
2							2
3							3
4							4
5							5
6							6
7							7
8							8
9							9
10							10
11							11
12							12
13							13
14							14
15							15
16							16
17							17
18							18
19							19
20							20
21							21
22							22
23							23
24							24
25							25
26							26
27							27
28							28
29							29
30							30
31							31
32							32
33							33
34							34
35							35
36							36

Mastery Problem (Continued)

Mastery Problem (Concluded)

Challenge Problem

Challenge Problem (Concluded)

Exercise 6Apx-1A

a. ____________ g. ____________

b. ____________ h. ____________

c. ____________ i. ____________

d. ____________ j. ____________

e. ____________ k. ____________

f. ____________

Problem 6Apx-2A

Exercise 6Apx-1B

a. ____________________

b. ____________________

c. ____________________

d. ____________________

e. ____________________

f. ____________________

g. ____________________

h. ____________________

i. ____________________

j. ____________________

k. ____________________

Problem 6Apx-2B

Name ______________________________

Comprehensive Problem 1: The Accounting Cycle

1.

GENERAL JOURNAL

PAGE 1

	DATE		DESCRIPTION	POST. REF.	DEBIT	CREDIT	
1							1
2							2
3							3
4							4
5							5
6							6
7							7
8							8
9							9
10							10
11							11
12							12
13							13
14							14
15							15
16							16
17							17
18							18
19							19
20							20
21							21
22							22
23							23
24							24
25							25
26							26
27							27
28							28
29							29
30							30
31							31
32							32
33							33
34							34

Comprehensive Problem 1 (Continued)

GENERAL JOURNAL

PAGE 2

DATE	DESCRIPTION	POST. REF.	DEBIT	CREDIT

Name ______________________________

Comprehensive Problem 1 (Continued)

GENERAL JOURNAL

PAGE 3

	DATE	DESCRIPTION	POST. REF.	DEBIT	CREDIT	
1						1
2						2
3						3
4						4
5						5
6						6
7						7
8						8
9						9
10						10
11						11
12						12
13						13
14						14
15						15
16						16
17						17
18						18
19						19
20						20
21						21
22						22
23						23
24						24
25						25
26						26
27						27
28						28
29						29
30						30
31						31
32						32
33						33
34						34
35						35

Comprehensive Problem 1 (Continued)

GENERAL JOURNAL

PAGE 4

	DATE		DESCRIPTION	POST. REF.	DEBIT	CREDIT	
1							1
2							2
3							3
4							4
5							5
6							6
7							7
8							8
9							9
10							10
11							11

2., 6., and 11.

GENERAL LEDGER

ACCOUNT Cash ACCOUNT NO. 101

DATE		ITEM	POST. REF.	DEBIT	CREDIT	BALANCE	
						DEBIT	CREDIT

Comprehensive Problem 1 (Continued)

ACCOUNT Office Supplies ACCOUNT NO. 142

DATE		ITEM	POST. REF.	DEBIT	CREDIT	BALANCE	
						DEBIT	CREDIT

ACCOUNT Food Supplies ACCOUNT NO. 144

DATE		ITEM	POST. REF.	DEBIT	CREDIT	BALANCE	
						DEBIT	CREDIT

ACCOUNT Prepaid Insurance ACCOUNT NO. 145

DATE		ITEM	POST. REF.	DEBIT	CREDIT	BALANCE	
						DEBIT	CREDIT

ACCOUNT Fishing Boats ACCOUNT NO. 181

DATE		ITEM	POST. REF.	DEBIT	CREDIT	BALANCE	
						DEBIT	CREDIT

Comprehensive Problem 1 (Continued)

ACCOUNT Accumulated Depreciation—Fishing Boats ACCOUNT NO. 181.1

DATE		ITEM	POST. REF.	DEBIT	CREDIT	BALANCE	
						DEBIT	CREDIT

ACCOUNT Accounts Payable ACCOUNT NO. 202

DATE		ITEM	POST. REF.	DEBIT	CREDIT	BALANCE	
						DEBIT	CREDIT

ACCOUNT Wages Payable ACCOUNT NO. 219

DATE		ITEM	POST. REF.	DEBIT	CREDIT	BALANCE	
						DEBIT	CREDIT

ACCOUNT Bob Night, Capital ACCOUNT NO. 311

DATE		ITEM	POST. REF.	DEBIT	CREDIT	BALANCE	
						DEBIT	CREDIT

Name ______________________________

Comprehensive Problem 1 (Continued)

ACCOUNT Bob Night, Drawing ACCOUNT NO. 312

DATE	ITEM	POST. REF.	DEBIT	CREDIT	BALANCE DEBIT	BALANCE CREDIT

ACCOUNT Income Summary ACCOUNT NO. 313

DATE	ITEM	POST. REF.	DEBIT	CREDIT	BALANCE DEBIT	BALANCE CREDIT

ACCOUNT Registration Fees ACCOUNT NO. 401

DATE	ITEM	POST. REF.	DEBIT	CREDIT	BALANCE DEBIT	BALANCE CREDIT

Comprehensive Problem 1 (Continued)

ACCOUNT Wages Expense ACCOUNT NO. 511

DATE	ITEM	POST. REF.	DEBIT	CREDIT	BALANCE DEBIT	BALANCE CREDIT

ACCOUNT Rent Expense ACCOUNT NO. 521

DATE	ITEM	POST. REF.	DEBIT	CREDIT	BALANCE DEBIT	BALANCE CREDIT

ACCOUNT Office Supplies Expense ACCOUNT NO. 523

DATE	ITEM	POST. REF.	DEBIT	CREDIT	BALANCE DEBIT	BALANCE CREDIT

ACCOUNT Food Supplies Expense ACCOUNT NO. 524

DATE	ITEM	POST. REF.	DEBIT	CREDIT	BALANCE DEBIT	BALANCE CREDIT

Comprehensive Problem 1 (Continued)

ACCOUNT Phone Expense ACCOUNT NO. 525

DATE	ITEM	POST. REF.	DEBIT	CREDIT	BALANCE DEBIT	BALANCE CREDIT

ACCOUNT Utilities Expense ACCOUNT NO. 533

DATE	ITEM	POST. REF.	DEBIT	CREDIT	BALANCE DEBIT	BALANCE CREDIT

ACCOUNT Insurance Expense ACCOUNT NO. 535

DATE	ITEM	POST. REF.	DEBIT	CREDIT	BALANCE DEBIT	BALANCE CREDIT

ACCOUNT Postage Expense ACCOUNT NO. 536

DATE	ITEM	POST. REF.	DEBIT	CREDIT	BALANCE DEBIT	BALANCE CREDIT

ACCOUNT Depreciation Expense—Fishing Boats ACCOUNT NO. 542

DATE	ITEM	POST. REF.	DEBIT	CREDIT	BALANCE DEBIT	BALANCE CREDIT

Comprehensive Problem 1 (Continued)

3. and 4.

	ACCOUNT TITLE	TRIAL BALANCE		ADJUSTMENTS	
		DEBIT	CREDIT	DEBIT	CREDIT
1					
2					
3					
4					
5					
6					
7					
8					
9					
10					
11					
12					
13					
14					
15					
16					
17					
18					
19					
20					
21					
22					
23					
24					
25					
26					
27					
28					
29					
30					
31					

Name ______________________________

Comprehensive Problem 1 (Continued)

____

____

____

ADJUSTED TRIAL BALANCE		INCOME STATEMENT		BALANCE SHEET		
DEBIT	CREDIT	DEBIT	CREDIT	DEBIT	CREDIT	
						1
						2
						3
						4
						5
						6
						7
						8
						9
						10
						11
						12
						13
						14
						15
						16
						17
						18
						19
						20
						21
						22
						23
						24
						25
						26
						27
						28
						29
						30
						31

Comprehensive Problem 1 (Continued)

7.

8.

Comprehensive Problem 1 (Continued)

9.

Comprehensive Problem 1 (Continued)

5. and 10.

GENERAL JOURNAL

PAGE 5

	DATE		DESCRIPTION	POST. REF.	DEBIT	CREDIT	
1							1
2							2
3							3
4							4
5							5
6							6
7							7
8							8
9							9
10							10
11							11
12							12
13							13
14							14
15							15
16							16
17							17
18							18
19							19
20							20
21							21
22							22
23							23
24							24
25							25
26							26
27							27
28							28
29							29
30							30
31							31
32							32
33							33
34							34
35							35

Comprehensive Problem 1 (Concluded)

GENERAL JOURNAL

PAGE 6

	DATE		DESCRIPTION	POST. REF.	DEBIT	CREDIT	
1							1
2							2
3							3
4							4
5							5
6							6
7							7
8							8
9							9

12.

ACCOUNT	ACCT. NO.	DEBIT BALANCE	CREDIT BALANCE

Comprehensive Problem 1, Period 2: The Accounting Cycle

1.

GENERAL JOURNAL

PAGE 5

	DATE		DESCRIPTION	POST. REF.	DEBIT	CREDIT	
1							1
2							2
3							3
4							4
5							5
6							6
7							7
8							8
9							9
10							10
11							11
12							12
13							13
14							14
15							15
16							16
17							17
18							18
19							19
20							20
21							21
22							22
23							23
24							24
25							25
26							26
27							27
28							28
29							29
30							30
31							31
32							32
33							33
34							34
35							35

Comprehensive Problem 1, Period 2 (Continued)

GENERAL JOURNAL

PAGE 6

DATE	DESCRIPTION	POST. REF.	DEBIT	CREDIT

Comprehensive Problem 1, Period 2 (Continued)

GENERAL JOURNAL

PAGE 7

	DATE	DESCRIPTION	POST. REF.	DEBIT	CREDIT	
1						1
2						2
3						3
4						4
5						5
6						6
7						7
8						8
9						9
10						10
11						11
12						12
13						13
14						14
15						15
16						16
17						17
18						18
19						19
20						20
21						21
22						22
23						23
24						24
25						25
26						26
27						27
28						28
29						29
30						30
31						31
32						32
33						33
34						34

Comprehensive Problem 1, Period 2 (Continued)

2., 6., and 11.

GENERAL LEDGER

ACCOUNT Cash ACCOUNT NO. 101

DATE		ITEM	POST. REF.	DEBIT	CREDIT	BALANCE DEBIT	BALANCE CREDIT
20-- Apr.	30	Balance	✓			130,650.00	

ACCOUNT Accounts Receivable ACCOUNT NO. 122

DATE		ITEM	POST. REF.	DEBIT	CREDIT	BALANCE DEBIT	BALANCE CREDIT

Comprehensive Problem 1, Period 2 (Continued)

ACCOUNT Office Supplies ACCOUNT NO. 142

DATE		ITEM	POST. REF.	DEBIT	CREDIT	BALANCE DEBIT	BALANCE CREDIT
20-- Apr.	30	Balance	✓			100 00	

ACCOUNT Food Supplies ACCOUNT NO. 144

DATE		ITEM	POST. REF.	DEBIT	CREDIT	BALANCE DEBIT	BALANCE CREDIT
20-- Apr.	30	Balance	✓			8000 00	

ACCOUNT Prepaid Insurance ACCOUNT NO. 145

DATE		ITEM	POST. REF.	DEBIT	CREDIT	BALANCE DEBIT	BALANCE CREDIT
20-- Apr.	30	Balance	✓			7500 00	

ACCOUNT Prepaid Subscriptions ACCOUNT NO. 146

DATE		ITEM	POST. REF.	DEBIT	CREDIT	BALANCE DEBIT	BALANCE CREDIT

Comprehensive Problem 1, Period 2 (Continued)

ACCOUNT Land ACCOUNT NO. 161

DATE		ITEM	POST. REF.	DEBIT	CREDIT	BALANCE DEBIT	BALANCE CREDIT

ACCOUNT Buildings ACCOUNT NO. 171

DATE		ITEM	POST. REF.	DEBIT	CREDIT	BALANCE DEBIT	BALANCE CREDIT

ACCOUNT Accumulated Depreciation—Buildings ACCOUNT NO. 171.1

DATE		ITEM	POST. REF.	DEBIT	CREDIT	BALANCE DEBIT	BALANCE CREDIT

ACCOUNT Fishing Boats ACCOUNT NO. 181

DATE		ITEM	POST. REF.	DEBIT	CREDIT	BALANCE DEBIT	BALANCE CREDIT
20-- Apr.	30	Balance	✓			60,000.00	

Comprehensive Problem 1, Period 2 (Continued)

ACCOUNT Accumulated Depreciation—Fishing Boats ACCOUNT NO. 181.1

DATE		ITEM	POST. REF.	DEBIT	CREDIT	BALANCE DEBIT	BALANCE CREDIT
20-- Apr.	30	Balance	✓				1,000 00

ACCOUNT Surround Sound System ACCOUNT NO. 182

DATE		ITEM	POST. REF.	DEBIT	CREDIT	BALANCE DEBIT	BALANCE CREDIT

ACCOUNT Accumulated Depreciation—Surround Sound System ACCOUNT NO. 182.1

DATE		ITEM	POST. REF.	DEBIT	CREDIT	BALANCE DEBIT	BALANCE CREDIT

ACCOUNT Big Screen TV ACCOUNT NO. 183

DATE		ITEM	POST. REF.	DEBIT	CREDIT	BALANCE DEBIT	BALANCE CREDIT

ACCOUNT Accumulated Depreciation—Big Screen TV ACCOUNT NO. 183.1

DATE		ITEM	POST. REF.	DEBIT	CREDIT	BALANCE DEBIT	BALANCE CREDIT

Comprehensive Problem 1, Period 2 (Continued)

ACCOUNT Accounts Payable ACCOUNT NO. 202

DATE		ITEM	POST. REF.	DEBIT	CREDIT	BALANCE DEBIT	BALANCE CREDIT
20-- Apr.	30	Balance	✓				66,500.00

ACCOUNT Wages Payable ACCOUNT NO. 219

DATE		ITEM	POST. REF.	DEBIT	CREDIT	BALANCE DEBIT	BALANCE CREDIT
20-- Apr.	30	Balance	✓				5,000.00

ACCOUNT Bob Night, Capital ACCOUNT NO. 311

DATE		ITEM	POST. REF.	DEBIT	CREDIT	BALANCE DEBIT	BALANCE CREDIT
20-- Apr.	30	Balance	✓				138,250.00

ACCOUNT Bob Night, Drawing ACCOUNT NO. 312

DATE		ITEM	POST. REF.	DEBIT	CREDIT	BALANCE DEBIT	BALANCE CREDIT

Comprehensive Problem 1, Period 2 (Continued)

ACCOUNT Income Summary ACCOUNT NO. 313

DATE		ITEM	POST. REF.	DEBIT	CREDIT	BALANCE	
						DEBIT	CREDIT

ACCOUNT Registration Fees ACCOUNT NO. 401

DATE		ITEM	POST. REF.	DEBIT	CREDIT	BALANCE	
						DEBIT	CREDIT

ACCOUNT Vending Commission Revenue ACCOUNT NO. 404

DATE		ITEM	POST. REF.	DEBIT	CREDIT	BALANCE	
						DEBIT	CREDIT

ACCOUNT Wages Expense ACCOUNT NO. 511

DATE		ITEM	POST. REF.	DEBIT	CREDIT	BALANCE	
						DEBIT	CREDIT

Comprehensive Problem 1, Period 2 (Continued)

ACCOUNT Advertising Expense ACCOUNT NO. 512

DATE		ITEM	POST. REF.	DEBIT	CREDIT	BALANCE DEBIT	BALANCE CREDIT

ACCOUNT Rent Expense ACCOUNT NO. 521

DATE		ITEM	POST. REF.	DEBIT	CREDIT	BALANCE DEBIT	BALANCE CREDIT

ACCOUNT Office Supplies Expense ACCOUNT NO. 523

DATE		ITEM	POST. REF.	DEBIT	CREDIT	BALANCE DEBIT	BALANCE CREDIT

ACCOUNT Food Supplies Expense ACCOUNT NO. 524

DATE		ITEM	POST. REF.	DEBIT	CREDIT	BALANCE DEBIT	BALANCE CREDIT

Comprehensive Problem 1, Period 2 (Continued)

ACCOUNT Phone Expense ACCOUNT NO. 525

DATE		ITEM	POST. REF.	DEBIT	CREDIT	BALANCE DEBIT	BALANCE CREDIT

ACCOUNT Utilities Expense ACCOUNT NO. 533

DATE		ITEM	POST. REF.	DEBIT	CREDIT	BALANCE DEBIT	BALANCE CREDIT

ACCOUNT Insurance Expense ACCOUNT NO. 535

DATE		ITEM	POST. REF.	DEBIT	CREDIT	BALANCE DEBIT	BALANCE CREDIT

ACCOUNT Postage Expense ACCOUNT NO. 536

DATE		ITEM	POST. REF.	DEBIT	CREDIT	BALANCE DEBIT	BALANCE CREDIT

Comprehensive Problem 1, Period 2 (Continued)

ACCOUNT Repair Expense ACCOUNT NO. 537

DATE		ITEM	POST. REF.	DEBIT	CREDIT	BALANCE	
						DEBIT	CREDIT

ACCOUNT Depreciation Expense—Buildings ACCOUNT NO. 540

DATE		ITEM	POST. REF.	DEBIT	CREDIT	BALANCE	
						DEBIT	CREDIT

ACCOUNT Depreciation Expense—Surround Sound System ACCOUNT NO. 541

DATE		ITEM	POST. REF.	DEBIT	CREDIT	BALANCE	
						DEBIT	CREDIT

ACCOUNT Depreciation Expense—Fishing Boats ACCOUNT NO. 542

DATE		ITEM	POST. REF.	DEBIT	CREDIT	BALANCE	
						DEBIT	CREDIT

Comprehensive Problem 1, Period 2 (Continued)

ACCOUNT Depreciation Expense—Big Screen TV ACCOUNT NO. 543

DATE		ITEM	POST. REF.	DEBIT	CREDIT	BALANCE DEBIT	BALANCE CREDIT

ACCOUNT Satellite Programming Expense ACCOUNT NO. 546

DATE		ITEM	POST. REF.	DEBIT	CREDIT	BALANCE DEBIT	BALANCE CREDIT

ACCOUNT Subscriptions Expense ACCOUNT NO. 548

DATE		ITEM	POST. REF.	DEBIT	CREDIT	BALANCE DEBIT	BALANCE CREDIT

Comprehensive Problem 1, Period 2 (Continued)
3. and 4.

	ACCOUNT TITLE	TRIAL BALANCE		ADJUSTMENTS	
		DEBIT	CREDIT	DEBIT	CREDIT
1					
2					
3					
4					
5					
6					
7					
8					
9					
10					
11					
12					
13					
14					
15					
16					
17					
18					
19					
20					
21					
22					
23					
24					
25					
26					
27					
28					
29					
30					
31					
32					
33					
34					
35					
36					
37					
38					
39					
40					

Comprehensive Problem 1, Period 2 (Continued)

ADJUSTED TRIAL BALANCE		INCOME STATEMENT		BALANCE SHEET		
DEBIT	CREDIT	DEBIT	CREDIT	DEBIT	CREDIT	
						1
						2
						3
						4
						5
						6
						7
						8
						9
						10
						11
						12
						13
						14
						15
						16
						17
						18
						19
						20
						21
						22
						23
						24
						25
						26
						27
						28
						29
						30
						31
						32
						33
						34
						35
						36
						37
						38
						39
						40

Comprehensive Problem 1, Period 2 (Continued)

5.

GENERAL JOURNAL

PAGE 8

DATE		DESCRIPTION	POST. REF.	DEBIT	CREDIT

Comprehensive Problem 1, Period 2 (Continued)

7.

8.

Comprehensive Problem 1, Period 2 (Continued)

9.

Name ____________________

Comprehensive Problem 1, Period 2 (Continued)

10.

GENERAL JOURNAL

PAGE 9

DATE		DESCRIPTION	POST. REF.	DEBIT	CREDIT

Comprehensive Problem 1, Period 2 (Concluded)

12.

ACCOUNT TITLE	ACCT. NO.	DEBIT BALANCE	CREDIT BALANCE

Exercise 7-1A

1. ____________________
2. ____________________
3. ____________________
4. ____________________
5. ____________________
6. ____________________
7. ____________________

Exercise 7-2A

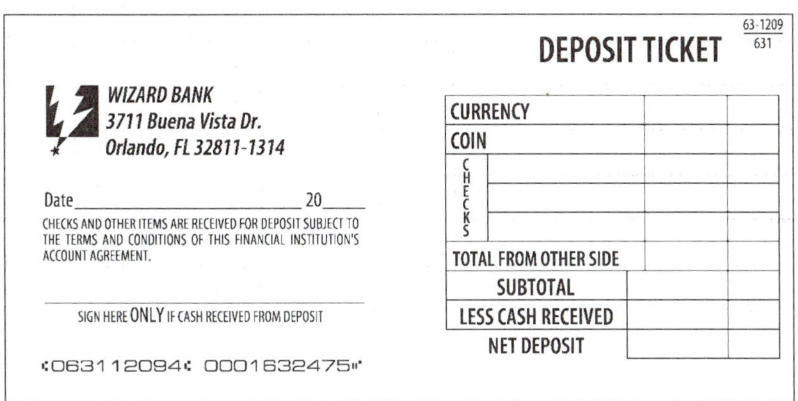

DEPOSIT TICKET 63-1209/631

WIZARD BANK
3711 Buena Vista Dr.
Orlando, FL 32811-1314

Date ______________________ 20____

CHECKS AND OTHER ITEMS ARE RECEIVED FOR DEPOSIT SUBJECT TO THE TERMS AND CONDITIONS OF THIS FINANCIAL INSTITUTION'S ACCOUNT AGREEMENT.

SIGN HERE ONLY IF CASH RECEIVED FROM DEPOSIT

⑆063112094⑆ 0001632475⑈

CURRENCY		
COIN		
CHECKS		
TOTAL FROM OTHER SIDE		
SUBTOTAL		
LESS CASH RECEIVED		
NET DEPOSIT		

Exercise 7-3A

No. 1

DATE ______________ 20____
TO ____________________
FOR ____________________

ACCT. ____________________

	DOLLARS	CENTS
BAL BRO'T FOR'D		
AMT. DEPOSITED		
TOTAL		
AMT. THIS CHECK		
BAL CAR'D FOR'D		

No. 1 63-1209/631

______________________ 20________

PAY TO THE ORDER OF ______________________________________ $ __________

____ Dollars

WIZARD BANK
3711 Buena Vista Dr.
Orlando, FL 32811-1314

FOR CLASSROOM USE ONLY

MEMO ______________________ BY ______________________

⑆063112094⑆ 0001632475⑈

Exercise 7-4A

	Ending Bank Balance	Ending Checkbook Balance
1.		
2.		
3.		
4.		
5.		
6.		
7.		

Exercise 7-5A

GENERAL JOURNAL

PAGE

	DATE		DESCRIPTION	POST. REF.	DEBIT	CREDIT	
1							1
2							2
3							3
4							4
5							5
6							6
7							7
8							8
9							9
10							10
11							11
12							12
13							13
14							14
15							15
16							16
17							17
18							18
19							19
20							20
21							21

Name ______________________________

Exercise 7-6A

GENERAL JOURNAL

PAGE

DATE		DESCRIPTION	POST. REF.	DEBIT	CREDIT

Exercise 7-7A

GENERAL JOURNAL

PAGE

DATE		DESCRIPTION	POST. REF.	DEBIT	CREDIT

Name ________________________________

Problem 7-8A

1.

Problem 7-8A (Concluded)

2.

GENERAL JOURNAL

PAGE

	DATE		DESCRIPTION	POST. REF.	DEBIT	CREDIT	
1							1
2							2
3							3
4							4
5							5
6							6
7							7
8							8
9							9
10							10
11							11
12							12
13							13
14							14
15							15

Problem 7-9A

1.

Problem 7-9A (Concluded)

2.

GENERAL JOURNAL

PAGE

	DATE		DESCRIPTION	POST. REF.	DEBIT	CREDIT	
1							1
2							2
3							3
4							4
5							5
6							6
7							7
8							8
9							9
10							10
11							11
12							12
13							13
14							14
15							15
16							16
17							17
18							18
19							19

Problem 7-10A

1. and 3.

GENERAL JOURNAL

PAGE

	DATE		DESCRIPTION	POST. REF.	DEBIT	CREDIT	
1							1
2							2
3							3
4							4
5							5
6							6
7							7
8							8
9							9
10							10
11							11
12							12
13							13

Problem 7-10A (Concluded)

2. and 3.

PETTY CASH PAYMENTS FOR MONTH OF 20-- PAGE

					DISTRIBUTION OF PAYMENTS								
	DAY	DESCRIPTION	VOU. NO.	TOTAL AMOUNT	OFFICE SUPPLIES	POSTAGE EXPENSE	CHARIT. CONTRIB. EXPENSE	PHONE EXPENSE	TRAVEL & ENTER. EXPENSE	MISC. EXPENSE	ACCOUNT	AMOUNT	
1													1
2													2
3													3
4													4
5													5
6													6
7													7
8													8
9													9
10													10
11													11
12													12
13													13
14													14
15													15
16													16
17													17
18													18
19													19
20													20
21													21
22													22

Name ______________________________

Problem 7-11A

1.

GENERAL JOURNAL

PAGE 8

	DATE		DESCRIPTION	POST. REF.	DEBIT	CREDIT	
1							1
2							2
3							3
4							
5							
6							6
7							7
8							8
9							9
10							10
11							11
12							12
13							13
14							14
15							15
16							16
17							17
18							18
19							19
20							20
21							21
22							22
23							23

2.

ACCOUNT ______________________________ ACCOUNT NO. __________

DATE		ITEM	POST. REF.	DEBIT	CREDIT	BALANCE	
						DEBIT	CREDIT

3. The balance represents:

____

Exercise 7-1B

1. ____________________
2. ____________________
3. ____________________
4. ____________________
5. ____________________
6. ____________________
7. ____________________

Exercise 7-2B

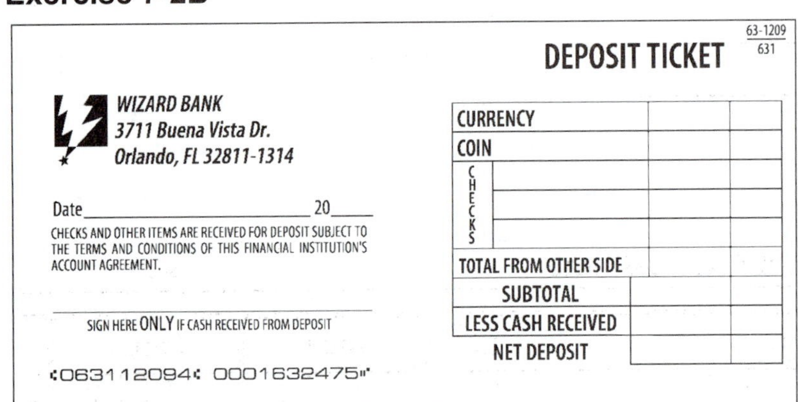

DEPOSIT TICKET

63-1209
631

WIZARD BANK
3711 Buena Vista Dr.
Orlando, FL 32811-1314

Date ____________________ 20____

CHECKS AND OTHER ITEMS ARE RECEIVED FOR DEPOSIT SUBJECT TO THE TERMS AND CONDITIONS OF THIS FINANCIAL INSTITUTION'S ACCOUNT AGREEMENT.

SIGN HERE ONLY IF CASH RECEIVED FROM DEPOSIT

⑆063112094⑆ 0001632475⑈

CURRENCY		
COIN		
CHECKS		
TOTAL FROM OTHER SIDE		
SUBTOTAL		
LESS CASH RECEIVED		
NET DEPOSIT		

Exercise 7-3B

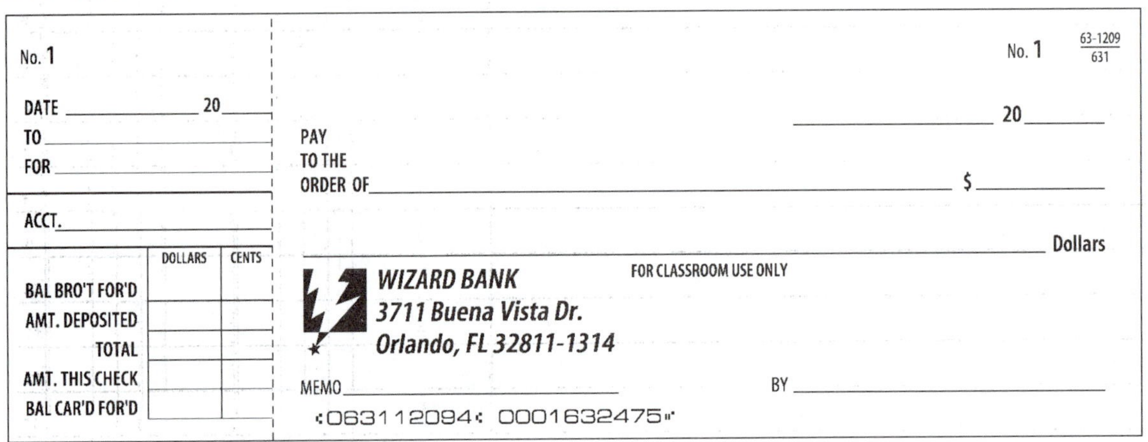

No. 1

DATE ____________ 20____
TO ____________
FOR ____________

ACCT. ____________

	DOLLARS	CENTS
BAL BRO'T FOR'D		
AMT. DEPOSITED		
TOTAL		
AMT. THIS CHECK		
BAL CAR'D FOR'D		

No. 1

63-1209
631

____________ 20____

PAY TO THE ORDER OF ____________________ $ ________

____________________ Dollars

WIZARD BANK
3711 Buena Vista Dr.
Orlando, FL 32811-1314

FOR CLASSROOM USE ONLY

MEMO ____________ BY ____________

⑆063112094⑆ 0001632475⑈

Name ____________________

Exercise 7-4B

	Ending Bank Balance	Ending Checkbook Balance
1.		
2.		
3.		
4.		
5.		
6.		
7.		

Exercise 7-5B

GENERAL JOURNAL PAGE

	DATE		DESCRIPTION	POST. REF.	DEBIT	CREDIT	
1							1
2							2
3							3
4							4
5							5
6							6
7							7
8							8
9							9
10							10
11							11
12							12
13							13
14							14
15							15
16							16
17							17
18							18
19							19
20							20
21							21

Exercise 7-6B

GENERAL JOURNAL

PAGE

DATE		DESCRIPTION	POST. REF.	DEBIT	CREDIT

Name ______________________________

Exercise 7-7B

GENERAL JOURNAL

PAGE

	DATE		DESCRIPTION	POST. REF.	DEBIT	CREDIT	
1							1
2							2
3							3
4							4
5							5
6							6
7							7
8							8
9							9
10							10
11							11
12							12
13							13
14							14
15							15
16							16
17							17
18							18
19							19
20							20
21							21
22							22
23							23
24							24
25							25
26							26
27							27
28							28
29							29
30							30
31							31
32							32
33							33
34							34
35							35
36							36

Problem 7-8B

1.

Problem 7-8B (Concluded)

2.

GENERAL JOURNAL

PAGE

	DATE	DESCRIPTION	POST. REF.	DEBIT	CREDIT	
1						1
2						2
3						3
4						4
5						5
6						6
7						7
8						8
9						9
10						10
11						11
12						12
13						13
14						14
15						15

Problem 7-9B

1.

Problem 7-9B (Concluded)

2.

GENERAL JOURNAL

PAGE

DATE		DESCRIPTION	POST. REF.	DEBIT	CREDIT

Problem 7-10B

1. and 3.

GENERAL JOURNAL

PAGE

	DATE		DESCRIPTION	POST. REF.	DEBIT	CREDIT	
1							1
2							2
3							3
4							4
5							5
6							6
7							7
8							8
9							9
10							10
11							11
12							12
13							13

Problem 7-10B (Concluded)

2. and 3.

PETTY CASH PAYMENTS FOR MONTH OF 20-- PAGE

	DAY	DESCRIPTION	VOU. NO.	TOTAL AMOUNT	DISTRIBUTION OF PAYMENTS								
					OFFICE SUPPLIES	POSTAGE EXPENSE	CHARIT. CONTRIB. EXPENSE	PHONE EXPENSE	TRAVEL & ENTER. EXPENSE	MISC. EXPENSE	ACCOUNT	AMOUNT	
1													1
2													2
3													3
4													4
5													5
6													6
7													7
8													8
9													9
10													10
11													11
12													12
13													13
14													14
15													15
16													16
17													17
18													18
19													19
20													20
21													21
22													22

Problem 7-11B

1.

GENERAL JOURNAL

PAGE 8

	DATE		DESCRIPTION	POST. REF.	DEBIT	CREDIT	
1							1
2							2
3							3
4							4
5							5
6							6
7							7
8							8
9							9
10							10
11							11
12							12
13							13
14							14
15							15
16							16
17							17
18							18
19							19
20							20
21							21
22							22
23							23

2.

ACCOUNT ACCOUNT NO.

DATE		ITEM	POST. REF.	DEBIT	CREDIT	BALANCE	
						DEBIT	CREDIT

3. The balance represents:

Mastery Problem

1.

PETTY CASH PAYMENTS FOR MONTH OF 20-- PAGE

					Distribution of Payments								
	DAY	DESCRIPTION	VOU. NO.	TOTAL AMOUNT	TRUCK EXPENSE	POSTAGE EXPENSE	CHARIT. CONTRIB. EXPENSE	PHONE EXPENSE	ADVERT. EXPENSE.	MISC. EXPENSE	ACCOUNT	AMOUNT	
1													1
2													2
3													3
4													4
5													5
6													6
7													7
8													8
9													9
10													10
11													11
12													12
13													13
14													14
15													15
16													16
17													17
18													18
19													19
20													20
21													21
22													22

Mastery Problem (Continued)

2. and 3.

GENERAL JOURNAL

PAGE 1

DATE		DESCRIPTION	POST. REF.	DEBIT	CREDIT

Mastery Problem (Concluded)

GENERAL JOURNAL

PAGE 2

	DATE		DESCRIPTION	POST. REF.	DEBIT	CREDIT	
1							1
2							2
3							3
4							4
5							5
6							6
7							7
8							8
9							9
10							10
11							11
12							12
13							13
14							14

3.

Challenge Problem

1. Panera Bakery

GENERAL JOURNAL PAGE

DATE	DESCRIPTION	POST. REF.	DEBIT	CREDIT

Name ______________________________

Challenge Problem (Concluded)

2. Lawrence Bank

GENERAL JOURNAL PAGE

	DATE		DESCRIPTION	POST. REF.	DEBIT	CREDIT	
1							1
2							2
3							3
4							4
5							5
6							6
7							7
8							8
9							9
10							10
11							11
12							12
13							13
14							14
15							15
16							16
17							17
18							18
19							19
20							20
21							21
22							22
23							23
24							24
25							25
26							26
27							27
28							28
29							29

APPENDIX: Internal Controls

Exercise 7Apx-1A

1. ____

____

2. ____

____

3. ____

____

4. ____

____

5. ____

____

Exercise 7Apx-2A

1. ____

2. ____

3. ____

4. ____

5. ____

Exercise 7Apx-3A

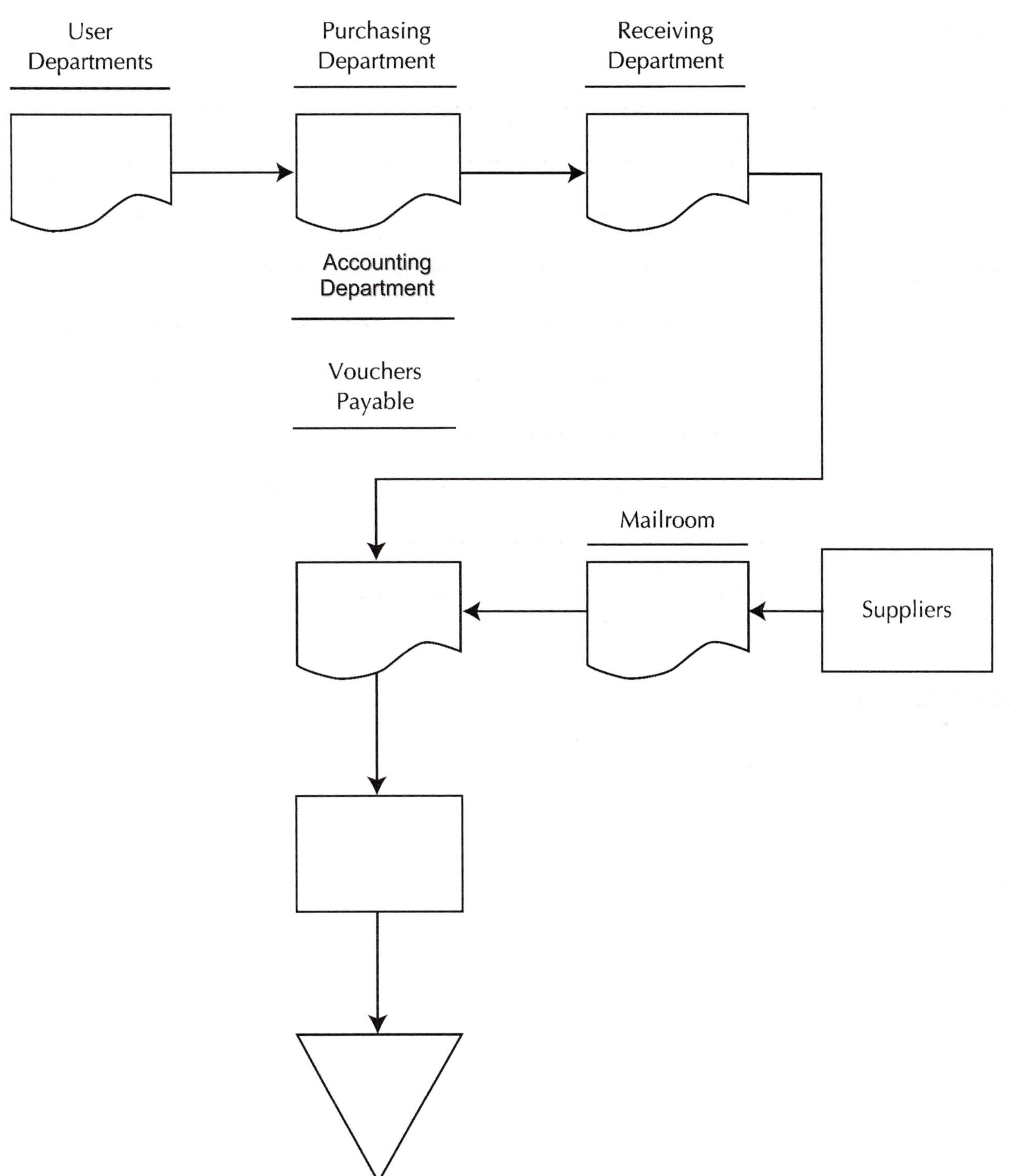

Problem 7Apx-4A

1. ____________________

____

2. ____________________

____

3. ____________________

____

4. ____________________

____

Exercise 7Apx-1B

1. ____________________

____

2. ____________________

____

3. ____________________

____

4. ____________________

____

Exercise 7Apx-2B

1. ____

2. ____

3. ____

4. ____

Exercise 7Apx-3B

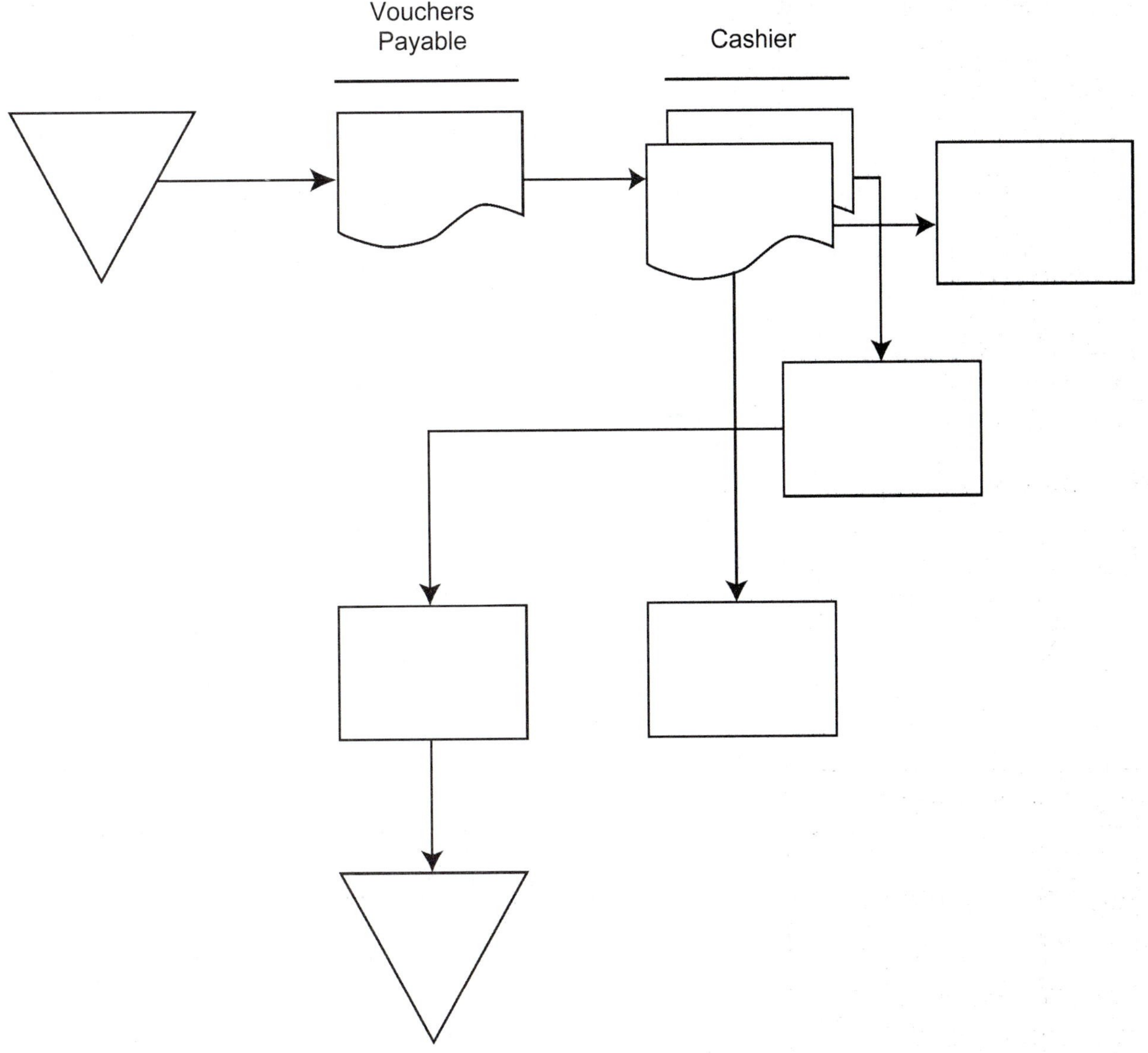

Problem 7Apx-4B

1. ______________________________

____

2. ______________________________

____

3. ______________________________

____

4. ______________________________

____

Exercise 8-1A

____

____

____

____

Exercise 8-2A

____

____

____

____

____

____

____

Exercise 8-3A

	Marital Status	Total Weekly Earnings	Number of Allowances	Amount of Withholding
a.	S	$347.60	2	
b.	S	451.50	1	
c.	M	481.15	3	
d.	S	490.52	0	
e.	M	691.89	5	

Exercise 8-4A

Cumul. Pay Before Current Weekly Payroll	Current Gross Pay	Year-to-Date Earnings	Soc. Sec. Maximum	Amount Over Max. Soc. Sec.	Amount Subject to Soc. Sec.	Soc. Sec. Tax Withheld	Medicare Tax Withheld
$ 22,000	$1,700		$118,500				
54,000	4,200		118,500				
115,900	3,925		118,500				
117,900	4,600		118,500				

Exercise 8-5A

a. ____________ regular hours × $10 per hour ____________

b. ____________ overtime hours × $15 per hour ____________

c. Total gross wages ____________

d. Federal income tax withholding (from tax tables in Figure 8-4) ____________

e. Social Security withholding at 6.2% ____________

f. Medicare withholding at 1.45% ____________

g. Total withholding ____________

h. Net pay ____________

Exercise 8-6A

GENERAL JOURNAL PAGE

	DATE		DESCRIPTION	POST. REF.	DEBIT	CREDIT	
1							1
2							2
3							3
4							4
5							5
6							6
7							7
8							8
9							9

Exercise 8-7A

GENERAL JOURNAL PAGE

	DATE		DESCRIPTION	POST. REF.	DEBIT	CREDIT	
1							1
2							2
3							3
4							4
5							5
6							6
7							7
8							8
9							9

Name ______________________

Problem 8-8A

1.

2.

GENERAL JOURNAL PAGE

DATE		DESCRIPTION	POST. REF.	DEBIT	CREDIT

Problem 8-9A

1.

PAYROLL REGISTER

	NAME	NO. ALLOW.	MARIT. STATUS	EARNINGS: REGULAR	EARNINGS: OVERTIME	EARNINGS: TOTAL	EARNINGS: CUMULATIVE TOTAL	TAXABLE EARNINGS: UNEMPLOY. COMP.	TAXABLE EARNINGS: SOCIAL SECURITY
1									
2									
3									
4									
5									
6									
7									
8									
9									
10									
11									
12									
13									
14									

Name ______________________

Problem 8-9A (Concluded)

FOR PERIOD ENDED 20--

DEDUCTIONS								
FEDERAL INCOME TAX	SOCIAL SECURITY TAX	MEDICARE TAX	CITY TAX	HEALTH INSUR.	OTHER	TOTAL	NET PAY	CK. NO.
									1
									2
									3
									4
									5
									6
									7
									8
									9
									10
									11
									12
									13
									14

2.

GENERAL JOURNAL

PAGE

	DATE	DESCRIPTION	POST. REF.	DEBIT	CREDIT	
1						1
2						2
3						3
4						4
5						5
6						6
7						7
8						8
9						9
10						10
11						11
12						12
13						13
14						14

Problem 8-10A

EMPLOYEE EARNINGS RECORD

20 -- PERIOD ENDED	EARNINGS				TAXABLE EARNINGS		DEDUCTIONS	
	REGULAR	OVERTIME	TOTAL	CUMULATIVE TOTAL	UNEMPLOY. COMP.	SOCIAL SECURITY	FEDERAL INCOME TAX	SOCIAL SECURITY TAX

GENDER		DEPARTMENT	OCCUPATION	SOCIAL SECURITY NO.	MARITAL STATUS	ALLOW-ANCES
M	F					

Name ______________________________

Problem 8-10A (Concluded)

FOR PERIOD ENDED 20--

DEDUCTIONS						
MEDICARE TAX	CITY TAX	HEALTH INSURANCE	OTHER	TOTAL	CK. NO.	AMOUNT

PAY RATE	DATE OF BIRTH	DATE HIRED	NAME/ADDRESS	EMP. NO.

Exercise 8-1B

Exercise 8-2B

Exercise 8-3B

	Marital Status	Total Weekly Earnings	Number of Allowances	Amount of Withholding
a.	M	$546.00	4	
b.	M	390.00	1	
c.	S	461.39	2	
d.	M	522.88	2	
e.	S	612.00	0	

Exercise 8-4B

Cumul. Pay Before Current Weekly Payroll	Current Gross Pay	Year-to-Date Earnings	Soc. Sec. Maximum	Amount Over Max. Soc. Sec.	Amount Subject to Soc. Sec.	Soc. Sec. Tax Withheld	Medicare Tax Withheld
$ 31,000	$1,500		$118,500				
53,000	2,860		118,500				
115,600	3,140		118,500				
117,900	2,920		118,500				

Exercise 8-5B

a. __________ regular hours × $12 per hour __________

b. __________ overtime hours × $18 per hour __________

c. Total gross wages __________

d. Federal income tax withholding (from tax tables in Figure 8-4) __________

e. Social Security withholding at 6.2% __________

f. Medicare withholding at 1.45% __________

g. Total withholding __________

h. Net pay __________

Exercise 8-6B

GENERAL JOURNAL PAGE

	DATE		DESCRIPTION	POST. REF.	DEBIT	CREDIT	
1							1
2							2
3							3
4							4
5							5
6							6
7							7
8							8
9							9
10							10
11							11
12							12
13							13
14							14
15							15
16							16
17							17
18							18
19							19
20							20
21							21
22							22

Exercise 8-7B

GENERAL JOURNAL PAGE

	DATE		DESCRIPTION	POST. REF.	DEBIT	CREDIT	
1							1
2							2
3							3
4							4
5							5
6							6
7							7
8							8
9							9
10							10
11							11
12							12
13							13

Problem 8-8B

1.

Name ______________________

Problem 8-8B (Concluded)

2.

GENERAL JOURNAL

PAGE

DATE		DESCRIPTION	POST. REF.	DEBIT	CREDIT

Problem 8-9B

1.

PAYROLL REGISTER

	NAME	NO. ALLOW.	MARIT. STATUS	EARNINGS				TAXABLE EARNINGS	
				REGULAR	OVERTIME	TOTAL	CUMULATIVE TOTAL	UNEMPLOY. COMP.	SOCIAL SECURITY
1									
2									
3									
4									
5									
6									
7									
8									
9									
10									
11									
12									
13									
14									

Name ______________________

Problem 8-9B (Concluded)

FOR PERIOD ENDED 20--

DEDUCTIONS									
FEDERAL INCOME TAX	SOCIAL SECURITY TAX	MEDICARE TAX	CITY TAX	HEALTH INSUR.	OTHER	TOTAL	NET PAY	CK. NO.	
									1
									2
									3
									4
									5
									6
									7
									8
									9
									10
									11
									12
									13
									14

2.

GENERAL JOURNAL

PAGE

	DATE	DESCRIPTION	POST. REF.	DEBIT	CREDIT	
1						1
2						2
3						3
4						4
5						5
6						6
7						7
8						8
9						9
10						10
11						11
12						12
13						13
14						14

Problem 8-10B

EMPLOYEE EARNINGS RECORD

20 -- PERIOD ENDED	EARNINGS				TAXABLE EARNINGS		DEDUCTIONS	
	REGULAR	OVERTIME	TOTAL	CUMULATIVE TOTAL	UNEMPLOY. COMP.	SOCIAL SECURITY	FEDERAL INCOME TAX	SOCIAL SECURITY TAX

GENDER		DEPARTMENT	OCCUPATION	SOCIAL SECURITY NO.	MARITAL STATUS	ALLOW-ANCES
M	F					

Name ______________________________

Problem 8-10B (Concluded)

FOR PERIOD ENDED 20--

DEDUCTIONS						CK. NO.	AMOUNT
MEDICARE TAX	CITY TAX	HEALTH INSURANCE	OTHER		TOTAL		

PAY RATE	DATE OF BIRTH	DATE HIRED	NAME/ADDRESS	EMP. NO.

Mastery Problem

1.

PAYROLL REGISTER

	NAME	NO. ALLOW.	MARIT. STATUS	EARNINGS: REGULAR	EARNINGS: OVERTIME	EARNINGS: TOTAL	EARNINGS: CUMULATIVE TOTAL	TAXABLE EARNINGS: UNEMPLOY. COMP.	TAXABLE EARNINGS: SOCIAL SECURITY
1									
2									
3									
4									
5									
6									
7									
8									
9									
10									
11									
12									
13									
14									

3.

EMPLOYEE EARNINGS RECORD

20 -- PERIOD ENDED	EARNINGS: REGULAR	EARNINGS: OVERTIME	EARNINGS: TOTAL	EARNINGS: CUMULATIVE TOTAL	TAXABLE EARNINGS: UNEMPLOY. COMP.	TAXABLE EARNINGS: SOCIAL SECURITY	FEDERAL INCOME TAX
11/4	330 00	33 00	363 00	6,145 50	363 00	363 00	5 00
11/11	440 00	49 50	489 50	6,635 00	489 50	489 50	17 00
11/18							
11/25							

GENDER		DEPARTMENT	OCCUPATION	SOCIAL SECURITY NO.	MARITAL STATUS
M	F				

Mastery Problem (Continued)

FOR PERIOD ENDED 20--

DEDUCTIONS																	
FEDERAL INCOME TAX		SOCIAL SECURITY TAX		MEDICARE TAX		STATE INCOME TAX		HEALTH INSURANCE		CREDIT UNION		TOTAL		NET PAY		CK. NO.	
																	1
																	2
																	3
																	4
																	5
																	6
																	7
																	8
																	9
																	10
																	11
																	12
																	13
																	14

FOR PERIOD ENDED 20--

DEDUCTIONS												NET PAY		
SOCIAL SECURITY TAX		MEDICARE TAX		STATE INCOME TAX		HEALTH INSURANCE		CREDIT UNION		TOTAL		CK. NO.	AMOUNT	
22	51	5	26	12	71			72	60	118	08	121	244	92
30	35	7	10	17	13			97	90	169	48	229	320	02

ALLOWANCES	PAY RATE	DATE OF BIRTH	DATE HIRED	NAME/ADDRESS	EMP. NO.

Mastery Problem (Concluded)

2.

GENERAL JOURNAL

PAGE

DATE		DESCRIPTION	POST. REF.	DEBIT	CREDIT

Name ______________________________

Challenge Problem

1.

GENERAL JOURNAL PAGE

	DATE		DESCRIPTION	POST. REF.	DEBIT	CREDIT	
1							1
2							2
3							3
4							4
5							5
6							6
7							7
8							8
9							9
10							10

2.

Exercise 9-1A

GENERAL JOURNAL PAGE

	DATE		DESCRIPTION	POST. REF.	DEBIT	CREDIT	
1							1
2							2
3							3
4							4
5							5
6							6
7							7

Exercise 9-2A

GENERAL JOURNAL PAGE

	DATE		DESCRIPTION	POST. REF.	DEBIT	CREDIT	
1							1
2							2
3							3
4							4
5							5
6							6
7							7

Exercise 9-3A

Name	Current Earnings	Taxable Earnings: Unemploy. Comp.	Taxable Earnings: Social Security
Jordahl			
Keesling			
Palmer			
Soltis			
Stout			
Xia			
Total			

GENERAL JOURNAL PAGE

	DATE		DESCRIPTION	POST. REF.	DEBIT	CREDIT	
1							1
2							2
3							3
4							4
5							5
6							6
7							7

Exercise 9-4A

Exercise 9-5A

GENERAL JOURNAL PAGE

DATE	DESCRIPTION	POST. REF.	DEBIT	CREDIT

Exercise 9-6A

1.

GENERAL JOURNAL PAGE

DATE	DESCRIPTION	POST. REF.	DEBIT	CREDIT

2.

GENERAL JOURNAL PAGE

DATE	DESCRIPTION	POST. REF.	DEBIT	CREDIT

Problem 9-7A

1.

Name	Current Earnings	Taxable Earnings Unemploy. Comp.	Taxable Earnings Social Security
Click, Katelyn			
Coombs, Michelle			
Faus, Erin			
Lenihan, Marcus			
McMahon, Drew			
Newell, Marg			
Stevens, Matt			
Total			

2.

GENERAL JOURNAL

PAGE

	DATE		DESCRIPTION	POST. REF.	DEBIT	CREDIT	
1							1
2							2
3							3
4							4
5							5
6							6
7							7
8							8
9							9
10							10

Name ______________________________

Problem 9-8A

1.

GENERAL JOURNAL

PAGE

DATE		DESCRIPTION	POST. REF.	DEBIT	CREDIT

Problem 9-8A (Continued)

GENERAL JOURNAL

PAGE

DATE	DESCRIPTION	POST. REF.	DEBIT	CREDIT

Problem 9-8A (Concluded)

2.

Cash	101

Employee Federal Income Tax Payable	211

Social Security Tax Payable	212

Medicare Tax Payable	213

Savings Bond Deductions Payable	218

FUTA Tax Payable	221

SUTA Tax Payable	222

Wages and Salaries Expense	511

Payroll Taxes Expense	530

Problem 9-9A

1.

GENERAL JOURNAL

PAGE

	DATE		DESCRIPTION	POST. REF.	DEBIT	CREDIT	
1							1
2							2
3							3
4							4
5							5
6							6

2.

GENERAL JOURNAL

PAGE

	DATE		DESCRIPTION	POST. REF.	DEBIT	CREDIT	
1							1
2							2
3							3
4							4
5							5
6							6

Problem 9-9A (Concluded)

3.

GENERAL JOURNAL PAGE

	DATE		DESCRIPTION	POST. REF.	DEBIT	CREDIT	
1							1
2							2
3							3
4							4
5							5

Exercise 9-1B

GENERAL JOURNAL PAGE

	DATE		DESCRIPTION	POST. REF.	DEBIT	CREDIT	
1							1
2							2
3							3
4							4
5							5
6							6
7							7
8							8
9							9

Exercise 9-2B

GENERAL JOURNAL

PAGE

	DATE		DESCRIPTION	POST. REF.	DEBIT	CREDIT	
1							1
2							2
3							3
4							4
5							5
6							6
7							7
8							8

Exercise 9-3B

		Taxable Earnings	
Name	**Current Earnings**	**Unemploy. Comp.**	**Social Security**
Carlson			
Delgado			
Lewis			
Nixon			
Shippe			
Watts			
Total			

Name ______________________________

Exercise 9-3B (Concluded)

GENERAL JOURNAL PAGE

	DATE		DESCRIPTION	POST. REF.	DEBIT	CREDIT	
1							1
2							2
3							3
4							4
5							5
6							6
7							7

Exercise 9-4B: See page WP-302.

Exercise 9-5B

GENERAL JOURNAL PAGE

	DATE		DESCRIPTION	POST. REF.	DEBIT	CREDIT	
1							1
2							2
3							3
4							4
5							5
6							6
7							7
8							8
9							9
10							10
11							11
12							12
13							13
14							14

Exercise 9-4B

Exercise 9-6B

1.

GENERAL JOURNAL PAGE

	DATE		DESCRIPTION	POST. REF.	DEBIT	CREDIT	
1							1
2							2
3							3
4							4
5							5

2.

GENERAL JOURNAL PAGE

	DATE		DESCRIPTION	POST. REF.	DEBIT	CREDIT	
1							1
2							2
3							3
4							4
5							5

Problem 9-7B

1.

Name	Current Earnings	Taxable Earnings: Unemploy. Comp.	Taxable Earnings: Social Security
Ackers, Alice			
Conley, Dorothy			
Davis, James			
Lawrence, Kevin			
Rawlings, Judy			
Tanaka, Sumio			
Vadillo, Raynette			
Total			

2.

GENERAL JOURNAL

PAGE

	DATE		DESCRIPTION	POST. REF.	DEBIT	CREDIT	
1							1
2							2
3							3
4							4
5							5
6							6
7							7
8							8
9							9
10							10
11							11
12							12

Problem 9-8B

1.

GENERAL JOURNAL

PAGE

DATE	DESCRIPTION	POST. REF.	DEBIT	CREDIT

Name ____________________

Problem 9-8B (Continued)

GENERAL JOURNAL

PAGE

DATE	DESCRIPTION	POST. REF.	DEBIT	CREDIT

Problem 9-8B (Concluded)

2.

Cash 101

Employee Federal Income Tax Payable 211

Social Security Tax Payable 212

Medicare Tax Payable 213

Savings Bond Deductions Payable 218

FUTA Tax Payable 221

SUTA Tax Payable 222

Wages and Salaries Expense 511

Payroll Taxes Expense 530

Name ______________________________

Problem 9-9B

1.

GENERAL JOURNAL

PAGE

	DATE		DESCRIPTION	POST. REF.	DEBIT	CREDIT	
1							1
2							2
3							3
4							4
5							5
6							6

2.

GENERAL JOURNAL

PAGE

	DATE		DESCRIPTION	POST. REF.	DEBIT	CREDIT	
1							1
2							2
3							3
4							4
5							5
6							6

Problem 9-9B (Concluded)

3.

GENERAL JOURNAL

PAGE

	DATE		DESCRIPTION	POST. REF.	DEBIT	CREDIT	
1							1
2							2
3							3
4							4

Name ______________________________

Mastery Problem

1., 2., and 3.

GENERAL JOURNAL

PAGE

DATE	DESCRIPTION	POST. REF.	DEBIT	CREDIT

Mastery Problem (Concluded)

GENERAL JOURNAL

PAGE

	DATE		DESCRIPTION	POST. REF.	DEBIT	CREDIT	
1							1
2							2
3							3
4							4
5							5
6							6
7							7
8							8
9							9
10							10
11							11
12							12
13							13
14							14
15							15
16							16
17							17
18							18
19							19
20							20
21							21
22							22
23							23
24							24
25							25
26							26
27							27
28							28
29							29
30							30
31							31
32							32
33							33
34							34
35							35

Name ____________________

Challenge Problem

1.

2.

GENERAL JOURNAL PAGE

	DATE		DESCRIPTION	POST. REF.	DEBIT	CREDIT	
1							1
2							2
3							3
4							4
5							5
6							6
7							7

3.

Exercise 10-1A

1. ______________________
2. ______________________
3. ______________________
4. ______________________
5. ______________________
6. ______________________

Exercise 10-2A

1.

Cash

Accounts Receivable

Sales Tax Payable

Sales

Sales Returns and Allowances

Sales Discounts

2.

Cash

Accounts Receivable

Sales Tax Payable

Sales

Sales Returns and Allowances

Sales Discounts

Exercise 10-2A (Concluded)

3.

Cash

Accounts Receivable

Sales Tax Payable

Sales

Sales Returns and Allowances

Sales Discounts

4.

Cash

Accounts Receivable

Sales Tax Payable

Sales

Sales Returns and Allowances

Sales Discounts

5.

Cash

Accounts Receivable

Sales Tax Payable

Sales

Sales Returns and Allowances

Sales Discounts

Exercise 10-3A

Exercise 10-4A

GENERAL JOURNAL PAGE

	DATE		DESCRIPTION	POST. REF.	DEBIT	CREDIT	
1							1
2							2
3							3
4							4
5							5
6							6
7							7
8							8
9							9
10							10
11							11
12							12
13							13
14							14
15							15
16							16
17							17
18							18
19							19
20							20

Exercise 10-4A (Concluded)

GENERAL JOURNAL

PAGE

	DATE	DESCRIPTION	POST. REF.	DEBIT	CREDIT	
21						21
22						22
23						23
24						24
25						25
26						26
27						27
28						28

Exercise 10-5A

GENERAL JOURNAL

PAGE

	DATE	DESCRIPTION	POST. REF.	DEBIT	CREDIT	
1						1
2						2
3						3
4						4
5						5
6						6
7						7
8						8
9						9
10						10
11						11
12						12
13						13
14						14
15						15
16						16
17						17
18						18
19						19
20						20
21						21
22						22

Exercise 10-6A

GENERAL JOURNAL

PAGE 60

	DATE		DESCRIPTION	POST. REF.	DEBIT	CREDIT	
1							1
2							2
3							3
4							4
5							5
6							6
7							7
8							8
9							9
10							10
11							11
12							12
13							13
14							14
15							15

GENERAL LEDGER

ACCOUNT Accounts Receivable ACCOUNT NO. 122

DATE		ITEM	POST. REF.	DEBIT	CREDIT	BALANCE DEBIT	BALANCE CREDIT
20-- June	1	Balance	✓			4 2 0 0 00	

ACCOUNT Sales Returns and Allowances ACCOUNT NO. 401.1

DATE		ITEM	POST. REF.	DEBIT	CREDIT	BALANCE DEBIT	BALANCE CREDIT

Exercise 10-6A (Concluded)

ACCOUNTS RECEIVABLE LEDGER

NAME John B. Abramowitz

ADDRESS 3201 West Judkins Road, Seattle, WA 98201-1079

DATE		ITEM	POST. REF.	DEBIT	CREDIT	BALANCE
20-- June	1	Balance	✓			850.00

NAME L. B. Gruder

ADDRESS 44 Western Blvd., Spokane, WA 98601-4092

DATE		ITEM	POST. REF.	DEBIT	CREDIT	BALANCE
20-- June	1	Balance	✓			428.00

NAME Marie L. Perez

ADDRESS 158 West Adams Point, Bellevue, WA 98401-0663

DATE		ITEM	POST. REF.	DEBIT	CREDIT	BALANCE
20-- June	1	Balance	✓			1018.00

Exercise 10-7A

GENERAL JOURNAL

PAGE

	DATE	DESCRIPTION	POST. REF.	DEBIT	CREDIT	
1						1
2						2
3						3
4						4
5						5
6						6
7						7
8						8
9						9
10						10
11						11
12						12
13						13
14						14
15						15
16						16
17						17
18						18
19						19
20						20
21						21
22						22

Exercise 10-8A

Problem 10-9A

1.

GENERAL JOURNAL

PAGE 15

	DATE		DESCRIPTION	POST. REF.	DEBIT	CREDIT	
1							1
2							2
3							3
4							4
5							5
6							6
7							7
8							8
9							9
10							10
11							11
12							12
13							13
14							14
15							15
16							16
17							17
18							18
19							19
20							20
21							21
22							22
23							23
24							24
25							25
26							26
27							27
28							28
29							29
30							30
31							31
32							32
33							33
34							34

Problem 10-9A (Continued)

2.

GENERAL LEDGER

ACCOUNT Accounts Receivable ACCOUNT NO. 122

DATE	ITEM	POST. REF.	DEBIT	CREDIT	BALANCE DEBIT	BALANCE CREDIT

ACCOUNT Sales Tax Payable ACCOUNT NO. 231

DATE	ITEM	POST. REF.	DEBIT	CREDIT	BALANCE DEBIT	BALANCE CREDIT

ACCOUNT Sales ACCOUNT NO. 401

DATE	ITEM	POST. REF.	DEBIT	CREDIT	BALANCE DEBIT	BALANCE CREDIT

Problem 10-9A (Concluded)

ACCOUNTS RECEIVABLE LEDGER

NAME Hassad Co.

ADDRESS 1225 W. Temperance Street, Elletsville, IN 47429-9976

DATE		ITEM	POST. REF.	DEBIT	CREDIT	BALANCE

NAME Helsinki, Inc.

ADDRESS 125 Fishers Drive, Noblesville, IN 47870-8867

DATE		ITEM	POST. REF.	DEBIT	CREDIT	BALANCE

NAME Jung Manufacturing Co.

ADDRESS 8825 Old State Road, Bloomington, IN 47401-8823

DATE		ITEM	POST. REF.	DEBIT	CREDIT	BALANCE

NAME Ardis Myler

ADDRESS 2100 Greer Lane, Bedford, IN 47421-8876

DATE		ITEM	POST. REF.	DEBIT	CREDIT	BALANCE

Problem 10-10A

1.

GENERAL JOURNAL

PAGE 20

DATE		DESCRIPTION	POST. REF.	DEBIT	CREDIT

Problem 10-10A (Continued)

GENERAL JOURNAL

PAGE 21

	DATE		DESCRIPTION	POST. REF.	DEBIT	CREDIT	
1							1
2							2
3							3
4							4
5							5
6							6
7							7
8							8
9							9
10							10
11							11
12							12
13							13
14							14
15							15
16							16
17							17
18							18
19							19
20							20
21							21
22							22
23							23
24							24
25							25
26							26
27							27
28							28
29							29
30							30
31							31
32							32
33							33
34							34

Problem 10-10A (Continued)

2.

GENERAL LEDGER

ACCOUNT Cash ACCOUNT NO. 101

DATE		ITEM	POST. REF.	DEBIT	CREDIT	BALANCE DEBIT	BALANCE CREDIT
20-- Dec.	1	Balance	✓			9,862.00	

ACCOUNT Accounts Receivable ACCOUNT NO. 122

DATE		ITEM	POST. REF.	DEBIT	CREDIT	BALANCE DEBIT	BALANCE CREDIT
20-- Dec.	1	Balance	✓			9,352.00	

Problem 10-10A (Continued)

ACCOUNT Sales Tax Payable ACCOUNT NO. 231

DATE	ITEM	POST. REF.	DEBIT	CREDIT	BALANCE DEBIT	BALANCE CREDIT

ACCOUNT Sales ACCOUNT NO. 401

DATE	ITEM	POST. REF.	DEBIT	CREDIT	BALANCE DEBIT	BALANCE CREDIT

ACCOUNT Sales Returns and Allowances ACCOUNT NO. 401.1

DATE	ITEM	POST. REF.	DEBIT	CREDIT	BALANCE DEBIT	BALANCE CREDIT

ACCOUNT Bank Credit Card Expense ACCOUNT NO. 513

DATE	ITEM	POST. REF.	DEBIT	CREDIT	BALANCE DEBIT	BALANCE CREDIT

Problem 10-10A (Continued)

ACCOUNTS RECEIVABLE LEDGER

NAME Michael Anderson

ADDRESS 233 West 11th Avenue, Detroit, MI 59500-1154

DATE		ITEM	POST. REF.	DEBIT	CREDIT	BALANCE
20-- Dec.	1	Balance	✓			2,480 00

NAME Ansel Manufacturing

ADDRESS 284 West 88 Street, Detroit, MI 59522-1168

DATE		ITEM	POST. REF.	DEBIT	CREDIT	BALANCE
20-- Dec.	1	Balance	✓			982 00

NAME J. Gorbea

ADDRESS P.O. Box 864, Detroit, MI 59552-0864

DATE		ITEM	POST. REF.	DEBIT	CREDIT	BALANCE
20-- Dec.	1	Balance	✓			880 00

Problem 10-10A (Concluded)

NAME Rachel Carson

ADDRESS 11312 Fourteenth Avenue South, Detroit, MI 59221-1142

DATE		ITEM	POST. REF.	DEBIT	CREDIT	BALANCE
20-- Dec.	1	Balance	✓			3,200.00

NAME Tom Wilson

ADDRESS 100 NW Seward St., Detroit, MI 59210-1337

DATE		ITEM	POST. REF.	DEBIT	CREDIT	BALANCE
20-- Dec.	1	Balance	✓			1,810.00

Name ______________________________

Problem 10-11A

1.

GENERAL JOURNAL

PAGE 7

DATE		DESCRIPTION	POST. REF.	DEBIT	CREDIT

Problem 10-11A (Continued)

GENERAL JOURNAL

PAGE 8

	DATE		DESCRIPTION	POST. REF.	DEBIT	CREDIT	
1							1
2							2
3							3
4							4
5							5
6							6
7							7
8							8
9							9
10							10
11							11
12							12
13							13
14							14
15							15
16							16
17							17
18							18
19							19
20							20
21							21
22							22
23							23
24							24
25							25
26							26
27							27
28							28
29							29
30							30
31							31
32							32
33							33
34							34

Problem 10-11A (Continued)

GENERAL JOURNAL

PAGE 9

	DATE		DESCRIPTION	POST. REF.	DEBIT	CREDIT	
1							1
2							2
3							3
4							4
5							5
6							6
7							7
8							8
9							9
10							10

2.

GENERAL LEDGER

ACCOUNT Cash ACCOUNT NO. 101

DATE		ITEM	POST. REF.	DEBIT	CREDIT	BALANCE DEBIT	BALANCE CREDIT
20-- Mar.	1	Balance	✓			9,586.00	

Problem 10-11A (Continued)

ACCOUNT Accounts Receivable ACCOUNT NO. 122

DATE		ITEM	POST. REF.	DEBIT	CREDIT	BALANCE DEBIT	BALANCE CREDIT
20-- Mar.	1	Balance	✓			1,016 00	

ACCOUNT Sales Tax Payable ACCOUNT NO. 231

DATE		ITEM	POST. REF.	DEBIT	CREDIT	BALANCE DEBIT	BALANCE CREDIT

Problem 10-11A (Continued)

ACCOUNT Sales ACCOUNT NO. 401

DATE		ITEM	POST. REF.	DEBIT	CREDIT	BALANCE DEBIT	BALANCE CREDIT

ACCOUNT Sales Returns and Allowances ACCOUNT NO. 401.1

DATE		ITEM	POST. REF.	DEBIT	CREDIT	BALANCE DEBIT	BALANCE CREDIT

ACCOUNTS RECEIVABLE LEDGER

NAME Donachie & Co.

ADDRESS 1424 Jackson Creek Road, Nashville, IN 47448-2245

DATE		ITEM	POST. REF.	DEBIT	CREDIT	BALANCE

Problem 10-11A (Concluded)

NAME Eck Bakery

ADDRESS 6422 E. Bender Road, Bloomington, IN 47401-7756

DATE		ITEM	POST. REF.	DEBIT	CREDIT	BALANCE

NAME R. J. Kibubu, Inc.

ADDRESS 3315 Longview Avenue, Bloomington, IN 47401-7223

DATE		ITEM	POST. REF.	DEBIT	CREDIT	BALANCE

NAME Whitaker Group

ADDRESS 2300 E. National Road, Cumberland, IN 46229-4824

DATE		ITEM	POST. REF.	DEBIT	CREDIT	BALANCE
20-- Mar.	1	Balance	✓			1,016 00

Problem 10-12A

Name ____________________

Exercise 10-1B

1. ____________________
2. ____________________
3. ____________________
4. ____________________
5. ____________________
6. ____________________

Exercise 10-2B

1.

Cash

Accounts Receivable

Sales Tax Payable

Sales

Sales Returns and Allowances

Sales Discounts

2.

Cash

Accounts Receivable

Sales Tax Payable

Sales

Sales Returns and Allowances

Sales Discounts

Exercise 10-2B (Concluded)

3.

Cash

Accounts Receivable

Sales Tax Payable

Sales

Sales Returns and Allowances

Sales Discounts

4.

Cash

Accounts Receivable

Sales Tax Payable

Sales

Sales Returns and Allowances

Sales Discounts

5.

Cash

Accounts Receivable

Sales Tax Payable

Sales

Sales Returns and Allowances

Sales Discounts

Exercise 10-3B

Exercise 10-4B

GENERAL JOURNAL PAGE

	DATE		DESCRIPTION	POST. REF.	DEBIT	CREDIT	
1							1
2							2
3							3
4							4
5							5
6							6
7							7
8							8
9							9
10							10
11							11
12							12
13							13
14							14
15							15
16							16
17							17
18							18
19							19
20							20

Exercise 10-4B (Concluded)

GENERAL JOURNAL

PAGE

DATE		DESCRIPTION	POST. REF.	DEBIT	CREDIT

Exercise 10-5B

GENERAL JOURNAL

PAGE

DATE		DESCRIPTION	POST. REF.	DEBIT	CREDIT

Exercise 10-6B

GENERAL JOURNAL

PAGE 60

	DATE		DESCRIPTION	POST. REF.	DEBIT	CREDIT	
1							1
2							2
3							3
4							4
5							5
6							6
7							7
8							8
9							9
10							10
11							11
12							12
13							13
14							14

GENERAL LEDGER

ACCOUNT Accounts Receivable ACCOUNT NO. 122

DATE		ITEM	POST. REF.	DEBIT	CREDIT	BALANCE	
						DEBIT	CREDIT
20-- June	1	Balance	✓			3 9 0 0 00	

ACCOUNT Sales Returns and Allowances ACCOUNT NO. 401.1

DATE		ITEM	POST. REF.	DEBIT	CREDIT	BALANCE	
						DEBIT	CREDIT

Exercise 10-6B (Concluded)

ACCOUNTS RECEIVABLE LEDGER

NAME John B. Adams

ADDRESS 127 Strawberry Lane, Manchester, CT 06040-0865

DATE		ITEM	POST. REF.	DEBIT	CREDIT	BALANCE
20-- June	1	Balance	✓			850 00

NAME L. B. Greene

ADDRESS 2254 Blackrock, Bronx, NY 10472-1974

DATE		ITEM	POST. REF.	DEBIT	CREDIT	BALANCE
20-- June	1	Balance	✓			428 00

NAME Marie L. Phillips

ADDRESS 334 Fern St., W. Hartford, CT 06119-2314

DATE		ITEM	POST. REF.	DEBIT	CREDIT	BALANCE
20-- June	1	Balance	✓			1018 00

Name ______________________

Exercise 10-7B

GENERAL JOURNAL PAGE 1

	DATE		DESCRIPTION	POST. REF.	DEBIT	CREDIT	
1							1
2							2
3							3
4							4
5							5
6							6
7							7
8							8
9							9
10							10
11							11
12							12
13							13
14							14
15							15
16							16
17							17
18							18
19							19
20							20
21							21
22							22
23							23

Exercise 10-8B

Problem 10-9B

1.

GENERAL JOURNAL

PAGE 15

DATE		DESCRIPTION	POST. REF.	DEBIT	CREDIT

Problem 10-9B (Continued)

2.

GENERAL LEDGER

ACCOUNT Accounts Receivable ACCOUNT NO. 122

DATE		ITEM	POST. REF.	DEBIT	CREDIT	BALANCE	
						DEBIT	CREDIT

ACCOUNT Sales Tax Payable ACCOUNT NO. 231

DATE		ITEM	POST. REF.	DEBIT	CREDIT	BALANCE	
						DEBIT	CREDIT

ACCOUNT Sales ACCOUNT NO. 401

DATE		ITEM	POST. REF.	DEBIT	CREDIT	BALANCE	
						DEBIT	CREDIT

Problem 10-9B (Concluded)

ACCOUNTS RECEIVABLE LEDGER

NAME Dvorak Manufacturing

ADDRESS 2105 Williams Drive, Muncie, IN 47304-2437

DATE		ITEM	POST. REF.	DEBIT	CREDIT	BALANCE

NAME Saga, Inc.

ADDRESS 1453 Parnell Avenue, Indianapolis, IN 46201-6870

DATE		ITEM	POST. REF.	DEBIT	CREDIT	BALANCE

NAME Vinnie Ward

ADDRESS 308 So. Muirhead Drive, Okemos, MI 48864-5356

DATE		ITEM	POST. REF.	DEBIT	CREDIT	BALANCE

NAME Zapata Co.

ADDRESS 789 N. Stafford Dr., Bloomington, IN 47401-6201

DATE		ITEM	POST. REF.	DEBIT	CREDIT	BALANCE

Name ______________________________

Problem 10-10B

1.

GENERAL JOURNAL

PAGE 20

	DATE		DESCRIPTION	POST. REF.	DEBIT	CREDIT	
1							1
2							2
3							3
4							4
5							5
6							6
7							7
8							8
9							9
10							10
11							11
12							12
13							13
14							14
15							15
16							16
17							17
18							18
19							19
20							20
21							21
22							22
23							23
24							24
25							25
26							26
27							27
28							28
29							29
30							30
31							31
32							32
33							33
34							34

Problem 10-10B (Continued)

GENERAL JOURNAL

PAGE 21

DATE	DESCRIPTION	POST. REF.	DEBIT	CREDIT

Problem 10-10B (Continued)

2.

GENERAL LEDGER

ACCOUNT Cash ACCOUNT NO. 101

DATE		ITEM	POST. REF.	DEBIT	CREDIT	BALANCE DEBIT	BALANCE CREDIT
20-- Jan.	1	Balance	✓			2,890.75	

ACCOUNT Accounts Receivable ACCOUNT NO. 122

DATE		ITEM	POST. REF.	DEBIT	CREDIT	BALANCE DEBIT	BALANCE CREDIT
20-- Jan.	1	Balance	✓			6,300.00	

Problem 10-10B (Continued)

ACCOUNT Sales Tax Payable ACCOUNT NO. 231

DATE		ITEM	POST. REF.	DEBIT	CREDIT	BALANCE	
						DEBIT	CREDIT

ACCOUNT Sales ACCOUNT NO. 401

DATE		ITEM	POST. REF.	DEBIT	CREDIT	BALANCE	
						DEBIT	CREDIT

ACCOUNT Sales Returns and Allowances ACCOUNT NO. 401.1

DATE		ITEM	POST. REF.	DEBIT	CREDIT	BALANCE	
						DEBIT	CREDIT

ACCOUNT Bank Credit Card Expense ACCOUNT NO. 513

DATE		ITEM	POST. REF.	DEBIT	CREDIT	BALANCE	
						DEBIT	CREDIT

Problem 10-10B (Continued)

ACCOUNTS RECEIVABLE LEDGER

NAME Ray Boyd

ADDRESS 229 SE 65th Avenue, Portland, OR 97215-1451

DATE		ITEM	POST. REF.	DEBIT	CREDIT	BALANCE
20-- Jan.	1	Balance	✓			1,400.00

NAME Dazai Manufacturing

ADDRESS 447 6th Avenue, Flagstaff, AZ 86004-6842

DATE		ITEM	POST. REF.	DEBIT	CREDIT	BALANCE
20-- Jan.	1	Balance	✓			318.00

NAME Clint Hassell

ADDRESS 1462 N. Steves Blvd., Los Cruces, NM 88012-7791

DATE		ITEM	POST. REF.	DEBIT	CREDIT	BALANCE
20-- Jan.	1	Balance	✓			815.00

Problem 10-10B (Concluded)

NAME Jan Sowada

ADDRESS 5997 Blackgold Lane, Grapevine, TX 76051-2366

DATE		ITEM	POST. REF.	DEBIT	CREDIT	BALANCE
20-- Jan.	1	Balance	✓			1 4 8 1 00

NAME Robert Zehnle

ADDRESS 6881 Seneca Drive, San Diego, CA 92127-8671

DATE		ITEM	POST. REF.	DEBIT	CREDIT	BALANCE
20-- Jan.	1	Balance	✓			2 2 8 6 00

Name ______________________________

Problem 10-11B

1.

GENERAL JOURNAL

PAGE 7

DATE		DESCRIPTION	POST. REF.	DEBIT	CREDIT

Problem 10-11B (Continued)

GENERAL JOURNAL

PAGE 8

DATE		DESCRIPTION	POST. REF.	DEBIT	CREDIT

Problem 10-11B (Continued)

2.

GENERAL LEDGER

ACCOUNT Cash ACCOUNT NO. 101

DATE		ITEM	POST. REF.	DEBIT	CREDIT	BALANCE DEBIT	BALANCE CREDIT
20-- Apr.	1	Balance	✓			2,864.54	

ACCOUNT Accounts Receivable ACCOUNT NO. 122

DATE		ITEM	POST. REF.	DEBIT	CREDIT	BALANCE DEBIT	BALANCE CREDIT
20-- Apr.	1	Balance	✓			2,726.25	

Problem 10-11B (Continued)

ACCOUNT Sales Tax Payable ACCOUNT NO. 231

DATE		ITEM	POST. REF.	DEBIT	CREDIT	BALANCE	
						DEBIT	CREDIT

ACCOUNT Sales ACCOUNT NO. 401

DATE		ITEM	POST. REF.	DEBIT	CREDIT	BALANCE	
						DEBIT	CREDIT

ACCOUNT Sales Returns and Allowances ACCOUNT NO. 401.1

DATE		ITEM	POST. REF.	DEBIT	CREDIT	BALANCE	
						DEBIT	CREDIT

Problem 10-11B (Concluded)

ACCOUNTS RECEIVABLE LEDGER

NAME O. L. Meyers

ADDRESS 119 Hartford Turnpike, Vernon, CT 06066-0113

DATE		ITEM	POST. REF.	DEBIT	CREDIT	BALANCE

NAME Kelsay Munkres

ADDRESS 233 Cambridge Dr., Branford, CT 06405-9276

DATE		ITEM	POST. REF.	DEBIT	CREDIT	BALANCE
20-- Apr.	1	Balance	✓			482 00

NAME Andrew Plaa

ADDRESS 51 Bissell Ave., Old Saybrook, CT 06475-0212

DATE		ITEM	POST. REF.	DEBIT	CREDIT	BALANCE

NAME Melissa Richfield

ADDRESS 1107 Silver Lane, East Hartford, CT 06108-1907

DATE		ITEM	POST. REF.	DEBIT	CREDIT	BALANCE
20-- Apr.	1	Balance	✓			2244 25

Problem 10-12B

Mastery Problem

1.

GENERAL JOURNAL

PAGE 7

DATE		DESCRIPTION	POST. REF.	DEBIT	CREDIT

Mastery Problem (Continued)

GENERAL JOURNAL

PAGE 8

	DATE	DESCRIPTION	POST. REF.	DEBIT	CREDIT	
1						1
2						2
3						3
4						4
5						5
6						6
7						7
8						8
9						9
10						10
11						11
12						12
13						13
14						14
15						15
16						16
17						17
18						18
19						19
20						20
21						21
22						22
23						23
24						24
25						25
26						26
27						27
28						28
29						29
30						30
31						31
32						32
33						33
34						34

Mastery Problem (Continued)

GENERAL JOURNAL

PAGE 9

	DATE		DESCRIPTION	POST. REF.	DEBIT	CREDIT	
1							1
2							2
3							3
4							4
5							5
6							6
7							7
8							8
9							9
10							10
11							11
12							12
13							13
14							14
15							15
16							16
17							17
18							18
19							19
20							20
21							21
22							22
23							23
24							24
25							25
26							26
27							27
28							28
29							29
30							30
31							31
32							32
33							33
34							34

Mastery Problem (Continued)

GENERAL JOURNAL

PAGE 10

	DATE		DESCRIPTION	POST. REF.	DEBIT	CREDIT	
1							1
2							2
3							3
4							4
5							5
6							6
7							7
8							8
9							9
10							10

2.

GENERAL LEDGER

ACCOUNT Cash ACCOUNT NO. 101

DATE		ITEM	POST. REF.	DEBIT	CREDIT	BALANCE DEBIT	BALANCE CREDIT
20-- Sept.	1	Balance	✓			23,500.25	

Mastery Problem (Continued)

ACCOUNT Accounts Receivable ACCOUNT NO. 122

DATE		ITEM	POST. REF.	DEBIT	CREDIT	BALANCE DEBIT	BALANCE CREDIT
20-- Sept.	1	Balance	✓			8,50 75	

ACCOUNT Notes Payable ACCOUNT NO. 201

DATE		ITEM	POST. REF.	DEBIT	CREDIT	BALANCE DEBIT	BALANCE CREDIT
20-- Sept.	1	Balance	✓				2,500 00

Mastery Problem (Continued)

ACCOUNT Sales Tax Payable ACCOUNT NO. 231

DATE		ITEM	POST. REF.	DEBIT	CREDIT	BALANCE DEBIT	BALANCE CREDIT
20-- Sept.	1	Balance	✓				9 0 9 90

ACCOUNT Sales ACCOUNT NO. 401

DATE		ITEM	POST. REF.	DEBIT	CREDIT	BALANCE DEBIT	BALANCE CREDIT
20-- Sept.	1	Balance	✓				13 0 5 0 48

Mastery Problem (Continued)

ACCOUNT Sales Returns and Allowances ACCOUNT NO. 401.1

DATE		ITEM	POST. REF.	DEBIT	CREDIT	BALANCE DEBIT	BALANCE CREDIT
20-- Sept.	1	Balance	✓			86 00	

ACCOUNT Boarding and Grooming Revenue ACCOUNT NO. 402

DATE		ITEM	POST. REF.	DEBIT	CREDIT	BALANCE DEBIT	BALANCE CREDIT
20-- Sept.	1	Balance	✓				2,115 00

ACCOUNTS RECEIVABLE LEDGER

NAME All American Day Camp

ADDRESS 3025 Old Mill Run, Bloomington, IN 47408-1080

DATE		ITEM	POST. REF.	DEBIT	CREDIT	BALANCE

Mastery Problem (Continued)

NAME Rosa Alanso

ADDRESS 2541 East 2nd Street, Bloomington, IN 47401-5356

DATE		ITEM	POST. REF.	DEBIT	CREDIT	BALANCE
20-- Sept.	1	Balance	✓			456 00

NAME Ed Cochran

ADDRESS 2669 Windcrest Drive, Bloomington, IN 47401-5446

DATE		ITEM	POST. REF.	DEBIT	CREDIT	BALANCE
20-- Sept.	1	Balance	✓			63 25

NAME Joe Gloy

ADDRESS 1458 Parnell Avenue, Muncie, IN 47304-2682

DATE		ITEM	POST. REF.	DEBIT	CREDIT	BALANCE
20-- Sept.	1	Balance	✓			273 25

NAME Susan Hays

ADDRESS 1424 Jackson Creek Road, Nashville, IN 47448-2245

DATE		ITEM	POST. REF.	DEBIT	CREDIT	BALANCE

Mastery Problem (Continued)

NAME Ken Shank

ADDRESS 6422 E. Bender Road, Bloomington, IN 47401-7756

DATE		ITEM	POST. REF.	DEBIT	CREDIT	BALANCE

NAME Tully Shaw

ADDRESS 3315 Longview Avenue, Bloomington, IN 47401-7223

DATE		ITEM	POST. REF.	DEBIT	CREDIT	BALANCE

NAME Nancy Truelove

ADDRESS 2300 E. National Road, Cumberland, IN 46229-4824

DATE		ITEM	POST. REF.	DEBIT	CREDIT	BALANCE
20-- Sept.	1	Balance	✓			58.25

NAME Jean Warkentin

ADDRESS 1813 Deep Well Court, Bloomington, IN 47401-5124

DATE		ITEM	POST. REF.	DEBIT	CREDIT	BALANCE

Mastery Problem (Concluded)

3.

4.

Challenge Problem

GENERAL JOURNAL

PAGE

DATE		DESCRIPTION	POST. REF.	DEBIT	CREDIT

Exercise 11-1A

1. ______________________
2. Purchase order
3. ______________________
4. ______________________

Exercise 11-2A

1.

____

____

____

____

2.

____

____

____

____

3.

GENERAL JOURNAL

PAGE

	DATE		DESCRIPTION	POST. REF.	DEBIT	CREDIT	
1							1
2							2
3							3
4							4
5							5
6							6
7							7
8							8
9							9
10							10
11							11
12							12
13							13
14							14
15							15

Exercise 11-3A

1.

Cash

Accounts Payable

Purchases

Purchases Returns and Allowances

Purchases Discounts

Freight-In

2.

Cash

Accounts Payable

Purchases

Purchases Returns and Allowances

Purchases Discounts

Freight-In

Name ______________________________

Exercise 11-3A (Concluded)

3.

Cash

Accounts Payable

Purchases

Purchases Returns and Allowances

Purchases Discounts

Freight-In

4.

Cash

Accounts Payable

Purchases

Purchases Returns and Allowances

Purchases Discounts

Freight-In

Exercise 11-4A

Name ______________________

Exercise 11-5A

GENERAL JOURNAL

PAGE

DATE		DESCRIPTION	POST. REF.	DEBIT	CREDIT

Exercise 11-6A

GENERAL JOURNAL

PAGE 3

	DATE		DESCRIPTION	POST. REF.	DEBIT	CREDIT	
1							1
2							2
3							3
4							4
5							5
6							6
7							7
8							8
9							9
10							10
11							11
12							12

GENERAL LEDGER

ACCOUNT Accounts Payable ACCOUNT NO. 202

DATE		ITEM	POST. REF.	DEBIT	CREDIT	BALANCE DEBIT	BALANCE CREDIT
20-- July	1	Balance	✓				10,650.00

ACCOUNT Purchases Returns and Allowances ACCOUNT NO. 501.1

DATE		ITEM	POST. REF.	DEBIT	CREDIT	BALANCE DEBIT	BALANCE CREDIT

Name ____________________

Exercise 11-6A (Concluded)

ACCOUNTS PAYABLE LEDGER

NAME Datamagic

ADDRESS

DATE		ITEM	POST. REF.	DEBIT	CREDIT	BALANCE
20-- July	1	Balance	✓			2,600 00

NAME Starcraft Industries

ADDRESS

DATE		ITEM	POST. REF.	DEBIT	CREDIT	BALANCE
20-- July	1	Balance	✓			4,300 00

NAME XYZ, Inc.

ADDRESS

DATE		ITEM	POST. REF.	DEBIT	CREDIT	BALANCE
20-- July	1	Balance	✓			3,750 00

Exercise 11-7A

GENERAL JOURNAL

PAGE 16

	DATE		DESCRIPTION	POST. REF.	DEBIT	CREDIT	
1							1
2							2
3							3
4							4
5							5
6							6
7							7
8							8
9							9
10							10
11							11
12							12
13							13
14							14
15							15
16							16
17							17
18							18
19							19
20							20
21							21

Exercise 11-8A

Name ____________________

Problem 11-9A

1.

GENERAL JOURNAL

PAGE 16

	DATE		DESCRIPTION	POST. REF.	DEBIT	CREDIT	
1							1
2							2
3							3
4							4
5							5
6							6
7							7
8							8
9							9
10							10
11							11
12							12
13							13
14							14
15							15
16							16
17							17
18							18
19							19
20							20
21							21
22							22
23							23
24							24
25							25
26							26
27							27
28							28
29							29
30							30
31							31
32							32
33							33
34							34

Problem 11-9A (Continued)

2.

GENERAL LEDGER

ACCOUNT Accounts Payable ACCOUNT NO. 202

DATE		ITEM	POST. REF.	DEBIT	CREDIT	BALANCE	
						DEBIT	CREDIT

ACCOUNT Purchases ACCOUNT NO. 501

DATE		ITEM	POST. REF.	DEBIT	CREDIT	BALANCE	
						DEBIT	CREDIT

ACCOUNTS PAYABLE LEDGER

NAME

ADDRESS

DATE		ITEM	POST. REF.	DEBIT	CREDIT	BALANCE

Problem 11-9A (Concluded)

NAME

ADDRESS

DATE		ITEM	POST. REF.	DEBIT	CREDIT	BALANCE

NAME

ADDRESS

DATE		ITEM	POST. REF.	DEBIT	CREDIT	BALANCE

NAME

ADDRESS

DATE		ITEM	POST. REF.	DEBIT	CREDIT	BALANCE

NAME

ADDRESS

DATE		ITEM	POST. REF.	DEBIT	CREDIT	BALANCE

Problem 11-10A

1.

GENERAL JOURNAL PAGE 9

DATE		DESCRIPTION	POST. REF.	DEBIT	CREDIT

Problem 11-10A (Continued)

GENERAL JOURNAL

PAGE 10

	DATE		DESCRIPTION	POST. REF.	DEBIT	CREDIT	
1							1
2							2
3							3
4							4
5							5

2.

GENERAL LEDGER

ACCOUNT Cash ACCOUNT NO. 101

DATE		ITEM	POST. REF.	DEBIT	CREDIT	BALANCE DEBIT	BALANCE CREDIT
20-- May	1	Balance	✓			40,000.00	

ACCOUNT Accounts Payable ACCOUNT NO. 202

DATE		ITEM	POST. REF.	DEBIT	CREDIT	BALANCE DEBIT	BALANCE CREDIT
20-- May	1	Balance	✓				20,000.00

Problem 11-10A (Continued)

ACCOUNT Purchases ACCOUNT NO. 501

DATE		ITEM	POST. REF.	DEBIT	CREDIT	BALANCE DEBIT	BALANCE CREDIT

ACCOUNT Purchases Discounts ACCOUNT NO. 501.2

DATE		ITEM	POST. REF.	DEBIT	CREDIT	BALANCE DEBIT	BALANCE CREDIT

ACCOUNT Freight-In ACCOUNT NO. 502

DATE		ITEM	POST. REF.	DEBIT	CREDIT	BALANCE DEBIT	BALANCE CREDIT

ACCOUNT Rent Expense ACCOUNT NO. 521

DATE		ITEM	POST. REF.	DEBIT	CREDIT	BALANCE DEBIT	BALANCE CREDIT

ACCOUNT Utilities Expense ACCOUNT NO. 533

DATE		ITEM	POST. REF.	DEBIT	CREDIT	BALANCE DEBIT	BALANCE CREDIT

Problem 11-10A (Concluded)

ACCOUNTS PAYABLE LEDGER

NAME Fantastic Toys

ADDRESS

DATE		ITEM	POST. REF.	DEBIT	CREDIT	BALANCE
20-- May	1	Balance	✓			5,200.00

NAME Goya Outlet

ADDRESS

DATE		ITEM	POST. REF.	DEBIT	CREDIT	BALANCE
20-- May	1	Balance	✓			3,800.00

NAME Mueller's Distributors

ADDRESS

DATE		ITEM	POST. REF.	DEBIT	CREDIT	BALANCE
20-- May	1	Balance	✓			3,600.00

NAME Van Kooning

ADDRESS

DATE		ITEM	POST. REF.	DEBIT	CREDIT	BALANCE
20-- May	1	Balance	✓			7,400.00

Problem 11-11A

1.

GENERAL JOURNAL

PAGE 16

DATE	DESCRIPTION	POST. REF.	DEBIT	CREDIT

Name ______________________________

Problem 11-11A (Continued)

GENERAL JOURNAL

PAGE 17

	DATE		DESCRIPTION	POST. REF.	DEBIT	CREDIT	
1							1
2							2
3							3
4							4
5							5
6							6
7							7
8							8
9							9
10							10
11							11
12							12
13							13
14							14
15							15
16							16
17							17
18							18
19							19
20							20
21							21
22							22
23							23
24							24
25							25
26							26
27							27
28							28
29							29
30							30
31							31
32							32
33							33
34							34

Problem 11-11A (Continued)

2.

GENERAL LEDGER

ACCOUNT Cash ACCOUNT NO. 101

DATE		ITEM	POST. REF.	DEBIT	CREDIT	BALANCE DEBIT	BALANCE CREDIT
20-- July	1	Balance	✓			21,000.00	

ACCOUNT Accounts Payable ACCOUNT NO. 202

DATE		ITEM	POST. REF.	DEBIT	CREDIT	BALANCE DEBIT	BALANCE CREDIT

Problem 11-11A (Continued)

ACCOUNT Purchases ACCOUNT NO. 501

DATE		ITEM	POST. REF.	DEBIT	CREDIT	BALANCE	
						DEBIT	CREDIT

ACCOUNT Purchases Returns and Allowances ACCOUNT NO. 501.1

DATE		ITEM	POST. REF.	DEBIT	CREDIT	BALANCE	
						DEBIT	CREDIT

ACCOUNT Purchases Discounts ACCOUNT NO. 501.2

DATE		ITEM	POST. REF.	DEBIT	CREDIT	BALANCE	
						DEBIT	CREDIT

ACCOUNT Rent Expense ACCOUNT NO. 521

DATE		ITEM	POST. REF.	DEBIT	CREDIT	BALANCE	
						DEBIT	CREDIT

Problem 11-11A (Concluded)

ACCOUNTS PAYABLE LEDGER

NAME

ADDRESS

DATE		ITEM	POST. REF.	DEBIT	CREDIT	BALANCE

NAME

ADDRESS

DATE		ITEM	POST. REF.	DEBIT	CREDIT	BALANCE

NAME

ADDRESS

DATE		ITEM	POST. REF.	DEBIT	CREDIT	BALANCE

NAME

ADDRESS

DATE		ITEM	POST. REF.	DEBIT	CREDIT	BALANCE

Problem 11-12A

Exercise 11-1B

1. ______

2. ______

3. ______

4. ______

Exercise 11-2B

1.

2.

3.

GENERAL JOURNAL PAGE

	DATE		DESCRIPTION	POST. REF.	DEBIT	CREDIT	
1							1
2							2
3							3
4							4
5							5
6							6
7							7
8							8
9							9
10							10
11							11
12							12
13							13
15							15

Exercise 11-3B

1.

Cash	

Accounts Payable	

Purchases	

Purchases Returns and Allowances	

Purchases Discounts	

Freight-In	

2.

Cash	

Accounts Payable	

Purchases	

Purchases Returns and Allowances	

Purchases Discounts	

Freight-In	

Exercise 11-3B (Concluded)

3.

Cash

Accounts Payable

Purchases

Purchases Returns and Allowances

Purchases Discounts

Freight-In

4.

Cash

Accounts Payable

Purchases

Purchases Returns and Allowances

Purchases Discounts

Freight-In

Exercise 11-4B

Exercise 11-5B

GENERAL JOURNAL

PAGE

DATE		DESCRIPTION	POST. REF.	DEBIT	CREDIT

Name ______________________________

Exercise 11-6B

GENERAL JOURNAL

PAGE 3

	DATE		DESCRIPTION	POST. REF.	DEBIT	CREDIT	
1							1
2							2
3							3
4							4
5							5
6							6
7							7
8							8
9							9
10							10
11							11
12							12

GENERAL LEDGER

ACCOUNT Accounts Payable ACCOUNT NO. 202

DATE		ITEM	POST. REF.	DEBIT	CREDIT	BALANCE DEBIT	BALANCE CREDIT
20-- Mar.	1	Balance	✓				8 3 5 0 00

ACCOUNT Purchases Returns and Allowances ACCOUNT NO. 501.1

DATE		ITEM	POST. REF.	DEBIT	CREDIT	BALANCE DEBIT	BALANCE CREDIT

Exercise 11-6B (Concluded)

ACCOUNTS PAYABLE LEDGER

NAME A & D Arms

ADDRESS

DATE		ITEM	POST. REF.	DEBIT	CREDIT	BALANCE
20-- Mar.	1	Balance	✓			2,300.00

NAME Mighty Mansion

ADDRESS

DATE		ITEM	POST. REF.	DEBIT	CREDIT	BALANCE
20-- Mar.	1	Balance	✓			1,450.00

NAME Tower Industries

ADDRESS

DATE		ITEM	POST. REF.	DEBIT	CREDIT	BALANCE
20-- Mar.	1	Balance	✓			4,600.00

Name ______________________

Exercise 11-7B

GENERAL JOURNAL

PAGE 16

	DATE		DESCRIPTION	POST. REF.	DEBIT	CREDIT	
1							1
2							2
3							3
4							4
5							5
6							6
7							7
8							8
9							9
10							10
11							11
12							12
13							13
14							14
15							15
16							16
17							17
18							18
19							19
20							20
21							21

Exercise 11-8B

Problem 11-9B

1.

GENERAL JOURNAL

PAGE 16

	DATE		DESCRIPTION	POST. REF.	DEBIT	CREDIT	
1							1
2							2
3							3
4							4
5							5
6							6
7							7
8							8
9							9
10							10
11							11
12							12
13							13
14							14
15							15
16							16
17							17
18							18
19							19
20							20
21							21
22							22
23							23
24							24
25							25
26							26
27							27
28							28
29							29
30							30
31							31
32							32
33							33
34							34

Problem 11-9B (Continued)

2.

GENERAL LEDGER

ACCOUNT Accounts Payable ACCOUNT NO. 202

DATE		ITEM	POST. REF.	DEBIT	CREDIT	BALANCE DEBIT	BALANCE CREDIT

ACCOUNT Purchases ACCOUNT NO. 501

DATE		ITEM	POST. REF.	DEBIT	CREDIT	BALANCE DEBIT	BALANCE CREDIT

ACCOUNTS PAYABLE LEDGER

NAME

ADDRESS

DATE		ITEM	POST. REF.	DEBIT	CREDIT	BALANCE

Problem 11-9B (Concluded)

NAME

ADDRESS

DATE		ITEM	POST. REF.	DEBIT	CREDIT	BALANCE

NAME

ADDRESS

DATE		ITEM	POST. REF.	DEBIT	CREDIT	BALANCE

NAME

ADDRESS

DATE		ITEM	POST. REF.	DEBIT	CREDIT	BALANCE

NAME

ADDRESS

DATE		ITEM	POST. REF.	DEBIT	CREDIT	BALANCE

Name ______________________________

Problem 11-10B

1.

GENERAL JOURNAL

PAGE 9

DATE		DESCRIPTION	POST. REF.	DEBIT	CREDIT

Problem 11-10B (Continued)

GENERAL JOURNAL

PAGE 10

	DATE		DESCRIPTION	POST. REF.	DEBIT	CREDIT	
1							1
2							2
3							3
4							4
5							5

2.

GENERAL LEDGER

ACCOUNT Cash ACCOUNT NO. 101

DATE		ITEM	POST. REF.	DEBIT	CREDIT	BALANCE DEBIT	BALANCE CREDIT
20-- May	1	Balance	✓			40 0 0 0 00	

ACCOUNT Accounts Payable ACCOUNT NO. 202

DATE		ITEM	POST. REF.	DEBIT	CREDIT	BALANCE DEBIT	BALANCE CREDIT
20-- May	1	Balance	✓				20 0 0 0 00

Problem 11-10B (Continued)

ACCOUNT Purchases ACCOUNT NO. 501

DATE	ITEM	POST. REF.	DEBIT	CREDIT	BALANCE DEBIT	BALANCE CREDIT

ACCOUNT Purchases Discounts ACCOUNT NO. 501.2

DATE	ITEM	POST. REF.	DEBIT	CREDIT	BALANCE DEBIT	BALANCE CREDIT

ACCOUNT Freight-In ACCOUNT NO. 502

DATE	ITEM	POST. REF.	DEBIT	CREDIT	BALANCE DEBIT	BALANCE CREDIT

ACCOUNT Rent Expense ACCOUNT NO. 521

DATE	ITEM	POST. REF.	DEBIT	CREDIT	BALANCE DEBIT	BALANCE CREDIT

ACCOUNT Utilities Expense ACCOUNT NO. 533

DATE	ITEM	POST. REF.	DEBIT	CREDIT	BALANCE DEBIT	BALANCE CREDIT

Problem 11-10B (Concluded)

ACCOUNTS PAYABLE LEDGER

NAME Cortez Distributors

ADDRESS

DATE		ITEM	POST. REF.	DEBIT	CREDIT	BALANCE
20-- May	1	Balance	✓			4 2 0 0 00

NAME Indra & Velga

ADDRESS

DATE		ITEM	POST. REF.	DEBIT	CREDIT	BALANCE
20-- May	1	Balance	✓			6 8 0 0 00

NAME Toy Corner

ADDRESS

DATE		ITEM	POST. REF.	DEBIT	CREDIT	BALANCE
20-- May	1	Balance	✓			4 6 0 0 00

NAME Troutman Outlet

ADDRESS

DATE		ITEM	POST. REF.	DEBIT	CREDIT	BALANCE
20-- May	1	Balance	✓			4 4 0 0 00

Name ______________________________

Problem 11-11B

1.

GENERAL JOURNAL

PAGE 16

DATE		DESCRIPTION	POST. REF.	DEBIT	CREDIT

Problem 11-11B (Continued)

GENERAL JOURNAL

PAGE 17

	DATE		DESCRIPTION	POST. REF.	DEBIT	CREDIT	
1							1
2							2
3							3
4							4
5							5
6							6
7							7
8							8
9							9
10							10
11							11
12							12
13							13
14							14
15							15
16							16
17							17
18							18
19							19
20							20
21							21
22							22
23							23
24							24
25							25
26							26
27							27
28							28
29							29
30							30
31							31
32							32
33							33
34							34

Problem 11-11B (Continued)

2.

GENERAL LEDGER

ACCOUNT Cash ACCOUNT NO. 101

DATE		ITEM	POST. REF.	DEBIT	CREDIT	BALANCE DEBIT	BALANCE CREDIT
20-- July	1	Balance	✓			20,000.00	

ACCOUNT Accounts Payable ACCOUNT NO. 202

DATE		ITEM	POST. REF.	DEBIT	CREDIT	BALANCE DEBIT	BALANCE CREDIT

Problem 11-11B (Continued)

ACCOUNT Purchases ACCOUNT NO. 501

DATE		ITEM	POST. REF.	DEBIT	CREDIT	BALANCE	
						DEBIT	CREDIT

ACCOUNT Purchases Returns and Allowances ACCOUNT NO. 501.1

DATE		ITEM	POST. REF.	DEBIT	CREDIT	BALANCE	
						DEBIT	CREDIT

ACCOUNT Purchases Discounts ACCOUNT NO. 501.2

DATE		ITEM	POST. REF.	DEBIT	CREDIT	BALANCE	
						DEBIT	CREDIT

ACCOUNT Rent Expense ACCOUNT NO. 521

DATE		ITEM	POST. REF.	DEBIT	CREDIT	BALANCE	
						DEBIT	CREDIT

Problem 11-11B (Concluded)

ACCOUNTS PAYABLE LEDGER

NAME

ADDRESS

DATE		ITEM	POST. REF.	DEBIT	CREDIT	BALANCE

NAME

ADDRESS

DATE		ITEM	POST. REF.	DEBIT	CREDIT	BALANCE

NAME

ADDRESS

DATE		ITEM	POST. REF.	DEBIT	CREDIT	BALANCE

NAME

ADDRESS

DATE		ITEM	POST. REF.	DEBIT	CREDIT	BALANCE

Problem 11-12B

Name ______________________________

Mastery Problem

1.

GENERAL JOURNAL

PAGE 16

	DATE		DESCRIPTION	POST. REF.	DEBIT	CREDIT	
1							1
2							2
3							3
4							4
5							5
6							6
7							7
8							8
9							9
10							10
11							11
12							12
13							13
14							14
15							15
16							16
17							17
18							18
19							19
20							20
21							21
22							22
23							23
24							24
25							25
26							26
27							27
28							28
29							29
30							30
31							31
32							32
33							33
34							34

Mastery Problem (Continued)

GENERAL JOURNAL

PAGE 17

	DATE		DESCRIPTION	POST. REF.	DEBIT	CREDIT	
1							1
2							2
3							3
4							4
5							5
6							6
7							7
8							8
9							9
10							10
11							11
12							12
13							13
14							14
15							15
16							16
17							17
18							18
19							19
20							20
21							21
22							22
23							23
24							24
25							25
26							26
27							27
28							28
29							29
30							30
31							31
32							32
33							33
34							34

Mastery Problem (Continued)

2.

GENERAL LEDGER

ACCOUNT Cash ACCOUNT NO. 101

DATE		ITEM	POST. REF.	DEBIT	CREDIT	BALANCE DEBIT	BALANCE CREDIT
20-- June	1	Balance	✓			32,200.00	

ACCOUNT Accounts Payable ACCOUNT NO. 202

DATE		ITEM	POST. REF.	DEBIT	CREDIT	BALANCE DEBIT	BALANCE CREDIT
20-- June	1	Balance	✓				2,000.00

Mastery Problem (Continued)

ACCOUNT M. French, Drawing ACCOUNT NO. 312

DATE		ITEM	POST. REF.	DEBIT	CREDIT	BALANCE DEBIT	BALANCE CREDIT
20-- June	1	Balance	✓			18,000.00	

ACCOUNT Purchases ACCOUNT NO. 501

DATE		ITEM	POST. REF.	DEBIT	CREDIT	BALANCE DEBIT	BALANCE CREDIT
20-- June	1	Balance	✓			67,021.66	

ACCOUNT Purchases Returns and Allowances ACCOUNT NO. 501.1

DATE		ITEM	POST. REF.	DEBIT	CREDIT	BALANCE DEBIT	BALANCE CREDIT
20-- June	1	Balance	✓				2,315.23

ACCOUNT Purchases Discounts ACCOUNT NO. 501.2

DATE		ITEM	POST. REF.	DEBIT	CREDIT	BALANCE DEBIT	BALANCE CREDIT
20-- June	1	Balance	✓				905.00

Mastery Problem (Continued)

ACCOUNT Freight-In ACCOUNT NO. 502

DATE		ITEM	POST. REF.	DEBIT	CREDIT	BALANCE DEBIT	BALANCE CREDIT
20-- June	1	Balance	✓			5 2 2 60	

ACCOUNT Rent Expense ACCOUNT NO. 521

DATE		ITEM	POST. REF.	DEBIT	CREDIT	BALANCE DEBIT	BALANCE CREDIT
20-- June	1	Balance	✓			3 1 2 5 00	

ACCOUNT Utilities Expense ACCOUNT NO. 533

DATE		ITEM	POST. REF.	DEBIT	CREDIT	BALANCE DEBIT	BALANCE CREDIT
20-- June	1	Balance	✓			1 5 2 2 87	

ACCOUNTS PAYABLE LEDGER

NAME Broadway Publishing, Inc.

ADDRESS 2300 Goodman, Cincinnati, OH 45219-2901

DATE		ITEM	POST. REF.	DEBIT	CREDIT	BALANCE

Mastery Problem (Continued)

NAME Irving Publishing Company

ADDRESS 5200 N. Keystone Ave., Indianapolis, IN 46220-1986

DATE		ITEM	POST. REF.	DEBIT	CREDIT	BALANCE

NAME Northeastern Publishing Co.

ADDRESS 874 Crescent Drive, Flint, MI 48503-7564

DATE		ITEM	POST. REF.	DEBIT	CREDIT	BALANCE
20-- June	1	Balance	✓			2,000.00

NAME Riley Publishing Co.

ADDRESS 5675 Pulaski Road, Chicago, IL 60629-6705

DATE		ITEM	POST. REF.	DEBIT	CREDIT	BALANCE

Mastery Problem (Concluded)

3.

4.

Challenge Problem

GENERAL JOURNAL

PAGE

DATE		DESCRIPTION	POST. REF.	DEBIT	CREDIT

Exercise 11Apx-1A

1.

GENERAL JOURNAL

PAGE

	DATE		DESCRIPTION	POST. REF.	DEBIT	CREDIT	
1							1
2							2
3							3
4							4
5							5
6							6
7							7
8							8
9							9
10							10
11							11
12							12
13							13
14							14
15							15
16							16

2.

1							1
2							2
3							3
4							4
5							5
6							6
7							7
8							8
9							9
10							10
11							11
12							12
13							13
14							14
15							15
16							16

Exercise 11Apx-1B

1.

GENERAL JOURNAL

PAGE

DATE		DESCRIPTION	POST. REF.	DEBIT	CREDIT

2.

Exercise 12-1A

		Journal
a.	Sold merchandise on account.	
b.	Purchased delivery truck on account for use in the business.	
c.	Received payment from customer on account.	
d.	Purchased merchandise on account.	
e.	Issued check in payment of electric bill.	
f.	Recorded depreciation on factory building.	

Exercise 12-2A

SALES JOURNAL PAGE

DATE	SALE NO.	TO WHOM SOLD	POST. REF.	ACCOUNTS RECEIVABLE DEBIT	SALES CREDIT	SALES TAX PAYABLE CREDIT

Exercise 12-3A

CASH RECEIPTS JOURNAL PAGE

	DATE	ACCOUNT CREDITED	POST. REF.	GENERAL CREDIT	ACCOUNTS RECEIVABLE CREDIT	SALES CREDIT	SALES TAX PAYABLE CREDIT	CASH DEBIT	
1									1
2									2
3									3
4									4
5									5
6									6
7									7
8									8
9									9
10									10
11									11

Exercise 12-4A

PURCHASES JOURNAL

PAGE

DATE	INVOICE NO.	FROM WHOM PURCHASED	POST. REF.	PURCHASES DEBIT ACCTS. PAY. CREDIT

Exercise 12-5A

CASH PAYMENTS JOURNAL

PAGE

DATE	CK. NO.	ACCOUNT DEBITED	POST. REF.	GENERAL DEBIT	ACCOUNTS PAYABLE DEBIT	PURCHASES DEBIT	PURCHASES DISCOUNTS CREDIT	CASH CREDIT

Problem 12-6A

1.

SALES JOURNAL

PAGE 8

DATE	SALE NO.	TO WHOM SOLD	POST. REF.	ACCOUNTS RECEIVABLE DEBIT	SALES CREDIT	SALES TAX PAYABLE CREDIT

2.

GENERAL LEDGER

ACCOUNT Accounts Receivable ACCOUNT NO. 122

DATE	ITEM	POST. REF.	DEBIT	CREDIT	BALANCE DEBIT	BALANCE CREDIT

ACCOUNT Sales Tax Payable ACCOUNT NO. 231

DATE	ITEM	POST. REF.	DEBIT	CREDIT	BALANCE DEBIT	BALANCE CREDIT

Problem 12-6A (Concluded)

ACCOUNT Sales ACCOUNT NO. 401

DATE		ITEM	POST. REF.	DEBIT	CREDIT	BALANCE DEBIT	BALANCE CREDIT

ACCOUNTS RECEIVABLE LEDGER

NAME Hassan Co.

ADDRESS 1225 W. Temperance Street, Ellettsville, IN 47429-9976

DATE		ITEM	POST. REF.	DEBIT	CREDIT	BALANCE

NAME Habrock, Inc.

ADDRESS 125 Fishers Dr., Noblesville, IN 47870-8867

DATE		ITEM	POST. REF.	DEBIT	CREDIT	BALANCE

NAME Jeter Manufacturing Co.

ADDRESS 8825 Old State Road, Bloomington, IN 47401-8823

DATE		ITEM	POST. REF.	DEBIT	CREDIT	BALANCE

NAME Seth Mowbray

ADDRESS 2100 Greer Lane, Bedford, IN 47421-8876

DATE		ITEM	POST. REF.	DEBIT	CREDIT	BALANCE

Problem 12-7A

1.

GENERAL JOURNAL

PAGE 8

DATE		DESCRIPTION	POST. REF.	DEBIT	CREDIT

Problem 12-7A (Continued)

CASH RECEIPTS JOURNAL

	DATE	ACCOUNT CREDITED	POST. REF.	GENERAL CREDIT	ACCOUNTS RECEIVABLE CREDIT
1					
2					
3					
4					
5					
6					
7					
8					
9					
10					
11					
12					
13					
14					
15					
16					
17					
18					
19					
20					
21					
22					
23					
24					
25					
26					
27					
28					

Name ______________________________

Problem 12-7A (Continued)

PAGE 10

SALES CREDIT	SALES TAX PAYABLE CREDIT	BANK CREDIT CARD EXPENSE DEBIT	CASH DEBIT	
				1
				2
				3
				4
				5
				6
				7
				8
				9
				10
				11
				12
				13
				14
				15
				16
				17
				18
				19
				20
				21
				22
				23
				24
				25
				26
				27
				28

Problem 12-7A (Continued)

2.

GENERAL LEDGER

ACCOUNT Cash ACCOUNT NO. 101

DATE		ITEM	POST. REF.	DEBIT	CREDIT	BALANCE DEBIT	BALANCE CREDIT
20-- Dec.	1	Balance	✓			9,862.00	

ACCOUNT Accounts Receivable ACCOUNT NO. 122

DATE		ITEM	POST. REF.	DEBIT	CREDIT	BALANCE DEBIT	BALANCE CREDIT
20-- Dec.	1	Balance	✓			9,352.00	

ACCOUNT Sales Tax Payable ACCOUNT NO. 231

DATE		ITEM	POST. REF.	DEBIT	CREDIT	BALANCE DEBIT	BALANCE CREDIT

ACCOUNT Sales ACCOUNT NO. 401

DATE		ITEM	POST. REF.	DEBIT	CREDIT	BALANCE DEBIT	BALANCE CREDIT

Problem 12-7A (Continued)

ACCOUNT Sales Returns and Allowances ACCOUNT NO. 401.1

DATE		ITEM	POST. REF.	DEBIT	CREDIT	BALANCE	
						DEBIT	CREDIT

ACCOUNT Bank Credit Card Expense ACCOUNT NO. 513

DATE		ITEM	POST. REF.	DEBIT	CREDIT	BALANCE	
						DEBIT	CREDIT

ACCOUNTS RECEIVABLE LEDGER

NAME Michael Anderson

ADDRESS 233 West 11th Avenue, Detroit, MI 59500-1154

DATE		ITEM	POST. REF.	DEBIT	CREDIT	BALANCE
20-- Dec.	1	Balance	✓			2,480.00

NAME Ansel Manufacturing

ADDRESS 284 West 88 Street, Detroit, MI 59522-1168

DATE		ITEM	POST. REF.	DEBIT	CREDIT	BALANCE
20-- Dec.	1	Balance	✓			982.00

Problem 12-7A (Concluded)

NAME J. Gorbea

ADDRESS P.O. Box 864, Detroit, MI 59552-0864

DATE		ITEM	POST. REF.	DEBIT	CREDIT	BALANCE
20-- Dec.	1	Balance	✓			880 00

NAME Rachel Carson

ADDRESS 11312 Fourteenth Avenue South, Detroit, MI 59221-1142

DATE		ITEM	POST. REF.	DEBIT	CREDIT	BALANCE
20-- Dec.	1	Balance	✓			3,200 00

NAME Tom Wilson

ADDRESS 100 NW Seward St., Detroit, MI 59210-1337

DATE		ITEM	POST. REF.	DEBIT	CREDIT	BALANCE
20-- Dec.	1	Balance	✓			1,810 00

Problem 12-8A

1.

SALES JOURNAL

PAGE 6

DATE	SALE NO.	TO WHOM SOLD	POST. REF.	ACCOUNTS RECEIVABLE DEBIT	SALES CREDIT	SALES TAX PAYABLE CREDIT

CASH RECEIPTS JOURNAL

PAGE 9

	DATE	ACCOUNT CREDITED	POST. REF.	GENERAL CREDIT	ACCOUNTS RECEIVABLE CREDIT	SALES CREDIT	SALES TAX PAYABLE CREDIT	CASH DEBIT	
1									1
2									2
3									3
4									4
5									5
6									6
7									7
8									8
9									9

Problem 12-8A (Continued)

GENERAL JOURNAL

PAGE 5

	DATE		DESCRIPTION	POST. REF.	DEBIT	CREDIT	
1							1
2							2
3							3
4							4
5							5
6							6
7							7
8							8
9							9
10							10
11							11
12							12
13							13
14							14

2.

GENERAL LEDGER

ACCOUNT Cash ACCOUNT NO. 101

DATE		ITEM	POST. REF.	DEBIT	CREDIT	BALANCE	
						DEBIT	CREDIT
20-- Mar.	1	Balance	✓			9,741.00	

ACCOUNT Accounts Receivable ACCOUNT NO. 122

DATE		ITEM	POST. REF.	DEBIT	CREDIT	BALANCE	
						DEBIT	CREDIT
20-- Mar.	1	Balance	✓			10,58.25	

Problem 12-8A (Continued)

ACCOUNT Sales Tax Payable ACCOUNT NO. 231

DATE		ITEM	POST. REF.	DEBIT	CREDIT	BALANCE	
						DEBIT	CREDIT

ACCOUNT Sales ACCOUNT NO. 401

DATE		ITEM	POST. REF.	DEBIT	CREDIT	BALANCE	
						DEBIT	CREDIT

ACCOUNT Sales Returns and Allowances ACCOUNT NO. 401.1

DATE		ITEM	POST. REF.	DEBIT	CREDIT	BALANCE	
						DEBIT	CREDIT

Problem 12-8A (Concluded)

ACCOUNTS RECEIVABLE LEDGER

NAME Able & Co.

ADDRESS 1424 Jackson Creek Road, Nashville, IN 47448-2245

DATE		ITEM	POST. REF.	DEBIT	CREDIT	BALANCE

NAME Blevins Bakery

ADDRESS 6422 E. Bender Road, Bloomington, IN 47401-7756

DATE		ITEM	POST. REF.	DEBIT	CREDIT	BALANCE

NAME R. J. Kalas, Inc.

ADDRESS 3315 Longview Avenue, Bloomington, IN 47401-7223

DATE		ITEM	POST. REF.	DEBIT	CREDIT	BALANCE

NAME Thompson Group

ADDRESS 2300 E. National Road, Cumberland, IN 46229-4824

DATE		ITEM	POST. REF.	DEBIT	CREDIT	BALANCE
20-- Mar.	1	Balance	✓			1 0 5 8 25

Problem 12-9A

1.

PURCHASES JOURNAL

PAGE 7

	DATE	INVOICE NO.	FROM WHOM PURCHASED	POST. REF.	PURCHASES DEBIT ACCTS. PAY. CREDIT	
1						1
2						2
3						3
4						4
5						5
6						6
7						7
8						8
9						9
10						10
11						11
12						12
13						13
14						14

2.

GENERAL LEDGER

ACCOUNT Accounts Payable ACCOUNT NO. 202

DATE	ITEM	POST. REF.	DEBIT	CREDIT	BALANCE	
					DEBIT	CREDIT

ACCOUNT Purchases ACCOUNT NO. 501

DATE	ITEM	POST. REF.	DEBIT	CREDIT	BALANCE	
					DEBIT	CREDIT

Problem 12-9A (Concluded)

ACCOUNTS PAYABLE LEDGER

NAME

ADDRESS

DATE		ITEM	POST. REF.	DEBIT	CREDIT	BALANCE

NAME

ADDRESS

DATE		ITEM	POST. REF.	DEBIT	CREDIT	BALANCE

NAME

ADDRESS

DATE		ITEM	POST. REF.	DEBIT	CREDIT	BALANCE

NAME

ADDRESS

DATE		ITEM	POST. REF.	DEBIT	CREDIT	BALANCE

NAME

ADDRESS

DATE		ITEM	POST. REF.	DEBIT	CREDIT	BALANCE

Name ______________________________

Problem 12-10A

1.

GENERAL LEDGER

ACCOUNT Accounts Payable — ACCOUNT NO. 202

DATE		ITEM	POST. REF.	DEBIT	CREDIT	BALANCE DEBIT	BALANCE CREDIT

ACCOUNT Purchases — ACCOUNT NO. 501

DATE		ITEM	POST. REF.	DEBIT	CREDIT	BALANCE DEBIT	BALANCE CREDIT

2.

ACCOUNTS PAYABLE LEDGER

NAME

ADDRESS

DATE		ITEM	POST. REF.	DEBIT	CREDIT	BALANCE

NAME

ADDRESS

DATE		ITEM	POST. REF.	DEBIT	CREDIT	BALANCE

Problem 12-10A (Concluded)

NAME

ADDRESS

DATE		ITEM	POST. REF.	DEBIT	CREDIT	BALANCE

NAME

ADDRESS

DATE		ITEM	POST. REF.	DEBIT	CREDIT	BALANCE

NAME

ADDRESS

DATE		ITEM	POST. REF.	DEBIT	CREDIT	BALANCE

Problem 12-11A

1.

CASH PAYMENTS JOURNAL

PAGE 6

	DATE	CK. NO.	ACCOUNT DEBITED	POST. REF.	GENERAL DEBIT	ACCOUNTS PAYABLE DEBIT	PURCHASES DEBIT	PURCHASES DISCOUNTS CREDIT	CASH CREDIT	
1										1
2										2
3										3
4										4
5										5
6										6
7										7
8										8
9										9
10										10
11										11
12										12

2.

GENERAL LEDGER

ACCOUNT Cash ACCOUNT NO. 101

DATE		ITEM	POST. REF.	DEBIT	CREDIT	BALANCE DEBIT	BALANCE CREDIT
20-- May	1	Balance	✓			40,000.00	

ACCOUNT Accounts Payable ACCOUNT NO. 202

DATE		ITEM	POST. REF.	DEBIT	CREDIT	BALANCE DEBIT	BALANCE CREDIT
20-- May	1	Balance	✓				20,000.00

Problem 12-11A (Continued)

ACCOUNT Purchases ACCOUNT NO. 501

DATE		ITEM	POST. REF.	DEBIT	CREDIT	BALANCE	
						DEBIT	CREDIT

ACCOUNT Purchases Discounts ACCOUNT NO. 501.2

DATE		ITEM	POST. REF.	DEBIT	CREDIT	BALANCE	
						DEBIT	CREDIT

ACCOUNT Freight-In ACCOUNT NO. 502

DATE		ITEM	POST. REF.	DEBIT	CREDIT	BALANCE	
						DEBIT	CREDIT

ACCOUNT Rent Expense ACCOUNT NO. 521

DATE		ITEM	POST. REF.	DEBIT	CREDIT	BALANCE	
						DEBIT	CREDIT

ACCOUNT Utilities Expense ACCOUNT NO. 533

DATE		ITEM	POST. REF.	DEBIT	CREDIT	BALANCE	
						DEBIT	CREDIT

Problem 12-11A (Concluded)

ACCOUNTS PAYABLE LEDGER

NAME Fantastic Toys

ADDRESS

DATE		ITEM	POST. REF.	DEBIT	CREDIT	BALANCE
20-- May	1	Balance	✓			5,200.00

NAME Goya Outlet

ADDRESS

DATE		ITEM	POST. REF.	DEBIT	CREDIT	BALANCE
20-- May	1	Balance	✓			3,800.00

NAME Mueller's Distributors

ADDRESS

DATE		ITEM	POST. REF.	DEBIT	CREDIT	BALANCE
20-- May	1	Balance	✓			3,600.00

NAME Van Kooning

ADDRESS

DATE		ITEM	POST. REF.	DEBIT	CREDIT	BALANCE
20-- May	1	Balance	✓			7,400.00

Problem 12-12A

1. **PURCHASES JOURNAL** PAGE 7

DATE	INVOICE NO.	FROM WHOM PURCHASED	POST. REF.	PURCHASES DEBIT ACCTS. PAY. CREDIT

CASH PAYMENTS JOURNAL PAGE 9

DATE	CK. NO.	ACCOUNT DEBITED	POST. REF.	GENERAL DEBIT	ACCOUNTS PAYABLE DEBIT	PURCHASES DEBIT	PURCHASES DISCOUNTS CREDIT	CASH CREDIT

Name ____________________

Problem 12-12A (Continued)

GENERAL JOURNAL

PAGE 3

	DATE		DESCRIPTION	POST. REF.	DEBIT	CREDIT	
1							1
2							2
3							3
4							4
5							5
6							6
7							7
8							8
9							9
10							10

2.

GENERAL LEDGER

ACCOUNT Cash ACCOUNT NO. 101

DATE		ITEM	POST. REF.	DEBIT	CREDIT	BALANCE DEBIT	BALANCE CREDIT
20-- July	1	Balance	✓			20,000.00	

ACCOUNT Accounts Payable ACCOUNT NO. 202

DATE		ITEM	POST. REF.	DEBIT	CREDIT	BALANCE DEBIT	BALANCE CREDIT

Problem 12-12A (Continued)

ACCOUNT F. Flint, Drawing ACCOUNT NO. 312

DATE		ITEM	POST. REF.	DEBIT	CREDIT	BALANCE DEBIT	BALANCE CREDIT

ACCOUNT Purchases ACCOUNT NO. 501

DATE		ITEM	POST. REF.	DEBIT	CREDIT	BALANCE DEBIT	BALANCE CREDIT

ACCOUNT Purchases Returns and Allowances ACCOUNT NO. 501.1

DATE		ITEM	POST. REF.	DEBIT	CREDIT	BALANCE DEBIT	BALANCE CREDIT

ACCOUNT Purchases Discounts ACCOUNT NO. 501.2

DATE		ITEM	POST. REF.	DEBIT	CREDIT	BALANCE DEBIT	BALANCE CREDIT

ACCOUNT Rent Expense ACCOUNT NO. 521

DATE		ITEM	POST. REF.	DEBIT	CREDIT	BALANCE DEBIT	BALANCE CREDIT

Problem 12-12A (Concluded)

ACCOUNTS PAYABLE LEDGER

NAME

ADDRESS

DATE		ITEM	POST. REF.	DEBIT	CREDIT	BALANCE

NAME

ADDRESS

DATE		ITEM	POST. REF.	DEBIT	CREDIT	BALANCE

NAME

ADDRESS

DATE		ITEM	POST. REF.	DEBIT	CREDIT	BALANCE

NAME

ADDRESS

DATE		ITEM	POST. REF.	DEBIT	CREDIT	BALANCE

Exercise 12-1B

		Journal
a.	Issued credit memo to customer for merchandise returned.	
b.	Sold merchandise for cash.	
c.	Purchased merchandise on account.	
d.	Issued checks to employees in payment of wages.	
e.	Purchased factory supplies on account.	
f.	Sold merchandise on account.	

Exercise 12-2B

SALES JOURNAL

PAGE

DATE	SALE NO.	TO WHOM SOLD	POST. REF.	ACCOUNTS RECEIVABLE DEBIT	SALES CREDIT	SALES TAX PAYABLE CREDIT

Exercise 12-3B

CASH RECEIPTS JOURNAL

PAGE

	DATE	ACCOUNT CREDITED	POST. REF.	GENERAL CREDIT	ACCOUNTS RECEIVABLE CREDIT	SALES CREDIT	SALES TAX PAYABLE CREDIT	CASH DEBIT	
1									1
2									2
3									3
4									4
5									5
6									6
7									7
8									8
9									9
10									10
11									11

Name ______________________________

Exercise 12-4B

PURCHASES JOURNAL

PAGE

	DATE	INVOICE NO.	FROM WHOM PURCHASED	POST. REF.	PURCHASES DEBIT ACCTS. PAY. CREDIT	
1						1
2						2
3						3
4						4
5						5
6						6
7						7
8						8
9						9
10						10
11						11

Exercise 12-5B

CASH PAYMENTS JOURNAL

PAGE

	DATE	CK. NO.	ACCOUNT DEBITED	POST. REF.	GENERAL DEBIT	ACCOUNTS PAYABLE DEBIT	PURCHASES DEBIT	PURCHASES DISCOUNTS CREDIT	CASH CREDIT	
1										1
2										2
3										3
4										4
5										5
6										6
7										7
8										8
9										9
10										10
11										11
12										12
13										13

Problem 12-6B

1.

SALES JOURNAL

PAGE 8

DATE		SALE NO.	TO WHOM SOLD	POST. REF.	ACCOUNTS RECEIVABLE DEBIT	SALES CREDIT	SALES TAX PAYABLE CREDIT

2.

GENERAL LEDGER

ACCOUNT Accounts Receivable ACCOUNT NO. 122

DATE		ITEM	POST. REF.	DEBIT	CREDIT	BALANCE	
						DEBIT	CREDIT

ACCOUNT Sales Tax Payable ACCOUNT NO. 231

DATE		ITEM	POST. REF.	DEBIT	CREDIT	BALANCE	
						DEBIT	CREDIT

Problem 12-6B (Concluded)

ACCOUNT Sales ACCOUNT NO. 401

DATE		ITEM	POST. REF.	DEBIT	CREDIT	BALANCE	
						DEBIT	CREDIT

ACCOUNTS RECEIVABLE LEDGER

NAME Dvorak Manufacturing Co.

ADDRESS 2105 Williams Drive, Muncie, IN 47304-2437

DATE		ITEM	POST. REF.	DEBIT	CREDIT	BALANCE

NAME Saga, Inc.

ADDRESS 1453 Parnell Avenue, Indianapolis, IN 46201-6870

DATE		ITEM	POST. REF.	DEBIT	CREDIT	BALANCE

NAME Vinnie Ward

ADDRESS 308 So. Muirhead Drive, Okemos, MI 48864-5356

DATE		ITEM	POST. REF.	DEBIT	CREDIT	BALANCE

NAME Zapata Co.

ADDRESS 789 N. Stafford Dr., Bloomington, IN 47401-6201

DATE		ITEM	POST. REF.	DEBIT	CREDIT	BALANCE

Problem 12-7B

1.

CASH RECEIPTS JOURNAL

	DATE		ACCOUNT CREDITED	POST. REF.	GENERAL CREDIT	ACCOUNTS RECEIVABLE CREDIT
1						
2						
3						
4						
5						
6						
7						
8						
9						
10						
11						
12						
13						
14						
15						
16						
17						
18						
19						
20						
21						
22						
23						
24						
25						
26						
27						
28						

Problem 12-7B (Continued)

PAGE 10

	SALES CREDIT	SALES TAX PAYABLE CREDIT	BANK CREDIT CARD EXPENSE DEBIT	CASH DEBIT
1				
2				
3				
4				
5				
6				
7				
8				
9				
10				
11				
12				
13				
14				
15				
16				
17				
18				
19				
20				
21				
22				
23				
24				
25				
26				
27				
28				

Problem 12-7B (Continued)

GENERAL JOURNAL

PAGE 8

DATE		DESCRIPTION	POST. REF.	DEBIT	CREDIT

Problem 12-7B (Continued)

2.

GENERAL LEDGER

ACCOUNT Cash ACCOUNT NO. 101

DATE		ITEM	POST. REF.	DEBIT	CREDIT	BALANCE DEBIT	BALANCE CREDIT
20-- Jan.	1	Balance	✓			2,890.75	

ACCOUNT Accounts Receivable ACCOUNT NO. 122

DATE		ITEM	POST. REF.	DEBIT	CREDIT	BALANCE DEBIT	BALANCE CREDIT
20-- Jan.	1	Balance	✓			6,300.00	

ACCOUNT Sales Tax Payable ACCOUNT NO. 231

DATE		ITEM	POST. REF.	DEBIT	CREDIT	BALANCE DEBIT	BALANCE CREDIT

ACCOUNT Sales ACCOUNT NO. 401

DATE		ITEM	POST. REF.	DEBIT	CREDIT	BALANCE DEBIT	BALANCE CREDIT

Problem 12-7B (Continued)

ACCOUNT Sales Returns and Allowances ACCOUNT NO. 401.1

DATE		ITEM	POST. REF.	DEBIT	CREDIT	BALANCE	
						DEBIT	CREDIT

ACCOUNT Bank Credit Card Expense ACCOUNT NO. 513

DATE		ITEM	POST. REF.	DEBIT	CREDIT	BALANCE	
						DEBIT	CREDIT

ACCOUNTS RECEIVABLE LEDGER

NAME Ray Boyd

ADDRESS 229 SE 65th Avenue, Portland, OR 97215-1451

DATE		ITEM	POST. REF.	DEBIT	CREDIT	BALANCE
20-- Jan.	1	Balance	✓			1,400.00

NAME Dazai Manufacturing

ADDRESS 447 6th Avenue, Flagstaff, AZ 86004-6842

DATE		ITEM	POST. REF.	DEBIT	CREDIT	BALANCE
20-- Jan.	1	Balance	✓			318.00

Problem 12-7B (Concluded)

NAME Clint Hassell

ADDRESS 1462 N. Steves Blvd., Los Cruces, NM 88012-7791

DATE		ITEM	POST. REF.	DEBIT	CREDIT	BALANCE
20-- Jan.	1	Balance	✓			815 00

NAME Jan Sowada

ADDRESS 5997 Blackgold Lane, Grapevine, TX 76051-2366

DATE		ITEM	POST. REF.	DEBIT	CREDIT	BALANCE
20-- Jan.	1	Balance	✓			1481 00

NAME Robert Zehnle

ADDRESS 6881 Seneca Drive, San Diego, CA 92127-8671

DATE		ITEM	POST. REF.	DEBIT	CREDIT	BALANCE
20-- Jan.	1	Balance	✓			2286 00

Problem 12-8B

1.

SALES JOURNAL

PAGE 6

DATE		SALE NO.	TO WHOM SOLD	POST. REF.	ACCOUNTS RECEIVABLE DEBIT	SALES CREDIT	SALES TAX PAYABLE CREDIT

CASH RECEIPTS JOURNAL

PAGE 9

	DATE		ACCOUNT CREDITED	POST. REF.	GENERAL CREDIT	ACCOUNTS RECEIVABLE CREDIT	SALES CREDIT	SALES TAX PAYABLE CREDIT	CASH DEBIT	
1										1
2										2
3										3
4										4
5										5
6										6
7										7
8										8
9										9

Problem 12-8B (Continued)

GENERAL JOURNAL

PAGE 5

	DATE		DESCRIPTION	POST. REF.	DEBIT	CREDIT	
1							1
2							2
3							3
4							4
5							5
6							6
7							7
8							8
9							9
10							10
11							11
12							12
13							13
14							14

2.

GENERAL LEDGER

ACCOUNT Cash ACCOUNT NO. 101

DATE		ITEM	POST. REF.	DEBIT	CREDIT	BALANCE	
						DEBIT	CREDIT
20-- Apr.	1	Balance	✓			28,645.4	

ACCOUNT Accounts Receivable ACCOUNT NO. 122

DATE		ITEM	POST. REF.	DEBIT	CREDIT	BALANCE	
						DEBIT	CREDIT
20-- Apr.	1	Balance	✓			27,262.5	

Problem 12-8B (Continued)

ACCOUNT Sales Tax Payable ACCOUNT NO. 231

DATE		ITEM	POST. REF.	DEBIT	CREDIT	BALANCE	
						DEBIT	CREDIT

ACCOUNT Sales ACCOUNT NO. 401

DATE		ITEM	POST. REF.	DEBIT	CREDIT	BALANCE	
						DEBIT	CREDIT

ACCOUNT Sales Returns and Allowances ACCOUNT NO. 401.1

DATE		ITEM	POST. REF.	DEBIT	CREDIT	BALANCE	
						DEBIT	CREDIT

Problem 12-8B (Concluded)

ACCOUNTS RECEIVABLE LEDGER

NAME O. L. Meyers

ADDRESS 119 Hartford Turnpike, Vernon, CT 06066-0113

DATE		ITEM	POST. REF.	DEBIT	CREDIT	BALANCE
20-- Apr.	1	Balance	✓			2,186.00

NAME Kelsay Munkres

ADDRESS 233 Cambridge Dr., Branford, CT 06405-9276

DATE		ITEM	POST. REF.	DEBIT	CREDIT	BALANCE
20-- Apr.	1	Balance	✓			482.00

NAME Andrew Plaa

ADDRESS 51 Bissell Ave., Old Saybrook, CT 06475-0212

DATE		ITEM	POST. REF.	DEBIT	CREDIT	BALANCE

NAME Melissa Richfield

ADDRESS 1107 Silver Lane, East Hartford, CT 06108-1907

DATE		ITEM	POST. REF.	DEBIT	CREDIT	BALANCE
20-- Apr.	1	Balance	✓			58.25

Problem 12-9B

1.

PURCHASES JOURNAL

PAGE 7

	DATE	INVOICE NO.	FROM WHOM PURCHASED	POST. REF.	PURCHASES DEBIT ACCTS. PAY. CREDIT	
1						1
2						2
3						3
4						4
5						5
6						6
7						7
8						8
9						9
10						10
11						11
12						12
13						13
14						14

2.

GENERAL LEDGER

ACCOUNT Accounts Payable ACCOUNT NO. 202

DATE	ITEM	POST. REF.	DEBIT	CREDIT	BALANCE	
					DEBIT	CREDIT

ACCOUNT Purchases ACCOUNT NO. 501

DATE	ITEM	POST. REF.	DEBIT	CREDIT	BALANCE	
					DEBIT	CREDIT

Problem 12-9B (Concluded)

ACCOUNTS PAYABLE LEDGER

NAME

ADDRESS

DATE		ITEM	POST. REF.	DEBIT	CREDIT	BALANCE

NAME

ADDRESS

DATE		ITEM	POST. REF.	DEBIT	CREDIT	BALANCE

NAME

ADDRESS

DATE		ITEM	POST. REF.	DEBIT	CREDIT	BALANCE

NAME

ADDRESS

DATE		ITEM	POST. REF.	DEBIT	CREDIT	BALANCE

NAME

ADDRESS

DATE		ITEM	POST. REF.	DEBIT	CREDIT	BALANCE

Problem 12-10B

1.

GENERAL LEDGER

ACCOUNT Accounts Payable ACCOUNT NO. 202

DATE		ITEM	POST. REF.	DEBIT	CREDIT	BALANCE DEBIT	BALANCE CREDIT

ACCOUNT Purchases ACCOUNT NO. 501

DATE		ITEM	POST. REF.	DEBIT	CREDIT	BALANCE DEBIT	BALANCE CREDIT

2.

ACCOUNTS PAYABLE LEDGER

NAME

ADDRESS

DATE		ITEM	POST. REF.	DEBIT	CREDIT	BALANCE

NAME

ADDRESS

DATE		ITEM	POST. REF.	DEBIT	CREDIT	BALANCE

Problem 12-10B (Concluded)

NAME

ADDRESS

DATE		ITEM	POST. REF.	DEBIT	CREDIT	BALANCE

NAME

ADDRESS

DATE		ITEM	POST. REF.	DEBIT	CREDIT	BALANCE

NAME

ADDRESS

DATE		ITEM	POST. REF.	DEBIT	CREDIT	BALANCE

Problem 12-11B

1.

CASH PAYMENTS JOURNAL

PAGE 6

	DATE		CK. NO.	ACCOUNT DEBITED	POST. REF.	GENERAL DEBIT	ACCOUNTS PAYABLE DEBIT	PURCHASES DEBIT	PURCHASES DISCOUNTS CREDIT	CASH CREDIT	
1											1
2											2
3											3
4											4
5											5
6											6
7											7
8											8
9											9
10											10
11											11
12											12

2.

GENERAL LEDGER

ACCOUNT Cash — ACCOUNT NO. 101

DATE		ITEM	POST. REF.	DEBIT	CREDIT	BALANCE DEBIT	BALANCE CREDIT
20-- May	1	Balance	✓			40 0 0 0 00	

ACCOUNT Accounts Payable — ACCOUNT NO. 202

DATE		ITEM	POST. REF.	DEBIT	CREDIT	BALANCE DEBIT	BALANCE CREDIT
20-- May	1	Balance	✓				20 0 0 0 00

Name ______________________________

Problem 12-11B (Continued)

ACCOUNT Purchases ACCOUNT NO. 501

DATE		ITEM	POST. REF.	DEBIT	CREDIT	BALANCE	
						DEBIT	CREDIT

ACCOUNT Purchases Discounts ACCOUNT NO. 501.2

DATE		ITEM	POST. REF.	DEBIT	CREDIT	BALANCE	
						DEBIT	CREDIT

ACCOUNT Freight-In ACCOUNT NO. 502

DATE		ITEM	POST. REF.	DEBIT	CREDIT	BALANCE	
						DEBIT	CREDIT

ACCOUNT Rent Expense ACCOUNT NO. 521

DATE		ITEM	POST. REF.	DEBIT	CREDIT	BALANCE	
						DEBIT	CREDIT

ACCOUNT Utilities Expense ACCOUNT NO. 533

DATE		ITEM	POST. REF.	DEBIT	CREDIT	BALANCE	
						DEBIT	CREDIT

Problem 12-11B (Concluded)

ACCOUNTS PAYABLE LEDGER

NAME Cortez Distributors

ADDRESS

DATE		ITEM	POST. REF.	DEBIT	CREDIT	BALANCE
20-- May	1	Balance	✓			4,200.00

NAME Indra & Velga

ADDRESS

DATE		ITEM	POST. REF.	DEBIT	CREDIT	BALANCE
20-- May	1	Balance	✓			6,800.00

NAME Toy Corner

ADDRESS

DATE		ITEM	POST. REF.	DEBIT	CREDIT	BALANCE
20-- May	1	Balance	✓			4,600.00

NAME Troutman Outlet

ADDRESS

DATE		ITEM	POST. REF.	DEBIT	CREDIT	BALANCE
20-- May	1	Balance	✓			4,400.00

Name ______________________________

Problem 12-12B

1.

PURCHASES JOURNAL

PAGE 7

	DATE	INVOICE NO.	FROM WHOM PURCHASED	POST. REF.	PURCHASES DEBIT ACCTS. PAY. CREDIT	
1						1
2						2
3						3
4						4
5						5
6						6
7						7
8						8
9						9
10						10

CASH PAYMENTS JOURNAL

PAGE 9

	DATE	CK. NO.	ACCOUNT DEBITED	POST. REF.	GENERAL DEBIT	ACCOUNTS PAYABLE DEBIT	PURCHASES DEBIT	PURCHASES DISCOUNTS CREDIT	CASH CREDIT	
1										1
2										2
3										3
4										4
5										5
6										6
7										7
8										8
9										9
10										10
11										11
12										12

Problem 12-12B (Continued)

GENERAL JOURNAL

PAGE 3

	DATE		DESCRIPTION	POST. REF.	DEBIT	CREDIT	
1							1
2							2
3							3
4							4
5							5
6							6
7							7
8							8
9							9
10							10

2.

GENERAL LEDGER

ACCOUNT Cash ACCOUNT NO. 101

DATE		ITEM	POST. REF.	DEBIT	CREDIT	BALANCE DEBIT	BALANCE CREDIT
20-- July	1	Balance	✓			20 0 0 0 00	

ACCOUNT Accounts Payable ACCOUNT NO. 202

DATE		ITEM	POST. REF.	DEBIT	CREDIT	BALANCE DEBIT	BALANCE CREDIT

Name ______________________

Problem 12-12B (Continued)

ACCOUNT D. Mueller, Drawing ACCOUNT NO. 312

DATE		ITEM	POST. REF.	DEBIT	CREDIT	BALANCE	
						DEBIT	CREDIT

ACCOUNT Purchases ACCOUNT NO. 501

DATE		ITEM	POST. REF.	DEBIT	CREDIT	BALANCE	
						DEBIT	CREDIT

ACCOUNT Purchases Returns and Allowances ACCOUNT NO. 501.1

DATE		ITEM	POST. REF.	DEBIT	CREDIT	BALANCE	
						DEBIT	CREDIT

ACCOUNT Purchases Discounts ACCOUNT NO. 501.2

DATE		ITEM	POST. REF.	DEBIT	CREDIT	BALANCE	
						DEBIT	CREDIT

ACCOUNT Rent Expense ACCOUNT NO. 521

DATE		ITEM	POST. REF.	DEBIT	CREDIT	BALANCE	
						DEBIT	CREDIT

Problem 12-12B (Concluded)

ACCOUNTS PAYABLE LEDGER

NAME

ADDRESS

DATE		ITEM	POST. REF.	DEBIT	CREDIT	BALANCE

NAME

ADDRESS

DATE		ITEM	POST. REF.	DEBIT	CREDIT	BALANCE

NAME

ADDRESS

DATE		ITEM	POST. REF.	DEBIT	CREDIT	BALANCE

NAME

ADDRESS

DATE		ITEM	POST. REF.	DEBIT	CREDIT	BALANCE

Name ______________________________

Mastery Problem

1.

SALES JOURNAL

PAGE 7

	DATE		SALE NO.	TO WHOM SOLD	POST. REF.	ACCOUNTS RECEIVABLE DEBIT	SALES CREDIT	SALES TAX PAYABLE CREDIT	
1									1
2									2
3									3
4									4
5									5
6									6
7									7
8									8

CASH RECEIPTS JOURNAL

PAGE 10

	DATE		ACCOUNT CREDITED	POST. REF.	GENERAL CREDIT	ACCOUNTS RECEIVABLE CREDIT	SALES CREDIT	SALES TAX PAYABLE CREDIT	CASH DEBIT	
1										1
2										2
3										3
4										4
5										5
6										6
7										7
8										8
9										9
10										10
11										11
12										12
13										13

Mastery Problem (Continued)

PURCHASES JOURNAL

PAGE 6

	DATE		INVOICE NO.	FROM WHOM PURCHASED	POST. REF.	PURCHASES DEBIT ACCTS. PAY. CREDIT	
1							1
2							2
3							3
4							4
5							5
6							6
7							7
8							8
9							9
10							10
11							11

CASH PAYMENTS JOURNAL

PAGE 11

	DATE		CK. NO.	ACCOUNT DEBITED	POST. REF.	GENERAL DEBIT	ACCOUNTS PAYABLE DEBIT	PURCHASES DEBIT	PURCHASES DISCOUNTS CREDIT	CASH CREDIT	
1											1
2											2
3											3
4											4
5											5
6											6
7											7
8											8
9											9
10											10
11											11
12											12
13											13

Name ______________________________

Mastery Problem (Continued)

GENERAL JOURNAL

PAGE 5

	DATE		DESCRIPTION	POST. REF.	DEBIT	CREDIT	
1							1
2							2
3							3
4							4
5							5
6							6
7							7
8							8
9							9
10							10
11							11
12							12

2.

GENERAL LEDGER

ACCOUNT Cash ACCOUNT NO. 101

DATE		ITEM	POST. REF.	DEBIT	CREDIT	BALANCE DEBIT	BALANCE CREDIT
20-- Oct.	1	Balance	✓			18,225.00	

ACCOUNT Accounts Receivable ACCOUNT NO. 122

DATE		ITEM	POST. REF.	DEBIT	CREDIT	BALANCE DEBIT	BALANCE CREDIT
20-- Oct.	1	Balance	✓			9,619.00	

Mastery Problem (Continued)

ACCOUNT Accounts Payable ACCOUNT NO. 202

DATE		ITEM	POST. REF.	DEBIT	CREDIT	BALANCE DEBIT	BALANCE CREDIT
20-- Oct.	1	Balance	✓				5 1 2 0 00

ACCOUNT Sales Tax Payable ACCOUNT NO. 231

DATE		ITEM	POST. REF.	DEBIT	CREDIT	BALANCE DEBIT	BALANCE CREDIT

ACCOUNT Sales ACCOUNT NO. 401

DATE		ITEM	POST. REF.	DEBIT	CREDIT	BALANCE DEBIT	BALANCE CREDIT

ACCOUNT Sales Returns and Allowances ACCOUNT NO. 401.1

DATE		ITEM	POST. REF.	DEBIT	CREDIT	BALANCE DEBIT	BALANCE CREDIT

Name ______________________________

Mastery Problem (Continued)

ACCOUNT Purchases ACCOUNT NO. 501

DATE		ITEM	POST. REF.	DEBIT	CREDIT	BALANCE DEBIT	BALANCE CREDIT

ACCOUNT Purchases Returns and Allowances ACCOUNT NO. 501.1

DATE		ITEM	POST. REF.	DEBIT	CREDIT	BALANCE DEBIT	BALANCE CREDIT

ACCOUNT Purchases Discounts ACCOUNT NO. 501.2

DATE		ITEM	POST. REF.	DEBIT	CREDIT	BALANCE DEBIT	BALANCE CREDIT

ACCOUNT Wages Expense ACCOUNT NO. 511

DATE		ITEM	POST. REF.	DEBIT	CREDIT	BALANCE DEBIT	BALANCE CREDIT

ACCOUNT Phone Expense ACCOUNT NO. 525

DATE		ITEM	POST. REF.	DEBIT	CREDIT	BALANCE DEBIT	BALANCE CREDIT

Mastery Problem (Continued)

ACCOUNTS RECEIVABLE LEDGER

NAME David's Decorating

ADDRESS 12 Jude Lane, Hartford, CT 06117

DATE		ITEM	POST. REF.	DEBIT	CREDIT	BALANCE
20-- Oct.	1	Balance	✓			3,340.00

NAME Meg Johnson

ADDRESS 700 Hobbes Dr., Avon, CT 06108

DATE		ITEM	POST. REF.	DEBIT	CREDIT	BALANCE
20-- Oct.	1	Balance	✓			4,000.00

NAME Elizabeth Shoemaker

ADDRESS 52 Juniper Road, Hartford, CT 06118

DATE		ITEM	POST. REF.	DEBIT	CREDIT	BALANCE
20-- Oct.	1	Balance	✓			279.00

NAME Leigh Summers

ADDRESS 5200 Hamilton Ave., Hartford, CT 06111

DATE		ITEM	POST. REF.	DEBIT	CREDIT	BALANCE
20-- Oct.	1	Balance	✓			2,000.00

Mastery Problem (Concluded)

ACCOUNTS PAYABLE LEDGER

NAME Flower Wholesalers

ADDRESS 43 Lucky Lane, Bristol, CT 06007

DATE		ITEM	POST. REF.	DEBIT	CREDIT	BALANCE
20-- Oct.	1	Balance	✓			1,500.00

NAME Jill Hand

ADDRESS 1009 Drake Rd., Farmington, CT 06082

DATE		ITEM	POST. REF.	DEBIT	CREDIT	BALANCE
20-- Oct.	1	Balance	✓			500.00

NAME Seidl Enterprises

ADDRESS 888 Anders Street, Newington, CT 06789

DATE		ITEM	POST. REF.	DEBIT	CREDIT	BALANCE

NAME Vases Etc.

ADDRESS 34 Harry Ave., East Hartford, CT 05234

DATE		ITEM	POST. REF.	DEBIT	CREDIT	BALANCE
20-- Oct.	1	Balance	✓			3,120.00

Challenge Problem

1.

GENERAL JOURNAL

PAGE

	DATE		DESCRIPTION	POST. REF.	DEBIT	CREDIT	
1							1
2							2
3							3
4							4
5							5
6							6
7							7
8							8
9							9
10							10
11							11
12							12
13							13
14							14
15							15
16							16
17							17
18							18
19							19
20							20
21							21
22							22
23							23
24							24
25							25
26							26
27							27
28							28
29							29
30							30
31							31
32							32
33							33
34							34

Name ________________________________

Challenge Problem (Continued)

GENERAL JOURNAL

PAGE

	DATE	DESCRIPTION	POST. REF.	DEBIT	CREDIT	
1						1
2						2
3						3
4						4
5						5
6						6
7						7
8						8
9						9
10						10
11						11
12						12
13						13
14						14
15						15
16						16
17						17
18						18
19						19
20						20
21						21
22						22
23						23
24						24
25						25
26						26
27						27
28						28
29						29
30						30
31						31
32						32
33						33
34						34

Challenge Problem (Continued)

GENERAL JOURNAL

PAGE

	DATE		DESCRIPTION	POST. REF.	DEBIT	CREDIT	
1							1
2							2
3							3
4							4
5							5
6							6
7							7
8							8
9							9
10							10
11							11
12							12
13							13
14							14
15							15
16							16
17							17
18							18
19							19
20							20
21							21
22							22
23							23
24							24
25							25
26							26
27							27
28							28
29							29
30							30
31							31
32							32
33							33
34							34

Name ______________________________

Challenge Problem (Concluded)

2.

SALES JOURNAL

PAGE

CASH RECEIPTS JOURNAL

PAGE

PURCHASES JOURNAL

PAGE

CASH PAYMENTS JOURNAL

PAGE

Exercise 13-1A

	Year 1	Year 2
Ending merchandise inventory		
Beginning merchandise inventory		
Cost of goods sold		
Gross profit		
Net income		
Ending owner's capital		

Exercise 13-2A

GENERAL JOURNAL PAGE

	DATE	DESCRIPTION	POST. REF.	DEBIT	CREDIT	
1						1
2						2
3						3
4						4
5						5
6						6
7						7
8						8
9						9
10						10
11						11
12						12
13						13
14						14
15						15
16						16
17						17
18						18
19						19
20						20
21						21
22						22
23						23

Exercise 13-3A

GENERAL JOURNAL

PAGE

DATE		DESCRIPTION	POST. REF.	DEBIT	CREDIT

Exercise 13-4A

Exercise 13-5A

Problem 13-6A

1. FIFO Inventory Method

Date 20-1/ 20-2		Cost of Goods Sold			Cost of Ending Inventory		
		Units	Unit Price	Total	Units	Unit Price	Total

2. LIFO Inventory Method

Date 20-1/ 20-2		Cost of Goods Sold			Cost of Ending Inventory		
		Units	Unit Price	Total	Units	Unit Price	Total

Problem 13-6A (Concluded)

3.

4. **Specific Identification Method**

Date 20-1/ 20-2		Cost of Goods Sold Units	Unit Price	Total	Cost of Ending Inventory Units	Unit Price	Total

Problem 13-7A

1.

a. FIFO Inventory Method

Date 20--		Cost of Goods Sold Units	Unit Price	Total	Cost of Ending Inventory Units	Unit Price	Total

b. LIFO Inventory Method

Date 20--		Cost of Goods Sold Units	Unit Price	Total	Cost of Ending Inventory Units	Unit Price	Total

Problem 13-7A (Concluded)

Problem 13-8A

Problem 13-9A

1. and 2.

	Cost	Retail

Exercise 13-1B

	Year 1	Year 2
Ending merchandise inventory		
Beginning merchandise inventory		
Cost of goods sold		
Gross profit		
Net income		
Ending owner's capital		

Exercise 13-2B

GENERAL JOURNAL

PAGE

DATE		DESCRIPTION	POST. REF.	DEBIT	CREDIT

Exercise 13-3B

GENERAL JOURNAL PAGE

	DATE		DESCRIPTION	POST. REF.	DEBIT	CREDIT	
1							1
2							2
3							3
4							4
5							5
6							6
7							7
8							8
9							9
10							10
11							11
12							12
13							13
14							14
15							15
16							16
17							17
18							18
19							19
20							20
21							21
22							22
23							23

Exercise 13-4B

Exercise 13-5B

Problem 13-6B

1. FIFO Inventory Method

Date 20-1/ 20-2		Cost of Goods Sold Units	Unit Price	Total	Cost of Ending Inventory Units	Unit Price	Total

2. LIFO Inventory Method

Date 20-1/ 20-2		Cost of Goods Sold Units	Unit Price	Total	Cost of Ending Inventory Units	Unit Price	Total

Problem 13-6B (Concluded)

3.

4. Specific Identification Method

Date 20-1/ 20-2		Cost of Goods Sold Units	Unit Price	Total	Cost of Ending Inventory Units	Unit Price	Total

Problem 13-7B

1.

a. FIFO Inventory Method

Date 20--		Cost of Goods Sold Units	Unit Price	Total	Cost of Ending Inventory Units	Unit Price	Total

b. LIFO Inventory Method

Date 20--		Cost of Goods Sold Units	Unit Price	Total	Cost of Ending Inventory Units	Unit Price	Total

Problem 13-7B (Concluded)

Problem 13-8B

Problem 13-9B

1. and 2.

	Cost	Retail

Mastery Problem

1.

a. FIFO Inventory Method

Date 20-2		Cost of Goods Sold Units	Unit Price	Total	Cost of Ending Inventory Units	Unit Price	Total

b. LIFO Inventory Method

Date 20-2		Cost of Goods Sold Units	Unit Price	Total	Cost of Ending Inventory Units	Unit Price	Total

Mastery Problem (Concluded)

Name ______________________________

Challenge Problem

20-1	FIFO Units	FIFO Cost/Unit	FIFO Cost	LIFO Units	LIFO Cost/Unit	LIFO Cost

Details of Cost of Goods Sold 20-1	FIFO Units	FIFO Cost/Unit	FIFO Cost	LIFO Units	LIFO Cost/Unit	LIFO Cost

Challenge Problem (Concluded)

20-2	FIFO Units	FIFO Cost/Unit	FIFO Cost	LIFO Units	LIFO Cost/Unit	LIFO Cost

Details of Cost of Goods Sold 20-2	FIFO Units	FIFO Cost/Unit	FIFO Cost	LIFO Units	LIFO Cost/Unit	LIFO Cost

Name ______________________________

APPENDIX: PERPETUAL INVENTORY METHOD: LIFO AND MOVING-AVERAGE METHODS

Exercise 13Apx-1A

1. Perpetual LIFO

	Purchases			Cost of Goods Sold				Inventory on Hand				
Date	Units	Cost/ Unit	Total	Units	Cost/ Unit	CGS	Cum. CGS	Layer	Units	Cost/ Unit	Layer Cost	Total

2. Perpetual Moving-Average

	Purchases			Cost of Goods Sold				Inventory on Hand and Average Cost per Unit			
Date	Units	Cost/ Unit	Total	Units	Cost/ Unit	CGS	Cum. CGS	Cost of Purchase or (Sale)	Cost of Inventory on Hand	Units on Hand	Average Cost/ Unit

Problem 13Apx-2A

1. Perpetual LIFO

	Purchases			Cost of Goods Sold				Inventory on Hand				
Date	Units	Cost/ Unit	Total	Units	Cost/ Unit	CGS	Cum. CGS	Layer	Units	Cost/ Unit	Layer Cost	Total

Problem 13Apx-2A (Concluded)

2. Perpetual Moving-Average

	Purchases			Cost of Goods Sold				Inventory on Hand and Average Cost per Unit			
Date	Units	Cost/ Unit	Total	Units	Cost/ Unit	CGS	Cum. CGS	Cost of Purchase or (Sale)	Cost of Inventory on Hand	Units on Hand	Average Cost/ Unit

Exercise 13Apx-1B

1. Perpetual LIFO

	Purchases			Cost of Goods Sold				Inventory on Hand				
Date	Units	Cost/ Unit	Total	Units	Cost/ Unit	CGS	Cum. CGS	Layer	Units	Cost/ Unit	Layer Cost	Total

2. Perpetual Moving-Average

	Purchases			Cost of Goods Sold				Inventory on Hand and Average Cost per Unit			
Date	Units	Cost/ Unit	Total	Units	Cost/ Unit	CGS	Cum. CGS	Cost of Purchase or (Sale)	Cost of Inventory on Hand	Units on Hand	Average Cost/ Unit

Name ______________________________

Problem 13Apx-2B

1. Perpetual LIFO

	Purchases			Cost of Goods Sold				Inventory on Hand				
Date	Units	Cost/ Unit	Total	Units	Cost/ Unit	CGS	Cum. CGS	Layer	Units	Cost/ Unit	Layer Cost	Total

Problem 13Apx-2B (Concluded)

2. Perpetual Moving-Average

	Purchases			Cost of Goods Sold				Inventory on Hand and Average Cost per Unit			
Date	Units	Cost/ Unit	Total	Units	Cost/ Unit	CGS	Cum. CGS	Cost of Purchase or (Sale)	Cost of Inventory on Hand	Units on Hand	Average Cost/ Unit

Name ______________________________

Exercise 14-1A

Merchandise Inventory

Income Summary

Exercise 14-2A

Exercise 14-3A

Cash

Unearned Ticket Revenue

Ticket Revenue

Exercise 14-4A

1., 2., and 3.

Kevin's

Work

For Year Ended

	ACCOUNT TITLE	TRIAL BALANCE DEBIT	TRIAL BALANCE CREDIT	ADJUSTMENTS DEBIT	ADJUSTMENTS CREDIT
1	Merchandise Inventory	40,000.00			
12	Income Summary				
13	Purchases	90,000.00			
14	Purchases Returns and Allow.		2,000.00		
15	Purchases Discounts		3,000.00		
16	Freight-In	500.00			
17					
18					

Exercise 14-4A (Concluded)

Gift Shop

Sheet (Partial)

December 31, 20--

ADJUSTED TRIAL BALANCE		INCOME STATEMENT		BALANCE SHEET		
DEBIT	CREDIT	DEBIT	CREDIT	DEBIT	CREDIT	
						1
						12
						13
						14
						15
						16
						17
						18

4.

Exercise 14-5A

Exercise 14-6A

GENERAL JOURNAL

PAGE

	DATE		DESCRIPTION	POST. REF.	DEBIT	CREDIT	
1							1
2							2
3							3
4							4
5							5
6							6
7							7
8							8
9							9
10							10
11							11
12							12
13							13
14							14
15							15
16							16
17							17
18							18
19							19
20							20
21							21
22							22
23							23
24							24
25							25
26							26
27							27

Exercise 14-7A

GENERAL JOURNAL

PAGE

	DATE		DESCRIPTION	POST. REF.	DEBIT	CREDIT	
1							1
2							2
3							3
4							4
5							5
6							6
7							7
8							8
9							9
10							10
11							11
12							12
13							13
14							14
15							15
16							16
17							17
18							18
19							19

Exercise 14-8A

GENERAL JOURNAL

PAGE

	DATE		DESCRIPTION	POST. REF.	DEBIT	CREDIT	
1							1
2							2
3							3
4							4
5							5
6							6
7							7
8							8
9							9
10							10
11							11

Problem 14-9A

1. and 2.

Venice Beach

Work

For Year Ended

	ACCOUNT TITLE	TRIAL BALANCE DEBIT	TRIAL BALANCE CREDIT	ADJUSTMENTS DEBIT	ADJUSTMENTS CREDIT
1	Cash	20,000.00			
2	Accounts Receivable	14,000.00			
3	Merchandise Inventory	25,000.00			
4	Supplies	8,000.00			
5	Prepaid Insurance	5,400.00			
6	Land	30,000.00			
7	Building	50,000.00			
8	Accumulated Depr.—Building		20,000.00		
9	Store Equipment	35,000.00			
10	Accumulated Depr.—Store Equip.		14,000.00		
11	Accounts Payable		9,600.00		
12	Wages Payable				
13	Sales Tax Payable		5,900.00		
14	Unearned Rent Revenue		8,900.00		
15	Mortgage Payable		45,000.00		
16	M. Young, Capital		65,410.00		
17	M. Young, Drawing	26,000.00			
18	Income Summary				
19	Sales		118,000.00		
20	Sales Returns and Allowances	1,700.00			
21	Rent Revenue				
22	Purchases	27,000.00			
23	Purchases Returns and Allow.		1,400.00		
24	Purchases Discounts		1,800.00		
25	Freight-In	2,100.00			
26	Wages Expense	32,000.00			
27	Advertising Expense	3,600.00			
28	Supplies Expense				
29	Phone Expense	1,350.00			
30	Utilities Expense	8,000.00			
31	Insurance Expense				
32	Depreciation Expense—Building				
33	Depreciation Exp.—Store Equip.				
34	Miscellaneous Expense	860.00			
35		290,010.00	290,010.00		
36					
37					
38					

Problem 14-9A (Continued)

Kite Shop

Sheet

December 31, 20--

ADJUSTED TRIAL BALANCE		INCOME STATEMENT		BALANCE SHEET		
DEBIT	CREDIT	DEBIT	CREDIT	DEBIT	CREDIT	
						1
						2
						3
						4
						5
						6
						7
						8
						9
						10
						11
						12
						13
						14
						15
						16
						17
						18
						19
						20
						21
						22
						23
						24
						25
						26
						27
						28
						29
						30
						31
						32
						33
						34
						35
						36
						37
						38

Problem 14-9A (Concluded)

3.

GENERAL JOURNAL

PAGE

DATE		DESCRIPTION	POST. REF.	DEBIT	CREDIT

Problem 14-10A

1. and 2. (See pages 518 and 519.)

3.

GENERAL JOURNAL

PAGE

	DATE	DESCRIPTION	POST. REF.	DEBIT	CREDIT	
1						1
2						2
3						3
4						4
5						5
6						6
7						7
8						8
9						9
10						10
11						11
12						12
13						13
14						14
15						15
16						16
17						17
18						18
19						19
20						20
21						21
22						22
23						23
24						24
25						25
26						26
27						27
28						28
29						29
30						30
31						31
32						32
33						33
34						34

Problem 14-10A (Continued)

1. and 2.

Cascade Bicycle

Work

For Year Ended

	ACCOUNT TITLE	TRIAL BALANCE DEBIT	TRIAL BALANCE CREDIT	ADJUSTMENTS DEBIT	ADJUSTMENTS CREDIT
1	Cash	23,000.00			
2	Accounts Receivable	15,000.00			
3	Merchandise Inventory	31,000.00			
4	Supplies	7,200.00			
5	Prepaid Insurance	4,600.00			
6	Land	28,000.00			
7	Building	53,000.00			
8	Accumulated Depr.—Building		17,000.00		
9	Store Equipment	27,000.00			
10	Accumulated Depr.—Store Equip.		9,000.00		
11	Accounts Payable		3,800.00		
12	Wages Payable				
13	Sales Tax Payable		3,050.00		
14	Unearned Storage Revenue		5,600.00		
15	Mortgage Payable		42,000.00		
16	D. Lamond, Capital		165,760.00		
17	D. Lamond, Drawing	33,000.00			
18	Income Summary				
19	Sales		51,000.00		
20	Sales Returns and Allowances	2,400.00			
21	Storage Revenue				
22	Purchases	21,000.00			
23	Purchases Returns and Allow.		1,300.00		
24	Purchases Discounts		1,900.00		
25	Freight-In	1,800.00			
26	Wages Expense	35,000.00			
27	Advertising Expense	5,700.00			
28	Supplies Expense				
29	Phone Expense	2,200.00			
30	Utilities Expense	9,600.00			
31	Insurance Expense				
32	Depreciation Expense—Building				
33	Depreciation Exp.—Store Equip.				
34	Miscellaneous Expense	910.00			
35		300,410.00	300,410.00		
36					
37					
38					

Problem 14-10A (Concluded)

Shop
Sheet
December 31, 20--

ADJUSTED TRIAL BALANCE		INCOME STATEMENT		BALANCE SHEET		
DEBIT	CREDIT	DEBIT	CREDIT	DEBIT	CREDIT	
						1
						2
						3
						4
						5
						6
						7
						8
						9
						10
						11
						12
						13
						14
						15
						16
						17
						18
						19
						20
						21
						22
						23
						24
						25
						26
						27
						28
						29
						30
						31
						32
						33
						34
						35
						36
						37
						38

Problem 14-11A

1.

Stark Street Computers
Work Sheet (Partial)
For Year Ended December 31, 20--

	ACCOUNT TITLE	TRIAL BALANCE		ADJUSTMENTS		ADJUSTED TRIAL BALANCE		
		DEBIT	CREDIT	DEBIT	CREDIT	DEBIT	CREDIT	
1	Cash	18,000.00				18,000.00		1
2	Accounts Receivable	11,000.00				11,000.00		2
3	Merchandise Inventory	25,000.00				35,000.00		3
4	Supplies	8,000.00				2,820.00		4
5	Prepaid Insurance	5,400.00				1,225.00		5
6	Land	27,000.00				27,000.00		6
7	Building	48,000.00				48,000.00		7
8	Accum. Depr.—Building		20,000.00				27,000.00	8
9	Store Equipment	33,000.00				33,000.00		9
10	Accum. Depr.—Store Equip.		8,700.00				12,800.00	10
11	Accounts Payable		6,400.00				6,400.00	11
12	Wages Payable						1,300.00	12
13	Sales Tax Payable		5,700.00				5,700.00	13
14	Unearned Repair Rev.		8,200.00				1,800.00	14
15	Mortgage Payable		44,000.00				44,000.00	15
16	L. Cowart, Capital		80,025.00				80,025.00	16
17	L. Cowart, Drawing	35,000.00				35,000.00		17
18	Income Summary					25,000.00	35,000.00	18
19	Sales		122,000.00				122,000.00	19
20	Sales Returns and Allow.	2,250.00				2,250.00		20
21	Repair Revenue						6,400.00	21
22	Purchases	29,750.00				29,750.00		22
23	Purchases Ret. and Allow.		1,850.00				1,850.00	23
24	Purchases Discounts		1,425.00				1,425.00	24
25	Freight-In	3,200.00				3,200.00		25
26	Wages Expense	37,000.00				38,300.00		26
27	Advertising Expense	4,125.00				4,125.00		27
28	Supplies Expense					5,180.00		28
29	Phone Expense	1,650.00				1,650.00		29
30	Utilities Expense	9,150.00				9,150.00		30
31	Insurance Expense					4,175.00		31
32	Depr. Exp.—Building					7,000.00		32
33	Depr. Exp.—Store Equip.					4,100.00		33
34	Miscellaneous Expense	775.00				775.00		34
35		298,300.00	298,300.00			345,700.00	345,700.00	35
36								36
37								37
38								38

Problem 14-11A (Concluded)

2.

GENERAL JOURNAL PAGE

	DATE		DESCRIPTION	POST. REF.	DEBIT	CREDIT	
1							1
2							2
3							3
4							4
5							5
6							6
7							7
8							8
9							9
10							10
11							11
12							12
13							13
14							14
15							15
16							16
17							17
18							18
19							19
20							20
21							21
22							22
23							23
24							24
25							25
26							26
27							27
28							28
29							29
30							30
31							31
32							32
33							33
34							34
35							35

Problem 14-12A

1.

Lewis Music

Work

For Year Ended

	ACCOUNT TITLE	TRIAL BALANCE DEBIT	TRIAL BALANCE CREDIT	ADJUSTMENTS DEBIT	ADJUSTMENTS CREDIT
1	Cash	27,000.00			
2	Accounts Receivable	13,300.00			
3	Merchandise Inventory	34,000.00			
4	Supplies	5,300.00			
5	Prepaid Insurance	6,100.00			
6	Land	31,000.00			
7	Building	52,000.00			
8	Accumulated Depr.—Building		17,000.00		
9	Store Equipment	39,000.00			
10	Accumulated Depr.—Store Equip.		11,900.00		
11	Accounts Payable		6,250.00		
12	Wages Payable				
13	Sales Tax Payable		6,200.00		
14	Unearned Rent Revenue		7,400.00		
15	Mortgage Payable		46,000.00		
16	H. Lewis, Capital		111,620.00		
17	H. Lewis, Drawing	37,000.00			
18	Income Summary				
19	Sales		136,000.00		
20	Sales Returns and Allowances	3,500.00			
21	Rent Revenue				
22	Purchases	39,000.00			
23	Purchases Returns and Allow.		2,530.00		
24	Purchases Discounts		1,975.00		
25	Freight-In	2,650.00			
26	Wages Expense	42,000.00			
27	Advertising Expense	4,175.00			
28	Supplies Expense				
29	Phone Expense	1,980.00			
30	Utilities Expense	7,945.00			
31	Insurance Expense				
32	Depreciation Expense—Building				
33	Depreciation Exp.—Store Equip.				
34	Miscellaneous Expense	925.00			
35		346,875.00	346,875.00		
36	Net Income				
37					
38					

Problem 14-12A (Continued)

Store
Sheet
December 31, 20--

ADJUSTED TRIAL BALANCE		INCOME STATEMENT		BALANCE SHEET		
DEBIT	CREDIT	DEBIT	CREDIT	DEBIT	CREDIT	
				27,000.00		1
				13,300.00		2
				38,000.00		3
				1,500.00		4
				1,785.00		5
				31,000.00		6
				52,000.00		7
					21,145.00	8
				39,000.00		9
					14,875.00	10
					6,250.00	11
					875.00	12
					6,200.00	13
					3,175.00	14
					46,000.00	15
					111,620.00	16
				37,000.00		17
		34,000.00	38,000.00			18
			136,000.00			19
		3,500.00				20
			4,225.00			21
		39,000.00				22
			2,530.00			23
			1,975.00			24
		2,650.00				25
		42,875.00				26
		4,175.00				27
		3,800.00				28
		1,980.00				29
		7,945.00				30
		4,315.00				31
		4,145.00				32
		2,975.00				33
		925.00				34
		152,285.00	182,730.00	240,585.00	210,140.00	35
		30,445.00			30,445.00	36
		182,730.00	182,730.00	240,585.00	240,585.00	37
						38

Problem 14-12A (Continued)

2.

GENERAL JOURNAL

PAGE

	DATE	DESCRIPTION	POST. REF.	DEBIT	CREDIT	
1						1
2						2
3						3
4						4
5						5
6						6
7						7
8						8
9						9
10						10
11						11
12						12
13						13
14						14
15						15
16						16
17						17
18						18
19						19
20						20
21						21
22						22
23						23
24						24
25						25
26						26
27						27
28						28
29						29
30						30
31						31
32						32
33						33
34						34

Problem 14-12A (Concluded)

3.

Exercise 14-1B

Merchandise Inventory

Income Summary

Exercise 14-2B

Exercise 14-3B

Cash

Unearned Ticket Revenue

Ticket Revenue

Exercise 14-4B

1., 2., 3., and 4. (See pages 528 and 529.)

Exercise 14-5B

Exercise 14-6B

GENERAL JOURNAL

PAGE

	DATE		DESCRIPTION	POST. REF.	DEBIT	CREDIT	
1							1
2							2
3							3
4							4
5							5
6							6
7							7
8							8
9							9
10							10
11							11
12							12
13							13
14							14
15							15
16							16
17							17
18							18
19							19
20							20
21							21
22							22
23							23
24							24
25							25
26							26
27							27

Exercise 14-4B

1., 2., and 3.

Nicole's

Work

For Year Ended

	ACCOUNT TITLE	TRIAL BALANCE DEBIT	TRIAL BALANCE CREDIT	ADJUSTMENTS DEBIT	ADJUSTMENTS CREDIT
1	Merchandise Inventory	30 0 0 0 00			
12	Income Summary				
13	Purchases	85 0 0 0 00			
14	Purchases Returns and Allow.		2 2 0 0 00		
15	Purchases Discounts		2 5 0 0 00		
16	Freight-In	1 0 0 00			
17					
18					

Name ______________________________

Exercise 14-4B (Concluded)

Gift Shop

Sheet (Partial)

December 31, 20--

ADJUSTED TRIAL BALANCE		INCOME STATEMENT		BALANCE SHEET		
DEBIT	CREDIT	DEBIT	CREDIT	DEBIT	CREDIT	
						1
						12
						13
						14
						15
						16
						17
						18

4.

Exercise 14-7B

GENERAL JOURNAL

PAGE

	DATE		DESCRIPTION	POST. REF.	DEBIT	CREDIT	
1							1
2							2
3							3
4							4
5							5
6							6
7							7
8							8
9							9
10							10
11							11
12							12
13							13
14							14
15							15
16							16
17							17
18							18
19							19
20							20
21							21

Exercise 14-8B

GENERAL JOURNAL

PAGE

	DATE		DESCRIPTION	POST. REF.	DEBIT	CREDIT	
1							1
2							2
3							3
4							4
5							5
6							6
7							7
8							8
9							9
10							10

Problem 14-9B

1. and 2. (See pages 532 and 533.)

3.

GENERAL JOURNAL

PAGE

DATE		DESCRIPTION	POST. REF.	DEBIT	CREDIT

Problem 14-9B (Continued)

1. and 2.

Basket

Work

For Year Ended

	ACCOUNT TITLE	TRIAL BALANCE DEBIT	TRIAL BALANCE CREDIT	ADJUSTMENTS DEBIT	ADJUSTMENTS CREDIT
1	Cash	25,000.00			
2	Accounts Receivable	8,100.00			
3	Merchandise Inventory	32,000.00			
4	Supplies	7,100.00			
5	Prepaid Insurance	3,600.00			
6	Land	40,000.00			
7	Building	45,000.00			
8	Accumulated Depr.—Building		16,000.00		
9	Store Equipment	27,000.00			
10	Accumulated Depr.—Store Equip.		5,500.00		
11	Accounts Payable		3,600.00		
12	Wages Payable				
13	Sales Tax Payable		6,200.00		
14	Unearned Decorating Revenue		6,300.00		
15	Mortgage Payable		36,000.00		
16	L. Palermo, Capital		112,050.00		
17	L. Palermo, Drawing	31,000.00			
18	Income Summary				
19	Sales		125,000.00		
20	Sales Returns and Allowances	2,600.00			
21	Decorating Revenue				
22	Purchases	38,000.00			
23	Purchases Returns and Allow.		2,200.00		
24	Purchases Discounts		1,700.00		
25	Freight-In	1,900.00			
26	Wages Expense	38,000.00			
27	Advertising Expense	4,200.00			
28	Supplies Expense				
29	Phone Expense	1,870.00			
30	Utilities Expense	8,400.00			
31	Insurance Expense				
32	Depreciation Expense—Building				
33	Depreciation Exp.—Store Equip.				
34	Miscellaneous Expense	780.00			
35		314,550.00	314,550.00		
36					
37					
38					

Problem 14-9B (Concluded)

Corner
Sheet
December 31, 20--

ADJUSTED TRIAL BALANCE		INCOME STATEMENT		BALANCE SHEET		
DEBIT	CREDIT	DEBIT	CREDIT	DEBIT	CREDIT	
						1
						2
						3
						4
						5
						6
						7
						8
						9
						10
						11
						12
						13
						14
						15
						16
						17
						18
						19
						20
						21
						22
						23
						24
						25
						26
						27
						28
						29
						30
						31
						32
						33
						34
						35
						36
						37
						38

Problem 14-10B

1. and 2.

Oregon Bike

Work

For Year Ended

	ACCOUNT TITLE	TRIAL BALANCE DEBIT	TRIAL BALANCE CREDIT	ADJUSTMENTS DEBIT	ADJUSTMENTS CREDIT
1	Cash	27,000.00			
2	Accounts Receivable	12,000.00			
3	Merchandise Inventory	39,000.00			
4	Supplies	6,200.00			
5	Prepaid Insurance	5,800.00			
6	Land	32,000.00			
7	Building	58,000.00			
8	Accumulated Depr.—Building		27,000.00		
9	Store Equipment	31,000.00			
10	Accumulated Depr.—Store Equip.		14,000.00		
11	Accounts Payable		4,900.00		
12	Wages Payable				
13	Sales Tax Payable		2,900.00		
14	Unearned Rent Revenue		6,100.00		
15	Mortgage Payable		49,000.00		
16	C. Moody, Capital		169,500.00		
17	C. Moody, Drawing	36,000.00			
18	Income Summary				
19	Sales		58,000.00		
20	Sales Returns and Allowances	3,300.00			
21	Rent Revenue				
22	Purchases	19,000.00			
23	Purchases Returns and Allow.		900.00		
24	Purchases Discounts		1,450.00		
25	Freight-In	800.00			
26	Wages Expense	47,000.00			
27	Advertising Expense	6,200.00			
28	Supplies Expense				
29	Phone Expense	1,860.00			
30	Utilities Expense	8,100.00			
31	Insurance Expense				
32	Depreciation Expense—Building				
33	Depreciation Exp.—Store Equip.				
34	Miscellaneous Expense	490.00			
35		333,750.00	333,750.00		
36					
37					
38					

Name ______________________________

Problem 14-10B (Continued)

Company

Sheet

December 31, 20--

ADJUSTED TRIAL BALANCE		INCOME STATEMENT		BALANCE SHEET	
DEBIT	CREDIT	DEBIT	CREDIT	DEBIT	CREDIT

Problem 14-10B (Concluded)

3.

GENERAL JOURNAL

PAGE

DATE		DESCRIPTION	POST. REF.	DEBIT	CREDIT

Name ______________________________

Problem 14-11B

1.

Burnside Auto Parts
Work Sheet (Partial)
For Year Ended December 31, 20--

	ACCOUNT TITLE	TRIAL BALANCE		ADJUSTMENTS		ADJUSTED TRIAL BALANCE		
		DEBIT	CREDIT	DEBIT	CREDIT	DEBIT	CREDIT	
1	Cash	21,000.00				21,000.00		
2	Accounts Receivable	8,300.00				8,300.00		
3	Merchandise Inventory	32,000.00				36,000.00		
4	Supplies	6,150.00				1,865.00		
5	Prepaid Insurance	5,925.00				1,835.00		5
6	Land	41,750.00				41,750.00		6
7	Building	43,000.00				43,000.00		7
8	Accum. Depr.—Building		24,000.00				27,500.00	8
9	Store Equipment	25,400.00				25,400.00		9
10	Accum. Depr.—Store Equip.		12,400.00				14,750.00	10
11	Accounts Payable		8,100.00				8,100.00	11
12	Wages Payable						980.00	12
13	Sales Tax Payable		5,200.00				5,200.00	13
14	Unearn. Rent-A-Junk Rev.		7,950.00				2,350.00	14
15	Mortgage Payable		26,000.00				26,000.00	15
16	B. Davis, Capital		109,130.00				109,130.00	16
17	B. Davis, Drawing	40,000.00				40,000.00		17
18	Income Summary					32,000.00	36,000.00	18
19	Sales		123,500.00				123,500.00	19
20	Sales Returns and Allow.	2,860.00				2,860.00		20
21	Rent-A-Junk Revenue						5,600.00	21
22	Purchases	32,525.00				32,525.00		22
23	Purchases Ret. and Allow.		2,150.00				2,150.00	23
24	Purchases Discounts		2,400.00				2,400.00	24
25	Freight-In	3,175.00				3,175.00		25
26	Wages Expense	44,175.00				45,155.00		26
27	Advertising Expense	3,275.00				3,275.00		27
28	Supplies Expense					4,285.00		28
29	Phone Expense	2,200.00				2,200.00		29
30	Utilities Expense	8,250.00				8,250.00		30
31	Insurance Expense					4,090.00		31
32	Depr. Exp.—Building					3,500.00		32
33	Depr. Exp.—Store Equip.					2,350.00		33
34	Miscellaneous Expense	845.00				845.00		34
35		320,830.00	320,830.00			363,660.00	363,660.00	35
36								36
37								37
38								38

Problem 14-11B (Concluded)

2.

GENERAL JOURNAL

PAGE

	DATE	DESCRIPTION	POST. REF.	DEBIT	CREDIT	
1						1
2						2
3						3
4						4
5						5
6						6
7						7
8						8
9						9
10						10
11						11
12						12
13						13
14						14
15						15
16						16
17						17
18						18
19						19
20						20
21						21
22						22
23						23
24						24
25						25
26						26
27						27
28						28
29						29
30						30
31						31
32						32
33						33
34						34

Name ______________________________

Problem 14-12B

1. (See pages 540 and 541.)
2.

GENERAL JOURNAL

PAGE

DATE		DESCRIPTION	POST. REF.	DEBIT	CREDIT

Problem 14-12B (Continued)

1.

Diamond Music

Work

For Year Ended

	ACCOUNT TITLE	TRIAL BALANCE DEBIT	TRIAL BALANCE CREDIT	ADJUSTMENTS DEBIT	ADJUSTMENTS CREDIT
1	Cash	31,000.00			
2	Accounts Receivable	11,980.00			
3	Merchandise Inventory	33,600.00			
4	Supplies	7,140.00			
5	Prepaid Insurance	5,985.00			
6	Land	36,200.00			
7	Building	51,850.00			
8	Accumulated Depr.—Building		13,590.00		
9	Store Equipment	32,675.00			
10	Accumulated Depr.—Store Equip.		10,290.00		
11	Accounts Payable		5,895.00		
12	Wages Payable				
13	Sales Tax Payable		6,375.00		
14	Unearned Rent Revenue		8,850.00		
15	Mortgage Payable		42,400.00		
16	N. Diamond, Capital		116,350.00		
17	N. Diamond, Drawing	39,500.00			
18	Income Summary				
19	Sales		148,000.00		
20	Sales Returns and Allowances	2,800.00			
21	Rent Revenue				
22	Purchases	40,700.00			
23	Purchases Returns and Allow.		2,775.00		
24	Purchases Discounts		2,325.00		
25	Freight-In	1,875.00			
26	Wages Expense	47,000.00			
27	Advertising Expense	4,695.00			
28	Supplies Expense				
29	Phone Expense	2,250.00			
30	Utilities Expense	6,825.00			
31	Insurance Expense				
32	Depreciation Expense—Building				
33	Depreciation Exp.—Store Equip.				
34	Miscellaneous Expense	775.00			
35		356,850.00	356,850.00		
36	Net Income				
37					
38					

Problem 14-12B (Continued)

Store

Sheet

December 31, 20--

ADJUSTED TRIAL BALANCE		INCOME STATEMENT		BALANCE SHEET	
DEBIT	CREDIT	DEBIT	CREDIT	DEBIT	CREDIT
				31,000.00	
				11,980.00	
				39,100.00	
				1,965.00	
				1,235.00	
				36,200.00	
				51,850.00	
					18,875.00
				32,675.00	
					14,755.00
					5,895.00
					1,250.00
					6,375.00
					2,930.00
					42,400.00
					116,350.00
				39,500.00	
		33,600.00	39,100.00		
			148,000.00		
		2,800.00			
			5,920.00		
		40,700.00			
			2,775.00		
			2,325.00		
		1,875.00			
		48,250.00			
		4,695.00			
		5,175.00			
		2,250.00			
		6,825.00			
		4,750.00			
		5,285.00			
		4,465.00			
		775.00			
		161,445.00	198,120.00	245,505.00	208,830.00
		36,675.00			36,675.00
		198,120.00	198,120.00	245,505.00	245,505.00

Problem 14-12B (Concluded)

3.

Name ______________________________

Mastery Problem

1. (See pages 544 and 545 for work sheet.)
2.

GENERAL JOURNAL

PAGE

DATE		DESCRIPTION	POST. REF.	DEBIT	CREDIT

Mastery Problem (Continued)

1.

Waikiki Surf

Work

For Year Ended

	ACCOUNT TITLE	TRIAL BALANCE DEBIT	TRIAL BALANCE CREDIT	ADJUSTMENTS DEBIT	ADJUSTMENTS CREDIT
1	Cash	30,000.00			
2	Accounts Receivable	22,500.00			
3	Merchandise Inventory	57,000.00			
4	Supplies	2,700.00			
5	Prepaid Insurance	3,600.00			
6	Land	15,000.00			
7	Building	135,000.00			
8	Accumulated Depr.—Building		24,000.00		
9	Store Equipment	75,000.00			
10	Accumulated Depr.—Store Equip.		22,500.00		
11	Notes Payable		7,500.00		
12	Accounts Payable		15,000.00		
13	Wages Payable				
14	Unearned Boat Rental Revenue		33,000.00		
15	J. Neff, Capital		233,700.00		
16	J. Neff, Drawing	30,000.00			
17	Income Summary				
18	Sales		300,750.00		
19	Sales Returns and Allowances	1,800.00			
20	Boat Rental Revenue				
21	Purchases	157,500.00			
22	Purchases Returns and Allow.		1,200.00		
23	Purchases Discounts		1,500.00		
24	Freight-In	450.00			
25	Wages Expense	63,000.00			
26	Advertising Expense	11,250.00			
27	Supplies Expense				
28	Phone Expense	5,250.00			
29	Utilities Expense	18,000.00			
30	Insurance Expense				
31	Depreciation Expense—Building				
32	Depreciation Exp.—Store Equip.				
33	Miscellaneous Expense	10,875.00			
34	Interest Expense	225.00			
35		639,150.00	639,150.00		
36					
37					
38					

Mastery Problem (Concluded)

Shop

Sheet

December 31, 20--

ADJUSTED TRIAL BALANCE		INCOME STATEMENT		BALANCE SHEET		
DEBIT	CREDIT	DEBIT	CREDIT	DEBIT	CREDIT	
						1
						2
						3
						4
						5
						6
						7
						8
						9
						10
						11
						12
						13
						14
						15
						16
						17
						18
						19
						20
						21
						22
						23
						24
						25
						26
						27
						28
						29
						30
						31
						32
						33
						34
						35
						36
						37
						38

Challenge Problem

APPENDIX: EXPENSE METHOD OF ACCOUNTING FOR PREPAID EXPENSES

Exercise 14Apx-1A

GENERAL JOURNAL PAGE

	DATE		DESCRIPTION	POST. REF.	DEBIT	CREDIT	
1							1
2							2
3							3
4							4
5							5
6							6
7							7
8							8
9							9
10							10
11							11
12							12

Exercise 14Apx-1B

GENERAL JOURNAL PAGE

	DATE		DESCRIPTION	POST. REF.	DEBIT	CREDIT	
1							1
2							2
3							3
4							4
5							5
6							6
7							7
8							8
9							9
10							10
11							11
12							12

Name ______________________________

Exercise 15-1A

Exercise 15-2A

Exercise 15-3A

Exercise 15-4A

Exercise 15-5A

1.

GENERAL JOURNAL

PAGE

DATE	DESCRIPTION	POST. REF.	DEBIT	CREDIT

Exercise 15-5A (Concluded)

2.

J. M. Gimbel, Capital

Exercise 15-6A

GENERAL JOURNAL PAGE

	DATE		DESCRIPTION	POST. REF.	DEBIT	CREDIT	
1							1
2							2
3							3
4							4
5							5

Exercise 15-7A

DATE	WITHOUT REVERSING ENTRY	WITH REVERSING ENTRY
Adjusting Entry:		
Closing Entry:		
Reversing Entry:		
Payment of Payroll:		

Wages Expense

Wages Expense

Wages Payable

Wages Payable

Cash

Cash

Problem 15-8A

1.

Problem 15-8A (Continued)

2.

Problem 15-8A (Concluded)

3.

Problem 15-9A

Name ______________________________

Problem 15-10A

1. (See pages 562 and 563)
2., 3., and 5.

GENERAL JOURNAL

PAGE

DATE		DESCRIPTION	POST. REF.	DEBIT	CREDIT

Problem 15-10A (Continued)

2., 3., and 5.

GENERAL JOURNAL PAGE

DATE		DESCRIPTION	POST. REF.	DEBIT	CREDIT

Problem 15-10A (Continued)

4.

ACCOUNT	DEBIT BALANCE	CREDIT BALANCE

Problem 15-10A (Continued)

1.

Vicki's Fabric

Work

For Year Ended

		TRIAL BALANCE		ADJUSTMENTS	
		DEBIT	CREDIT	DEBIT	CREDIT
1	Cash	28,000.00			
2	Accounts Receivable	14,200.00			
3	Merchandise Inventory	33,000.00			
4	Supplies	1,600.00			
5	Prepaid Insurance	900.00			
6	Equipment	6,600.00			
7	Accumulated Depr.—Equipment		1,000.00		
8	Accounts Payable		15,620.00		
9	Wages Payable				
10	Sales Tax Payable		850.00		
11	Unearned Revenue		5,000.00		
12	Vicki Roberts, Capital		71,200.00		
13	Vicki Roberts, Drawing	21,610.00			
14	Income Summary				
15	Sales		74,500.00		
16	Sales Returns and Allowances	1,850.00			
17	Interest Revenue		1,200.00		
18	Purchases	41,500.00			
19	Purchases Returns and Allow.		1,800.00		
20	Purchases Discounts		830.00		
21	Freight-In	660.00			
22	Wages Expense	14,880.00			
23	Advertising Expense	810.00			
24	Supplies Expense				
25	Phone Expense	1,210.00			
26	Utilities Expense	3,240.00			
27	Insurance Expense				
28	Depreciation Expense—Equip.				
29	Miscellaneous Expense	920.00			
30	Interest Expense	1,020.00			
31		172,000.00	172,000.00		
32					
33					

Name ______________________________

Problem 15-10A (Concluded)

Store

Sheet

December 31, 20-1

ADJUSTED TRIAL BALANCE		INCOME STATEMENT		BALANCE SHEET	
DEBIT	CREDIT	DEBIT	CREDIT	DEBIT	CREDIT

Exercise 15-1B

Exercise 15-2B

Name ______________________________

Exercise 15-3B

Exercise 15-4B

Exercise 15-5B

1. **GENERAL JOURNAL** PAGE

DATE		DESCRIPTION	POST. REF.	DEBIT	CREDIT

Exercise 15-5B (Concluded)

2.

L. Marlow, Capital

Name ______________________________

Exercise 15-6B

GENERAL JOURNAL PAGE

	DATE		DESCRIPTION	POST. REF.	DEBIT	CREDIT	
1							1
2							2
3							3
4							4
5							5

Exercise 15-7B

DATE	WITHOUT REVERSING ENTRY	WITH REVERSING ENTRY
Adjusting Entry:		
Closing Entry:		
Reversing Entry:		
Payment of Payroll:		

Wages Expense

Wages Expense

Wages Payable

Wages Payable

Cash

Cash

Problem 15-8B

1.

Problem 15-8B (Continued)

2.

Problem 15-8B (Concluded)

3.

Name ______________________________

Problem 15-9B

Problem 15-10B

1.

Darby Kite

Work

For Year Ended

		TRIAL BALANCE		ADJUSTMENTS	
		DEBIT	CREDIT	DEBIT	CREDIT
1	Cash	11,700.00			
2	Accounts Receivable	11,200.00			
3	Merchandise Inventory	25,000.00			
4	Supplies	1,200.00			
5	Prepaid Insurance	800.00			
6	Equipment	5,400.00			
7	Accumulated Depr.—Equipment		800.00		
8	Accounts Payable		7,100.00		
9	Wages Payable				
10	Sales Tax Payable		250.00		
11	Unearned Revenue		3,000.00		
12	M. D. Akins, Capital		50,000.00		
13	M. D. Akins, Drawing	10,500.00			
14	Income Summary				
15	Sales		55,490.00		
16	Sales Returns and Allowances	1,450.00			
17	Purchases	34,500.00			
18	Purchases Returns and Allow.		1,100.00		
19	Purchases Discounts		630.00		
20	Freight-In	360.00			
21	Wages Expense	10,880.00			
22	Advertising Expense	740.00			
23	Supplies Expense				
24	Phone Expense	1,100.00			
25	Utilities Expense	2,300.00			
26	Insurance Expense				
27	Depreciation Expense—Equip.				
28	Miscellaneous Expense	320.00			
29	Interest Expense	920.00			
30		118,370.00	118,370.00		
31					
33					

Problem 15-10B (Continued)

Store

Sheet

December 31, 20-1

ADJUSTED TRIAL BALANCE		INCOME STATEMENT		BALANCE SHEET		
DEBIT	CREDIT	DEBIT	CREDIT	DEBIT	CREDIT	
						1
						2
						3
						4
						5
						6
						7
						8
						9
						10
						11
						12
						13
						14
						15
						16
						17
						18
						19
						20
						21
						22
						23
						24
						25
						26
						27
						28
						29
						30
						31
						32

Problem 15-10B (Continued)

2., 3., and 5.

GENERAL JOURNAL

PAGE

DATE		DESCRIPTION	POST. REF.	DEBIT	CREDIT

Name ______________________________

Problem 15-10B (Continued)

GENERAL JOURNAL

PAGE

	DATE		DESCRIPTION	POST. REF.	DEBIT	CREDIT	
1							1
2							2
3							3
4							4
5							5
6							6
7							7
8							8
9							9
10							10
11							11
12							12
13							13
14							14
15							15
16							16
17							17
18							18
19							19
20							20
21							21
22							22
23							23
24							24
25							25
26							26
27							27
28							28
29							29
30							30
31							31
32							32
33							33
34							34

Problem 15-10B (Concluded)

4.

ACCOUNT	DEBIT BALANCE	CREDIT BALANCE

Mastery Problem

1.

Mastery Problem (Continued)

2.

Mastery Problem (Continued)

3.

Mastery Problem (Continued)

4.

Mastery Problem (Concluded)

6. and 7.

GENERAL JOURNAL

PAGE 4

DATE		DESCRIPTION	POST. REF.	DEBIT	CREDIT

Mastery Problem (Continued)

5.

GENERAL JOURNAL

PAGE 3

	DATE		DESCRIPTION	POST. REF.	DEBIT	CREDIT	
1							1
2							2
3							3
4							4
5							5
6							6
7							7
8							8
9							9
10							10
11							11
12							12
13							13
14							14
15							15
16							16
17							17
18							18
19							19
20							20
21							21
22							22

Should the adjustment be reversed? ______________________________

Name ______________________________

Challenge Problem

Comprehensive Problem 2—General Journal Based, Part 1

Requirements 2. and 3.

GENERAL JOURNAL

PAGE 3

DATE		DESCRIPTION	POST. REF.	DEBIT	CREDIT

Comprehensive Problem 2—General Journal Based, Part 1 (Requirements 2. and 3. Concluded)

GENERAL JOURNAL

PAGE 4

	DATE		DESCRIPTION	POST. REF.	DEBIT	CREDIT	
1							1
2							2
3							3
4							4
5							5
6							6
7							7
8							8
9							9
10							10
11							11
12							12
13							13
14							14
15							15
16							16
17							17

Requirements 1., 2., 3., 6., 7., and 9.

GENERAL LEDGER

ACCOUNT Cash ACCOUNT NO. 101

DATE		ITEM	POST. REF.	DEBIT	CREDIT	BALANCE DEBIT	BALANCE CREDIT
20-1 Dec.	16	Balance	✓			9 7 0 5 00	

Name ______________________________

Comprehensive Problem 2—General Journal Based, Part 1 (Requirements 1., 2., 3., 6., 7., and 9. Continued)

ACCOUNT Accounts Receivable ACCOUNT NO. 122

DATE		ITEM	POST. REF.	DEBIT	CREDIT	BALANCE DEBIT	BALANCE CREDIT
20-1 Dec.	16	Balance	✓			10,256.00	

ACCOUNT Merchandise Inventory ACCOUNT NO. 131

DATE		ITEM	POST. REF.	DEBIT	CREDIT	BALANCE DEBIT	BALANCE CREDIT
20-1 Dec.	16	Balance	✓			21,800.00	

ACCOUNT Supplies ACCOUNT NO. 141

DATE		ITEM	POST. REF.	DEBIT	CREDIT	BALANCE DEBIT	BALANCE CREDIT
20-1 Dec.	16	Balance	✓			1,035.00	

ACCOUNT Prepaid Insurance ACCOUNT NO. 145

DATE		ITEM	POST. REF.	DEBIT	CREDIT	BALANCE DEBIT	BALANCE CREDIT
20-1 Dec.	16	Balance	✓			1,380.00	

Comprehensive Problem 2—General Journal Based, Part 1 (Requirements 1., 2., 3., 6., 7., and 9. Continued)

ACCOUNT Land ACCOUNT NO. 161

DATE		ITEM	POST. REF.	DEBIT	CREDIT	BALANCE DEBIT	BALANCE CREDIT
20-1 Dec.	16	Balance	✓			8,700.00	

ACCOUNT Building ACCOUNT NO. 171

DATE		ITEM	POST. REF.	DEBIT	CREDIT	BALANCE DEBIT	BALANCE CREDIT
20-1 Dec.	16	Balance	✓			52,000.00	

ACCOUNT Accumulated Depreciation—Building ACCOUNT NO. 171.1

DATE		ITEM	POST. REF.	DEBIT	CREDIT	BALANCE DEBIT	BALANCE CREDIT
20-1 Dec.	16	Balance	✓				9,200.00

ACCOUNT Store Equipment ACCOUNT NO. 181

DATE		ITEM	POST. REF.	DEBIT	CREDIT	BALANCE DEBIT	BALANCE CREDIT
20-1 Dec.	16	Balance	✓			28,750.00	

Comprehensive Problem 2—General Journal Based, Part 1 (Requirements 1., 2., 3., 6., 7., and 9. Continued)

ACCOUNT Accumulated Depreciation—Store Equipment ACCOUNT NO. 181.1

DATE		ITEM	POST. REF.	DEBIT	CREDIT	BALANCE DEBIT	BALANCE CREDIT
20-1 Dec.	16	Balance	✓				9,300.00

ACCOUNT Accounts Payable ACCOUNT NO. 202

DATE		ITEM	POST. REF.	DEBIT	CREDIT	BALANCE DEBIT	BALANCE CREDIT
20-1 Dec.	16	Balance	✓				3,600.00

ACCOUNT Wages Payable ACCOUNT NO. 219

DATE		ITEM	POST. REF.	DEBIT	CREDIT	BALANCE DEBIT	BALANCE CREDIT

Comprehensive Problem 2—General Journal Based, Part 1 (Requirements 1., 2., 3., 6., 7., and 9. Continued)

ACCOUNT Sales Tax Payable ACCOUNT NO. 231

DATE		ITEM	POST. REF.	DEBIT	CREDIT	BALANCE DEBIT	BALANCE CREDIT
20-1 Dec.	16	Balance	✓				1,378.00

ACCOUNT Mortgage Payable ACCOUNT NO. 251

DATE		ITEM	POST. REF.	DEBIT	CREDIT	BALANCE DEBIT	BALANCE CREDIT
20-1 Dec.	16	Balance	✓				12,525.00

ACCOUNT Tom Jones, Capital ACCOUNT NO. 311

DATE		ITEM	POST. REF.	DEBIT	CREDIT	BALANCE DEBIT	BALANCE CREDIT
20-1 Dec.	16	Balance	✓				90,000.00

ACCOUNT Tom Jones, Drawing ACCOUNT NO. 312

DATE		ITEM	POST. REF.	DEBIT	CREDIT	BALANCE DEBIT	BALANCE CREDIT
20-1 Dec.	16	Balance	✓			8,500.00	

Comprehensive Problem 2—General Journal Based, Part 1 (Requirements 1., 2., 3., 6., 7., and 9. Continued)

ACCOUNT Income Summary ACCOUNT NO. 313

DATE		ITEM	POST. REF.	DEBIT	CREDIT	BALANCE DEBIT	BALANCE CREDIT

ACCOUNT Sales ACCOUNT NO. 401

DATE		ITEM	POST. REF.	DEBIT	CREDIT	BALANCE DEBIT	BALANCE CREDIT
20-1 Dec.	16	Balance	✓				124 9 0 0 00

ACCOUNT Sales Returns and Allowances ACCOUNT NO. 401.1

DATE		ITEM	POST. REF.	DEBIT	CREDIT	BALANCE DEBIT	BALANCE CREDIT
20-1 Dec.	16	Balance	✓			1 4 3 0 00	

Comprehensive Problem 2—General Journal Based, Part 1 (Requirements 1., 2., 3., 6., 7., and 9. Continued)

ACCOUNT Purchases ACCOUNT NO. 501

DATE		ITEM	POST. REF.	DEBIT	CREDIT	BALANCE DEBIT	BALANCE CREDIT
20-1 Dec.	16	Balance	✓			64,400.00	

ACCOUNT Purchases Returns and Allowances ACCOUNT NO. 501.1

DATE		ITEM	POST. REF.	DEBIT	CREDIT	BALANCE DEBIT	BALANCE CREDIT
20-1 Dec.	16	Balance	✓				460.00

ACCOUNT Purchases Discounts ACCOUNT NO. 501.2

DATE		ITEM	POST. REF.	DEBIT	CREDIT	BALANCE DEBIT	BALANCE CREDIT
20-1 Dec.	16	Balance	✓				698.00

ACCOUNT Freight-In ACCOUNT NO. 502

DATE		ITEM	POST. REF.	DEBIT	CREDIT	BALANCE DEBIT	BALANCE CREDIT
20-1 Dec.	16	Balance	✓			175.00	

Comprehensive Problem 2—General Journal Based, Part 1 (Requirements 1., 2., 3., 6., 7., and 9. Continued)

ACCOUNT Wages Expense ACCOUNT NO. 511

DATE		ITEM	POST. REF.	DEBIT	CREDIT	BALANCE DEBIT	BALANCE CREDIT
20-1 Dec.	16	Balance	✓			26,100 00	

ACCOUNT Advertising Expense ACCOUNT NO. 512

DATE		ITEM	POST. REF.	DEBIT	CREDIT	BALANCE DEBIT	BALANCE CREDIT
20-1 Dec.	16	Balance	✓			4,700 00	

ACCOUNT Supplies Expense ACCOUNT NO. 524

DATE		ITEM	POST. REF.	DEBIT	CREDIT	BALANCE DEBIT	BALANCE CREDIT

ACCOUNT Phone Expense ACCOUNT NO. 525

DATE		ITEM	POST. REF.	DEBIT	CREDIT	BALANCE DEBIT	BALANCE CREDIT
20-1 Dec.	16	Balance	✓			2,180 00	

Comprehensive Problem 2—General Journal Based, Part 1 (Requirements 1., 2., 3., 6., 7., and 9. Continued)

ACCOUNT Utilities Expense ACCOUNT NO. 533

DATE		ITEM	POST. REF.	DEBIT	CREDIT	BALANCE DEBIT	BALANCE CREDIT
20-1 Dec.	16	Balance	✓			6,900.00	

ACCOUNT Insurance Expense ACCOUNT NO. 535

DATE		ITEM	POST. REF.	DEBIT	CREDIT	BALANCE DEBIT	BALANCE CREDIT

ACCOUNT Depreciation Expense—Building ACCOUNT NO. 540

DATE		ITEM	POST. REF.	DEBIT	CREDIT	BALANCE DEBIT	BALANCE CREDIT

ACCOUNT Depreciation Expense—Store Equipment ACCOUNT NO. 541

DATE		ITEM	POST. REF.	DEBIT	CREDIT	BALANCE DEBIT	BALANCE CREDIT

Comprehensive Problem 2—General Journal Based, Part 1 (Requirements 1., 2., 3., 6., 7., and 9. Continued)

ACCOUNT Miscellaneous Expense ACCOUNT NO. 549

DATE		ITEM	POST. REF.	DEBIT	CREDIT	BALANCE DEBIT	BALANCE CREDIT
20-1 Dec.	16	Balance	✓			2,700 00	

ACCOUNT Interest Expense ACCOUNT NO. 551

DATE		ITEM	POST. REF.	DEBIT	CREDIT	BALANCE DEBIT	BALANCE CREDIT
20-1 Dec.	16	Balance	✓			1,350 00	

ACCOUNTS RECEIVABLE LEDGER

NAME Martha Boyle

ADDRESS 12 Jude Lane, Hartford, CT 06117

DATE		ITEM	POST. REF.	DEBIT	CREDIT	BALANCE
20-1 Dec.	16	Balance	✓			3,796 00

NAME Anne Clark

ADDRESS 52 Juniper Road, Hartford, CT 06118

DATE		ITEM	POST. REF.	DEBIT	CREDIT	BALANCE
20-1 Dec.	16	Balance	✓			2,100 00

Comprehensive Problem 2—General Journal Based, Part 1 (Requirements 1., 2., 3., 6., 7., and 9. Continued)

NAME John Dempsey

ADDRESS 700 Hobbes Dr., Avon, CT 06108

DATE		ITEM	POST. REF.	DEBIT	CREDIT	BALANCE
20-1 Dec.	16	Balance	✓			1,560.00

NAME Kim Fields

ADDRESS 5200 Hamilton Ave., Hartford, CT 06117

DATE		ITEM	POST. REF.	DEBIT	CREDIT	BALANCE
20-1 Dec.	16	Balance	✓			—

NAME Lucy Greene

ADDRESS 236 Bally Lane, Simsbury, CT 06123

DATE		ITEM	POST. REF.	DEBIT	CREDIT	BALANCE
20-1 Dec.	16	Balance	✓			2,800.00

Comprehensive Problem 2—General Journal Based, Part 1 (Requirements 1., 2., 3., 6., 7., and 9. Concluded)

ACCOUNTS PAYABLE LEDGER

NAME Evans Essentials

ADDRESS 34 Harry Ave., East Hartford, CT 05234

DATE		ITEM	POST. REF.	DEBIT	CREDIT	BALANCE
20-1 Dec.	16	Balance	✓			3,600.00

NAME Nathen Co.

ADDRESS 1009 Drake Rd., Farmington, CT 06082

DATE		ITEM	POST. REF.	DEBIT	CREDIT	BALANCE
20-1 Dec.	16	Balance	✓			—

NAME Owen Enterprises

ADDRESS 43 Lucky Lane, Bristol, CT 06007

DATE		ITEM	POST. REF.	DEBIT	CREDIT	BALANCE
20-1 Dec.	16	Balance	✓			—

NAME West Wholesalers

ADDRESS 888 Anders Street, Newington, CT 06789

DATE		ITEM	POST. REF.	DEBIT	CREDIT	BALANCE
20-1 Dec.	16	Balance	✓			—

Comprehensive Problem 2—General Journal Based, Part 1

Requirement 4.

This page intentionally left blank.

Comprehensive Problem 2—General Journal Based, Part 1

Requirement 5.

		TRIAL BALANCE		ADJUSTMENTS	
		DEBIT	CREDIT	DEBIT	CREDIT
1					
2					
3					
4					
5					
6					
7					
8					
9					
10					
11					
12					
13					
14					
15					
16					
17					
18					
19					
20					
21					
22					
23					
24					
25					
26					
27					
28					
29					
30					
31					
32					
33					
34					
35					
36					

Name ______________________________

Comprehensive Problem 2—General Journal Based, Part 1
(Requirement 5. Continued)

ADJUSTED TRIAL BALANCE		INCOME STATEMENT		BALANCE SHEET		
DEBIT	CREDIT	DEBIT	CREDIT	DEBIT	CREDIT	
						1
						2
						3
						4
						5
						6
						7
						8
						9
						10
						11
						12
						13
						14
						15
						16
						17
						18
						19
						20
						21
						22
						23
						24
						25
						26
						27
						28
						29
						30
						31
						32
						33
						34
						35
						36

Comprehensive Problem 2—General Journal Based, Part 1
(Requirement 5. Continued)

Name ______________________________

Comprehensive Problem 2—General Journal Based, Part 1
(Requirement 5. Continued)

Comprehensive Problem 2—General Journal Based, Part 1
(Requirement 5. Concluded)

Name ______________________________

Comprehensive Problem 2—General Journal Based, Part 1

Requirement 6.

GENERAL JOURNAL

PAGE 5

DATE	DESCRIPTION	POST. REF.	DEBIT	CREDIT

Comprehensive Problem 2—General Journal Based, Part 1

Requirements 7. and 9.

GENERAL JOURNAL

PAGE 6

	DATE		DESCRIPTION	POST. REF.	DEBIT	CREDIT	
1							1
2							2
3							3
4							4
5							5
6							6
7							7
8							8
9							9
10							10
11							11
12							12
13							13
14							14
15							15
16							16
17							17
18							18
19							19
20							20
21							21
22							22
23							23
24							24
25							25
26							26
27							27
28							28
29							29
30							30
31							31
32							32
33							33
34							34

Name ____________________

Comprehensive Problem 2—General Journal Based, Part 1

Requirement 8.

ACCOUNT	DEBIT BALANCE	CREDIT BALANCE

Comprehensive Problem 2—General Journal Based, Part 2

Requirements 2. and 3.

GENERAL JOURNAL

PAGE 1

DATE		DESCRIPTION	POST. REF.	DEBIT	CREDIT

Name ______________________________

Comprehensive Problem 2—General Journal Based, Part 2 (Requirements 2. and 3. Concluded)

GENERAL JOURNAL

PAGE 2

	DATE		DESCRIPTION	POST. REF.	DEBIT	CREDIT	
1							1
2							2
3							3
4							4
5							5
6							6
7							7
8							8
9							9
10							10
11							11
12							12
13							13
14							14
15							15
16							16
17							17
18							18
19							19
20							20
21							21
22							22
23							23
24							24
25							25
26							26
27							27
28							28
29							29
30							30
31							31
32							32
33							33
34							34
35							35
36							36
37							37
38							38
39							39

Comprehensive Problem 2—General Journal Based, Part 2

Requirements 1., 2., 3., 6., and 7.

GENERAL LEDGER

ACCOUNT Cash ACCOUNT NO. 101

DATE		ITEM	POST. REF.	DEBIT	CREDIT	BALANCE DEBIT	BALANCE CREDIT
20-2 Jan.	1	Balance	✓			12,548.00	

ACCOUNT Accounts Receivable ACCOUNT NO. 122

DATE		ITEM	POST. REF.	DEBIT	CREDIT	BALANCE DEBIT	BALANCE CREDIT
20-2 Jan.	1	Balance	✓			7,203.00	

Name ______________________________

Comprehensive Problem 2—General Journal Based, Part 2 (Requirements 1., 2., 3., 6., and 7. Continued)

ACCOUNT Merchandise Inventory ACCOUNT NO. 131

DATE		ITEM	POST. REF.	DEBIT	CREDIT	BALANCE DEBIT	BALANCE CREDIT
20-2 Jan.	1	Balance	✓			19,700.00	

ACCOUNT Supplies ACCOUNT NO. 141

DATE		ITEM	POST. REF.	DEBIT	CREDIT	BALANCE DEBIT	BALANCE CREDIT
20-2 Jan.	1	Balance	✓			525.00	

ACCOUNT Prepaid Insurance ACCOUNT NO. 145

DATE		ITEM	POST. REF.	DEBIT	CREDIT	BALANCE DEBIT	BALANCE CREDIT
20-2 Jan.	1	Balance	✓			1,000.00	

ACCOUNT Land ACCOUNT NO. 161

DATE		ITEM	POST. REF.	DEBIT	CREDIT	BALANCE DEBIT	BALANCE CREDIT
20-2 Jan.	1	Balance	✓			8,700.00	

Comprehensive Problem 2—General Journal Based, Part 2 (Requirements 1., 2., 3., 6., and 7. Continued)

ACCOUNT Building ACCOUNT NO. 171

DATE		ITEM	POST. REF.	DEBIT	CREDIT	BALANCE DEBIT	BALANCE CREDIT
20-2 Jan.	1	Balance	✓			52,000.00	

ACCOUNT Accumulated Depreciation—Building ACCOUNT NO. 171.1

DATE		ITEM	POST. REF.	DEBIT	CREDIT	BALANCE DEBIT	BALANCE CREDIT
20-2 Jan.	1	Balance	✓				10,000.00

ACCOUNT Store Equipment ACCOUNT NO. 181

DATE		ITEM	POST. REF.	DEBIT	CREDIT	BALANCE DEBIT	BALANCE CREDIT
20-2 Jan.	1	Balance	✓			28,750.00	

Comprehensive Problem 2—General Journal Based, Part 2 (Requirements 1., 2., 3., 6., and 7. Continued)

ACCOUNT Accumulated Depreciation—Store Equipment ACCOUNT NO. 181.1

DATE		ITEM	POST. REF.	DEBIT	CREDIT	BALANCE DEBIT	BALANCE CREDIT
20-2 Jan.	1	Balance	✓				9,750.00

ACCOUNT Accounts Payable ACCOUNT NO. 202

DATE		ITEM	POST. REF.	DEBIT	CREDIT	BALANCE DEBIT	BALANCE CREDIT
20-2 Jan.	1	Balance	✓				4,350.00

ACCOUNT Wages Payable ACCOUNT NO. 219

DATE		ITEM	POST. REF.	DEBIT	CREDIT	BALANCE DEBIT	BALANCE CREDIT

Comprehensive Problem 2—General Journal Based, Part 2 (Requirements 1., 2., 3., 6., and 7. Continued)

ACCOUNT Sales Tax Payable ACCOUNT NO. 231

DATE		ITEM	POST. REF.	DEBIT	CREDIT	BALANCE DEBIT	BALANCE CREDIT
20-2 Jan.	1	Balance	✓				1,518.00

ACCOUNT Mortgage Payable ACCOUNT NO. 251

DATE		ITEM	POST. REF.	DEBIT	CREDIT	BALANCE DEBIT	BALANCE CREDIT
20-2 Jan.	1	Balance	✓				12,525.00

ACCOUNT Tom Jones, Capital ACCOUNT NO. 311

DATE		ITEM	POST. REF.	DEBIT	CREDIT	BALANCE DEBIT	BALANCE CREDIT
20-2 Jan.	1	Balance	✓				91,953.00

ACCOUNT Tom Jones, Drawing ACCOUNT NO. 312

DATE		ITEM	POST. REF.	DEBIT	CREDIT	BALANCE DEBIT	BALANCE CREDIT

Name ______________________

Comprehensive Problem 2—General Journal Based, Part 2 (Requirements 1., 2., 3., 6., and 7. Continued)

ACCOUNT Income Summary ACCOUNT NO. 313

DATE	ITEM	POST. REF.	DEBIT	CREDIT	BALANCE DEBIT	BALANCE CREDIT

ACCOUNT Sales ACCOUNT NO. 401

DATE	ITEM	POST. REF.	DEBIT	CREDIT	BALANCE DEBIT	BALANCE CREDIT

ACCOUNT Sales Returns and Allowances ACCOUNT NO. 401.1

DATE	ITEM	POST. REF.	DEBIT	CREDIT	BALANCE DEBIT	BALANCE CREDIT

ACCOUNT Purchases ACCOUNT NO. 501

DATE	ITEM	POST. REF.	DEBIT	CREDIT	BALANCE DEBIT	BALANCE CREDIT

Comprehensive Problem 2—General Journal Based, Part 2
(Requirements 1., 2., 3., 6., and 7. Continued)

ACCOUNT Purchases Returns and Allowances ACCOUNT NO. 501.1

DATE	ITEM	POST. REF.	DEBIT	CREDIT	BALANCE DEBIT	BALANCE CREDIT

ACCOUNT Purchases Discounts ACCOUNT NO. 501.2

DATE	ITEM	POST. REF.	DEBIT	CREDIT	BALANCE DEBIT	BALANCE CREDIT

ACCOUNT Freight-In ACCOUNT NO. 502

DATE	ITEM	POST. REF.	DEBIT	CREDIT	BALANCE DEBIT	BALANCE CREDIT

Name ______________________________

Comprehensive Problem 2—General Journal Based, Part 2 (Requirements 1., 2., 3., 6., and 7. Continued)

ACCOUNT Wages Expense ACCOUNT NO. 511

DATE		ITEM	POST. REF.	DEBIT	CREDIT	BALANCE DEBIT	BALANCE CREDIT
20-2 Jan.	1	Balance	✓				3 3 0 00

ACCOUNT Advertising Expense ACCOUNT NO. 512

DATE		ITEM	POST. REF.	DEBIT	CREDIT	BALANCE DEBIT	BALANCE CREDIT

ACCOUNT Supplies Expense ACCOUNT NO. 524

DATE		ITEM	POST. REF.	DEBIT	CREDIT	BALANCE DEBIT	BALANCE CREDIT

ACCOUNT Phone Expense ACCOUNT NO. 525

DATE		ITEM	POST. REF.	DEBIT	CREDIT	BALANCE DEBIT	BALANCE CREDIT

Comprehensive Problem 2—General Journal Based, Part 2 (Requirements 1., 2., 3., 6., and 7. Continued)

ACCOUNT Utilities Expense ACCOUNT NO. 533

DATE	ITEM	POST. REF.	DEBIT	CREDIT	BALANCE	
					DEBIT	CREDIT

ACCOUNT Insurance Expense ACCOUNT NO. 535

DATE	ITEM	POST. REF.	DEBIT	CREDIT	BALANCE	
					DEBIT	CREDIT

ACCOUNT Depreciation Expense—Building ACCOUNT NO. 540

DATE	ITEM	POST. REF.	DEBIT	CREDIT	BALANCE	
					DEBIT	CREDIT

ACCOUNT Depreciation Expense—Store Equipment ACCOUNT NO. 541

DATE	ITEM	POST. REF.	DEBIT	CREDIT	BALANCE	
					DEBIT	CREDIT

Comprehensive Problem 2—General Journal Based, Part 2 (Requirements 1., 2., 3., 6., and 7. Continued)

ACCOUNT Miscellaneous Expense ACCOUNT NO. 549

DATE		ITEM	POST. REF.	DEBIT	CREDIT	BALANCE DEBIT	BALANCE CREDIT

ACCOUNT Interest Expense ACCOUNT NO. 551

DATE		ITEM	POST. REF.	DEBIT	CREDIT	BALANCE DEBIT	BALANCE CREDIT

ACCOUNTS RECEIVABLE LEDGER

NAME Martha Boyle

ADDRESS 12 Jude Lane, Hartford, CT 06117

DATE		ITEM	POST. REF.	DEBIT	CREDIT	BALANCE
20-2 Jan.	1	Balance	✓			1,323 00

NAME Anne Clark

ADDRESS 52 Juniper Road, Hartford, CT 06118

DATE		ITEM	POST. REF.	DEBIT	CREDIT	BALANCE
20-2 Jan.	1	Balance	✓			2,100 00

Comprehensive Problem 2—General Journal Based, Part 2 (Requirements 1., 2., 3., 6., and 7. Continued)

NAME John Dempsey

ADDRESS 700 Hobbes Dr., Avon, CT 06108

DATE		ITEM	POST. REF.	DEBIT	CREDIT	BALANCE
20-2 Jan.	1	Balance	✓			2,121.00

NAME Kim Fields

ADDRESS 5200 Hamilton Ave., Hartford, CT 06117

DATE		ITEM	POST. REF.	DEBIT	CREDIT	BALANCE
20-2 Jan.	1	Balance	✓			168.00

NAME Lucy Greene

ADDRESS 236 Bally Lane, Simsbury, CT 06123

DATE		ITEM	POST. REF.	DEBIT	CREDIT	BALANCE
20-2 Jan.	1	Balance	✓			1,491.00

Name ______________________

Comprehensive Problem 2—General Journal Based, Part 2 (Requirements 1., 2., 3., 6., and 7. Concluded)

ACCOUNTS PAYABLE LEDGER

NAME Evans Essentials

ADDRESS 34 Harry Ave., East Hartford, CT 05234

DATE		ITEM	POST. REF.	DEBIT	CREDIT	BALANCE
20-2 Jan.	1	Balance	✓			2 3 5 0 00

NAME Nathen Co.

ADDRESS 1009 Drake Rd., Farmington, CT 06082

DATE		ITEM	POST. REF.	DEBIT	CREDIT	BALANCE
20-2 Jan.	1	Balance	✓			8 0 0 00

NAME Owen Enterprises

ADDRESS 43 Lucky Lane, Bristol, CT 06007

DATE		ITEM	POST. REF.	DEBIT	CREDIT	BALANCE

NAME West Wholesalers

ADDRESS 888 Anders Street, Newington, CT 06789

DATE		ITEM	POST. REF.	DEBIT	CREDIT	BALANCE
20-2 Jan.	1	Balance	✓			1 2 0 0 00

Comprehensive Problem 2—General Journal Based, Part 2

Requirement 4.

This page intentionally left blank.

Comprehensive Problem 2—General Journal Based, Part 2

Requirement 5.

		TRIAL BALANCE		ADJUSTMENTS	
		DEBIT	CREDIT	DEBIT	CREDIT
1					
2					
3					
4					
5					
6					
7					
8					
9					
10					
11					
12					
13					
14					
15					
16					
17					
18					
19					
20					
21					
22					
23					
24					
25					
26					
27					
28					
29					
30					
31					
32					
33					
34					
35					
36					

Name ______________________________

Comprehensive Problem 2—General Journal Based, Part 2
(Requirement 5. Continued)

ADJUSTED TRIAL BALANCE		INCOME STATEMENT		BALANCE SHEET		
DEBIT	CREDIT	DEBIT	CREDIT	DEBIT	CREDIT	
						1
						2
						3
						4
						5
						6
						7
						8
						9
						10
						11
						12
						13
						14
						15
						16
						17
						18
						19
						20
						21
						22
						23
						24
						25
						26
						27
						28
						29
						30
						31
						32
						33
						34
						35
						36

Comprehensive Problem 2—General Journal Based, Part 2
(Requirement 5. Continued)

Comprehensive Problem 2—General Journal Based, Part 2
(Requirement 5. Continued)

Comprehensive Problem 2—General Journal Based, Part 2
(Requirement 5. Concluded)

Comprehensive Problem 2—General Journal Based, Part 2

Requirement 6.

GENERAL JOURNAL

PAGE 3

	DATE		DESCRIPTION	POST. REF.	DEBIT	CREDIT	
1							1
2							2
3							3
4							4
5							5
6							6
7							7
8							8
9							9
10							10
11							11
12							12
13							13
14							14
15							15
16							16
17							17
18							18
19							19
20							20
21							21
22							22
23							23
24							24
25							25
26							26
27							27
28							28
29							29
30							30
31							31
32							32
33							33
34							34

Comprehensive Problem 2—General Journal Based, Part 2

Requirement 7.

GENERAL JOURNAL

PAGE 4

DATE		DESCRIPTION	POST. REF.	DEBIT	CREDIT

Comprehensive Problem 2—General Journal Based, Part 2

Requirement 8.

ACCOUNT	DEBIT BALANCE	CREDIT BALANCE

Comprehensive Problem 2—Special Journals Based, Part 1

Requirements 2. and 3.

SALES JOURNAL

PAGE 6

DATE		SALE NO.	TO WHOM SOLD	POST. REF.	ACCOUNTS RECEIVABLE DEBIT	SALES CREDIT	SALES TAX PAYABLE CREDIT
20-1 Dec.	1-15		Cumulative Amount	✓	4,263.00	4,060.00	203.00

CASH RECEIPTS JOURNAL

PAGE 9

	DATE		ACCOUNT CREDITED	POST. REF.	GENERAL CREDIT	ACCOUNTS RECEIVABLE CREDIT	SALES CREDIT	SALES TAX PAYABLE CREDIT	CASH DEBIT	
1	20-1 Dec.	1-15	Cumulative Amt	✓		1,830.00	4,840.00	242.00	6,912.00	1
2										2
3										3
4										4
5										5
6										6
7										7

Comprehensive Problem 2—Special Journals Based, Part 1 (Requirements 2. and 3. Continued)

PURCHASES JOURNAL

PAGE 5

DATE		INVOICE NO.	FROM WHOM PURCHASED	POST. REF.	PURCHASES DEBIT ACCTS. PAY. CREDIT
20-1 Dec.	1-15		Cumulative Amount	✓	3900 00

CASH PAYMENTS JOURNAL

PAGE 10

DATE		CK. NO.	ACCOUNT DEBITED	POST. REF.	GENERAL DEBIT	ACCOUNTS PAYABLE DEBIT	PURCHASES DEBIT	PURCHASES DISCOUNTS CREDIT	CASH CREDIT
20-1 Dec.	1-15		Cumulative Amount	✓	1680 00	7150 00		123 00	8707 00

Comprehensive Problem 2—Special Journals Based, Part 1 (Requirements 2. and 3. Concluded)

GENERAL JOURNAL

PAGE 3

	DATE		DESCRIPTION	POST. REF.	DEBIT	CREDIT	
1							1
2							2
3							3
4							4
5							5
6							6
7							7
8							8
9							9
10							10
11							11
12							12

Requirements 1., 2., 3., 6., 7., and 9.

GENERAL LEDGER

ACCOUNT Cash ACCOUNT NO. 101

DATE		ITEM	POST. REF.	DEBIT	CREDIT	BALANCE DEBIT	BALANCE CREDIT
20-1 Dec.	16	Balance	✓			11 5 0 0 00	

ACCOUNT Accounts Receivable ACCOUNT NO. 122

DATE		ITEM	POST. REF.	DEBIT	CREDIT	BALANCE DEBIT	BALANCE CREDIT
20-1 Dec.	16	Balance	✓			7 8 2 3 00	

Comprehensive Problem 2—Special Journals Based, Part 1 (Requirements 1., 2., 3., 6., 7., and 9. Continued)

ACCOUNT Merchandise Inventory ACCOUNT NO. 131

DATE		ITEM	POST. REF.	DEBIT	CREDIT	BALANCE DEBIT	BALANCE CREDIT
20-1 Dec.	16	Balance	✓			21,800.00	

ACCOUNT Supplies ACCOUNT NO. 141

DATE		ITEM	POST. REF.	DEBIT	CREDIT	BALANCE DEBIT	BALANCE CREDIT
20-1 Dec.	16	Balance	✓			1,035.00	

ACCOUNT Prepaid Insurance ACCOUNT NO. 145

DATE		ITEM	POST. REF.	DEBIT	CREDIT	BALANCE DEBIT	BALANCE CREDIT
20-1 Dec.	16	Balance	✓			1,380.00	

ACCOUNT Land ACCOUNT NO. 161

DATE		ITEM	POST. REF.	DEBIT	CREDIT	BALANCE DEBIT	BALANCE CREDIT
20-1 Dec.	16	Balance	✓			8,700.00	

Name ______________________________

Comprehensive Problem 2—Special Journals Based, Part 1 (Requirements 1., 2., 3., 6., 7., and 9. Continued)

ACCOUNT Building ACCOUNT NO. 171

DATE		ITEM	POST. REF.	DEBIT	CREDIT	BALANCE DEBIT	BALANCE CREDIT
20-1 Dec.	16	Balance	✓			52 0 0 0 00	

ACCOUNT Accumulated Depreciation—Building ACCOUNT NO. 171.1

DATE		ITEM	POST. REF.	DEBIT	CREDIT	BALANCE DEBIT	BALANCE CREDIT
20-1 Dec.	16	Balance	✓				9 2 0 0 00

ACCOUNT Store Equipment ACCOUNT NO. 181

DATE		ITEM	POST. REF.	DEBIT	CREDIT	BALANCE DEBIT	BALANCE CREDIT
20-1 Dec.	16	Balance	✓			28 7 5 0 00	

ACCOUNT Accumulated Depreciation—Store Equipment ACCOUNT NO. 181.1

DATE		ITEM	POST. REF.	DEBIT	CREDIT	BALANCE DEBIT	BALANCE CREDIT
20-1 Dec.	16	Balance	✓				9 3 0 0 00

Comprehensive Problem 2—Special Journals Based, Part 1 (Requirements 1., 2., 3., 6., 7., and 9. Continued)

ACCOUNT Accounts Payable ACCOUNT NO. 202

DATE		ITEM	POST. REF.	DEBIT	CREDIT	BALANCE DEBIT	BALANCE CREDIT
20-1 Dec.	16	Balance	✓				6,850.00

ACCOUNT Wages Payable ACCOUNT NO. 219

DATE		ITEM	POST. REF.	DEBIT	CREDIT	BALANCE DEBIT	BALANCE CREDIT

ACCOUNT Sales Tax Payable ACCOUNT NO. 231

DATE		ITEM	POST. REF.	DEBIT	CREDIT	BALANCE DEBIT	BALANCE CREDIT
20-1 Dec.	16	Balance	✓				933.00

ACCOUNT Mortgage Payable ACCOUNT NO. 251

DATE		ITEM	POST. REF.	DEBIT	CREDIT	BALANCE DEBIT	BALANCE CREDIT
20-1 Dec.	16	Balance	✓				12,525.00

Name

Comprehensive Problem 2—Special Journals Based, Part 1 (Requirements 1., 2., 3., 6., 7., and 9. Continued)

ACCOUNT Tom Jones, Capital ACCOUNT NO. 311

DATE		ITEM	POST. REF.	DEBIT	CREDIT	BALANCE DEBIT	BALANCE CREDIT
20-1 Dec.	16	Balance	✓				90,000.00

ACCOUNT Tom Jones, Drawing ACCOUNT NO. 312

DATE		ITEM	POST. REF.	DEBIT	CREDIT	BALANCE DEBIT	BALANCE CREDIT
20-1 Dec.	16	Balance	✓			8,500.00	

ACCOUNT Income Summary ACCOUNT NO. 313

DATE		ITEM	POST. REF.	DEBIT	CREDIT	BALANCE DEBIT	BALANCE CREDIT

ACCOUNT Sales ACCOUNT NO. 401

DATE		ITEM	POST. REF.	DEBIT	CREDIT	BALANCE DEBIT	BALANCE CREDIT
20-1 Dec.	16	Balance	✓				116,000.00

Comprehensive Problem 2—Special Journals Based, Part 1 (Requirements 1., 2., 3., 6., 7., and 9. Continued)

ACCOUNT Sales Returns and Allowances ACCOUNT NO. 401.1

DATE		ITEM	POST. REF.	DEBIT	CREDIT	BALANCE DEBIT	BALANCE CREDIT
20-1 Dec.	16	Balance	✓			1,430.00	

ACCOUNT Purchases ACCOUNT NO. 501

DATE		ITEM	POST. REF.	DEBIT	CREDIT	BALANCE DEBIT	BALANCE CREDIT
20-1 Dec.	16	Balance	✓			60,500.00	

ACCOUNT Purchases Returns and Allowances ACCOUNT NO. 501.1

DATE		ITEM	POST. REF.	DEBIT	CREDIT	BALANCE DEBIT	BALANCE CREDIT
20-1 Dec.	16	Balance	✓				460.00

ACCOUNT Purchases Discounts ACCOUNT NO. 501.2

DATE		ITEM	POST. REF.	DEBIT	CREDIT	BALANCE DEBIT	BALANCE CREDIT
20-1 Dec.	16	Balance	✓				575.00

Comprehensive Problem 2—Special Journals Based, Part 1 (Requirements 1., 2., 3., 6., 7., and 9. Continued)

ACCOUNT Freight-In ACCOUNT NO. 502

DATE		ITEM	POST. REF.	DEBIT	CREDIT	BALANCE DEBIT	BALANCE CREDIT
20-1 Dec.	16	Balance	✓			1,7 5 00	

ACCOUNT Wages Expense ACCOUNT NO. 511

DATE		ITEM	POST. REF.	DEBIT	CREDIT	BALANCE DEBIT	BALANCE CREDIT
20-1 Dec.	16	Balance	✓			26,1 0 0 00	

ACCOUNT Advertising Expense ACCOUNT NO. 512

DATE		ITEM	POST. REF.	DEBIT	CREDIT	BALANCE DEBIT	BALANCE CREDIT
20-1 Dec.	16	Balance	✓			4,7 0 0 00	

ACCOUNT Supplies Expense ACCOUNT NO. 524

DATE		ITEM	POST. REF.	DEBIT	CREDIT	BALANCE DEBIT	BALANCE CREDIT

Comprehensive Problem 2—Special Journals Based, Part 1 (Requirements 1., 2., 3., 6., 7., and 9. Continued)

ACCOUNT Phone Expense ACCOUNT NO. 525

DATE		ITEM	POST. REF.	DEBIT	CREDIT	BALANCE DEBIT	BALANCE CREDIT
20-1 Dec.	16	Balance	✓			2,180.00	

ACCOUNT Utilities Expense ACCOUNT NO. 533

DATE		ITEM	POST. REF.	DEBIT	CREDIT	BALANCE DEBIT	BALANCE CREDIT
20-1 Dec.	16	Balance	✓			6,900.00	

ACCOUNT Insurance Expense ACCOUNT NO. 535

DATE		ITEM	POST. REF.	DEBIT	CREDIT	BALANCE DEBIT	BALANCE CREDIT

ACCOUNT Depreciation Expense—Building ACCOUNT NO. 540

DATE		ITEM	POST. REF.	DEBIT	CREDIT	BALANCE DEBIT	BALANCE CREDIT

Comprehensive Problem 2—Special Journals Based, Part 1 (Requirements 1., 2., 3., 6., 7., and 9. Continued)

ACCOUNT Depreciation Expense—Store Equipment ACCOUNT NO. 541

DATE		ITEM	POST. REF.	DEBIT	CREDIT	BALANCE DEBIT	BALANCE CREDIT

ACCOUNT Miscellaneous Expense ACCOUNT NO. 549

DATE		ITEM	POST. REF.	DEBIT	CREDIT	BALANCE DEBIT	BALANCE CREDIT
20-1 Dec.	16	Balance	✓			2,700.00	

ACCOUNT Interest Expense ACCOUNT NO. 551

DATE		ITEM	POST. REF.	DEBIT	CREDIT	BALANCE DEBIT	BALANCE CREDIT
20-1 Dec.	16	Balance	✓			1,350.00	

ACCOUNTS RECEIVABLE LEDGER

NAME Martha Boyle

ADDRESS 12 Jude Lane, Hartford, CT 06117

DATE		ITEM	POST. REF.	DEBIT	CREDIT	BALANCE
20-1 Dec.	16	Balance	✓			3,796.00

Comprehensive Problem 2—Special Journals Based, Part 1 (Requirements 1., 2., 3., 6., 7., and 9. Continued)

NAME Anne Clark

ADDRESS 52 Juniper Road, Hartford, CT 06118

DATE		ITEM	POST. REF.	DEBIT	CREDIT	BALANCE
20-1 Dec.	16	Balance	✓			2,100.00

NAME John Dempsey

ADDRESS 700 Hobbes Dr., Avon, CT 06108

DATE		ITEM	POST. REF.	DEBIT	CREDIT	BALANCE
20-1 Dec.	16	Balance	✓			1,560.00

NAME Kim Fields

ADDRESS 5200 Hamilton Ave., Hartford, CT 06117

DATE		ITEM	POST. REF.	DEBIT	CREDIT	BALANCE
20-1 Dec.	16	Balance	✓			—

NAME Lucy Greene

ADDRESS 236 Bally Lane, Simsbury, CT 06123

DATE		ITEM	POST. REF.	DEBIT	CREDIT	BALANCE
20-1 Dec.	16	Balance	✓			2,800.00

Comprehensive Problem 2—Special Journals Based, Part 1 (Requirements 1., 2., 3., 6., 7., and 9. Continued)

ACCOUNTS PAYABLE LEDGER

NAME Evans Essentials

ADDRESS 34 Harry Ave., East Hartford, CT 05234

DATE		ITEM	POST. REF.	DEBIT	CREDIT	BALANCE
20-1 Dec.	16	Balance	✓			3,600 00

NAME Nathen Co.

ADDRESS 1009 Drake Rd., Farmington, CT 06082

DATE		ITEM	POST. REF.	DEBIT	CREDIT	BALANCE
20-1 Dec.	16	Balance	✓			—

Comprehensive Problem 2—Special Journals Based, Part 1 (Requirements 1., 2., 3., 6., 7., and 9. Concluded)

NAME Owen Enterprises

ADDRESS 43 Lucky Lane, Bristol, CT 06007

DATE		ITEM	POST. REF.	DEBIT	CREDIT	BALANCE
20-1 Dec.	16	Balance	✓			

NAME West Wholesalers

ADDRESS 888 Anders Street, Newington, CT 06789

DATE		ITEM	POST. REF.	DEBIT	CREDIT	BALANCE
20-1 Dec.	16	Balance	✓			

Comprehensive Problem 2—Special Journals Based, Part 1

Requirement 4.

Comprehensive Problem 2—Special Journals Based, Part 1

Requirement 5.

		TRIAL BALANCE		ADJUSTMENTS	
		DEBIT	CREDIT	DEBIT	CREDIT
1					
2					
3					
4					
5					
6					
7					
8					
9					
10					
11					
12					
13					
14					
15					
16					
17					
18					
19					
20					
21					
22					
23					
24					
25					
26					
27					
28					
29					
30					
31					
32					
33					
34					
35					
36					

Comprehensive Problem 2—Special Journals Based, Part 1
(Requirement 5. Continued)

ADJUSTED TRIAL BALANCE		INCOME STATEMENT		BALANCE SHEET	
DEBIT	CREDIT	DEBIT	CREDIT	DEBIT	CREDIT

Comprehensive Problem 2—Special Journals Based, Part 1
(Requirement 5. Continued)

Name ______________________________

Comprehensive Problem 2—Special Journals Based, Part 1
(Requirement 5. Continued)

Comprehensive Problem 2—Special Journals Based, Part 1
(Requirement 5. Concluded)

Comprehensive Problem 2—Special Journals Based, Part 1

Requirement 6.

GENERAL JOURNAL

PAGE 5

	DATE		DESCRIPTION	POST. REF.	DEBIT	CREDIT	
1							1
2							2
3							3
4							4
5							5
6							6
7							7
8							8
9							9
10							10
11							11
12							12
13							13
14							14
15							15
16							16
17							17
18							18
19							19
20							20
21							21
22							22
23							23
24							24
25							25
26							26
27							27
28							28
29							29
30							30
31							31
32							32
33							33
34							34

Comprehensive Problem 2—Special Journals Based, Part 1

Requirements 7. and 9.

GENERAL JOURNAL

PAGE 6

	DATE		DESCRIPTION	POST. REF.	DEBIT	CREDIT	
1							1
2							2
3							3
4							4
5							5
6							6
7							7
8							8
9							9
10							10
11							11
12							12
13							13
14							14
15							15
16							16
17							17
18							18
19							19
20							20
21							21
22							22
23							23
24							24
25							25
26							26
27							27
28							28
29							29
30							30
31							31
32							32
33							33
34							34

Name ______________________

Comprehensive Problem 2—Special Journals Based, Part 1

Requirement 8.

ACCOUNT	DEBIT BALANCE	CREDIT BALANCE

Comprehensive Problem 2—Special Journals Based, Part 2

Requirements 2. and 3.

SALES JOURNAL

PAGE 7

DATE		SALE NO.	TO WHOM SOLD	POST. REF.	ACCOUNTS RECEIVABLE DEBIT	SALES CREDIT	SALES TAX PAYABLE CREDIT

CASH RECEIPTS JOURNAL

PAGE 10

	DATE		ACCOUNT CREDITED	POST. REF.	GENERAL CREDIT	ACCOUNTS RECEIVABLE CREDIT	SALES CREDIT	SALES TAX PAYABLE CREDIT	CASH DEBIT	
1										1
2										2
3										3
4										4
5										5
6										6
7										7
8										8
9										9

Comprehensive Problem 2—Special Journals Based, Part 2 (Requirements 2. and 3. Continued)

PURCHASES JOURNAL

PAGE 6

	DATE		INVOICE NO.	FROM WHOM PURCHASED	POST. REF.	PURCHASES DEBIT ACCTS. PAY. CREDIT	
1							1
2							2
3							3
4							4
5							5
6							6
7							7
8							8
9							9

CASH PAYMENTS JOURNAL

PAGE 11

	DATE		CK. NO.	ACCOUNT DEBITED	POST. REF.	GENERAL DEBIT	ACCOUNTS PAYABLE DEBIT	PURCHASES DEBIT	PURCHASES DISCOUNTS CREDIT	CASH CREDIT	
1											1
2											2
3											3
4											4
5											5
6											6
7											7
8											8
9											9
10											10
11											11
12											12
13											13

Comprehensive Problem 2—Special Journals Based, Part 2 (Requirements 2. and 3. Concluded)

GENERAL JOURNAL

PAGE 1

	DATE		DESCRIPTION	POST. REF.	DEBIT	CREDIT	
1							1
2							2
3							3
4							4
5							5
6							6
7							7
8							8
9							9
10							10
11							11
12							12

Requirements 1., 2., 3., 6., and 7.

GENERAL LEDGER

ACCOUNT Cash ACCOUNT NO. 101

DATE		ITEM	POST. REF.	DEBIT	CREDIT	BALANCE DEBIT	BALANCE CREDIT
20-2 Jan.	1	Balance	✓			12,548.00	

ACCOUNT Accounts Receivable ACCOUNT NO. 122

DATE		ITEM	POST. REF.	DEBIT	CREDIT	BALANCE DEBIT	BALANCE CREDIT
20-2 Jan.	1	Balance	✓			7,203.00	

Comprehensive Problem 2—Special Journals Based, Part 2 (Requirements 1., 2., 3., 6., and 7. Continued)

ACCOUNT Merchandise Inventory ACCOUNT NO. 131

DATE		ITEM	POST. REF.	DEBIT	CREDIT	BALANCE DEBIT	BALANCE CREDIT
20-2 Jan.	1	Balance	✓			19,700.00	

ACCOUNT Supplies ACCOUNT NO. 141

DATE		ITEM	POST. REF.	DEBIT	CREDIT	BALANCE DEBIT	BALANCE CREDIT
20-2 Jan.	1	Balance	✓			525.00	

ACCOUNT Prepaid Insurance ACCOUNT NO. 145

DATE		ITEM	POST. REF.	DEBIT	CREDIT	BALANCE DEBIT	BALANCE CREDIT
20-2 Jan.	1	Balance	✓			1,000.00	

ACCOUNT Land ACCOUNT NO. 161

DATE		ITEM	POST. REF.	DEBIT	CREDIT	BALANCE DEBIT	BALANCE CREDIT
20-2 Jan.	1	Balance	✓			870.00	

Comprehensive Problem 2—Special Journals Based, Part 2 (Requirements 1., 2., 3., 6., and 7. Continued)

ACCOUNT Building ACCOUNT NO. 171

DATE		ITEM	POST. REF.	DEBIT	CREDIT	BALANCE DEBIT	BALANCE CREDIT
20-2 Jan.	1	Balance	✓			52,000.00	

ACCOUNT Accumulated Depreciation—Building ACCOUNT NO. 171.1

DATE		ITEM	POST. REF.	DEBIT	CREDIT	BALANCE DEBIT	BALANCE CREDIT
20-2 Jan.	1	Balance	✓				10,000.00

ACCOUNT Store Equipment ACCOUNT NO. 181

DATE		ITEM	POST. REF.	DEBIT	CREDIT	BALANCE DEBIT	BALANCE CREDIT
20-2 Jan.	1	Balance	✓			28,750.00	

ACCOUNT Accumulated Depreciation—Store Equipment ACCOUNT NO. 181.1

DATE		ITEM	POST. REF.	DEBIT	CREDIT	BALANCE DEBIT	BALANCE CREDIT
20-2 Jan.	1	Balance	✓				9,750.00

Comprehensive Problem 2—Special Journals Based, Part 2 (Requirements 1., 2., 3., 6., and 7. Continued)

ACCOUNT Accounts Payable ACCOUNT NO. 202

DATE		ITEM	POST. REF.	DEBIT	CREDIT	BALANCE DEBIT	BALANCE CREDIT
20-2 Jan.	1	Balance	✓				4,350 00

ACCOUNT Wages Payable ACCOUNT NO. 219

DATE		ITEM	POST. REF.	DEBIT	CREDIT	BALANCE DEBIT	BALANCE CREDIT

ACCOUNT Sales Tax Payable ACCOUNT NO. 231

DATE		ITEM	POST. REF.	DEBIT	CREDIT	BALANCE DEBIT	BALANCE CREDIT
20-2 Jan.	1	Balance	✓				1,518 00

ACCOUNT Mortgage Payable ACCOUNT NO. 251

DATE		ITEM	POST. REF.	DEBIT	CREDIT	BALANCE DEBIT	BALANCE CREDIT
20-2 Jan.	1	Balance	✓				12,525 00

Comprehensive Problem 2—Special Journals Based, Part 2 (Requirements 1., 2., 3., 6., and 7. Continued)

ACCOUNT Tom Jones, Capital ACCOUNT NO. 311

DATE		ITEM	POST. REF.	DEBIT	CREDIT	BALANCE DEBIT	BALANCE CREDIT
20-2 Jan.	1	Balance	✓				91,953.00

ACCOUNT Tom Jones, Drawing ACCOUNT NO. 312

DATE		ITEM	POST. REF.	DEBIT	CREDIT	BALANCE DEBIT	BALANCE CREDIT

ACCOUNT Income Summary ACCOUNT NO. 313

DATE		ITEM	POST. REF.	DEBIT	CREDIT	BALANCE DEBIT	BALANCE CREDIT

ACCOUNT Sales ACCOUNT NO. 401

DATE		ITEM	POST. REF.	DEBIT	CREDIT	BALANCE DEBIT	BALANCE CREDIT

Comprehensive Problem 2—Special Journals Based, Part 2 (Requirements 1., 2., 3., 6., and 7. Continued)

ACCOUNT Sales Returns and Allowances ACCOUNT NO. 401.1

DATE		ITEM	POST. REF.	DEBIT	CREDIT	BALANCE DEBIT	BALANCE CREDIT

ACCOUNT Purchases ACCOUNT NO. 501

DATE		ITEM	POST. REF.	DEBIT	CREDIT	BALANCE DEBIT	BALANCE CREDIT

ACCOUNT Purchases Returns and Allowances ACCOUNT NO. 501.1

DATE		ITEM	POST. REF.	DEBIT	CREDIT	BALANCE DEBIT	BALANCE CREDIT

ACCOUNT Purchases Discounts ACCOUNT NO. 501.2

DATE		ITEM	POST. REF.	DEBIT	CREDIT	BALANCE DEBIT	BALANCE CREDIT

Comprehensive Problem 2—Special Journals Based, Part 2 (Requirements 1., 2., 3., 6., and 7. Continued)

ACCOUNT Freight-In ACCOUNT NO. 502

DATE		ITEM	POST. REF.	DEBIT	CREDIT	BALANCE DEBIT	BALANCE CREDIT

ACCOUNT Wages Expense ACCOUNT NO. 511

DATE		ITEM	POST. REF.	DEBIT	CREDIT	BALANCE DEBIT	BALANCE CREDIT
20-2 Jan.	1	Balance	✓				3 3 0 00

ACCOUNT Advertising Expense ACCOUNT NO. 512

DATE		ITEM	POST. REF.	DEBIT	CREDIT	BALANCE DEBIT	BALANCE CREDIT

ACCOUNT Supplies Expense ACCOUNT NO. 524

DATE		ITEM	POST. REF.	DEBIT	CREDIT	BALANCE DEBIT	BALANCE CREDIT

Name ____________________

Comprehensive Problem 2—Special Journals Based, Part 2 (Requirements 1., 2., 3., 6., and 7. Continued)

ACCOUNT Phone Expense ACCOUNT NO. 525

DATE		ITEM	POST. REF.	DEBIT	CREDIT	BALANCE	
						DEBIT	CREDIT

ACCOUNT Utilities Expense ACCOUNT NO. 533

DATE		ITEM	POST. REF.	DEBIT	CREDIT	BALANCE	
						DEBIT	CREDIT

ACCOUNT Insurance Expense ACCOUNT NO. 535

DATE		ITEM	POST. REF.	DEBIT	CREDIT	BALANCE	
						DEBIT	CREDIT

ACCOUNT Depreciation Expense—Building ACCOUNT NO. 540

DATE		ITEM	POST. REF.	DEBIT	CREDIT	BALANCE	
						DEBIT	CREDIT

ACCOUNT Depreciation Expense—Store Equipment ACCOUNT NO. 541

DATE		ITEM	POST. REF.	DEBIT	CREDIT	BALANCE	
						DEBIT	CREDIT

Comprehensive Problem 2—Special Journals Based, Part 2 (Requirements 1., 2., 3., 6., and 7. Continued)

ACCOUNT Miscellaneous Expense ACCOUNT NO. 549

DATE		ITEM	POST. REF.	DEBIT	CREDIT	BALANCE	
						DEBIT	CREDIT

ACCOUNT Interest Expense ACCOUNT NO. 551

DATE		ITEM	POST. REF.	DEBIT	CREDIT	BALANCE	
						DEBIT	CREDIT

ACCOUNTS RECEIVABLE LEDGER

NAME Martha Boyle

ADDRESS 12 Jude Lane, Hartford, CT 06117

DATE		ITEM	POST. REF.	DEBIT	CREDIT	BALANCE
20-2 Jan.	1	Balance	✓			1,323.00

NAME Anne Clark

ADDRESS 52 Juniper Road, Hartford, CT 06118

DATE		ITEM	POST. REF.	DEBIT	CREDIT	BALANCE
20-2 Jan.	1	Balance	✓			2,100.00

Comprehensive Problem 2—Special Journals Based, Part 2 (Requirements 1., 2., 3., 6., and 7. Continued)

NAME John Dempsey

ADDRESS 700 Hobbes Dr., Avon, CT 06108

DATE		ITEM	POST. REF.	DEBIT	CREDIT	BALANCE
20-2 Jan.	1	Balance	✓			2,121 00

NAME Kim Fields

ADDRESS 5200 Hamilton Ave., Hartford, CT 06117

DATE		ITEM	POST. REF.	DEBIT	CREDIT	BALANCE
20-2 Jan.	1	Balance	✓			168 00

NAME Lucy Greene

ADDRESS 236 Bally Lane, Simsbury, CT 06123

DATE		ITEM	POST. REF.	DEBIT	CREDIT	BALANCE
20-2 Jan.	1	Balance	✓			1,491 00

Comprehensive Problem 2—Special Journals Based, Part 2 (Requirements 1., 2., 3., 6., and 7. Concluded)

ACCOUNTS PAYABLE LEDGER

NAME Evans Essentials

ADDRESS 34 Harry Ave., East Hartford, CT 05234

DATE		ITEM	POST. REF.	DEBIT	CREDIT	BALANCE
20-2 Jan.	1	Balance	✓			2,350 00

NAME Nathen Co.

ADDRESS 1009 Drake Rd., Farmington, CT 06082

DATE		ITEM	POST. REF.	DEBIT	CREDIT	BALANCE
20-2 Jan.	1	Balance	✓			800 00

NAME Owen Enterprises

ADDRESS 43 Lucky Lane, Bristol, CT 06007

DATE		ITEM	POST. REF.	DEBIT	CREDIT	BALANCE

NAME West Wholesalers

ADDRESS 888 Anders Street, Newington, CT 06789

DATE		ITEM	POST. REF.	DEBIT	CREDIT	BALANCE
20-2 Jan.	1	Balance	✓			1,200 00

Name ______________________________

Comprehensive Problem 2—Special Journals Based, Part 2

Requirement 4.

Comprehensive Problem 2—Special Journals Based, Part 2

Requirement 5.

	Trial Balance		Adjustments	
	Debit	Credit	Debit	Credit

Name ______________________________

Comprehensive Problem 2—Special Journals Based, Part 2 (Requirement 5. Continued)

____

____

____

ADJUSTED TRIAL BALANCE		INCOME STATEMENT		BALANCE SHEET		
DEBIT	CREDIT	DEBIT	CREDIT	DEBIT	CREDIT	
						1
						2
						3
						4
						5
						6
						7
						8
						9
						10
						11
						12
						13
						14
						15
						16
						17
						18
						19
						20
						21
						22
						23
						24
						25
						26
						27
						28
						29
						30
						31
						32
						33
						34
						35
						36

Comprehensive Problem 2—Special Journals Based, Part 2
(Requirement 5. Continued)

Comprehensive Problem 2—Special Journals Based, Part 2
(Requirement 5. Continued)

Comprehensive Problem 2—Special Journals Based, Part 2
(Requirement 5. Concluded)

Name ______________________________

Comprehensive Problem 2—Special Journals Based, Part 2

Requirement 6.

GENERAL JOURNAL

PAGE 2

	DATE		DESCRIPTION	POST. REF.	DEBIT	CREDIT	
1							1
2							2
3							3
4							4
5							5
6							6
7							7
8							8
9							9
10							10
11							11
12							12
13							13
14							14
15							15
16							16
17							17
18							18
19							19
20							20
21							21
22							22
23							23
24							24
25							25
26							26
27							27
28							28
29							29
30							30
31							31
32							32
33							33
34							34

Comprehensive Problem 2—Special Journals Based, Part 2

Requirement 7.

GENERAL JOURNAL

PAGE 3

DATE		DESCRIPTION	POST. REF.	DEBIT	CREDIT

Name ______________________________

Comprehensive Problem 2—Special Journals Based, Part 2

Requirement 8.

ACCOUNT	DEBIT BALANCE	CREDIT BALANCE

NOTES

NOTES

NOTES

END PAGE OF
WORKING PAPERS